MOBILITY AND INEQUALITY

MOBILITY AND INEQUALITY

Frontiers of Research in
Sociology and Economics

*Edited by Stephen L. Morgan, David B. Grusky,
and Gary S. Fields*

STANFORD UNIVERSITY PRESS

STANFORD, CALIFORNIA

2006

Stanford University Press
Stanford, California
© 2006 by the Board of Trustees of the Leland Stanford
Junior University. All rights reserved.

Printed in the United States of America on acid-free,
archival-quality paper

Library of Congress Cataloging-in-Publication Data
Mobility and inequality : frontiers of research from so-
ciology and economics / edited by Stephen L. Morgan,
David B. Grusky, and Gary S. Fields.
    p.   cm.
Includes bibliographical references and index.
ISBN 0-8047-5249-4 (cloth : alk. paper)
1. Social mobility—Economic aspects.   2. Equality.
3. Income distribution.   I. Morgan, Stephen L.
II. Grusky, David B. III. Fields, Gary S.

    HT612.M63   2006
    305.5'13—dc22   2005020553

Original Printing 2006

Last figure below indicates year of this printing:
15   14   13   12   11   10   09   08   07   06

Typeset by G & S Book Services in10/14 Sabon

For our families

CONTENTS

TABLES AND FIGURES

Tables

Figures

ACKNOWLEDGMENTS

This volume originated as a series of presentations delivered at a conference in Ithaca, New York, entitled, *Frontiers in Social and Economic Mobility*. From March 27 to March 29 2003, sociologists and economists from more than a dozen universities gathered to discuss and advance questions such as: What is socioeconomic mobility? How do we measure it? How do we understand it? Funded jointly by the Center for the Study Inequality and the Poverty Inequality and Development Initiative at Cornell University, the conference was a great success, in large part thanks to the coordinating committee that included François Bourguignon and John Goldthorpe. We are deeply grateful to Ravi Kanbur for extending funds from the Poverty Inequality and Development Initiative, as well as the many conference participants for enhancing the lively discussion and debate. Jessica Henning coordinated all logistics for the conference, with the assistance of Alice Murdock, Sharon Sandlan, and Susan Meyer.

Following the conference, it was clear that a volume should be produced, and we then invited additional contributions from distinguished mobility researchers unable to attend the conference. Accordingly, five additional chapters were acquired, and a full manuscript was then compiled and submitted to Stanford University Press for review. At the Press, we thank Patricia Katayama and then Kate Wahl for showing initial interest, and then Paula England and George Farkas for reviewing the manuscript. Their detailed and provocative comments on the chapters of the volume are greatly appreciated.

Following a final round of revisions, Elizabeth Heitner then compiled the entire manuscript for transmittal to Stanford University Press. At Stanford UP, Cheryl Hauser expertly edited the manuscript. Judith Hibbard and her production team at Stanford UP took over, with Kelly Andronicos at Cornell assisting in the effort to resolve all of the lingering queries. We are grateful to this superb team.

MOBILITY AND INEQUALITY

PART ONE   OVERVIEW

CHAPTER ONE

Past Themes and Future Prospects for Research on Social and Economic Mobility

Stephen L. Morgan

For more than fifty years, edited volumes of original research from leading scholars of mobility have been published regularly—from Lipset and Bendix (1959) to Laumann (1970), Breiger (1990), Birdsall and Graham (2000), Corak (2004), Breen (2004), and Bowles, Gintis, and Osborne Groves (2005). The present volume follows in this tradition and yet is somewhat distinct because (1) it draws contributions from both sociology and economics and (2) it gives substantial explicit attention to the effects of inequality on mobility outcomes. The theme of mobility and inequality is timely, as labor market inequality in many industrialized societies has increased in the past thirty years. The integrative agenda is timely as well, as scholarship in sociology and economics has grown increasingly similar over the same time period. Sociologists and economists now engage similar substantive topics, many of which were formerly confined to their disciplines alone. And, as a result, each discipline has gained an appreciation for some of the differing conceptual and methodological tools that are deployed across the two disciplines.

In this overview chapter, I discuss the common intellectual foundations of mobility research in sociology and economics, connect these to the chapters of this volume, and then identify some unresolved questions that the contributions demonstrate should be engaged in future research. In the process, I argue that mobility research remains important to the social sciences, especially given recent and expected future developments in the structure of inequality.

I thank David B. Grusky and Gary Fields for helpful comments on the first draft of this chapter.

PAST THEMES OF MOBILITY RESEARCH AND THEIR INTERDISCIPLINARY ORIGINS

Although it would be misleading to claim that the mobility literature has emerged from interdisciplinary dialogue, common themes underlie its development across disciplines. Given the wide availability of excellent reviews of the mobility literature, I will confine my discussion to the most prominent themes and challenges identified by both sociology and economics.[1]

Mobility researchers from these two disciplines have explored a variety of related foundational questions on the definition of mobility, often framed by the question: "Mobility between what?" In sociology, this question is answered implicitly by adopting one of two basic approaches. For the first approach, mobility is modeled by accounting for movement between aggregated groupings of occupational titles, generally labeled social classes.[2] Accordingly, intergenerational mobility is analyzed via inspection of cross-classifications of parent's and their children's occupations. In the early literature, levels of mobility were summarized by alternative indices, often derived while analyzing alternative cross-classifications drawn from different societies or subgroups within a single society.[3] The later literature moved away from such representations, giving way to analyses of the fine structure of patterns of mobility. This work is best represented by the cross-national research of Erikson and Goldthorpe (1992), as brought up-to-date by Richard Breen and his team of researchers (see Breen 2004).

With the publication of Blau and Duncan's *American Occupational Structure* in 1967, a second approach to the study of mobility reached maturity, later labeled status attainment research. In this tradition, sociologists focus on the causes and consequences of differences in socioeconomic status (often defined as scores attached to occupational titles, based on the average educational attainment and earnings of incumbents; see Hauser and Warren 1997). In this tradition, levels of social mobility are measured by intergenerational correlations of socioeconomic status (see Hauser 1998; Jencks 1990), and these correlations are then decomposed using intervening variables in structural equation models.

In economics, the mobility literature is somewhat more unified in its implicit answer to the question "Mobility between what?" Much of the early work arose out of labor economics, based on the "unified approach to intergenerational mobility and inequality" (Becker and Tomes 1979:1154), which brought together human capital theory with dynastic investment models for family behavior. As with the status attainment tradition in sociology, economists working in this tradition sought single-number expressions for levels of mobility, generally intergenerational correlations of income, although usually estimated as elasticities from regressions of log earnings across generations (see Fields and Ok 1996; Solon 1999; Behrman 2000). More recently, however, economists have begun to focus as well on categorical representations of the structure of inequality, examining placement within the distribution of earnings, either using fixed categories across generations or relative ranks within income distributions (see Björklund and Jäntti 1997; Corak and Heisz 1999; Couch and Lillard 2004; Ermisch and Francesconi 2004; Gottschalk and Spolaore 2002; Grawe 2004). When analyzed as cross-classifications of quantiles, these methods are quite similar in spirit to the between-social-class mobility studies of sociology. Indeed, Björklund and Jäntti (1997) refer to income groups as income classes and reference the log-linear tradition of cross-national mobility research in sociology.[4]

No matter how this "Mobility between what?" question has been answered, a prominent concern of both disciplines has been the impact of structural change over time on mobility outcomes. In sociology, the extent to which over-time shifts in occupational distributions generate upward mobility has been studied extensively. Such outcomes were welcomed in the middle of the twentieth century, and elaborated in scholarship from both sociology (see Parsons 1960, 1970) and economics (see Kerr, Dunlop, Harbison, and Myers 1960) where it was argued that the growth of higher status occupations is an inevitable outcome of the process of industrialization (and also, by implication, that Marxist claims of the inevitability of class polarization under capitalism had been exaggerated). Perhaps reflecting the growing pessimism and radicalism of sociology in the 1960s and 1970s, such structurally induced upward mobility was deemed less theoretically meaningful than levels of mobility purged of these effects. The study of what came to be known as pure exchange mobility then became possible with the development of log-linear modeling techniques that could be used to ascertain margin-free measures of mobility (see Goodman 1965, 1968; Hauser 1978; Hauser and Grusky 1988). The resulting decompositions of total mobility into structural and exchange mobility can be regarded as the main triumph of sociological research on social mobility arrays during the last third of the twentieth century. Deploying these techniques, sociologists established conclusively that exchange mobility patterns are remarkably similar across most industrial societies (see Breen 2004; Erikson and Goldthorpe 1992; Grusky and Hauser 1984).[5]

In economics, the consequences of structural change for mobility patterns focused traditionally on the distributional effects of economic growth.[6] Following the classic conjecture of Kuznets (1955) that inequality rises with entry into industrialization but then moderates thereafter, empirical examination of the relationship between growth and the level of inequality has been a mainstay of the labor and development economics literatures. The types of mobility considered in this tradition, however, centered most commonly on gross distributional shifts in income along with income dynamics over the life course.

More recently, economists have become interested in the extent to which increasing inequalities within the labor markets of industrialized countries between the 1970s and the 1990s can be seen as less consequential to the extent that they have been accompanied by increasing chances of intergenerational mobility (see Welch 1999; Corak 2004). Relatedly, some economists have sought to determine the extent to which increasing chances of upward mobility sustain support for the market reforms in eastern Europe and the former Soviet Union that have tended to increase inequality (see Birdsall and Graham 2000). These interests have prompted others to work on the capacity to assess alternative economic systems by evaluating regimes of mobility opportunities alongside more traditional static representations of the distribution of inequality (see Roemer 1998; Stiglitz 2000).

Sociologists and economists have also focused on the process of intergenerational mobility. Both disciplines have intensified their efforts to study the effects of mental ability on educational attainment, the development of cognitive skills in schooling, and subsequent patterns of labor market success. Although these are old topics for both disciplines, the need to respond to *The Bell Curve* of Herrnstein and Murray (1994) served as a unifying event for empirical researchers from both disciplines (see Arrow, Bowles, and Durlauf 2000; Bowles, Gintis, and Osborne Groves 2005; Devlin, Fienberg, Resnick, and Roeder 1997). And, as I have described elsewhere (see Morgan 2005), in part because of this empirical work, economic and sociological research on educational attainment has grown more similar in the past decade. Economists have shown greater interest in long-run disadvantage and belief formation, and sociologists have shown greater interest in models of forward-looking, choice-driven behavior.

Beyond these core concerns of the intergenerational mobility literature, two final themes appear common to both disciplines. Sociologists and economists have considered whether intragenerational mobility should be modeled with the same conceptual and methodological apparatus as intergenerational mobility. On the one hand, if the ultimate destinations for mobility are groups of hierarchically organized social classes or income deciles, it should matter relatively little whether the origin positions of individuals are those of their parents or instead the first occupational positions or income levels secured on completion of educational training. On the other hand, the intervening mechanisms of both types of mobility remain rather distinct (i.e., educational attainment and the accumulation of cognitive skill in adolescence for intergenerational mobility versus labor market dynamics and organizational promotion schemes for intragenerational mobility). In sociology, intragenerational mobility is rarely studied as such anymore (see Sørensen 1975, 1978 for the beginning of the end in sociological research). Within economics, intragenerational income dynamics are still sometimes characterized as income mobility studies (see Fields 2001).

Finally, sociologists and economists have considered whether the mobility literature should focus primarily on descriptive methods and empirical analysis or instead on theoretical models of mobility processes. Between the descriptive focus on total mobility patterns and the turn toward log-linear modeling in sociology (i.e., between Lipset and Bendix 1959 and Grusky and Hauser 1984), a series of formal Markov models for mobility research was advanced in sociology (see Boudon 1973; MacFarland 1970; White 1970). The "Cornell Mobility Model" (McGinnis 1968), for example, elaborated basic first-order Markov processes in order to generate reasonably realistic models for intragenerational mobility patterns. These modelers conceded that they could not predict observed mobility patterns particularly well, but they nonetheless valorized the pursuit of parsimonious and explicit mathematical models. In the end, however, the descriptive tradition, exemplified best by log-linear model fitting, has dominated sociology since the late 1970s.

Economics has seen a similar movement from formal theory toward descriptive modeling. Formal models, such as those advanced by Becker and Tomes (1979, 1986), were subjected to empirical examination (e.g., Behrman and Taubman 1985; Peters 1992) and found less than complete. Formal modeling is still pursued (see Mulligan 1987; Piketty 2000), but the descriptive agenda has gained relative prominence in economics since the 1980s, in part because it would seem that the growth in inequality between positions in the labor market has brought empirical analysis more centrally to the core of all research in labor economics (see Katz and Autor 1999) and in part because of renewed interest in the effects of such inequality on cross-national mobility patterns (see Atkinson, Bourguignon, and Morrisson 1992; Burkhauser, Holtz-Eakin, and Rhody 1997; Corak 2004; Dearden, Machin, and Reed 1997; Jarvis and Jenkins 1998; Solon 1992). It may be reasonable to expect a movement back to more formal modeling of mobility, now that the descriptive agenda has been so successfully pursued.

THE CURRENT VOLUME

In the Part Two of the volume, two chapters analyze the level of mobility between generations and evaluate competing positions on how much mobility would be ideal. In "Would Equal Opportunity Mean More Mobility?," Christopher Jencks and Laura Tach consider the recent literature on inter-generational income mobility, building on classic questions that Jencks made famous in his two books from the 1970s—*Inequality* (Jencks 1972) and *Who Gets Ahead?* (Jencks 1979)—but with attention to the distributional justice and economic efficiency literature, in which he engaged in the interim (e.g., Jencks 1990). Jencks and Tach argue that approximately half of the correlation between incomes across generations can be attributed to genes and individual values. When then taking the position (based on the empirical social justice literature) that meritocracy should be understood as allowing for inequalities based only on "productivity enhancing traits," they argue convincingly that trends in intergenerational correlations of income are a poor reflection of trends toward achieving equality of opportunity. The lack of correspondence results from the "denominator problem" that underlies (literally) associations of this type. Jencks and Tach show that inter-generational correlations are a function of possibly countervailing effects of the advantages conferred by parents as well as all other sources of advantages. Given this indeterminacy, Jencks and Tach conclude by laying out an alternative agenda for how equal opportunity should be measured, arguing for straightforward but fine-grained investigation of the particular effects that establish intergenerational inheritance of economic status but still fall outside agreed on conceptions of what is meritocratic.

In "How Demanding Should Equality of Opportunity Be, and How Much Have We Achieved?," Valentino Dardanoni, Gary S. Fields, John Roemer, and Maria Laura Sanchez Puerta develop formal tests of equality of opportunity (building in part on Roemer 1998), which they then apply to data from the United States and from Britain (the Wisconsin Longitudinal Survey and the National Child Development Survey, respectively). Dardanoni and colleagues address some of the concerns developed by Jencks and Tach in the preceding chapter, using quantile regression and non-parametric moment comparisons to test finely (but somewhat indirectly) for mobility patterns consistent with four specific channels by which parents affect the income opportunities of their children—social connections, the inculcation of beliefs and investment in skills, genetic inheritance of ability, and the cultivation of preferences and aspirations. They find no support for equality of opportunity in Britain and very weak support in the United States.

In the Part Three of the volume, three chapters reengage the classic "Mobility between what?" question from the sociological literature on intergenerational mobility. In "Does the Sociological Approach to Studying Social Mobility Have a Future?," David B. Grusky and Kim A. Weeden renew their challenge to "big class" models in sociology (see Grusky and Sørensen 1998 and Grusky and Weeden 2001), arguing for the utility and elegance of studying underlying mechanisms of immobility with reference to smaller aggregations of occupational titles. To the extent that mobility processes are more complex than can be captured by simple 7-by-7 or even 11-by-11 tables of social classes, there is much to be said for this approach (but see Goldthorpe's comment on Grusky and Weeden 2001 for a rejoinder). In their chapter for this volume, Grusky and Weeden lay out an agenda for settling the debate. First, they specify the three core assumptions of the sociological literature on mobility that they see as matters of convention (and perhaps matters of faith): (1) the inequality space resolves into classes; (2) inequality is transmitted through classes; and (3) classes are big. They then argue that these assumptions are empirical statements, amenable to the empirical tests that they specify. The entailed agenda of such analysis, they contend, may help to further the joint agenda of both sociological and economic research on mobility, by establishing a tractable model of constrained multidimensionalism.

In "The Economic Basis of Social Class," John Goldthorpe and Abigail McKnight then offer a defense of the social class schema that has become the dominant classification for cross-national mobility research (following on Goldthorpe 1987 and then Erikson and Goldthorpe 1992), but this time highlighting the economic sensibility of the classification. Extending the arguments of Goldthorpe (2000) and Erikson and Goldthorpe (2002), they regard big classes as having (by and large) already passed the sorts of tests proposed by Grusky and Weeden in the previous chapter. To the extent that the dimensions of most concern in the Grusky-Weeden model can be said to be employment relations, Goldthorpe and McKnight make a case that is convincing.

Finally, in "Mobility: What? When? How?," Andrew Abbott offers a wide-ranging discussion that challenges the entire enterprise of modeling intergenerational mobility via cross-generational occupational classifications from two arbitrary points in time. Consistent with his research on sequence analysis and task niches in the ecology of professionalization, he argues for alternative forms of aggregation that preserve the essential nature of mobility outcomes as career trajectories in a moving field of changing occupational destinations. His multidimensionalism is of an entirely different sort than the one pitched by Grusky and Weeden, emphasizing contingencies through time rather than across endowments, working conditions, and outcomes (except insofar as his entire schema could be situated within the outcomes space of Grusky and Weeden).

In Part Four of the volume, five contributions investigate specific mechanisms of intergenerational mobility, examining the ways in which educational outcomes are related to cognitive skills, demographic processes, decision-making orientations, and changing levels of inequality. In "Inequality of Conditions and Intergenerational Mobility: Changing Patterns of Educational Attainment in the United States," I offer, with my coauthor Young-Mi Kim, an empirical analysis that challenges the position that inequality of family background resources necessarily regulates levels of intergenerational mobility. We show that the resource differentials that grew in the United States in the 1980s and 1990s cannot easily account for the accentuation of class differences in patterns of educational attainment.

In "Family Attainment Norms and Educational Stratification in the United States and Taiwan: The Effects of Parents' School Transitions," Robert D. Mare and Huey-Chi Chang test for subtle differences across both countries in the nonlinear effects of parental education on children's educational attainments. Beyond further demonstrating the utility of the educational transitions model that Mare pioneered, Mare and Chang develop the case that parental education affects children's educational attainments in two distinct ways: (1) by way of total completed education and (2) as a function of whether parents progressed successfully through the particular educational transition being modeled. This proposal formalizes the notion that parents' schooling represents a floor under the attainments of children, with a separable effect on children's own behavior, which is manifest either as rule following or direct socialization. Mare and Chang then show that, for both the United States and Taiwan, this specific nonlinear coding of parents' education fits the data better than alternatives. And, across the two societies, they use the effect sizes to explain important gender differences in educational stratification, noting in particular how the floor effect operates primarily for fathers in Taiwan and is transmitted only to sons. In the United States, where educational stratification has more closely approached a type of gender neutrality in process, the effects of mothers' and fathers' educational histories are similar (and for both boys and girls).

Next, Richard Breen and Meir Yaish offer "Testing the Breen-Goldthorpe Model of Educational Decision Making," which extends and then evaluates favorably the influential model proposed in Breen and Goldthorpe (1997) for the persistence of inequality of educational attainment across generations. Using data from the National Child Development Study (also analyzed by Dardanoni and colleagues in Chapter 3), they offer support for the crucial "relative risk aversion" assumption that generates the model's behavioral predictions. Notably, the chapter is an advance over prior versions of the Breen and Goldthorpe (1997) model itself, resting more solidly on a foundation that should be convincing to those who accept the generality of prospect theory.

In "Mental Ability—Uni or Multidimensional? An Analysis of Effects," David Epstein and Christopher Winship analyze the subscales of intelligence test scores, testing for differential effects on education and labor market outcomes. Building on prior work (see Winship and Korenman 1997), they find considerable reason to question unidimensional assumptions about the nature of intelligence and its effects on lifetime success. They show that quantitative ability and possibly verbal ability are the most important predictors of educational attainment, but that neither has direct effects on economic success. In contrast, they show that "fluent production" is the most important direct predictor of economic success, and yet it has no appreciable effects on educational attainment. Reconciling this set of findings, they speculate that education may serve as a relatively accurate signal to employers of individuals' quantitative and verbal abilities. Why education does not signal the fluent production that is (seemingly) of interest to employers as well may represent a critique of the U.S. education system, but this is a topic for further investigation.

For the last chapter of the section, Flavio Cunha, James J. Heckman, and Salvador Navarro offer "Counterfactual Analysis of Inequality and Social Mobility," in which they fault the mobility literature for its descriptive focus, arguing for greater attention to the underlying counterfactual causal effects that generate intergenerational correlations of income and socioeconomic status (and with reference to the large literature that Heckman and his many colleagues have developed; see Heckman and Krueger 2003). This chapter, much like the two from the first part of the volume, demonstrates the need to separate systematic and chance determinants of socioeconomic attainments when modeling intergenerational mobility. And, touching more deeply on issues of causality, the chapter demonstrates that the mechanisms that have generated immobility in the past are amenable to change in the future, but that such changes may not necessarily alter levels of mobility.

The volume concludes with three chapters on the contexts of mobility that demonstrate the need to consider macroeconomic conditions when assessing the causes and consequences of income dynamics, vulnerability to poverty, and absolute levels of well-being. In "Estimating Individual Vulnerability to Poverty with Pseudo-Panel Data," François Bourguignon, Chor-ching Goh, and Dae Il Kim present a methodology for estimating the probability of falling below a poverty threshold, conditional on one's current level of earnings, using repeated cross-sectional data. Comparing their estimates to benchmarks from genuine panel data on Korea, they demonstrate the effectiveness of their approach. They thereby contribute a new set of techniques for investigating a crucial set of mobility outcomes: income dynamics in developing countries where only cross-sectional data are available but where the globalization literature suggests macroeconomic dynamics have substantial effects on vulnerable populations of relatively low-skilled workers.

In "Happiness Pays: An Analysis of Well-Being, Income, and Health Based on Russian Panel Data," Carol Graham, Andrew Eggers, and Sandip Sukhtankar estimate the consequences of a different type of shock—the causal pathway between unexplained earnings residuals and future earnings growth. They argue, with evidence from Russia, that individual-level shocks to earnings levels are directly related to levels of happiness, and happiness in turn is directly related to further wage gains. Their chapter suggests that the recent interest in the behavioral dynamics of the earnings process may yield substantial insight for the economics literature.

In the final chapter of the volume, "The Panel-of-Countries Approach to Explaining Income Inequality: An Interdisciplinary Research Agenda," Anthony B. Atkinson and Andrea Brandolini draw on more than two-dozen studies from both economics and sociology on the relationship between macroeconomic dynamics and the income distribution. They develop a theoretical framework for understanding the common findings and substantial variation found in the literature. And, especially when considered alongside the common themes developed in the prior two chapters, it is a fitting conclusion to the volume, as it lays out an agenda for further progress in understanding the evolution of inequality around the globe, with full recognition that we may be witnessing a crucial period of development in structures of inequality in advanced industrial, postindustrial, and developing societies.

FUTURE PROSPECTS FOR ENGAGEMENT AND DEVELOPMENT OF THESE THEMES

Mobility research represents one of the oldest areas of empirical research in the social sciences. And, if it is defined broadly to include the empirical literature on inequality and poverty, then it is also one of the largest. However, despite this depth of engagement, many important and well-established questions remain open for investigation. Each of the four parts of this volume focuses on areas that demand further research, and the contributions themselves make clear which specific questions need to be answered. In conclusion, I will discuss three broad areas that demand engagement, before ending the chapter with a discussion of the new frontiers that are opening up for cross-national studies of mobility processes.

First, the contributions to the volume demonstrate that we must refine the methods by which the amount of mobility is measured, not just for descriptive work, but also for tracking changes in mobility in response to policy interventions. As Chapter 11 by Cunha, Heckman, and Navarro demonstrates, refined and sustained attempts to prosecute causal questions on the mechanisms of mobility can clarify why we see the particular patterns of mobility outcomes that we do. And, as Jencks and Tach and then Dardanoni and colleagues demonstrate, a deeper knowledge of mobility mechanisms is needed if we wish to determine the range of possible mobility outcomes, and how we might design assessments to determine the effectiveness and attractiveness of policies that promote equality of opportunity (however defined).

Second, we must continue to reevaluate positions on the appropriate units of analysis and summary measures for mobility research. There is no inherent need to break with past tools that have shown their merit, such as intergenerational cross-classifications of big social classes or intergenerational elasticities of family income. Indeed, there is value in understanding the reasons why some of these tools have proven so useful in the past (as revealed, for example, in Goldthorpe and McKnight's chapter that shows how well their class schema reflects basic employment relations). But, should these tools be outperformed, such as by more refined social class categories or non-parametric estimates of intergenerational elasticities, then consistency with the past literature must be sacrificed.

Finally, as the final three chapters demonstrate, we need to continue to pursue an integration of the mobility literature with broader perspectives on the evolution of structures of inequality, paying particular attention to the macroeconomic conditions that shape national labor markets. Although data limitations are substantial, as we will probably never have enough data on enough countries covering enough time periods to definitively determine the relevance of economic dynamics for mobility outcomes, we can make a great deal of progress by following the strategies set forth in those chapters.

Aside from further engagement of these classic themes, new frontiers are opening up for the study of social and economic mobility. The mobility literature of the mid-twentieth century was driven in important ways by three very large issues, much more consequential than scholarly inquiry: (1) the development of advanced industrialism in much of the northern hemisphere, (2) the transition to postcolonial independence in much of the southern hemisphere, and (3) the global competition between capitalism and communism. New concerns are now emerging, and although different, the new ones are nearly as dramatic: (1) the emergence of new varieties of industrialism in developing societies, (2) the transition to postindustrialism in advanced industrialized societies, and (3) a new era of global economic relations that is still in formation.

The last three chapters of this volume directly reflect these new frontiers more than the prior chapters, and yet the sort of work represented by the first eleven chapters is what must be undertaken with the latest data in order to come to grips with the new trends. In particular, patterns of globalization entail sectoral shifts in employment within most countries. Even if these shifts represent nothing more than the latest developments in the long and largely positive history of industrialization, their effects on patterns of social and economic mobility must be examined further. And, as nations at the periphery of global trade exhibit new of forms of industrialization, a new wave of studies of the early industrialization process will be needed. There is no guarantee that the received wisdom on the industrialization process, as revealed by developments in OECD countries, will be confirmed in these new cases.

These structural changes in the labor markets of countries throughout the world are accompanied by new patterns of development in the institutional levers that regulate mobility patterns. Intergenerational mobility remains contingent on the contours of educational systems, and these continue to develop in ways only partly attributable to evolving domestic economies. Intragenerational mobility remains contingent on within-organization vacancy opportunities along with the availability of between-organization intermediaries to buffer the effects of economic dislocations. One could lay out a nearly endless list of unresolved issues such as these that demand attention, and we hope that the following chapters of this volume will inspire scholars in sociology and economics to do so.

Notes

1. For general and comprehensive reviews of the mobility literature in sociology and economics, see Atkinson and Bourguignon (2000), Bendix and Lipset (1966), Breen (2004), Breiger (1995), Fields (2001), Grusky (2001), Piketty (2000), Solon (1999), and Treiman and Ganzeboom (1998).

2. For a comprehensive treatment of the social class literature, as it relates to this tradition of mobility analysis, see Grusky and Sørensen (1998).

3. Following upon Sorokin (1927) and Lipset and Bendix (1959), competing measures of mobility were developed; see Boudon (1973) for an integrative summary.

4. Joseph Schumpeter's writings on mobility represent an early confluence of the sociological and economics literatures on mobility. In a passage cited frequently by both sociologists and economists, Schumpeter (1955:126) referred to social classes as hotels, writing that "each class resembles a hotel or an omnibus, always full, but always of different people." This statement is often misrepresented, under the claim that Schumpeter regarded mobility as movement between floors of a hotel.

5. Although patterns of association between fathers' and sons' occupations could be analyzed elegantly and with precision using log-linear techniques, there were some unintended consequences of the log-linear revolution. As noted by scholars who wished to continue to work with intergenerational correlations of socioeconomic status, structural mobility patterns were sometimes regarded as a nuisance (i.e., deserving of estimation, but only in order to reveal pure exchange mobility patterns).

6. At one point, sociologists (see, for example, Smelser and Lipset 1966) were interested in the consequences of economic growth for intergenerational mobility (and vice versa), above and beyond the structural mobility induced by expansion of the most favored social classes. But, as sociology has retreated in large measure from studying developing societies, so has the attention to the consequences of economic growth (although see Atkinson and Brandolini in this volume for some discussion of the literature that does remain; also see Breen 1997).

References

Arrow, Kenneth Joseph, Samuel Bowles, and Steven N. Durlauf, eds. 2000. *Meritocracy and Economic Inequality*. Princeton: Princeton University Press.

Atkinson, A. B., A. K. Maynard, and C. G. Trinder. 1983. *Parents and Children: Incomes in Two Generations*. London: Heinemann.

Atkinson, A. B., François Bourguignon, and Christian Morrisson. 1992. *Empirical Studies of Earnings Mobility*. Chur, Switzerland: Harwood Academic.

Atkinson, A. B., and François Bourguignon, eds. 2000. *Handbook of Income Distribution*, Vol. 1. Amsterdam: Elsevier.

Becker, Gary S., and Nigel Tomes. 1979. "An Equilibrium Theory of the Distribution of Income and Intergenerational Mobility." *Journal of Political Economy* 87:1153–89.

——— 1986. "Human Capital and the Rise and Fall of Families." *Journal of Labor Economics* 4:S1–S39.

Behrman, Jere, and Paul Taubman. 1985. "Intergenerational Earnings Mobility in the United States: Some Estimates and a Test of Becker's Intergenerational Endowments Model." *Review of Economics and Statistics* 67:144–51.

Behrman, Jere. 2000. "Social Mobility: Concepts and Measurement." Pp. 69–100 in *New Markets, New Opportunities? Economic and Social Mobility in a Changing World*, edited by N. Birdsall and C. Graham. Washington, DC: Brookings.

Bendix, Reinhard, and Seymour Martin Lipset, eds. 1953. *Class, Status, and Power: A Reader in Social Stratification*. Glencoe, IL: Free Press.

——— eds. 1966. *Class, Status, and Power: Social Stratification in Comparative Perspective*. New York: Free Press.

Birdsall, Nancy, and Carol Graham. 2000. *New Markets, New Opportunities? Economic and Social Mobility in a Changing World*. Washington, DC: Brookings.

Björklund, Anders, and Markus Jäntti. 1997. "Intergenerational Income Mobility in Sweden Compared to the United States." *American Economic Review* 87:1009–18.

Blau, Peter M., and Otis Dudley Duncan. 1967. *The American Occupational Structure.* New York: Wiley.

Boudon, Raymond. 1973. *Mathematical Structures of Social Mobility.* San Francisco: Jossey-Bass.

Bowles, Samuel, Herbert Gintis, and Melissa Osborne Groves. 2005. *Unequal Chances: Family Background and Economic Success.* Princeton, NJ: Princeton University Press.

Breen, Richard. 1997. "Inequality, Economic Growth and Social Mobility." *British Journal of Sociology* 48:429–49.

Breen, Richard, and John H. Goldthorpe. 1997. "Explaining Educational Differentials: Towards a Formal Rational Action Theory." *Rationality and Society* 9:275–305.

Breen, Richard, ed. 2004. *Social Mobility in Europe.* Oxford: Oxford University Press.

Breiger, Ronald L., ed. 1990. *Social Mobility and Social Structure.* Cambridge: Cambridge University Press.

——— 1990. "Introduction: On the Structural Analysis of Social Mobility." Pp. 1–23 in *Social Mobility and Social Structure*, edited by R. L. Breiger. Cambridge: Cambridge University Press.

Breiger, Ronald L. 1995. "Social Structure and the Phenomenology of Attainment." *Annual Review of Sociology* 21:115–36.

Burkhauser, Richard V., Douglas Holtz-Eakin, and Stephen E. Rhody. 1997. "Labor Earnings Mobility and Inequality in the United States and Germany During the Growth Years of the 1980s." *International Economic Review* 38:775–94.

Corak, Miles, and Andrew Heisz. 1999. "The Intergenerational Earnings and Income Mobility of Canadian Men: Evidence from Longitudinal Income Tax Data." *Journal of Human Resources* 34:504–33.

Corak, Miles, ed. 2004. *Generational Income Mobility in North America and Europe.* New York: Cambridge University Press.

Couch, Kenneth A., and Dean R. Lillard. 2004. "Non-Linear Patterns of Intergenerational Mobility in Germany and the United States." Pp. 190–206 in *Generational Income Mobility in North America and Europe*, edited by M. Corak. New York: Cambridge University Press.

Dearden, Lorraine, Stephen Machin, and Howard Reed. 1997. "Intergenerational Mobility in Britain." *Economic Journal* 107:47–66.

Devlin, Bernie, Stephen E. Fienberg, Daniel P. Resnick, and Kathryn Roeder, eds. 1997. *Intelligence, Genes, and Success: Scientists Respond to the Bell Curve.* New York: Springer.

Erikson, Robert, and John H. Goldthorpe. 1992. *The Constant Flux: A Study of Class Mobility in Industrial Societies.* Oxford: Oxford University Press.

———— 2002. "Intergenerational Inequality: A Sociological Perspective." *Journal of Economic Perspectives* 16:31–44.

Ermisch, John, and John Francesconi. 2004. "Intergenerational Mobility in Britain: New Evidence from the British Household Panel Survey." Pp. 147–89 in *Generational Income Mobility in North America and Europe*, edited by M. Corak. New York: Cambridge University Press.

Fields, Gary S., and Efe A. Ok. 1996. "The Meaning and Measurement of Income Mobility." *Journal of Economic Theory* 71:349–77.

Fields, Gary S. 2001. *Distribution and Development: A New Look at the Developing World*. New York: Russell Sage Foundation.

Goldthorpe, John H. 1987. *Social Mobility and Class Structure in Modern Britain*. Oxford: Clarendon.

———— 2000. *On Sociology: Numbers, Narratives, and the Integration of Research and Theory*. Oxford: Oxford University Press.

Goodman, Leo A. 1965. "On the Statistical Analysis of Mobility Tables." *American Journal of Sociology* 70:564–85.

———— 1968. "The Analysis of Cross-Classified Data: Independence, Quasi-Independence, and Interaction in Contingency Tables, with or without Missing Entries." *Journal of the American Statistical Association* 63:1091–131.

Gottschalk, Peter, and Enrico Spolaore. 2002. "On the Evaluation of Economic Mobility." *Review of Economic Studies* 69:191–208.

Grawe, Nathan D. 2004. "Intergenerational Mobility for Whom? The Experience of High- and Low-Earning Sons in International Perspective." Pp. 58–89 in *Generational Income Mobility in North America and Europe*, edited by M. Corak. New York: Cambridge University Press.

Grusky, David B., and Robert M. Hauser. 1984. "Comparative Social Mobility Revisited: Models of Convergence and Divergence in 16 Countries." *American Sociological Review* 49:19–38.

Grusky, David B., and Jesper B. Sørensen. 1998. "Can Class Analysis Be Salvaged?" *American Journal of Sociology* 103:1187–234.

Grusky, David B., ed. 2001. *Social Stratification: Class, Race, and Gender in Sociological Perspective*. Boulder, CO: Westview.

Grusky, David B., and Kim A. Weeden. 2001. "Decomposition without Death: A Research Agenda for a New Class Analysis." *Acta Sociologica* 44:203–18.

Hauser, Robert M. 1978. "A Structural Model of the Mobility Table." *Social Forces* 56:919–53.

Hauser, Robert M., and David B. Grusky. 1988. "Cross-National Variation in Occupational Distributions, Relative Mobility Chances, and Intergenerational Shifts in Occupational Distributions." *American Sociological Review* 53:723–41.

Hauser, Robert M., and John Robert Warren. 1997. "Socioeconomic Indexes for Occupations: A Review, Update and Critique." *Sociological Methodology* 27:177–298.

Hauser, Robert M. 1998. "Intergenerational Economic Mobility in the United States: Measures, Differentials and Trends." CDE Working Paper No. 98–12, University of Wisconsin-Madison.

Heckman, James J., and Alan B. Krueger. 2003. *Inequality in America: What Role for Human Capital Policies?* Cambridge: MIT Press.

Herrnstein, Richard J., and Charles A. Murray. 1994. *The Bell Curve: Intelligence and Class Structure in American Life*. New York: Free Press.

Jarvis, Sarah, and Stephen P. Jenkins. 1998. "How Much Income Mobility Is There in Britain?" *Economic Journal* 108:428–43.

Jencks, Christopher. 1972. *Inequality: A Reassessment of the Effect of Family and Schooling in America*. New York: Basic Books.

Jencks, Christopher 1979. *Who Gets Ahead? The Determinants of Economic Success in America*. New York: Basic Books.

Jencks, Christopher 1990. "What Is the True Rate of Social Mobility?" Pp. 103–30 in *Social Mobility and Social Structure*, edited by R. L. Breiger. Cambridge: Cambridge University Press.

Katz, Lawrence F. and David H. Autor. 1999. "Changes in the Wage Structure and Earnings Inequality." Pp. 1463–1555 in *Handbook of Labor Economics, Volume 3*, edited by O. C. Ashenfelter and D. Card. Amsterdam: Elsevier.

Kerr, Clark, John T. Dunlop, Frederick H. Harbison, and Charles A. Myers. 1960. *Industrialism and Industrial Man: The Problems of Labor and Management in Economic Growth*. Cambridge: Harvard University Press.

Kuznets, Simon. 1955. "Economic Growth and Income Inequality." *American Economic Review* 45:1–28.

Laumann, Edward O., ed. 1970. *Social Stratification: Research and Theory for the 1970s*. Indianapolis: Bobbs-Merrill.

Lipset, Seymour Martin, and Reinhard Bendix. 1959. *Social Mobility in Industrial Society*. Berkeley: University of California Press.

McFarland, David D. 1970. "Intragenerational Social Mobility as a Markov Process: Including a Time-Stationary Markovian Model That Explains Observed Declines in Mobility Rates over Time." *American Sociological Review* 35:463–76.

McGinnis, Robert. 1968. "A Stochastic Model of Social Mobility." *American Sociological Review* 33:712–22.

Morgan, Stephen L. 2005. *On the Edge of Commitment: Educational Attainment and Race in the United States*. Stanford, CA: Stanford University Press.

Mulligan, Casey B. 1997. *Parental Priorities and Economic Inequality*. Chicago: University of Chicago Press.

Parsons, Talcott. 1960. *Structure and Process in Modern Societies*. Glencoe, IL: Free Press.

——— 1970. "Equality and Inequality in Modern Society, or Social Stratification Revisited." Pp. 13–72 in *Social Stratification: Research and Theory for the 1970s*, edited by E. O. Laumann. Indianapolis: Bobbs-Merrill.

Peters, H. Elizabeth. 1992. "Patterns of Intergenerational Mobility in Income and Earnings." *Review of Economics and Statistics* 74:456–66.

Piketty, Thomas. 2000. "Theories of Persistent Inequality and Intergenerational Mobility." Pp. 429–76 in *Handbook of Income Distribution, Volume I*, edited by A. B. Atkinson and F. Bourguignon. Amsterdam: Elsevier.

Roemer, John E. 1998. *Equality of Opportunity*. Cambridge: Harvard University Press.

Schumpeter, Joseph A. 1955. *Imperialism and Social Classes: Two Essays*. New York: Meridian.

Smelser, Neil J., and Seymour Martin Lipset. 1966. *Social Structure and Mobility in Economic Development*. London: Routledge & K. Paul.

Solon, Gary. 1992. "Intergenerational Income Mobility in the United States." *American Economic Review* 82:393–408.

——— 1999. "Intergenerational Mobility in the Labor Market." Pp. 1761–800 in *Handbook of Labor Economics, Volume 3*, edited by O. C. Ashenfelter and D. Card. Amsterdam: Elsevier.

Sorokin, Pitirim A. 1927. *Social Mobility*. New York: Harper & Brothers.

Sørensen, Aage B. 1975. "The Structure of Intragenerational Mobility." *American Sociological Review* 40:456–71.

——— 1978. "Mathematical Models in Sociology." *Annual Review of Sociology* 4:345–71.

Stiglitz, Joseph E. 2000. "Reflections on Mobility and Social Justice, Economic Efficiency, and Individual Responsibility." Pp. 36–65 in *New Markets, New Opportunities? Economic and Social Mobility in a Changing World*, edited by N. Birdsall and C. Graham. Washington, DC: Brookings.

Treiman, Donald J., and Harry B. G. Ganzeboom. 1998. "The Fourth Generation of Comparative Stratification Research." Working Paper, University of California at Los Angeles.

Welch, Finis. 1999. "In Defense of Inequality." *American Economic Review* 89:1–17.

White, Harrison C. 1970. "Stayers and Movers." *American Journal of Sociology* 76:307–24.

Winship, Christopher, and Sanders Korenman. 1997. "Does Staying in School Make You Smarter? The Effect of Education on IQ in the Bell Curve." Pp. 215–34 in *Intelligence, Genes, and Success: Scientists Respond to the Bell Curve*, edited by B. Devlin, S. E. Fienberg, D. P. Resnick, and K. Roeder. New York: Springer.

PART TWO   HOW MUCH MOBILITY?

CHAPTER TWO

Would Equal Opportunity Mean More Mobility?

Christopher Jencks and Laura Tach

Adults' economic status is positively correlated with their parents' economic status in every society for which we have data, but no democratic society is entirely comfortable with this fact. As a result, all democratic societies have adopted policies aimed at reducing the effect of family background on life chances, and almost all parties of the left think governments should do even more. A poll of social scientists who study intergenerational mobility would probably find that they, too, want governments to be more aggressive about removing obstacles to economic mobility. Those who study the effects of family background on life chances are, after all, often drawn to the subject because they feel that the inheritance of economic disadvantages is unjust.

This chapter will make two main arguments. First, equal opportunity does not imply eliminating *all* sources of economic resemblance between parents and children. Specifically, equal opportunity does not require that society eliminate the effects of either inherited differences in ability, broadly defined, or inherited values regarding the importance of economic success relative to other goals. Our second main point, which follows directly from the first, is that the intergenerational correlation of economic status (which we denote as r_I) is not a good indicator of how close a society has come to equalizing opportunity. Measuring equality of opportunity requires data on *why* successful parents tend to have successful children. In particular, we

We are grateful to the Russell Sage Foundation for financial support and to Tom Cook, Miles Corak, Gosta Esping-Anderson, Michael Hout, Jane Mansbridge, Jal Mehta, Mathias Risse, Adam Swift, and Scott Winship for invaluable criticisms that led to drastic revisions of an earlier draft. Any remaining errors are our own.

must separate the contributions of genes and values from the contributions of child-rearing arrangements, educational institutions, and labor market practices that favor the well-born.

In the interest of brevity we denote the intergenerational correlation of adult earnings as r_{Iy} and the intergenerational correlation of occupational rank as r_{Isei}. These two measures are not good substitutes for one another. Reported values of r_{Iy} are higher in the United States than in most other rich countries, while reported values of r_{Isei} are lower in the United States than in most other rich countries (Corak 2004; Björklund and Jäntti 2000). In addition, we often cite data from papers by economists, who report the elasticity of children's earnings with respect to their parents' earnings rather than the correlation. We denote this elasticity as β_{Iy}. When earnings inequality is the same for fathers and sons, r_{Iy} will equal β_{Iy}, but that is not always the case.[1]

Section 1 presents evidence that most citizens of rich western democracies reject absolute economic equality and think that intelligence and skill should be rewarded, regardless of their source. But the citizens of rich democracies also think that economic inequality is fair only if there is equal opportunity. At least in America, we argue, legislators have resolved these potentially conflicting ideals by assuming that equal opportunity requires both meritocratic labor markets and an opportunity for everyone to acquire whatever traits the labor market rewards.

Section 2 briefly reviews what we know about how individual traits that affect economic success contribute to r_I. Section 3 discusses evidence about the role of genes, while Section 4 discusses the role of values. These sections tentatively conclude that the combined effect of inherited genes and values explains something like half of r_{Iy}.

Section 5 argues that meritocracy should be understood as a system in which "productivity enhancing traits" are the only source of earnings inequality, and that earnings inequality would be substantially lower in such a society than in most existing societies. Because r_I depends on the ratio of inherited inequality to total inequality, and because equal opportunity would reduce both, its effect on r_I is unpredictable. It follows that changes in r_I are an unreliable indicator of whether opportunity has become more or less equal. Section 6 concludes by suggesting that the best way to measure changes in equal opportunity is to track the effects of specific sources of intergenerational economic resemblance that offend our sense of justice, such as the effect of parental income on college enrollment rates or children's chances of seeing a doctor when they are sick.

I. WHEN IS THE INHERITANCE OF PRIVILEGE UNJUST?

Table 2.1 shows how adults in Japan, West Germany, Great Britain, and the United States responded to five questions about the acceptability of economic inequality in 1991. The data were collected by the International Social Justice Project (ISJP). The table shows the percentage of adults who agreed with each statement minus the percentage who disagreed. The negative numbers in the top two rows indicate that most respondents disagreed with these statements. The positive numbers in the bottom three rows indicate that almost all respondents agreed with these statements. Three points deserve attention:

- Most adults in rich democracies reject the proposition that distributing income equally is the fairest option. This is especially true in the United States.
- Most adults in rich democracies feel that workers deserve to earn more if they are "more intelligent or more skillful than others." This is especially true in the United States and Britain.[2]
- Almost all adults in West Germany, Britain, and the United States agree that economic inequality is fair, "but only if there are equal opportunities."

The ISJP also surveyed a number of East European nations in 1991, obtaining results remarkably similar to those in Table 2.1.

Table 2.1 does not tell us what the citizens of rich democracies mean by "equal opportunities." In America, however, the legislative record from 1960 to 2000 suggests that lawmakers thought equal opportunity had two components. First, employers should not reward workers for characteristics that do not affect their job performance. This ideal, which we call "meritocracy," led to legislation forbidding discrimination in hiring, promotions, and pay on the basis of race, ethnicity, gender, and many disabilities.[3] The second component of equal opportunity was the idea that every child should have an equal chance to develop the traits that employers value. This ideal is usually called "equal educational opportunity."

Although equal educational opportunity is a widely accepted ideal, there is no consensus about what it means.[4] Sometimes the term refers only to the opportunities that schools provide, but sometimes it subsumes the full range of opportunities available to children, including those provided by families and communities. This broader definition implies that society must

TABLE 2.1

Percentage of Adults Who Agreed Minus the Percentage Who
Disagreed with Five Statements about Distributive Justice: Japan,
West Germany, Great Britain, and the United States in 1991

Question	Japan	West Germany	Great Britain	United States
"The fairest way of distributing wealth and income would be to give everyone equal shares."	−39	−37	−32	−51
"It is just luck if some people are more intelligent or more skillful than others, so they don't deserve to earn more money."	−37	−27	−56	−66
"People who work hard deserve more money than those who do not."	86	89	93	89
"People are entitled to keep what they have earned even if this means some people will be wealthier than others."	56	83	72	88
"It's fair if people have more money and wealth, but only if there are equal opportunities."	40	72	71	74

SOURCE: International Social Justice Project, as reported in Marshall, Swift, and Roberts (1997:246).

either make families and communities more alike or find ways to offset the adverse effect of growing up in a disadvantaged family or community. To avoid confusion we refer to this broader ideal as equal developmental opportunity rather than equal educational opportunity.

Discussions of equal educational opportunity also tend to be vague about whose opportunities must be equalized. The term almost always implies that children from different racial and ethnic groups should have the same chance of acquiring valuable habits and skills, and most scholars assume that this principle also applies to children from different socioeconomic backgrounds. But while race and class are *not* acceptable sources of inequality, it is less clear what sources of inequality *are* acceptable in a world of equal opportunity. If equal educational opportunity literally means "no child left behind," it requires equal outcomes. But Table 2.1 shows that hardly anyone favors that goal.

A more common interpretation of equal educational opportunity is that all children should have the same opportunities to develop their innate abilities. This chapter adopts that definition, but with an important caveat. When people talk about differences in "innate ability" they usually have in mind genetic differences that have roughly the same additive effect in good and bad environments. If every child attends a better school, mean outcomes will rise but neither the dispersion of outcomes nor their correlation with children's genetic endowment will change much. But genes do not always work this way. If some children have an inherited tendency to myopia and some do not, giving all children eyeglasses will only help those who are myopic. Mean visual acuity will rise, and the dispersion will fall. Likewise, if a society stops marginalizing individuals on the basis of their physical appearance, mean earnings should rise and inequality should fall.

The idea that society should worry more about environmental than genetic differences also reflects the mistaken assumption that it is easier to overcome environmental than genetic disadvantages. In reality, however, environmental damage is often just as irreversible as genetic damage, and when that is the case the victims need compassionate help, not "equal opportunity." Indeed, we may eventually find it easier to treat many genetic disadvantages than to reverse the effects of childhood diseases or parental ineptitude. For now, however, we think it important to ask how much of r_I derives from genetic resemblance between parents and children, even though we recognize that the normative implications of such estimates are far from clear.

Another crucial question about equal opportunity is whether meritocracy requires that all individuals receive "equal pay for equal work" or whether this rule applies only to members of underrepresented minorities like black people and women. In this chapter we assume that meritocracy requires equal pay for all equally competent workers, even if they are not members of any identifiable minority. To see why we take this position, two examples are helpful.

In 1953 the wages of unionized Boston-area truck drivers varied by a factor of two, depending on what was in the driver's truck (Dunlop 1957). Delivering magazines was worth more than delivering beer, which in turn was worth more than delivering coal. Laundry and scrap metal were the least rewarding cargoes. Dunlop attributed these differences partly to variation in the wages of other workers in a driver's industry and partly to historical accidents. Although these wage differentials were not related in obvious ways to skill requirements, their effects were probably not random. Boston unions that controlled access to jobs usually favored applicants with relatives in the union. As a result, high-wage drivers were probably in a position to help their sons get similar jobs, raising r_I. Unions of this kind have declined since the 1950s, but employers still rely heavily on their current employees to fill vacancies. As a result, seemingly random variation in the wages paid to workers with the same skills will in practice benefit children with well-connected parents more than children without such connections.

Our second example involves lotteries. Lotteries make incomes more unequal, but in a random way. In recent decades Americans have invested a growing fraction of their income in lotteries. Suppose that by 2050 households were spending a quarter of their income on lottery tickets. This would make post-lottery income far more unequal than pre-lottery income without increasing the covariance between parental income and children's adult income, so r_I would fall. Some would argue that opportunity was also more equal, precisely because r_I had fallen and "anyone now has a chance to get rich." Others would argue that equal opportunity requires rewards based on merit, not luck. This chapter makes the second assumption, so we see lotteries as simultaneously lowering r_I and making opportunity less equal by making it less dependent on merit.

Despite these ambiguities, we think r_I would remain positive if economic success depended solely on job performance and all children had the same opportunity to develop their talents. This principle would be true partly because the citizens of an equal opportunity society would still get half their genes from their mother and half their genes from their father. As we shall see, genes currently influence workers' cognitive skills, personality traits, educational attainment, and labor market success. And as the second question in Table 2.1 indicates, most citizens of rich democracies seem to think that intelligence and skills should be rewarded even if they are due to "luck." [5] These beliefs would probably change if we knew how to neutralize the effects of disadvantageous genes and failed to do so, but that is not yet a common problem.

A second reason for believing that r_I would remain positive under equal opportunity is that even the weakest versions of democratic pluralism allow parents to pass along their distinctive values to their children (or at least to try). If parents value spending time with their families more than they value consumer goods or a big bank balance, their children will probably tend to have the same priorities. The same will be true of parents who value saving souls or artistic expression more than they value economic status. Such patterns would keep r_I positive even if genetic variation became unimportant. [6]

2. PROXIMATE CAUSES OF r_I

Many influential sociologists and economists have argued that parents pass along their advantages to their children primarily by helping their children acquire more education (see, for example, Becker 1964 and 1991; Blau and Duncan 1967). Some have argued that noncognitive traits play an equally important role in determining earnings and that such traits may also help explain r_I (Bowles and Gintis 1976; Mueser 1979; Heckman 2000). Recent evidence suggests that disparities in physical and mental health also contribute to r_I.

Education and Cognitive Skills

Surprisingly few surveys have good measures of both respondents' cognitive skills and their parents' income. The best source of such data is probably the Wisconsin Longitudinal Survey (WLS), which has been following a representative sample of that state's 1957 high school graduates. The WLS extracted data on parental income from Wisconsin's tax records for 1957 through 1960 and obtained children's eleventh grade scores on the Henmon-Nelson group IQ test from school records. Because the WLS was limited to high school graduates, it underestimates the role of low educational attainment in explaining adults' economic problems. Because Wisconsin was relatively prosperous and overwhelmingly white in 1957, the WLS also underrepresents respondents from extremely disadvantaged backgrounds. Our aim, however, is not to estimate r_I for the United States but to estimate the degree to which r_I can be explained by children's test scores and educational attainment.

Table 2.2 shows three measures of the association between parents' economic status in 1957 and their children's economic status in 1991:

    1. The coefficient of father's occupational status (SEI) in 1957 when predicting employed children's occupational status in 1992.[7]
    2. The coefficient of logged parental income for 1957–60 when predicting employed children's logged earnings in 1991.
    3. The coefficient of logged parental income for 1957–60 in an equation predicting children's logged family income in 1991.

Column 1 shows the bivariate coefficients of father's occupation and parental income with no controls. Column 2 shows the coefficients after controlling causally prior parental characteristics (father's education in the case of father's occupation; both father's education and father's occupation

TABLE 2.2

Coefficients of Father's Occupation and Family Income in 1957 when Predicting
Children's Occupation, Earnings, and Family Income in 1991–92
Using Various Controls in the Wisconsin Longitudinal Survey

Dependent and Independent Variable	(1)	(2)	(3)	(4)	(5)	(6)	(7)	N
1. Daughter's occupational SEI score in 1992 on father's occupational SEI score in 1957	.171 (.016)	.119 (.018)	.102 (.018)	.076 (.018)	.034 (.017)	.034 (.017)	.029 (.017)	2,961
2. Daughter's logged earnings in 1991 on parents' logged family income in 1957	.095 (.034)	.057 (.039)	.049 (.040)	.039 (.039)	.022 (.039)	.022 (.039)	.015 (.039)	2,264
3. Daughter's logged family income in 1991 on parents' logged family income in 1957	.152 (.028)	.094 (.031)	.082 (.032)	.073 (.031)	.061 (.031)	.058 (.031)	.053 (.031)	2,790
4. Son's occupational SEI score in 1992 on father's occupational SEI score in 1957	.309 (.019)	.232 (.022)	.212 (.023)	.153 (.021)	.092 (.019)	.070 (.019)	.069 (.019)	2,737
5. Son's logged earnings in 1991 on parents' logged family income in 1957	.207 (.023)	.125 (.026)	.125 (.026)	.114 (.026)	.094 (.025)	.093 (.025)	.095 (.025)	2,353
6. Son's logged family income in 1991 on parents' logged family income in 1957	.235 (.024)	.156 (.027)	.153 (.027)	.143 (.027)	.122 (.026)	.120 (.026)	.121 (.026)	2,576
Controls								
Father's education and (in rows 2, 3, 5, and 6) father's occupation		Yes	Yes	Yes	Yes	Yes	Yes	
Mother's education, number of siblings, and family structure			Yes	Yes	Yes	Yes	Yes	
Eleventh grade IQ score				Yes	Yes	Yes	Yes	
Educational attainment years, plus degree dummies					Yes	Yes	Yes	
Occupational aspirations in 1957						Yes	Yes	
"Big Five" personality traits in 1992							Yes	

SOURCE: Authors' tabulations using the Wisconsin Longitudinal Survey. Coefficients in bold are at least twice their standard error.

in the case of parental income). Column 3 adds measures of the mother's education, family size, and whether there were two parents in the home, all of which could be affected by the father's economic position prior to marrying. Column 4 adds the child's eleventh grade test score, while column 5 adds years of school completed and six dichotomous measures of whether the respondent held specific degrees. Column 6 adds a measure of occupational aspirations at the end of high school, which is a determinant of educational attainment but also has a significant effect on all outcomes except a daughter's earnings even with educational attainment controlled. Column 7 adds five measures of personality traits in 1992.

Once we take account of a daughter's test scores and education, her parents' income no longer has an economically or statistically significant effect on her own earnings or family income. Her father's occupational status does have a statistically significant effect, but because the coefficient is only 0.034, it is not economically important. Among daughters, therefore, the economic benefits of having a successful father are almost all attributable to the fact that daughters of such fathers have above-average cognitive skills and educational attainment.

The human capital story does not work as well for sons. About half the bivariate association between parental income and sons' earnings or family income remains unexplained after we control IQ and education (compare equations 1 and 5 in rows 5 and 6).[8] These controls also leave a third of the bivariate association between fathers' and sons' occupational standing unexplained.[9]

Noncognitive Habits and Skills

Bowles and Gintis (1976), Heckman (2000), and Osborne (2005) all argue that noncognitive traits explain part of r_I. Although this argument seems plausible, empirical tests have not yielded impressive results.[10] Osborne, for example, finds that adolescent males who say that hard work counts for more than luck have above-average earnings in adulthood. But after she controls men's test scores and educational attainment, locus of control explains only 4 percent of r_{Iy}.

The 1992 WLS follow-up also included measures of what psychologists call the "Big Five" (extraversion, agreeableness, conscientiousness, neuroticism, and openness). When we included these measures in equation 7 of Table 2.2 more than half of these thirty coefficients were significant. But these measures were so weakly correlated with father's occupation and parental income that they explained almost none of β_{Isei} or β_{Iy}.

Michael Olneck's follow-up of students who attended school in Kalamazoo, Michigan, yielded similar results. Tenth grade homeroom teachers rated Kalamazoo students on cooperativeness, dependability, executive ability, emotional control, industriousness, initiative, integrity, perseverance, and appearance. The correlations between these nine ratings and men's economic status when they were between the ages of 35 and 59 averaged 0.24 for occupational SEI and 0.18 for annual earnings (Jencks et al. 1979, Tables A5.3 and A5.4). But once again Kalamazoo teachers' ratings were so weakly correlated with family background that they explained a negligible fraction of r_I (Corcoran and Jencks 1979:75).

Duncan, Kalil, Mayer, Tepper, and Payne (2005) used measures of math skills, shyness, self-esteem, depression, and "mastery" during childhood or adolescence to predict a woman's mean family income when she was between the ages of 30 and 34. The income correlations with the four noncognitive measures averaged 0.12. The income correlation with adolescent math scores was 0.25. The authors could not calculate the noncognitive traits' contribution to r_{Iy}, but traits that correlate only 0.12 with adult income cannot contribute much to r_{Iy}.

Dunifon, Duncan, and Brooks-Gunn (2001) showed that annual interviewer ratings of how clean respondents' houses were in 1968–72 predicted both respondents' hourly wages and their children's hourly wages in 1994–96. After controlling other aspects of family background, a one standard deviation increase in cleanliness was associated with a 10 to 15 percent increase in both parents' and children's future earnings.

Antisocial behavior may play a larger role in explaining r_I. Incarceration is associated with a significant reduction in future earnings, even after controlling test scores and education (Western 2004). Incarceration is also correlated with family background, although we could not find estimates of its contribution to r_I.

Health

Parental income is positively correlated with children's health (Case, Lubotsky, and Paxson 2002). Children are healthier if they have a regular bedtime, if they wear seatbelts, if no one in their household smokes, and if their mother is not overweight, but these indicators explain only a tenth of the correlation between parents' income and their assessment of their child's health. The fact that low-income parents tend to have unhealthy children appears to play some role in explaining r_I (Case, Fertig, and Paxson 2004; Haas 2004).

3. GENES AND r_I.

In 1971 Richard Herrnstein published a controversial article in *The Atlantic* arguing that genes played a substantial role in explaining the transmission of economic advantages from one generation to the next. Herrnstein proposed a syllogism that we can rephrase thus:

- If genes affect IQ and if IQ affects economic success, then
- Economically successful parents will have more than their share of the genes that contribute to high IQ scores.
- Because children inherit half their genes from each parent, children of economically successful parents will also have more than their share of the genes that contribute to high IQ scores. Therefore
- Children of economically successful parents will have higher IQ scores and be more economically successful than children of less successful parents.

Although this argument is logically compelling, IQ explains only a modest fraction of the economic resemblance between parents and children. As a result, genetic influences on IQ do not explain much of the economic resemblance between parents and children (Jencks et al. 1972). But although Herrnstein exaggerated the importance of IQ, he may not have exaggerated the role of genes in economic success. We now know that genes affect a multitude of traits that can influence economic success, including not just test scores but physical and mental health, educational attainment, beauty, height, and weight. Herrnstein's argument can therefore be restated in more general form:

- If genetic variation affects any of the traits that labor markets reward, then
- Genetic variation will affect economic success.
- If the labor market still rewards the same traits a generation later and genes still affect these traits, then
- Biological children of successful parents will still tend to have traits that the labor market rewards, even if the children have no social contact with their parent.

This section argues that genetic similarities between parents and children account for something like two-fifths of r_{Iy}. But before turning to the evidence, we need to clarify what we mean when we say that genes "explain" something.

Genes can affect human skills and behavior in at least three distinct ways. First, genetic differences lead to physiological differences among individuals who grow up in the same environment, and these differences can affect both skills and behavior. Second, genetic differences affect the way members of a society treat one another. Third, genetic differences affect the environments that people choose or create for themselves. Consider math skills. Some children master math more easily than others, and some of this variation is traceable to genetic differences. The educational system accentuates these differences by assigning mathematically gifted students to more demanding classes and by encouraging them to attend college. At the same time, students who find math difficult preserve their self-respect by dismissing math as unimportant and dropping it at the first possible opportunity. Genes may also influence math skills indirectly. Plomin et al. (1990) report that preschool children's genetic endowment influences the amount of time they spend watching television. Once children start school, those who watch more television presumably have less time for math.

Because our genes affect both the way others treat us and the choices we make for ourselves, we cannot estimate genes' impact "holding the environment constant." We can control measurable features of the environment, but we can never rule out the possibility that genes also influence unmeasured features of the individual's environment. As a result, estimates of genes' explanatory power seldom distinguish their physiological effects from their social effects. Thus although we may be able to say that genes currently explain, say, 20 percent of the variation in earnings, we cannot infer that environment explains only 80 percent. Because genes influence people's environment, environmental variation could explain 100 percent the variation in earnings even though genes also explain 20 percent.

Genes and Earnings in Sweden

The most direct way to estimate genes' role in economic inheritance is to compare the value of r_I when parents raise their own biological children ($r_{I\text{-}b}$) to the value when parents raise children to whom they are not biologically related ($r_{I\text{-}nb}$). Björklund, Lindahl, and Plug (2004) have assembled such data for nearly 6,000 Swedish children adopted during the 1960s. Among children who grew up with their biological fathers, the intergenerational earnings elasticity ($\beta_{Iy\text{-}b}$) was 0.232.[11] Among children adopted before their first birthday, the elasticity of children's earnings with respect to their adoptive father's earnings ($\beta_{Iy\text{-}nb}$) was 0.139 ($\pm$0.033), a reduction of two-fifths. This difference between $\beta_{Iy\text{-}nb}$ and $\beta_{Iy\text{-}b}$ could reflect the fact that fathers and their adopted children have fewer genes in common, but it could also have other sources.[12]

Adoptions must usually be approved by social workers, who try to weed out unpromising applicants. If this form of selection succeeds, the correlation between income and parental competence should fall, lowering $\beta_{Iy\text{-}nb}$. One way to assess the magnitude of this bias is to look at the effect of biological fathers' incomes when they have no social contact with their children. Björklund and Chadwick (2003) report that if sons never lived with their biological fathers, the elasticity of a son's earnings with respect to his biological father's earnings is 0.09 (again, about two-fifths of $\beta_{Iy\text{-}b}$).[13]

Heritability Estimates for Earnings

We can also check these estimates using indirect methods. The fraction of the observed ("phenotypic") variance explained by genetic variation is commonly called "heritability" and denoted as h^2. The simplest way to think about h^2 is to imagine a sample of monozygotic (MZ) twins reared apart. MZ twins occur when an egg splits after fertilization, making the twins genetically identical. If MZ twins were separated immediately after their egg divided, transplanted to the wombs of randomly selected mothers, and raised by those mothers, the correlation between separated twins' characteristics (r_{MZA}) would tell us how much of the variation in each characteristic was traceable to genetic factors. In other words, r_{MZA} would equal h^2.

MZ twins are never raised in this way, but there are other ways of approximating h^2. One common method is to compare monozygotic and dizygotic twins. Dizygotic (DZ) twins occur when two separate eggs are fertilized simultaneously. As a result, DZ twins share only half their genes. If genes all had additive effects and there were no assortative mating, the earnings correlation between DZ twins separated at the moment of conception (r_{DZA}) would be $0.5h^2$. Assortative mating will raise r_{DZA} while nonadditive genetic effects will lower it, so r_{DZA} should not be too far from $0.5h^2$. If growing up together raises the correlation between MZ and DZ pairs by the same amount (e_T^2), the correlations between MZ and DZ twins reared together will be

$$r_{MZT} = r_{MZA} + e_T^2 = h^2 + e_T^2 \qquad (1)$$

$$r_{DZT} = r_{DZA} + e_T^2 \approx 0.5h^2 + e_T^2 \qquad (2)$$

Subtracting equation 2 from equation 1 and rearranging we get:

$$h^2 \simeq 2(r_{MZT} - r_{DZT}) \tag{3}$$

This approximation will be too high if nonadditive genetic effects are more important than assortative mating or if growing up together raises r_{MZA} more than r_{DZA}.[14]

Björklund, Jäntti, and Solon (2005) present data on Swedish twins' average earnings for 1987, 1990, and 1993. Using equation 3, $h^2 = 0.39$ for both male and female earnings. But for h^2 to be 0.39 the effect on twins of growing up together must be zero or even negative. Because the correlation between adopted siblings reared together averages 0.074, the hypothesis that growing up together does not make people's earnings more alike is implausible. When Björklund et al. drop this assumption and take account of their data on biological siblings and half-siblings reared together and apart, their best estimate of h^2 is 0.20 for men and 0.13 for women. In Sweden, therefore, the traditional "twin method" appears to overstate the heritability of earnings by a factor of about two for men and three for women. That could be because e_T^2 is larger for MZ than DZ twins or because assortative mating does not fully offset the various nonadditive effects of genes.

Parents and children also share half their genes, so if the effects of assortative mating offset the nonadditive effects of genes, the earnings correlation between biological parents and children who have no social contact ($r_{Iy\text{-}ba}$) should again be roughly $0.5h^2$. Thus, if h^2 is 0.20 for Swedish men, $r_{Iy\text{-}ba}$ should be roughly 0.10. This estimate appears consistent with Björklund and Chadwick's estimate that $\beta_{Iy\text{-}ba} = 0.09$ and with Björklund, Lindahl, and Plug's (2004) finding that $\beta_{Iy\text{-}b}$ exceeds $\beta_{Iy\text{-}nb}$ by 0.093. Our suggestion that genetic resemblance explains about two-fifths of β_{Iy} in Sweden is thus what we would expect if Björklund, Jäntti, and Solon's best estimate of h^2 were correct.

Is America Like Sweden?

Sacerdote (2004) estimated the intergenerational elasticity of household income for 1,413 Korean children adopted by American families during the 1970s and early 1980s and for 1,176 biological children raised in the same American families. Placement was random, but mean age at adoption was 21 months. The intergenerational household income elasticity was 0.161 (± 0.051) for biological children and -0.087 (± 0.037) for adopted children.

The significant negative elasticity for adopted children is an unresolved puzzle.

We have better American data on adopted children's educational attainment than on their income, and these data suggest that the role of genes in educational attainment is similar in the United States and Sweden. The 1992 WLS follow-up asked respondents about their children's educational attainment. When Plug (2004) regressed these children's educational attainment on their parents' attainment, the bivariate coefficients for mothers and fathers averaged 0.46 for the 15,871 biological children and 0.27 for the 610 adopted children. When Björklund, Lindahl, and Plug (2004) made similar calculations for Swedish children born in roughly the same period, the coefficients averaged 0.235 for biological families and 0.120 for adoptive families. An extra year of parental education was thus twice as important in Wisconsin as in Sweden. Nonetheless, the reductions in the coefficients among adopted children were about the same in Wisconsin (41 percent) as in Sweden (49 percent). (In Sacerdote's sample of Korean adoptees the reduction was 77 percent.)

The most representative earnings data on American twins comes from Paul Taubman's (1976) survey of twins who served in the armed forces during World War II. Using equation 3, h^2 for white men's 1973 earnings is 0.48.[15] If twin data overstate the heritability of men's earnings by a factor of two in the United States as well as Sweden, the true value of h^2 for white American men would have been about 0.24 and the predicted value of r_{ly} for biological sons who never lived with their fathers would have been about 0.12. Father-son elasticities for annual earnings were around 0.30 during the 1970s in the United States (Solon 1992), and the correlations were similar to the elasticities. If r_{ly} was about 0.12 for biological sons who had no contact with their father and 0.30 for sons who grew up with their fathers, genes would explain about two-fifths of r_{ly} in the United States as well as Sweden. The uncertainties surrounding these estimates are obvious.[16]

How Might Genes Influence Earnings?

The most direct way to assess genes' contribution to the various traits that link parents' economic status to their children's status is once again to compare children raised by biological and adoptive parents. We have already mentioned evidence suggesting that about two-fifths of educational resemblance between biological parents and children derives from genetic resemblance.

But Plug (2004) also shows that once parental education is controlled the *direct* effect of parental income on children's educational attainment is essentially identical for biological and adopted children.

Two small American samples provide analogous data on the association between parental SES (socioeconomic status) and children's IQ. The Texas adoption study compared 256 adopted children with 93 biological children reared in the same families. The Minnesota adoption study compared 150 late adolescents who had been adopted before their first birthday with 237 late adolescents raised in a different set of biological families. The two Minnesota samples were recruited in rather similar ways and had similar economic characteristics. The Texas and Minnesota studies both suggest that the association between parental SES and older children's IQ is reduced by about two-fifths when children are adopted.[17] Table 2.2 suggests, however, that IQ scores play a fairly modest role in explaining intergenerational economic inheritance. Comparing columns 2 and 4, for example, the reductions in β_{Isei} average about a third. For earnings and family income, the reductions in elasticities average 27 percent for daughters and 9 percent for sons. This pattern suggests that genes are not generating intergenerational economic resemblance primarily by influencing IQ.

Genes also influence noncognitive traits. Loehlin (2005) reports parent-child correlations for the "Big Five" averaging 0.13 in biological families, 0.10 for biological parents who did not raise their children, and 0.04 for adoptive parents and children. But this does not help us explain genes' contribution to r_{ly}, because the Big Five have little relationship to parents' economic success.

Physical and mental illnesses often have a significant genetic component, so when they affect earnings they can contribute to r_l. Case, Lubotsky, and Paxson (2002) found no evidence that the association between parental income and children's health was weaker when children were not biologically related to their parents, but their sample of nonbiological children was relatively small and many diseases with a genetic component only manifest themselves in adulthood, so the last word has not been written on this issue.

This survey leads us to two conclusions about genes and earnings. First, our best guess is that genes account for about two-fifths of r_{ly} in Sweden. We are inclined to think that the figure is similar in America, but the data are far less satisfactory. Second, the normative implications of such estimates depend on whether genes exert their influence through traits like "ability" that are widely seen as legitimate sources of economic inequality, or through traits like beauty and skin color that are not seen this way. We cannot yet answer that question.

4. VALUES AND r_I.

Individuals whose top priority is economic success tend to do better economically than individuals whose top priority is spending time with their children or shooting ducks. We have no data on the weight that adults assign to occupational standing or earnings relative to their other goals in life, but we do have data on a few elements of such a measure.

Time

Working reduces the time available for most other activities. Because economic success tends to require unusually long hours, it leaves even less time for everything else. Altonji and Dunn (2000) have investigated the intergenerational correlation of hours worked. After taking account of the positive relationship between wages and hours worked, which should control both the effect of wages on motivation to work and the effect of skills on the availability of work, they attribute the remaining variation in hours to individual preferences. Preferred hours account for 15 percent of the variation in annual earnings for sons and 56 percent for daughters. The effect of a father's preferences on his son's preferences explains only 4 percent of the covariance between fathers' and sons' annual earnings, but the effect of a mother's preferences explains 37 percent of the covariance between mothers' and daughters' earnings.

Location

Many people also want to live in the community where they grew up or in a nearby community with similar characteristics. Page and Solon (2003) have used the Panel Study of Income Dynamics (PSID) to compare the places where parents lived in 1968 to the places where their grown sons lived in 1987–91. Among sons raised in nonmetropolitan areas, 54 percent still lived in such an area as adults. Only 14 percent had moved to a major metropolitan area (more than a million residents). Among sons raised in major metropolitan areas, in contrast, 83 percent still lived in such an area, and only 6 percent had moved to a nonmetropolitan area. Sons raised in large metropolitan areas earned 46 percent more than sons raised in nonmetropolitan areas.

When Bonggeum Kim (personal communication, 3/17/04) controlled the size of the community and the region of the country in which a son was raised, the father-son earnings elasticity in the PSID fell from 0.447 to 0.315. The wage gap between large and small communities was partly attributable to cost-of-living differences, but this adjustment only lowered the father-son elasticity from 0.447 to 0.402 (Kim 2002). Kim (2004) argues that the remaining wage gap between large and small communities arises because skilled men move to larger places where their skills are more valuable. But skill differences between men raised in large and small communities are also partly endogenous. If children growing up in a small community want to stay there, they have little incentive to develop skills that would be valuable only if they moved.

Nonmonetary Job Characteristics

Workers also face trade-offs between maximizing their hourly wages and job characteristics like safety, job security, interesting work, and proximity to home. Jencks, Perman, and Rainwater (1988) constructed an index of jobs' nonmonetary rewards based on the way workers with different job characteristics rated their own job relative to an average job. A job's score on their index of nonmonetary characteristics correlated 0.50 with its pay. Workers' ratings of their own job correlated 0.48 with their pay and 0.62 with the value that the average worker assigned to the job's nonmonetary characteristics.

We have not found data on whether parents and children make similar trade-offs between jobs' monetary and nonmonetary rewards, but we would expect some resemblance. Fathers who are self-employed tend to have sons who are self-employed, even when the father and son work in different occupations (Klatzky and Hodge 1971). Parents who work in occupations that require a lot of education relative to their pay also tend to have children who do the same (Hauser and Warren 1997). Conversely, if parents always choose the best paid job they can find, their children are likely to have somewhat similar priorities.

What can we say about the importance of values to r_I based on currently available data? Altonji and Dunn find that preferences about hours vary more for daughters than for sons, and that daughters' priorities are more influenced by their mother's priorities than their father's. If we take account of inherited locational preferences, however, values probably explain at least a tenth of β_{Iy} even for sons. If that is the case, and if two-fifths of β_{Iy} in biological families is explained by genetic resemblance, the combined effects of genes and values would account for something like half of β_{Iy} among both sons and daughters. As with all guesses, however, caveat lector.

5. ESTIMATING r_I WHEN OPPORTUNITY IS EQUAL

Most thoughtful advocates of equal opportunity concede that r_I would probably be positive even if labor markets were completely meritocratic and developmental opportunities were completely equal. Nonetheless, most still assume that equal opportunity would make r_I substantially smaller than it is now.[18] Although that is possible, it is far from certain. Everything depends on the "denominator problem."

The easiest way to illustrate the denominator problem is to decompose the variance of economic success (Var Y) into the variance explained by a parent's success (Var $\hat{Y}$) and the variance not explained by the parent's success (Var Y_e). Because $r_{Iy}^2 = $ Var $\hat{Y}/$Var Y, decomposing Var Y yields:

$$r_{Iy}^2 = \text{Var } \hat{Y}/(\text{Var } \hat{Y} + \text{Var } Y_e) \tag{4}$$

If Var $\hat{Y}$ falls while Var Y_e remains constant, r_{Iy} must fall. This is the scenario that most advocates of equal opportunity envision. The "denominator problem" arises because equal opportunity can also affect Var Y_e. Indeed, if equal opportunity means that all workers with comparable performance-related attributes get equally desirable jobs, Var Y_e is likely to fall substantially. If Var Y_e falls proportionately more than Var $\hat{Y}$, then r_{Iy} will rise.

Consider Sweden between 1956 and 1970, when large employers and labor unions sought to eliminate wage differences between similar jobs in different industries, communities, and workplaces. Hibbs and Locking (2000) report that the squared coefficient of variation for blue collar industrial wages fell by 33 percent between 1962 and 1970. If these data were available back to 1956, the decline would presumably be even larger. We have no data on how this decline was allocated between Var $\hat{Y}$ and Var Y_e. Before 1956 blue collar fathers in high-wage workplaces were presumably helping their sons get jobs in the same place, so reducing wage differences between workplaces presumably lowered Var $\hat{Y}$. Blue collar sons also tended to live near their fathers, so reducing geographic wage differences presumably lowered Var $\hat{Y}$ too. Nonetheless, it is hard to imagine that such changes reduced Var $\hat{Y}$ by 33 percent. Thus if all else had remained equal, r_{ly} would probably have risen among blue collar fathers and sons.

One common response to this argument is that it illustrates the advantages of using β_l rather than r_l to measure inequality of opportunity. If workers cared only about absolute differences, this argument would be correct. But workers also care about their rank in the economic hierarchy.[19] Suppose, for example, that Sweden had cut β_l from 0.50 in 1950 to 0.25 in 1980 and had eliminated *all* other sources of variation in earnings. This change would have had two effects. First, the children of Sweden's best and worst paid workers in 1950 would have enjoyed more equal living standards in 1980. Second, the children of the best paid workers in 1950 would all, without exception, have been the best paid in 1980. Conversely, the worst paid workers in 1980 would all have been children of the worst paid workers in 1950. We doubt that many people would view such a change as a step toward more equal opportunity.

The American labor market is larger and more chaotic than the Swedish labor market, so an "equal pay for equal work" rule could have even more dramatic effects here than in Sweden. American workers' measured characteristics explained less than half the variation in their occupational rank and less than a third of the variation in their annual earnings during the 1960s and 1970s (Jencks et al. 1979), and the same is probably true today. Some of the remaining variation is traceable to unmeasured skills and personality traits, but earnings vary a lot even when we follow the same individual over time. Gottschalk and Moffitt (1994) found that a third of the variance in American workers' annual earnings was caused by year-to-year fluctuations around a worker's average earnings over the course of a decade. Some of these fluctuations presumably reflected changes in workers' preferred job characteristics, but some reflected the fact that the American labor market is not governed by the law of one price. Year-to-year fluctuations cannot be correlated with family background, which is fixed. Thus if meritocracy reduced fluctuations of this kind, r_{ly} would rise. Indeed, Solon's (1992) upward revision of r_{ly} flowed directly from his argument that economists should be concerned only with fathers' and sons' lifetime earnings and should treat year-to-year fluctuations like measurement error.

Eliminating variation in children's opportunities to develop their talents would also have unpredictable effects on r_l. If all children had the same opportunity to develop their innate abilities, some of the genes that now influence earnings would no longer do so. But *some* genes would still affect earnings by affecting performance. If we use G to denote the maximum potential earnings of individuals with a given set of productivity-related genes and use V to denote the fraction of potential earnings that individuals take in monetary form (rather than, say, leisure, safety, or interesting work), equal opportunity would mean that an individual's earnings were:

$$Y_i = V_i G_i \tag{5a}$$

Note the absence of an error term. Taking logarithms:

$$\ln Y_i = \ln V_i + \ln G_i \tag{5b}$$

In equilibrium, the variance of logged earnings would be the same for parents and children, so:

$$\text{Var}(\ln Y) = \text{Var}(\ln V) + \text{Var}(\ln G) + 2\text{Cov}(\ln V, \ln G) \tag{6}$$

Using the subscripts p and c to denote a parent and a child, the covariance of a parent's earnings with a child's earnings is:

$$\text{Cov}(\ln Y_p, \ln Y_c) = \text{Cov}(\ln V_p \ \ln V_c) + \text{Cov}(\ln V_p \ \ln G_c)$$
$$+ \text{Cov}(\ln V_c \ \ln G_p) + \text{Cov}(\ln G_p \ \ln G_c) \tag{7}$$

Dividing equation 7 by equation 6 the intergenerational earnings correlation in a society with equal opportunity ($r_{Iy\text{-}EO}$) is:

$$r_{Iy-EO} = \frac{\text{Cov}(\ln V_p \ \ln V_c) + \text{Cov}(\ln V_p \ \ln G_c) + \text{Cov}(\ln V_c \ \ln G_p) + \text{Cov}(\ln G_p \ \ln G_c)}{\text{Var}(\ln V) + \text{Var}(\ln G) + 2\text{Cov}(\ln V \ \ln G)} \tag{8}$$

We cannot estimate equation 8 from existing data. We know, for example, that individuals currently make trade-offs between earnings and jobs' nonmonetary characteristics (including hours of work). Otherwise there would be no missionaries and few actors. But we do not know how much of the variance in annual earnings is currently attributable to these trade-offs, so we cannot estimate $\text{Var}(\ln V)$. We also know that genetic differences currently explain some of the variation in hourly wages, but we do not know how much of this variation derives from differences in job performance, so we cannot estimate $\text{Var}(\ln G)$. The intergenerational correlation of $\ln V$ is likely to be positive, but we have no evidence on its magnitude. Nor do we know the correlations between ln V and ln G either within or across generations. Nor do we know how any of these parameters would change if labor markets were completely meritocratic and developmental opportunities were completely equal.

We can, however, get some sense of how large $r_{ly\text{-}EO}$ might be with a few simplifying assumptions. First, let Var(ln G) = M^2Var(ln V). Normalizing Var(ln V) to 1.00 then makes Var(ln G) = M^2. Second, assume that although high potential wages induce people to work more hours, working more hours also makes people put more weight on their job's nonmonetary characteristics, so that the individual level correlation of ln V with ln G is zero. Third, assume that ln V is also uncorrelated with ln G across generations. Fourth, assume that the intergenerational correlation of G is 0.50 and denote the intergenerational correlation of V as r_{IV}. Then equation 8 reduces to:

$$r_{ly\text{-}EO} = (r_{IV} + 0.5M^2)/(1 + M^2) \qquad (8a)$$

If there are *no* genetic limitations on potential earnings, $M = 0$ and $r_{ly\text{-}EO} = r_{IV}$. Now assume that r_{IV} is positive but small (say 0.2). If $M = 0.5$ rather than zero, $r_{ly\text{-}EO}$ will rise from 0.20 to 0.26. If productivity-related genes generate as much variance in earnings as values, $M = 1$ and $r_{ly\text{-}EO}$ rises to 0.35. If $M = 2$, $r_{ly\text{-}EO}$ rises to 0.44. If r_{IV} exceeds 0.20, $r_{ly\text{-}EO}$ will be correspondingly larger.

Corak (2004) suggests that intergenerational earnings elasticities currently exceed 0.4 in the United States, Britain, and France.[20] His estimates for Germany and Sweden are close to 0.3, and his estimates for Canada, Denmark, Finland, and Norway are less than 0.2. In countries like Canada, Denmark, Finland, and Norway, therefore, making labor markets more meritocratic and developmental opportunity more equal could easily raise r_I rather than lowering it. Whether such a change would make people feel that they lived in a more just society is unclear.

Our earlier argument suggested that positive values of r_I are not in themselves evidence that opportunities are unequal. This section suggests two further conclusions:

- The value of r_I can fall for either of two reasons: because parental success has less impact on children's success or because other sources of variation in economic success have become more important. Conversely, r_I can rise either because parental success is having more impact or because other sources of variation are becoming less important.

- Unless r_I is very high, declines in r_I do not necessarily mean that opportunity is becoming more equal, and increases in r_I do not necessarily mean that opportunity is becoming less equal.

Unlike our earlier conclusion, however, these conclusions rest on the potentially controversial assumption equal opportunity should reduce random variation in the earnings of individuals with the same skills and preferences.

6. HOW *CAN* WE MEASURE UNEQUAL OPPORTUNITY?

If we want to know whether opportunity is becoming more or less equal, we need to track the effects of the specific intergenerational linkages that violate our norms regarding meritocracy and developmental opportunity. In the case of the labor market, these mechanisms could include:

1. Random variation in the wages or working conditions of equivalent workers.
2. Employers who treat socioeconomic background as evidence of potential productivity.
3. Economically successful parents using their social networks to help their grown children find the best available job for someone with their abilities.

In the case of developmental opportunity, three other mechanisms are potentially relevant:

1. Economically successful adults making better use of the time they spend with their children to develop traits that the labor market rewards.
2. Economically successful parents spending more on goods and services that enhance their children's labor market prospects.
3. Economically successful parents living in places that provide more public good to children.

This section uses the last two mechanisms to suggest the kinds of measures we think potentially useful for assessing trends in equality of opportunity.

Effects of Family Income

Parental income is positively correlated with preschool children's school test scores and health status. Among older children parental income is also correlated with high school grades, high school graduation, college graduation, post-educational employment, staying out of prison, and marrying before having a baby. Such correlations may indicate that affluent parents use their money to buy goods and services that improve their children's life chances, but they may also reflect the influence of genetic endowment or parenting practices.

Susan Mayer's 1997 book, *What Money Can't Buy*, is the most comprehensive effort to separate the effects of parental income from other sources of r_I. Mayer investigated the effects of parental income on children's test performance, behavior problems, high school graduation rates, college attendance, and post-educational employment. She also looked at the effect of income on teenage daughters' fertility and their chances of having a child out of wedlock. Her findings for test performance illustrate her general approach. She found that a child's test performance between the ages of 5 and 7 was fairly strongly correlated with the parents' average income since the child's birth. But she also found that three-fifths of this correlation was explained by the fact that more affluent parents had higher test scores themselves, were better educated, had fewer children, had their children when they were older, and were more likely to be white.

Mayer also investigated whether other unmeasured factors could be influencing both parental income and children's test scores by comparing the correlation of children's test scores with their parents' average income before and after the test was given. If income were only a proxy for stable but unobserved parental characteristics that also influenced test performance, pretest and posttest incomes should be equally good predictors of test performance. If the entire correlation between pretest income and test performance were causal, there should be no correlation between posttest income and test performance once pretest income was controlled. Based on these comparisons Mayer concluded that three-quarters of the association between parental income and children's test performance was explained by other stable determinants of both test scores and income. The remaining quarter appeared to be a true effect of pretest parental income on children's scores.[21]

Mayer found broadly similar patterns when she investigated the impact of parental income on behavioral problems, high school graduation, having a child as a teenager, and becoming a single mother. Note that if parental income also had a small impact on many other outcomes, these small effects could ultimately explain a nontrivial fraction of r_{Iy}. Mayer also found one important exception to the rule of small effects. Children's chances of attending college were far more strongly related to their parents' income when the children were in high school than to parental income when children were in their twenties. This pattern suggests that parental income during high school really does affect college attendance.[22]

The fact that parental income affects college attendance should come as no surprise. Unlike learning math, finishing high school, or avoiding pregnancy, attending college usually requires someone to write a series of sizable checks. The fact that parental income during adolescence affects college attendance also rebuts the most common objection to Mayer's "before and after" method. Economists often argue that households adjust their current consumption in light of their expectations about their future income. If this were common, the "before and after" method would be misleading. But if parents who expected their income to rise often borrowed to help their children, financing higher education should be their top priority. The fact that family income during adolescence appears to matter more than subsequent income for college attendance suggests either that parents' expectations are seldom accurate or that such expectations have little influence on parents' willingness defray their children's college bills.

Mayer did not investigate the effect of parental income on children's health, and we have not seen any natural experiments that throw light on this question. Based on Mayer's findings about college attendance, we would expect parental income to have its largest health effects through medical care. We would also expect these effects to be much larger among the uninsured than the insured. Roughly a fifth of children in families with incomes less than twice the poverty line were uninsured in 2002. A third of these children had no usual source of care, and a sixth had not seen a doctor in the past year. Almost all insured children had a usual source of care, regardless of income.[23]

The Role of Government

Advocates of equal opportunity level two kinds of charges at governments: that they distribute public resources in ways that favor the rich over the poor, and that even when they give more to the poor they do not do as much as equal opportunity requires. Again, test scores are a good place to begin. The most popular explanation for test score differences between richer and poorer children is that school districts serving affluent children spend more per pupil. If this were the explanation, however, low-income children should learn more in districts with high per pupil expenditure. Three decades of research have failed to find such a relationship (Hanushek 2003).[24] In addition, if the link between parental income and children's school achievement reflected disparities in school spending, California's decision to equalize expenditure on rich and poor children should have made achievement scores more equal. That did not happen.[25]

The weak relationship between expenditures and test performance probably reflects the fact that effective teachers gravitate to schools that serve more advantaged (and more white) students regardless of whether these schools pay more or have smaller classes (Hanushek, Kain, and Rivkin 2004; Hanushek, Kain, O'Brien, and Rivkin 2004). As a result, schools that enroll children of successful parents can get their pick of teachers even if they spend no more than schools that enroll less privileged children. The only way to eliminate the correlation between parental income and teacher quality would be for schools serving disadvantaged students to pay far more than their competitors. That is not politically feasible in America's decentralized system.

Reducing the effect of parental income on college enrollment would be easier than reducing income's effect on teacher quality. Kane (1999) reports that when states raise tuition at their public colleges, the fraction of state residents entering college tends to fall, especially among students from low-income families. Since the 1960s, however, states have raised public college prices faster than most residents' incomes. A sixth of all children lived in families with money incomes below the federal poverty line in both 1967 and 2001. In 1967 tuition, room, and board at public colleges averaged 29 percent of poverty line. By 2001 the ratio had risen to 46 percent.[26] Most of this increase was driven by tuition charges, not room and board. Such increases presumably help explain why Ellwood and Kane (2000) found that the link between parental income and college entrance tightened between 1982 and 1992.

The legislators who raised state college tuition often defended their votes by arguing that affluent families could afford to pay more, and that poorer families could get federal financial aid. But the Pell Grant program, which has provided federal scholarships for low-income students since 1972, did not reduce the association between parental income and college attendance (Hansen 1983), perhaps because potential recipients could not know how much help they would get—or even whether they would qualify—until after they had been admitted to a college. The Social Security Administration's financial aid program for children of deceased, disabled, or retired beneficiaries, in contrast, told children how much help they could expect as soon as they became eligible. Perhaps for this reason, the Reagan Administration's decision to abolish the program led to a sharp decline in college attendance among children of widows (Dynarski 2003). Evidence of this kind suggests that reducing the effect of parental income on college attendance would probably be much easier than reducing the effect of parental income on access to the most effective elementary and secondary school teachers. All we would need to do is cut prices in a predictable and transparent way.

What about health care? Most nations provide almost all of their citizens with low-cost health care. In the United States, a sixth of the population lacked insurance in 2002, up from one a seventh in 1984. The effect of insurance on health is hard to estimate, because the causal connections run both ways. The cost of care deters the uninsured from seeking care when they are sick, but this effect can be masked by the fact that people with health problems are more likely to seek coverage.[27] The best way to identify the effect of coverage is therefore to ask what happens when more people become eligible for free care. Currie and Gruber (1996), for example, studied the effect of expanding Medicaid eligibility between 1984 and 1992. Children's chances of seeing a doctor increased faster in states where eligibility expanded more. Childhood deaths also fell faster in these states, suggesting that free care really saved lives.[28] Levy and Meltzer (2004) find that expanding insurance coverage usually improves adult health as well.

This brief review suggests that although parental income has a direct effect on many characteristics of children, its effects on outcomes that do not require significant cash expenditures are relatively small. But when significant cash expenditures *are* required, as they are for both college attendance and medical care for the uninsured, the effects of parental income are important. College graduation is probably the outcome with the strongest effect on children's economic prospects. Children's health and survival is probably the outcome that parents care most about. The fact that these outcomes depend on parental income has two important implications. First, the best currently available evidence suggests that more generous public programs could reduce the impact of parental income on both children's access to higher education and their access to medical care. The fact that the United States has done less than most rich democracies to reduce this relationship suggests that we should be skeptical about the claim that America has an unusually strong commitment to equal opportunity. Second, if we want to know whether a country is doing all that it can to equalize opportunity, changes in the effects of parental income on cash-dependent outcomes provide a better measure than changes in r_I.

Notes

1. Using y_p to denote the standard deviation of a parent's logged earnings and y_c to denote the standard deviation of a child's logged earnings, $r_I = \beta_I (\sigma_{yp}/\sigma_{yc})$. Because σ_y rises with age, σ_{yp} usually exceeds σ_{yc} and r_{Iy} usually exceeds β_{Iy} if parents were older than children when the earnings data were collected. But in countries where σ_y is rising over time, this bias may be offset if children's earnings are measured in a later period than parents' earnings.

2. If we denote the percentages in Table 2.1 as P_T, then if all respondents answered a given question the percentage who agreed would be $(P_T + 100)/2$. Table 2.1 therefore implies that about 17 percent of Americans and 37 percent of West Germans thought that individuals did not deserve to earn more just because they were more intelligent or more skillful, with the British and Japanese falling in between.

3. Michael Young (1958) invented the term meritocracy to describe a dystopia, but in America it has usually had positive rather than negative connotations.

4. See Jencks (1988) for a discussion of the diverse meanings that an elementary school teacher might assign to "equal educational opportunity" when allocating her time between different children in her classroom.

5. Some of those who said they disagreed with the statement in line 2 of Table 2.1 could, however, have been rejecting the factual premise that "it is just luck if some people are more intelligent or more skillful than others" rather than the moral inference ("so they don't deserve more money").

6. Roemer (1998) makes a similar argument for slightly different reasons.

7. Occupational SEI scores take their name from Duncan's (1961) "Socio-Economic Index for All Occupations," and are based on the educational attainment and earnings of workers in a given occupation. Measures of r_I based on SEI scores are consistently higher than measures of r_I based on either prestige rankings (Featherman, Jones, and Hauser 1975; Featherman and Hauser 1976) or an occupation's mean earnings (Hauser and Warren 1997).

8. Bowles, Gintis, and Osborne (2005) reach similar conclusions using other data.

9. Corcoran and Jencks (1979) present data from three surveys of men over the age of 30 suggesting that test scores and education typically explain 84 percent of the bivariate relationship between parental characteristics and grown sons' SEI scores. None of these surveys includes a measure of parental income.

10. Farkas (2003) provides a good review on this literature.

11. The elasticities of children's earnings with respect to father's earnings are 0.260 for sons and 0.203 for daughters. All elasticities are slightly higher when the mother's and father's earnings are summed.

12. Björklund et al. investigate and reject the hypothesis that selective placement plays a significant role in $\beta_{Iy\text{-}nb}$.

13. $\beta_{ly\text{-}nb}$ may not be a "pure" genetic effect if these biological fathers' earnings are also correlated with the quality of their children's early environment. Also the relationship between fathers' and sons' earnings is not linear in logs, so the elasticity for adopted sons is not necessarily representative of what one would obtain for all sons.

14. Critics of the twin method often argue that identical twins are treated more alike than fraternal twins, but this is not the right test. Identical twins reared apart are also treated more alike than random children, because their genes are more alike and genes influence the environment. The relevant test is whether the *increase* in environmental resemblance is greater when identical twins are reared together than when fraternal twins are reared together.

15. Orley Ashenfelter and his collaborators also collected data on twins' hourly wages in the 1990s. This sample overrepresents identical twins and probably overrepresents twins who remain close to one another as adults. Ashenfelter and Rouse (1998) provide details. Their analysis focuses on returns to schooling among identical twins, but Rouse (personal communication) reports that the MZ and DZ twin correlations for hourly wages were 0.63 and 0.37 respectively. Using equation 3, the implied heritability of hourly wages is $(0.63 - 0.37)/(1 - 0.5) = 0.52$. Miller, Mulvey, and Martin (1995) also present estimates of r_{MZ} and r_{DZ} for Australia, but their income estimates are based on the average earnings of workers in a given occupation.

16. For a somewhat different approach to estimating the genetic component of intergenerational economic resemblance see Bowles and Gintis (2002).

17. In Minnesota the multiple correlation of father's occupation and total parental income with adolescent children's IQ scores was 0.28 for biological children and 0.16 for adopted children (Scarr and Weinberg 1978). In Texas, the adoptive parents' SES (based on the father's occupation and both parents' educational attainment) correlated 0.17 with the biological children's IQ scores and 0.11 with the adopted children's scores between the ages of 13 and 24 (Loehlin, Horn, and Willerman 1989). There was some selective placement in both Minnesota and Texas, so some of the resemblance between adoptive parents and their adopted children is genetic in origin, but this bias appears to be tiny. One fairly consistent feature of comparisons between children reared by biological and adoptive parents is that the regression coefficient of a rearing parent's educational attainment in an equation predicting a child's IQ score drops more among adopted children than does the coefficient of father's occupation or family income. This is true in Scarr and Weinberg's (1978) Minnesota study and in the older studies reviewed by Jencks et al. (1972:276). Capron and Duyme's (1989) small but carefully selected sample of French adoptive parents also suggests that parents' SES has a sizable effect on their adopted children's IQ scores.

18. This generalization rests on three facts. First, we have made this argument to a number of audiences. No one has ever said that they were convinced, and

many have said they were not. We also received extensive written comments on earlier drafts of this chapter from thoughtful colleagues and anonymous referees. None of them were convinced either. Finally, we have never seen anyone else make this argument in print, although Swift (2004) raises some of the same issues.

19. Parducci (1995) reviews the algorithms that both experimental subjects and ordinary citizens use to assess the adequacy of economic rewards.

20. Mazumder (2001 and 2005) reports even higher elasticities, although these may reflect differences between the standard deviations for fathers and sons rather than high values of r_I.

21. Shea (2000) reached conclusions similar to Mayer's using union membership, job loss, and industry wage premiums as instrumental variables for identifying the true effects of parental income.

22. Children from low-income families can usually scrape together enough money to attend a local public college if they work while in college and borrow heavily. But these requirements make higher education far less attractive to poor students than to affluent students. Students who have to work will have little leisure, and students who have to borrow know that it will be a long time before their investment raises their standard of living. An affluent parent can eliminate these costs by paying the bills, making college attendance considerably more attractive.

23. The data in this paragraph are from National Center for Health Statistics (2004:254, 256, and 350). Among insured poor children, 94 percent had a usual source of care in 2001–02.

24. Card and Krueger (1996) present evidence that higher school spending affected adult earnings before World War II, but this claim is controversial (see the other papers collected in Burtless 1996).

25. See Downes (1992). For some contrary evidence see Card and Payne (1998).

26. Tuition is the mean for public four-year institutions other than universities and comes from National Center for Education Statistics (2002:359). Poverty thresholds are from U.S. Bureau of the Census (2000 and 2002).

27. This presumably explains why Case, Lubotsky, and Paxson did not find that insurance coverage explained any of the correlation between parental income and children's health.

28. Conley and Springer (2001) also found that infant mortality fell faster when OECD countries increased their health spending.

References

Altonji, Joseph, and Thomas Dunn. 2000. "An Intergenerational Model of Wages, Hours, and Earnings." *Journal of Human Resources* 35(2):221–58.

Ashenfelter, Orley, and Cecelia Rouse. 1998. "Income, Schooling, and Ability: Evidence from a New Sample of Identical Twins." *Quarterly Journal of Economics*, 113:253–84.

Becker, Gary. 1991. *A Treatise on the Family*, enlarged edition. Cambridge, MA: Harvard University Press.

Becker, Gary. 1964. *Human Capital*. Chicago: University of Chicago Press.

Björklund, Anders, and Markus Jäntti. 2000. "Intergenerational Mobility of Socio-economic Status in Comparative Perspective." *Nordic Journal of Political Economy* 26(1):3–33.

Björklund, Anders, and Laura Chadwick. 2003. "Intergenerational Income Mobility in Permanent and Separated Families," *Economics Letters* 80:239–46.

Björklund, Anders, Mikael Lindahl, and Erik Plug. 2004. "Intergenerational Effects in Sweden: What Can We Learn from Adoption Data?" Bonn, Germany: Institute for the Study of Labor, IZA Discussion Paper 1194.

Björklund, Anders, Markus Jäntti, and Gary Solon. 2005. "Influences of Nature and Nurture of Earnings: A Report on a Study of Various Sibling Types in Sweden," in Samuel Bowles, Herbert Gintis, and Melissa Osborne, eds., *Unequal Chances: Family Background and Economic Success*, Princeton University Press and Russell Sage.

Blau, Peter, and Otis Dudley Duncan. 1967. *The American Occupational Structure*. New York: Wiley.

Bowles, Samuel, and Herbert Gintis. 1976. *Schooling in Capitalist America*. New York: Basic Books.

Bowles, Samuel and Herbert Gintis. 2002. "The Inheritance of Inequality." *Journal of Economic Perspectives*. 16(3):3–30.

Bowles, Samuel, Herbert Gintis, and Melissa Osborne. 2001. "The Determinants of Earnings: A Behavioral Approach," *Journal of Economic Literature* (December) 39:1137–76.

Bowles, Samuel, Herbert Gintis, and Melissa Osborne. 2005. "Introduction" to Samuel Bowles, Herbert Gintis, and Melissa Osborne, eds., *Unequal Chances: Family Background and Economic Success*, Princeton University Press and Russell Sage.

Burtless, Gary, ed. 1996. *Does Money Matter? The Effect of School Resources on Student Achievement and Adult Success*. Washington, DC: Brookings.

Capron, Christiane, and Michel Duyme. 1989. "Assessment of Effects of Socioeconomic Status on IQ in a Full Cross-Fostering Study." *Nature*. (August 17) 340(6234):552–53.

Card, David, and Alan Krueger, 1996. "Labor Market Effects of School Quality: Theory and Evidence." *Does Money Matter? The Effect of School Resources on Student Achievement and Adult Success*, edited by Gary Burtless. Washington, DC: Brookings.

Card, David, and Abigail Payne. 1998. "School Finance Reform, The Distribution of School Spending, and the Distribution of SAT Scores." Cambridge: National Bureau of Economic Research, Working Paper 6766.

Case, Anne, Darren Lubotsky, and Christina Paxson. 2002. "Economic Status and Health in Childhood: The Origins of the Gradient." *American Economic Review* (December) 92(5):1308–34.

Case, Anne, Angela Fertig, and Christina Paxson. 2004. "The Lasting Impact of Childhood Health and Circumstance." Princeton, NJ: Princeton University. Center for Health and Wellbeing.

Conley, Dalton, and Kristen Springer. 2001. "Welfare State and Infant Mortality." *American Journal of Sociology* 107(3):768–807.

Currie, Janet, and John Gruber. 1996. "Health Insurance Eligibility, Utilization of Medical Care, and Child Health. *Quarterly Journal of Economics* (May) 111(2):431–66.

Corak, Miles. 2004. "Do Poor Children Become Poor Adults? Lessons for Public Policy from a Cross-Country Comparison of Earnings Mobility." Florence, Italy: UNICEF Innocenti Research Center.

Corcoran, Mary and Christopher Jencks. 1979. "The Effects of Family Background." Pp. 50–84 in *Who Gets Ahead: The Determinants of Economic Success in America*, edited by Christopher Jencks et al. New York: Basic Books.

Downes, Thomas. 1992. "Evaluating the Impact of School Finance Reform on the Provision of Public Education: The California Case." *National Tax Journal* 45(4):405–19.

Duncan, Otis Dudley. 1961. "A Socioeconomic Index for All Occupations." In Albert J. Reiss, *Occupations and Social Status*. Glencoe, IL: Free Press.

Duncan, Greg, Ariel Kalil, Susan E. Mayer, Robin Tepper, and Monique Payne. 2005. "The Apple Falls Even Closer to the Tree than We Thought." In *Unequal Chances: Family Background and Economic Success*, edited by Samuel Bowles, Herbert Gintis, and Melissa Osborne. Princeton University Press and Russell Sage.

Dunifon, Rachel, Greg Duncan, and Jeanne Brooks-Gunn. 2001. "As Ye Sweep, So Shall Ye Reap." *American Economic Review* (May) 91(2):150–54.

Dunlop, John. 1957. "The Task of Contemporary Wage Theory." In *New Concepts in Wage Determination*, edited by George Taylor and Frank Pierson. New York: McGraw-Hill.

Dynarski, Susan. 2003. "Does Aid Matter? Measuring the Effect of Student Aid on College Attendance and Completion." *American Economic Review* (March) 93(1):279–88.

Ellwood, David and Thomas Kane. 2000. "Who Is Getting a College Education? Family Background and the Growing Gaps in Enrollment." In *Securing the Future*, edited by Sheldon Danziger and Jane Waldfogel. New York: Russell Sage.

Farkas, George. 2003. "Cognitive Skills and Noncognitive Traits and Behaviors in Stratification Processes." *Annual Review of Sociology* 29:541–62.

Featherman, David, and Robert Hauser. 1976. "Prestige or Socioeconomic Scales in the Study of Occupational Achievement?" *Sociological Methods and Research* (May) 4(4):403–22.

Featherman, David, F. L. Jones, and Robert Hauser. 1975. "Assumptions of Social Mobility Research in the U.S.: The Case of Occupational Status." *Social Science Research* (December) 4:329–60.

Gottschalk, Peter and Robert Moffitt. 1994. "The Growth of Earnings Instability in the US Labor Market." *Brookings Papers on Economic Activity* (2):217–54.

Halsey, A. H., A. F. Heath, and J. M. Ridge. 1980. *Origins and Destinations.* Oxford: Clarendon Press.

Hansen, W. Lee. 1983. "Impact of Student Financial Aid on Access." In *The Crisis in Higher Education,* edited by Joseph Froomkin. New York: Academy of Political Science.

Hanushek, Eric. 2003. "The Failure of Input-Based Schooling Policies," *Economic Journal* (February) 113: F64–F98.

Hanushek, Eric, John Kain, and Steven Rivkin. 2004. "Why Public Schools Lose Teachers." *Journal of Human Resources* (Spring) 39(2):326–54.

Hanushek, Eric, John Kain, Daniel O'Brien, and Steven Rivkin. 2004. "The Market for Teacher Quality." National Bureau of Economic Research (July): http://www.nber.org/~confer/2004/si2004/ls/hanushek.pdf

Haas, Steven. 2004. "Health Selection in the Stratification Process: The Effect of Childhood Health on Educational Attainment, Labor Force Participation, and Earnings." Boston: Harvard School of Public Health, Department of Society, Human Development, and Health.

Hauser, Robert, and John Robert Warren. 1997. "Socioeconomic Indexes for Occupations: A Review, Update, and Critique." *Sociological Methodology* 27:177–298.

Heckman, James. 2000. "Policies that Foster Human Capital," *Research in Economics* 54:3–56.

Herrnstein, Richard. 1971. "IQ." *Atlantic Monthly* (September):43–64.

Hibbs, Douglas and Hakan Locking. 2000. "Wage Dispersion and Productive Efficiency: Evidence for Sweden." *Journal of Labor Economics* 18(4): 755–82.

Jencks, Christopher. 1988. "Whom Must We Treat Equally for Educational Opportunity to Be Equal?" *Ethics* (April) 98:518–33.

Jencks, Christopher, Marshall Smith, Henry Acland, Mary Jo Bane, David Cohen, Herbert Gintis, Barbara Heyns, and Stephan Michelson. 1972. *Inequality: A Reassessment of the Effect of Family and Schooling in America.* New York: Basic Books.

Jencks, Christopher, Susan Bartlett, Mary Corcoran. James Crouse, David Eaglesfield, Gregory Jackson, Kent McClelland, Peter Mueser, Michael Olneck,

Joseph Schwartz, Sherry Ward, and Jill Williams. 1979. *Who Gets Ahead: The Determinants of Economic Success in America.* New York: Basic Books.

Jencks, Christopher, Lauri Perman, and Lee Rainwater. 1988. "What Is a Good Job? A New Measure of Labor Market Success," *American Journal of Sociology* (May) 93: 1322–57.

Kane, Thomas. 1999. *The Price of Admission: Rethinking How Americans Pay for College.* Washington, DC: Brookings.

Kim, Bonggeum. 2002. "The Role of the Urban/Non-urban Cost-of-Living Difference in Measured Intergenerational Earnings Mobility." *Economics Letters* 77:9–14.

Kim, Bonggeum. 2004. "The Wage Gap between Metropolitan and Non-metropolitan Areas." Unpublished.

Klatzky, Sheila, and Robert W. Hodge. 1971. "A Canonical Correlation Analysis of Occupational Mobility." *Journal of the American Statistical Association* (March) 66(333):16–22.

Krueger, Alan. 1999. "Experimental Estimates of Education Production Functions." *Quarterly Journal of Economics* (May) 114:497–532.

Levy, Helen, and David Meltzer. 2004. "What Do We Really Know about Whether Health Insurance Affects Health?" Pp. 179–204 in *Health Policy and the Uninsured*, edited by Catherine McLaughlin. Washington, DC: Urban Institute Press.

Loehlin, John, Joseph Horn, and Lee Willerman. 1989. "Modeling IQ Changes: Evidence from the Texas Adoption Project." *Child Development* (August) 60(4):993–1004.

Loehlin, John. 2005. "Resemblance in Personality and Attitudes between Parents and Their Children: Genetic and Environmental Contributions." In *Unequal Chances: Family Background and Economic Success*, edited by Samuel Bowles, Herbert Gintis, and Melissa Osborne. Princeton University Press and Russell Sage.

Marshall, Gordon, Adam Swift, and Stephen Roberts. 1997. *Against the Odds: Social Class and Social Justice in Industrial Societies.* Oxford: Clarendon.

Mazumder, Bhashkar. 2001. "Earnings Mobility in the US: A New Look at Intergenerational Inequality." Chicago: Federal Reserve Bank of Chicago Working Paper 2001–18.

Mazumder, Bhashkar. 2005. "The Apple Falls Ever Closer to the Tree Than We Thought." pp. 80–99 in *Unequal Chances: Family Background and Economic Success,* edited by Samuel Bowles, Herbert Gintis, and Melissa Osborne. Princeton University Press and Russell Sage.

Mayer, Susan E. 1997. *What Money Can't Buy: Family Income and Children's Life Chances.* Cambridge, MA: Harvard University Press.

Miller, Paul, Charles Mulvey, and Nick Martin. 1995. "What Do Twins Reveal about the Economic Return to Education? A Comparison of Australian and U.S. Findings." *American Economic Review* (June) 85(3):586–99.

Mueser, Peter. 1979. "The Effects of Noncognitive Traits." In *Who Gets Ahead: The Determinants of Economic Success in America*, edited by Christopher Jencks et al. New York: Basic Books.

National Center for Education Statistics. 2002. *Digest of Education Statistics, 2001.* Washington, DC: Government Printing Office.

National Center for Health Statistics. 2004. *Health, United States, 2004.* Washington, DC: Government Printing Office.

Osborne, Melissa. 2005. "Personality and the Intergenerational Transmission of Economic Status." In *Unequal Chances: Family Background and Economic Success*, edited by Samuel Bowles, Herbert Gintis, and Melissa Osborne. Princeton University Press and Russell Sage.

Page, Marianne E., and Gary Solon. 2003. "Correlations between Brothers and Neighboring Boys in Their Adult Earnings: The Importance of Being Urban." *Journal of Labor Economics* 21(4):831–55.

Parducci, Allen. 1995. *Happiness, Pleasure, and Judgment: The Contextual Theory and Its Applications.* Mahwah, NJ: Lawrence Erlbaum.

Plomin, Robert, Robin Corley, J. C. DeFries, and D. W. Fulker. 1990. "Individual Differences in Television Viewing in Early Childhood: Nature as Well as Nurture." *Psychological Science* (November) 1(6): 371–77.

Plug, Erik. 2004. "Estimating the Effect of Mother's Schooling on Children's Schooling Using a Sample of Adoptees." *American Economic Review* (March) 94(1):358–68.

Roemer, John. 1998. *Equality of Opportunity.* Cambridge, MA: Harvard University Press.

Sacerdote, Bruce. 2004. "What Happens When We Randomly Assign Children to Families?" Cambridge: National Bureau of Economic Research, Working Paper 10894.

Scarr, Sandra, and Richard Weinberg. 1978. "The Influence of Family Background on Intellectual Attainment." *American Sociological Review.* 43 (October): 674–92.

Shea, John. 2000. "Does Parents' Money Matter?" *Journal of Public Economics* 77:155–84.

Solon, Gary. 1992. "Intergenerational Income Mobility in the United States." *American Economic Review* (June) 82 (3):393–408.

Swift, Adam. 2004. "Would Perfect Mobility Be Perfect?" *European Sociological Review* 20(1):1–11.

Taubman, Paul. 1976. "The Determinants of Earnings: Genetics, Family, and Other Environments: A Study of White Male Twins." *American Economic Review* 66 (5):858–70.

U.S. Census Bureau. 2000. "Poverty in the United States: 1999." *Current Population Reports*, P60-210. Washington, DC: Government Printing Office.

U.S. Census Bureau. 2002. "Poverty in the United States: 2001." *Current Population Reports*, P60-219. Washington, DC: Government Printing Office.

Western, Bruce. 2004. "The Effects of Incarceration on Wages and Employment." Princeton, NJ: Princeton University, Department of Sociology.

Young, Michael. 1958. *The Rise of the Meritocracy*. London: Thames and Hudson.

CHAPTER THREE

How Demanding Should Equality of Opportunity Be, and How Much Have We Achieved?

Valentino Dardanoni, Gary S. Fields, John E. Roemer, Maria Laura Sánchez Puerta

1. INTRODUCTION

This chapter proposes tests of various notions of equality of opportunity and applies them to intergenerational income data for the United States and Britain. Agreement is widespread that equality of opportunity holds in a society if the chances that individuals have to succeed depend only on their own efforts and not on extraneous circumstances that may inhibit or expand those chances. What is contentious, however, is what constitutes "effort" and "circumstances." Most people, we think, would say that the social connections of an individual's parents would be included among circumstances: equality of opportunity is incomplete if some individuals get ahead because they have well-connected parents. This and other channels through which circumstances affect income opportunities in an intergenerational context are discussed in Section 2.

Section 3 then formulates four, increasingly stringent criteria for equality of opportunity. In Section 4, we turn to an empirical implementation of these criteria to test for equality of opportunity in the United States and Britain. The results, presented in Section 5, provide only the weakest of support for equality of opportunity in the United States and no support at all in Britain.

Concluding remarks are presented in Section 6.

2. CIRCUMSTANCES, EFFORT, RESPONSIBILITY, AND CHANNELS FOR TRANSMISSION OF OPPORTUNITY

Recently, one of the authors has attempted to formalize a general conception of equality of opportunity, conceived of as "leveling the playing field"

(Roemer 1998, 2002). Five words comprise the language of that approach. The *objective* is the aspect of well-being for which the policymaker or society wants to equalize opportunities. In this chapter, the objective is the wage-earning capacity of individuals. *Circumstances* are the aspects of the environments of individuals that affect their achievement of the objective, *and* for which the society in question, or the policymaker, does *not* wish to hold individuals responsible. A *type* is the set of individuals in the society who share the same circumstances. *Effort* comprises the totality of actions of the individual that affect his or her achievement of the objective, and for which society *does* hold the individual responsible. Finally, the *instrument* is the policy that can be manipulated in order to change the value of the objective.

We are now ready to define the core concept of this chapter, namely, equality of opportunity (EOp). We shall say that equality of opportunity has been achieved when all those who expend the same degree of effort, regardless of their type, have the same chances of achieving the objective. In terms of the preceding language, EOp holds that differences in the values of the objective are ethically acceptable if they are due to differential effort but not if they are due to differential circumstances.

An *equal opportunity policy* is a value of the instrument that makes it the case that the achievement of the objective of individuals shall be a function only of their efforts, not of their circumstances. In other words, the instrument is used to compensate fully those with disadvantageous circumstances, so that, in the end, they have the same chances of acquiring high values of the objective as do those with advantageous circumstances.

In this chapter, we discuss four channels through which circumstances affect income opportunities in an intergenerational context:

C1. Parents affect the chances of their children through provision of *social connections*.

C2. Parents affect the chances of their children through formation of *beliefs and skills* in children through family culture and investment.

C3. Parents affect the chances of their children through genetic transmission of *native ability*.

C4. Parents affect the chances of their children through the instillation of *preferences and aspirations* in children.

Various notions of equality of opportunity are based on the ethical observer's choice of which of these channels to regard as circumstances and which are subsumed under effort.

3. FOUR LEVELS OF EQUALITY OF OPPORTUNITY

We have listed the four channels for transmission of opportunity—social connections, beliefs and skills, native ability, and preferences and aspirations—in what we believe most of us would choose as the right order for nested inclusion in the set of circumstances. We think that nearly all observers would regard differential family connections as a circumstance outside of the control of the individual. A somewhat smaller number of observers would be likely also to count a person as unfairly disadvantaged because of having been raised in a family that inculcated the children with pessimistic beliefs about what they could become, or that did not invest in their skills. Probably a smaller number still would also say that the children are not responsible for low innate ability. Finally, we think that few observers would treat the preferences and aspirations of children as falling outside their control.

We do not wish to be dogmatic about the ordering of these four channels and can see how some observers might wish to reverse the order of the last two. The reason that "family influence on preferences" is listed as the last channel is that we think that most people would say that an adult should be responsible for his preferences—in particular, with regard to pursuit of economic opportunities—even if those preferences are in large part the consequence of his upbringing. As one influential philosopher has written, a person should be held responsible for his preferences if and when he is glad he has them (Dworkin 1981). This definition excludes addictions and compulsions, which are preferences one would prefer not to have, but not income-occupational choice preferences, even if they were instilled in childhood. We shall denote by P^S those preferences that the individual has that are attributable to the self (hence the superscript "S"). In our analysis, the individual is always held responsible for these preferences. This is to be contrasted with the preferences that the individual has because of family influences, for which he or she may or may not be held responsible.

For the sake of argument, let us make two assumptions: first, that the four kinds of circumstances listed exhaust the set of parental influences on child incomes, and second, that the set of parental influences is "nested" in the preceding order, with regard to arguable inclusion in the set of circumstances for EOp policy. If so, then we have four associated conceptions of equality of opportunity, associated with four possible sets of circumstances:

EOp1: Circumstances = {C1}. Effort = {C2, C3, C4, P^S}.

EOp2: Circumstances = {C1, C2}. Effort = {C3, C4, P^S}.
EOp3: Circumstances = {C1, C2, C3}. Effort = {C4, P^S}.
EOp4: Circumstances = {C1, C2, C3, C4}. Effort = {P^S}.

Thus, when X is the number of channels designated as circumstances, EOpX denotes equality of opportunity when there are X channels.

4. TESTING THREE LEVELS OF EQUALITY OF OPPORTUNITY

A. Three Tests

As we do not have data that permit us to test for the effect of parental social connections, we will henceforth ignore EOp1. The tests for equality of opportunity at the other levels (EOpX, X = 2, 3, 4) proceed as follows.

Let Y denote the outcome variable and let m(.) denote a function or statistic by which the outcome variable is judged—for example, the cumulative distribution function or the mean of Y. Let $j = 1, \ldots, J$ be the values of the C2 channels, $k = 1, \ldots, K$ the values of the C3 channels, and $l = 1, \ldots, L$ the values of the C4 channels.

The most demanding criterion for equality of opportunity is EOp4. This test maintains that the distribution of the outcomes should be the same for all (*social connections*), *beliefs and skills*, *native ability*, and *preferences and aspirations* groups. That is:

$$\text{Test of EOp4: Are the numbers } m_{jkl} \text{ all the same,} \tag{1}$$
$$\text{for all values of } (j, k, l)?$$

If individuals are held to be responsible for the family-induced preferences and aspirations (C4) but not for the other intergenerational transmission channels (C1-C3), we move to the EOp3 criterion. The test for EOp3 maintains that the distribution of outcomes should be the same for all (*social connections*), *beliefs and skills*, and *native ability* groups within a preferences and aspirations category. In other words:

$$\text{Test of EOp3: For each choice of } l, \text{ are the numbers} \tag{2}$$
$$\{m_{jkl} \mid l \text{ fixed, } j = 1, \ldots J, k = 1, \ldots, K\} \text{ the same?}$$

Suppose that individuals are also held responsible for native ability. We then have the EOp2 criterion, the test for which is that the distribution of outcomes should be the same for all (*social connections* and) *beliefs and skills* groups. The corresponding test is then:

Test of EOp2: For each choice of *l* and *k*, are the numbers
$\{m_{jkl} \mid l, k \text{ fixed}, j = 1, \ldots, J\}$ the same?   (3)

As noted earlier, EOp4 is a more demanding criterion than most observers, we think, hold.

One final remark: we take it as axiomatic that no ethical observer would hold individuals responsible for the consequence of their parents' social connections or lack thereof. To hold individuals responsible for *everything* about their environments would comprise the extremely laissez-faire view that any person, regardless of his situation, can "pull himself up by his bootstraps," and so equality of opportunity would require only antidiscrimination legislation.

B. The U.S. and British Data Sets

These tests for equality of opportunity are performed on data for the United States and Britain. In the case of the United States, we use the Wisconsin Longitudinal Study (WLS). This is a long-term study of a random sample of 10,317 men and women who graduated from Wisconsin high schools in 1957. Survey data were collected from the original respondents or their parents in 1957, 1964, 1975, and 1992. These data provide a full record of social background, youthful aspirations, schooling, military service, family formation, labor market experiences, and social participation of the original respondents. The survey data from earlier years have been supplemented by mental ability tests, measures of school performance, and characteristics of communities of residence, schools and colleges, and employers and industries. The WLS sample is broadly representative of white, non-Hispanic American men and women who have completed at least a high school education. Among Americans aged 50 to 54 in 1990 and 1991, approximately 66 percent are non-Hispanic white persons who completed at least 12 years of schooling.

In the case of Britain, we use the National Child Development Survey (NCDS) and the British Cohort Survey (BCS). These data sets are two UK cohort studies targeting the population born in the UK respectively between 3–9 March 1958 and between 5–11 April 1970. Individuals were surveyed at different stages of their life, and information on their parental background was collected. The latest NCDSs were conducted in 1981, 1991, and 1999 when the cohort members were aged 23, 33, and 41, while the latest BCS was conducted in 1999.

In implementing these tests on U.S. and British data, the outcome variable is the individual's monthly income in the United States, and hourly wage in the UK. In the United States, we have two income variables y. The principal income variable for our analysis, y_1, is the labor market earnings of the individual high school graduate in 1992, which is the most recent round of the survey. The data set also includes, for the household that the individual lives in, the income from the labor market and other sources. This total income, expressed on a per capita basis, is our second income variable y_2. In the case of Britain, the data set only provides information on individual labor market hourly wage, which is the sole outcome variable for our analysis.

The explanatory variables for the two countries are similar. *Beliefs and skills* are proxied by parents' education. *Preferences and aspirations* are proxied by individual's education. *Native ability* is proxied by individual's IQ.

Before continuing, we comment on the commonly used test for equality of opportunity, which is to ask if the distribution of outcomes among children is independent of parents' outcome values, using as test whether the rows of the intergenerational transition matrix are equal. This test implies taking EOp4 as the appropriate definition of equality of opportunity. However, as we have suggested, most ethical observers would probably not endorse EOp4 as the appropriate notion of equal opportunity, and hence the usual test is far too demanding, as it is not associated with an ethical view that many people hold.

We turn now to two approaches for relating the outcome variables to the explanatory variables.

C. Implementing the Tests by Quantile Regression

In our first empirical approach, we use quantile regression to check the four hypotheses considered in this chapter. Quantile regression differs from ordinary regression in the following way. In ordinary regression, the regression equation gives the mean of the outcome variable conditional on the explanatory variables:

$$Y_{mean} \mid A, E, PE = a + b\,A + cE + dPE.$$

Quantile regression, in contrast, provides an equation for the qth quantile of the conditional distribution. Thus, the equation for the conditional median is

$$Y_{med} \mid A, E, PE = a_{med} + b_{med} A + c_{med} E + d_{med} PE.$$

In this study, we estimate the conditional distribution of the outcome variable Y at four different quantiles, $q = 0.20, 0.40, 0.60,$ and $0.80,$ and see how the conditional distribution of Y depends on the conditioning variables in correspondence of the chosen quantiles. Let

$$Y_q \mid A, E, PE = a_q + b_q A + c_q E + d_q PE. \quad q = 0.20, 0.40, 0.60, 0.80$$

denote the conditional quantiles of the outcome variable, conditional on individual's education, individual's ability, and parents' education. Positive values of b_q, c_q, and d_q mean that higher values of ability, education, or parents' education *raise* income at the qth quantile of the conditional income distribution. It is possible, and indeed our results below show, that b_q, c_q, and d_q are not all positive at all quantiles of the distribution.

Turning now to tests for equality of opportunity, the three tests can be implemented with the following quantile regression equations:

$$\text{Test of EOp4: For all q's, } b_q = c_q = d_q = 0. \tag{1a}$$

$$\text{Test of EOp3: For all q's, } c_q = d_q = 0. \tag{2a}$$

$$\text{Test of EOp2: For all q's, } d_q = 0. \tag{3a}$$

The advantage of quantile regression over ordinary regression is that the former provides a test for whether the *distributions* of the outcome variable are independent of various circumstances, instead of whether the means of those distributions are independent of circumstances.

Implementing the Tests Nonparametrically

In our second empirical approach, we dichotomize the parental education, ability, and individual education variables in order to have a small number of different populations that can be directly compared in a nonparametric fashion.

We implement the three dichotomous variables in the following ways. The first thing that the approach turns on is the implementation of *beliefs and skills*. We create two categories of parents, "advantaged" and "disadvantaged." In both countries, parents' education is expressed as the average of the education level of the two parents. In the United States, the advantaged parents are those who averaged at least a high school diploma. In Britain, the dividing line between advantaged and disadvantaged parents is the median of average education, 9.5 years. The second concept that we use is individual's *native ability*. We distinguish two "ability" groups, gauged by the score on an IQ test, and call them "highly able" and "less able" according to whether they fall above or below the median. Third, the approach identifies two different groups for *preferences and aspirations*, according to the education of the individual. In the United States, the "high preference" individuals are those with one or more year of college. In Britain, those with A-level education or higher are regarded as "high preference" and those with O-level education or less are regarded as "low preference."

Accordingly, the three equality of opportunity tests, in decreasing order of stringency, are:

Test of EOp4: For eight parents' education/IQ/individual's
education groups, $m_{111} = m_{112} = \ldots = m_{222}$.   (1^b)

Test of EOp3: For each individual's education group, the mean
incomes are the same for each parents' education/IQ
group: $m_{11l} = m_{12l} = m_{21l} = m_{22l}\, l = 1, 2$.   (2^b)

Test of EOp2: For each individual's education/IQ group,
the mean incomes are the same for each parents' education
group: $m_{1kl} = m_{1kl}\,|\,k = 1, 2, l = 1, 2$.   (3^b)

To test for the three levels of equality of opportunity EOp2, EOp3, and EOp4, we perform a main test and a number of robustness tests. The main test uses individual labor earnings y_1 as the outcome variable of interest and compares the means μ of the eight distribution functions.

The robustness tests use different income variables or different statistics. The first and second robustness tests compare median individual earnings and CDFs of individual earnings instead of means. Finally, the third and fourth tests compare mean incomes per capita, y_2, for the United States and mean log-earnings instead of earnings in dollars for both countries.

5. RESULTS

A. First Set of Results: Quantile Regression

Tables 3.1 and 3.2 present the results of the estimation of the conditional quantile regressions for the two countries. Table 3.1 reveals that all coefficients are significantly positive for all quantiles. Thus, all three equality of opportunity hypotheses are strongly rejected for the UK. On the other

TABLE 3.1

Quantile Regression Results for the UK
Dependent Variable: Logarithm of Wage

	20TH QUANTILE		40TH QUANTILE		60TH QUANTILE		80TH QUANTILE	
	Coefficient	Std Error	Coefficient	Std Error	Coefficient	Std Error	Coefficient	Std Error
Constant	1.33	.032***	1.59	.049***	1.77	.043***	1.97	.048***
Ability	.080	.006***	.090	.006***	.091	.007***	.092	.010***
Education	.170	.006***	.164	.006***	.144	.005***	.122	.007***
Parents' ed.	.011	.003***	.007	.005	.011	.004***	.017	.005***

*, **, *** mean 10, 5 and 1 percent level of significance.

TABLE 3.2
Quantile Regression Results for the United States
Dependent Variable: Earnings

	20TH QUANTILE		40TH QUANTILE		60TH QUANTILE		80TH QUANTILE	
	Coefficient	Std Error	Coefficient	Std Error	Coefficient	Std Error	Coefficient	Std Error
Constant	−32.413	3,483.6***	−35,511	2,487.9***	−32,059	2,949.3***	−46,891	5,269.8***
Ability	21.7	9.5**	44.9	13.7***	61.9	16.2***	98.1	19.7***
Education	3,112.3	266.7***	4,304.5	236.8***	4,427.7	232.7***	5,966.6	406.7***
Parents' ed.	−434.8	96.9***	−498.6	153.3***	−35.8	176.9	744.4	279.0***

*, **, *** mean 10, 5 and 1 percent level of significance.

hand, the results for the United States presented in Table 3.2 are somewhat mixed. Individual's own education and own ability always exhibit statistically significant positive effects. Thus, EOp4 and EOp3 are strongly rejected. However, parents' education exhibits mixed effects. The coefficients are *significantly negative* at the 20th and 40th percentile of the conditional earnings distribution, *statistically insignificant* at the 60th percentile of the conditional earnings distribution, and *significantly positive* at the 80th percentile of the conditional earnings distribution. Thus, the hypothesis that parents' education, after conditioning on own education and ability, has no effect on children's outcome is strongly rejected. However, the rejection is in an unexpected direction, with profound differences between the lower and higher sections of the conditional distribution.

In summary, the results using the quantile regression method are that (1) we reject equality of opportunity as defined by EOp4 and EOp3 for both countries, (2) we reject equality of opportunity as defined by EOp2 for Britain, and (3) our results do not permit us to conclude whether EOp2 holds for the U.S. population described by our data.

B. Second Set of Results: Nonparametric Approach

In this subsection we present the results for the tests of equality of opportunity with the nonparametric approach. We begin with the results for the main tests, from the most stringent to the least, followed by the results of the robustness tests performed. The United States results using this method are presented in Tables 3.3 and 3.4, the British results in Tables 3.5 and 3.6.

The result for the main tests for EOp3 and EOp4 is that we reject the null hypothesis at the 1 percent level of significance. This result is the same for both the United States and Britain.

The results for the main test for EOp2 differ for the United States and Britain. In the case of the U.S. data set, we reject the null hypothesis at the 5 percent level of significance but not at the 1 percent level. That is, using mean individual earnings in dollars, we can be 95 percent confident (but not 99 percent confident) that equality of opportunity is rejected. However, for the case of Britain, the result for the main test for EOp2 is that we reject the null hypothesis at the 1 percent level of significance.

In summary, the results for the main tests are that (1) we reject equality of opportunity as defined by EOp4 and EOp3 for both countries, (2) we reject equality of opportunity as defined by EOp2 for Britain, and (3) we find

TABLE 3.3
United States: Data for Tests of Equality of Opportunity

MAIN TEST: COMPARISON OF MEAN EARNINGS IN DOLLARS

	Group 1 mean = 48,405	Group 2 mean = 36,578	Group 3 mean = 26,415	Group 4 mean = 21,915	Group 5 mean = 43,288	Group 6 mean = 33,930	Group 7 mean = 24,389	Group 8 mean = 19,871
Group 1 (mean = 48,405)								
Group 2 (mean = 36,578)	$\mu_1 > \mu_2$***							
Group 3 (mean = 26,415)	$\mu_1 > \mu_3$***	$\mu_2 > \mu_3$***						
Group 4 (mean = 21,915)	$\mu_1 > \mu_4$***	$\mu_2 > \mu_4$***	$\mu_3 > \mu_4$***					
Group 5 (mean = 43,288)	$\mu_1 > \mu_5$**	$\mu_5 > \mu_2$***	$\mu_5 > \mu_3$***	$\mu_5 > \mu_4$***				
Group 6 (mean = 33,930)	$\mu_1 > \mu_6$***	$\mu_2 > \mu_6$	$\mu_6 > \mu_3$***	$\mu_6 > \mu_4$***	$\mu_5 > \mu_6$***			
Group 7 (mean = 24,389)	$\mu_1 > \mu_7$***	$\mu_2 > \mu_7$***	$\mu_3 > \mu_7$	$\mu_7 > \mu_4$**	$\mu_5 > \mu_7$***	$\mu_6 > \mu_7$***		
Group 8 (mean = 19,871)	$\mu_1 > \mu_8$***	$\mu_2 > \mu_8$***	$\mu_3 > \mu_8$***	$\mu_4 > \mu_8$**	$\mu_5 > \mu_8$***	$\mu_6 > \mu_8$***	$\mu_7 > \mu_8$***	

*, **, *** for 10, 5, 1 percent significance level respectively. H_0: means are equal.

	Group 1 median = 36,000	Group 2 median = 30,000	Group 3 median = 21,000	Group 4 median = 19,000	Group 5 median = 38,000	Group 6 median = 32,000	Group 7 median = 20,000	Group 8 median = 17,000
Group 1 (median = 36,000)								
Group 2 (median = 30,000)	$med_1 > med^{***}$							
Group 3 (median = 21,000)	$med_1 > med^{***}$	$med_2 > med_3^{***}$						
Group 4 (median = 19,000)	$med_1 > med^{***}$	$med_2 > med_4^{***}$	$med_3 > med_4^{*}$					
Group 5 (median = 38,000)	$med_5 > med_1$	$med_5 > med_2^{***}$	$med_4 > med_3^{***}$	$med_5 > me^{***}$				
Group 6 (median = 32,000)	$med_1 > med^{***}$	$med_6 > med_2$	$med_6 > med_3^{***}$	$med_6 > me^{***}$	$med_5 > med^{***}$			
Group 7 (median = 20,000)	$med_1 > med^{***}$	$med_2 > med_7^{***}$	$med_3 > med_7$	$med_7 > med_4$	$med_5 > med^{***}$	$med_6 > me^{***}$		
Group 8 (median = 17,000)	$med_1 > med^{***}$	$med_2 > med_8^{***}$	$med_3 > med_8^{**}$	$med_4 > med_8$	$med_5 > med^{***}$	$med_6 > me^{***}$	$med_7 > med^{***}$	

*, **, *** for 10, 5, 1 percent significance level respectively. H_0: medians are equal.

(continued)

TABLE 3.3
(continued)

ROBUSTNESS TEST 2: STOCHASTIC DOMINANCE IN DOLLARS

	Group 1	Group 2	Group 3	Group 4	Group 5	Group 6	Group 7	Group 8
Group 1								
Group 2	1 > FOD 2***							
Group 3	1 > FOD 3***	2 > SOD 3***						
Group 4	1 > FOD 4***	2 > FOD 4***	3 > SOD 4***					
Group 5	1 ~ 5	5 > SOD 2***	5 > FOD 3***	5 > FOD 4***				
Group 6	1 ~ 6***	2 ~ 6	6 > SOD 3***	6 > SOD 4***	5 > FOD 6***			
Group 7	1 > FOD 7***	2 > SOD 7***	3 ~ 7	7 > SOD 4***	5 > FOD 7***	6 > SOD 7***		
Group 8	1 > FOD 8***	2 > FOD 8***	3 > FOD 8***	4 ~ 8*	5 > SOD 8***	6 > SOD 8***	7 > FOD 8***	

*, **, *** for 10, 5, 1 percent significance level respectively. H_0: CDFs are equal.

ROBUSTNESS TEST 3: COMPARISON OF MEAN INCOME PER CAPITA IN DOLLARS (STRICTLY POSITIVE VALUES)

	Group 1 mean = 42,114	Group 2 mean = 33,021	Group 3 mean = 28,736	Group 4 mean = 23,743	Group 5 mean = 36,913	Group 6 mean = 30,929	Group 7 mean = 24,952	Group 8 mean = 21,529
Group 1 (mean = 42,114)								
Group 2 (mean = 33,021)	$\mu_1 > \mu_2$***							
Group 3 (mean = 28,736)	$\mu_1 > \mu_3$***	$\mu_2 > \mu_3$**						
Group 4 (mean = 23,743)	$\mu_1 > \mu_4$***	$\mu_2 > \mu_4$***	$\mu_3 > \mu_4$***					
Group 5 (mean = 36,913)	$\mu_1 > \mu_5$***	$\mu_5 > \mu_2$**	$\mu_5 > \mu_3$***	$\mu_5 > \mu_4$***				
Group 6 (mean = 30,929)	$\mu_1 > \mu_6$***	$\mu_2 > \mu_6$	$\mu_6 > \mu_3$	$\mu_6 > \mu_4$***	$\mu_5 > \mu_6$***			
Group 7 (mean = 24,952)	$\mu_1 > \mu_7$***	$\mu_2 > \mu_7$**	$\mu_3 > \mu_7$***	$\mu_7 > \mu_4$	$\mu_5 > \mu_7$***	$\mu_6 > \mu_7$***		
Group 8 (mean = 21,529)	$\mu_1 > \mu_8$***	$\mu_2 > \mu_8$	$\mu_3 > \mu_8$***	$\mu_4 > \mu_8$***	$\mu_5 > \mu_8$***	$\mu_6 > \mu_8$***	$\mu_7 > \mu_8$***	

*, **, *** for 10, 5, 1 percent significance level respectively. H_0: means are equal.

(continued)

TABLE 3.3
(continued)

ROBUSTNESS TEST 4: COMPARISON OF MEAN LOG-EARNINGS IN DOLLARS

	Group 1 mean = 9,330	Group 2 mean = 8,864	Group 3 mean = 8,339	Group 4 mean = 7,931	Group 5 mean = 9,440	Group 6 mean = 9,147	Group 7 mean = 8,342	Group 8 mean = 7,866
Group 1 (mean = 9,330)								
Group 2 (mean = 8,864)	$\mu_1 > \mu_2$**							
Group 3 (mean = 8,339)	$\mu_1 > \mu_3$***	$\mu_2 > \mu_3$**						
Group 4 (mean = 7,931)	$\mu_1 > \mu_4$***	$\mu_2 > \mu_4$***	$\mu_3 > \mu_4$*					
Group 5 (mean = 9,440)	$\mu_5 > \mu_1$	$\mu_5 > \mu_2$***	$\mu_5 > \mu_3$***	$\mu_5 > \mu_4$***				
Group 6 (mean = 9,147)	$\mu_1 > \mu_6$	$\mu_6 > \mu_2$	$\mu_6 > \mu_3$***	$\mu_6 > \mu_4$***	$\mu_5 > \mu_6$			
Group 7 (mean = 8,342)	$\mu_1 > \mu_7$***	$\mu_2 > \mu_7$***	$\mu_7 > \mu_3$	$\mu_7 > \mu_4$**	$\mu_5 > \mu_7$***	$\mu_6 > \mu_7$***		
Group 8 (mean = 7,866)	$\mu_1 > \mu_8$***	$\mu_2 > \mu_8$	$\mu_3 > \mu_8$***	$\mu_4 > \mu_8$	$\mu_5 > \mu_8$***	$\mu_6 > \mu_8$***	$\mu_7 > \mu_8$***	

*, **, *** for 10, 5, 1 percent significance level respectively. H_o: means are equal.

Group 1 = advantaged high ability high preference
Group 2 = advantaged low ability high preference
Group 3 = advantaged high ability low preference
Group 4 = advantaged low ability low preference
Group 5 = disadvantaged high ability high preference
Group 6 = disadvantaged low ability high preference
Group 7 = disadvantaged high ability low preference
Group 8 = disadvantaged low ability low preference

TABLE 3.4

United States: Summary of Tests of Equal Opportunity

		RESULTS OF MAIN TEST	RESULTS OF ROBUSTNESS TESTS			
			Test 1	Test 2	Test 3	Test 4
Test of EOp4	Are all 8 group means equal?	No	No	No	No	No
Test of EOp3	Within a preference group, are all four ability-type groups equal? (Group 1 = Group 2 = Group 5 = Group 6 & Group 3 = Group 4 = Group 7 = Group 8)	No	No	No	No	No
Test of EOp2	Within an ability-preference pair, are the four type comparisons equal? (Group 1 = Group 5 & Group 2 = Group 6 & Group 3 = Group 7 & Group 4 = Group 8)	Yes at the 1% level, no at the 5% level.	Yes at the 1 and 5% level, no at the 10% level.	Yes	No	Yes

NOTE: "Yes" = "Cannot reject that they are equal."
"No" = "Reject that they are equal."

About the Tests:
Main test: Mean earnings are equal.
Robustness test 1: Median earnings are equal.
Robustness test 2: CDFs are equal.
Robustness test 3: Mean incomes per capita are equal.
Robustness test 4: Mean log-earnings are equal.

Group 1 = advantaged high ability high preference
Group 2 = advantaged low ability high preference
Group 3 = advantaged high ability low preference
Group 4 = advantaged low ability low preference
Group 5 = disadvantaged high ability high preference
Group 6 = disadvantaged low ability high preference
Group 7 = disadvantaged high ability low preference
Group 8 = disadvantaged low ability low preference

TABLE 3.5
Britain: Data for Tests of Equality of Opportunity

COMPARISON OF MEANS IN DOLLARS (EARNINGS)

	Group 1 mean = 10.86	Group 2 mean = 9.15	Group 3 mean = 7.97	Group 4 mean = 6.70	Group 5 mean = 9.92	Group 6 mean = 8.19	Group 7 mean = 7.46	Group 8 mean = 6.50
Group 1 (mean = 10.86)								
Group 2 (mean = 9.15)	$\mu_1 > \mu_2$***							
Group 3 (mean = 7.97)	$\mu_1 > \mu_3$***	$\mu_2 > \mu_3$***						
Group 4 (mean = 6.70)	$\mu_1 > \mu_4$***	$\mu_2 > \mu_4$***	$\mu_3 > \mu_4$***					
Group 5 (mean = 9.92)	$\mu_1 > \mu_5$***	$\mu_2 > \mu_5$***	$\mu_5 > \mu_3$***	$\mu_5 > \mu_4$***				
Group 6 (mean = 8.19)	$\mu_1 > \mu_6$***	$\mu_2 > \mu_6$***	$\mu_6 > \mu_3$	$\mu_6 > \mu_4$***	$\mu_5 > \mu_6$***			
Group 7 (mean = 7.46)	$\mu_1 > \mu_7$***	$\mu_2 > \mu_7$***	$\mu_3 > \mu_7$**	$\mu_7 > \mu_4$***	$\mu_5 > \mu_7$***	$\mu_6 > \mu_7$***		
Group 8 (mean = 6.50)	$\mu_1 > \mu_8$***	$\mu_2 > \mu_8$***	$\mu_3 > \mu_8$***	$\mu_4 > \mu_8$	$\mu_5 > \mu_8$***	$\mu_6 > \mu_8$***	$\mu_7 > \mu_8$***	

*, **, *** for 10, 5, 1 percent significance level respectively. H_0: means are equal.

COMPARISON OF MEDIANS IN DOLLARS

	Group 1 median = 10.34	Group 2 median = 8.82	Group 3 median = 7.16	Group 4 median = 5.97	Group 5 median = 9.44	Group 6 median = 7.85	Group 7 median = 6.69	Group 8 median = 5.96
Group 1 (median = 10.34)								
Group 2 (median = 8.82)	$med_1 > med$***							
Group 3 (median = 7.16)	$med_1 > med$***	$med_2 > med_3$***						
Group 4 (median = 5.97)	$med_1 > med$***	$med_2 > med_4$***	$med_3 > med_4$***					
Group 5 (median = 9.44)	$med_1 > med$***	$med_5 > med_2$*	$med_4 > med_3$***	$med_5 > med_2$*				
Group 6 (median = 7.85)	$med_1 > med$***	$med_2 > med$***	$med_6 > med_3$**	$med_6 > med_3$**	$med_5 > med$***			
Group 7 (median = 6.69)	$med_1 > med$***	$med_2 > med$***	$med_3 > med_7$**	$med_7 > med_3$**	$med_5 > med$***	$med_6 > med$***		
Group 8 (median = 5.96)	$med_1 > med$***	$med_2 > med$***	$med_3 > med_8$***	$med_4 > med_8$	$med_5 > med$***	$med_6 > med$***	$med_7 > med$***	

*, **, *** for 10, 5, 1 percent significance level respectively. H_0: medians are equal.

(continued)

TABLE 3.5
(*continued*)

STOCHASTIC DOMINANCE IN DOLLARS

	Group 1	Group 2	Group 3	Group 4	Group 5	Group 6	Group 7	Group 8
Group 1								
Group 2	1 > SOD 2***							
Group 3	1 > FOD 3***	2 > SOD 3***						
Group 4	1 > FOD 4***	2 > SOD 4***	3 ~ 4***					
Group 5	1 ~ 5***	5 > SOD 2***	5 > SOD 3***	5 > SOD 4***				
Group 6	1 > FOD 6***	2 > SOD 6***	6 > SOD 3***	6 > SOD 4***	5 > SOD 6***			
Group 7	1 > FOD 7***	2 > SOD 7***	3 ~ 7**	7 > SOD 4***	5 > FOD 7***	6 > SOD 8***		
Group 8	1 > FOD 8***	2 > FOD 8***	3 > FOD 8***	4 > SOD 8	5 > FOD 8***	7 > FOD 8***	7 > SOD 8***	

*, **, *** for 10, 5, 1 percent significance level respectively. H_0: CDFs are equal.

COMPARISON OF MEANS IN DOLLARS (LOG-EARNINGS)

	Group 1 mean = 2.34	Group 2 mean = 2.18	Group 3 mean = 1.97	Group 4 mean = 1.79	Group 5 mean = 2.25	Group 6 mean = 2.06	Group 7 mean = 1.90	Group 8 mean = 1.79
Group 1 (mean = 2.34)								
Group 2 (mean = 2.18)	$\mu_1 > \mu_2$***							
Group 3 (mean = 1.97)	$\mu_1 > \mu_3$***	$\mu_2 > \mu_3$***						
Group 4 (mean = 1.79)	$\mu_1 > \mu_4$***	$\mu_2 > \mu_4$***	$\mu_3 > \mu_4$***					
Group 5 (mean = 2.25)	$\mu_1 > \mu_5$***	$\mu_5 > \mu_2$***	$\mu_5 > \mu_3$***	$\mu_5 > \mu_4$***				
Group 6 (mean = 2.06)	$\mu_1 > \mu_6$***	$\mu_6 > \mu_2$***	$\mu_6 > \mu_3$**	$\mu_6 > \mu_4$***	$\mu_5 > \mu_6$***			
Group 7 (mean = 1.90)	$\mu_1 > \mu_7$***	$\mu_2 > \mu_7$***	$\mu_3 > \mu_7$**	$\mu_7 > \mu_4$**	$\mu_5 > \mu_7$***	$\mu_6 > \mu_7$***		
Group 8 (mean = 1.79)	$\mu_1 > \mu_8$***	$\mu_2 > \mu_8$***	$\mu_3 > \mu_8$***	$\mu_4 > \mu_8$	$\mu_5 > \mu_8$***	$\mu_6 > \mu_8$***	$\mu_7 > \mu_8$***	

*, **, *** for 10, 5, 1 percent significance level respectively. H_0: means are equal.

Group 1 = advantaged high ability high preference
Group 2 = advantaged low ability high preference
Group 3 = advantaged high ability low preference
Group 4 = advantaged low ability low preference
Group 5 = disadvantaged high ability high preference
Group 6 = disadvantaged low ability high preference
Group 7 = disadvantaged high ability low preference
Group 8 = disadvantaged low ability low preference

TABLE 3.6

Britain: Summary of Tests of Equal Opportunity

	RESULTS OF MAIN TEST	RESULTS OF ROBUSTNESS TESTS		
		Test 1	Test 2	Test 3
Test of EOp4	Are all 8 group means equal?	No	No	No	No
Test of EOp3	Within a preference group, are all four ability-type groups equal?	No	No	No	No
Test of EOp2	Within an ability-preference pair, are the four type comparisons equal?	No	No	No	No

NOTE: "Yes" = "Cannot reject that they are equal."
"No" = "Reject that they are equal."

About the Tests:

Main test: Mean earnings are equal
Robustness test 1: Median earnings are equal
Robustness test 2: CDFs are equal
Robustness test 3: Mean log-earnings are equal.

Group 1 = advantaged high ability high preference
Group 2 = advantaged low ability high preference
Group 3 = advantaged high ability low preference
Group 4 = advantaged low ability low preference
Group 5 = disadvantaged high ability high preference
Group 6 = disadvantaged low ability high preference
Group 7 = disadvantaged high ability low preference
Group 8 = disadvantaged low ability low preference

weak evidence of equality of opportunity using criterion EOp2 for the case of the United States.

Turning now to the robustness tests, we conduct four different ones for each of the three criteria for equality of opportunity. In the case of Britain, all the available robustness tests (using median earnings, CDFs of individual earnings, and mean log-earnings) support the rejection of EOp4, EOp3, and EOp2 at all levels of significance. In the case of the United States, all the robustness tests (using median earnings, CDFs of individual earnings, mean incomes per capita, and mean log-earnings) support the rejection of EOp4 and EOp3 at all levels of significance. However, in the case of EOp2, the robustness tests for the United States produce additional weak evidence in favor of equality of opportunity. Of the four robustness tests, one (the income per capita test) rejects EOp2 at all significance levels, one (CDFs) rejects EOp2 at the 10 percent significance level, and the other two (median earnings and mean log-earnings) do not reject EOp2 at any significance level. Taken together, the main test and the four robustness tests do not decisively reject EOp2 for the United States, but they do not provide strong evidence in favor of it either.

6. CONCLUSION

In market economies like those of the United States and the UK, we should not expect equality of opportunity for prefiscal incomes to hold when native ability and years of education are taken to be "circumstances." That is to say, one would expect prefiscal income, to be sensitive to native ability and years of education, and hence it is no surprise that our results imply that EOp3 and EOp4 do not hold in either country.

One might, however, conjecture that the institution of public education would be sufficient to compensate children for parental disadvantage (as here proxied by the parents" educational level)—that is that equality of opportunity in the sense of EOp2 would hold. Our tests show that this is not the case in the UK; the results are more ambiguous with respect to the United States. One might cautiously suggest, based on this result, that the United States is a more meritocratic society than the UK, in the sense that the disadvantages associated with parental deficits are less important for the success of the child. Our data, however, are not sufficiently fine to allow us to distinguish between the effects of family *connections* and family *culture* on the future earnings of the child. It is likely that both are important. It is nevertheless conceivable that, in the UK, parents pass their jobs down to their children, in the United States they do not, and this explains the different results for EOp2. It is more likely, however, that family culture is important in both countries; as well, perhaps the fact that private education for the wealthy is more institutionalized in the UK than in the United States explains the "better" results for the United States in regard to EOp2.

Finally, we repeat our caveat with regard to the ethical view associated with asking whether the rows of the intergenerational transition matrix are the same. As such equality could only be expected to hold if EOp4 held, *given* the fact that the joint distribution of native ability and preferences/aspirations differs according to parental type, demanding that kind of equality corresponds to a particularly radical conception of what equalizing opportunities requires.

We hope that our discussion will stimulate others to assemble data sets with more precise measures of the salient characteristics of individuals and their families, so that tests for equality of opportunity may be performed that correspond to commonly held ethical views.

References

Dworkin, R. 1981. "What Is Equality? Part 2: Equality of Resources." *Philosophy & Public Affairs* 10:283–345.

Roemer, J. E. 1998. *Equality of Opportunity*. Cambridge, MA: Harvard University Press.

———— 2002. "Equality of Opportunity: A Progress Report." *Social Choice and Welfare* 19:455–71.

CHAPTER FOUR

Does the Sociological Approach to Studying Social Mobility Have a Future?

David B. Grusky and Kim A. Weeden

The analysis of social mobility tables has become one of the signature contributions of sociology over the last half-century. If sociology can count this tradition as one of its resounding successes, it is in part because a consensus over methods has allowed mobility analysts to turn to research rather than squabble endlessly over how it should be completed. Although the discipline is justifiably proud of this success, it is nonetheless useful to ask whether the long-standing methodological conventions within the subfield continue to serve the mobility analyst well. The time is ripe for such a reexamination because the latest wave of cross-national mobility research has all but come to a close (e.g., Erikson and Goldthorpe 1992; cf. Breen 2005a) and because new theoretical developments in economics allow us to reconsider our conventional methodological commitments in light of the strikingly different rationale for mobility research that economists typically offer. In this chapter, we expose some of the assumptions of sociological mobility research, ask whether they still can be defended, and outline in the process a new program of mobility research that sociologists and economists alike could embrace.

We concentrate, in particular, on the usefulness of applying conventional social class schemes to characterize the positions between which individuals can move. Within sociology, the mobility analyst typically proceeds by classifying parents and children in terms of "big-class" schemes that

The research reported here was supported by a National Science Foundation research grant (SBS-9906419) and with discretionary funds from Cornell University and Stanford University. We are grateful for the unusually helpful comments of Stephen L. Morgan and Young-Mi Kim. If any errors or misinterpretations remain, we are fully responsible for them.

comprise, for example, such categories as professionals, managers, routine nonmanuals, petty bourgeoisie, and skilled and unskilled manual workers (e.g., Goldthorpe 2000). The study of mobility then reduces to the study of transitions between cells in the matrices formed by cross-classifying the big-class categories of parents and children. As new statistical techniques have emerged, the resulting mobility array has been analyzed with increasingly sophisticated models, but the array itself has been constructed in much the same way for the last half-century.

We don't mean to suggest that all methodological debate has been eliminated within this subfield. For example, we have ourselves criticized the big-class convention in earlier essays (e.g., Grusky and Weeden 2001; Sørensen and Grusky 1996), but our critique has not so much challenged the class concept itself as the way it has been operationalized. That is, we have suggested that mobility analysis should be carried out with micro classes (i.e., detailed occupational categories) rather than big classes, because the former are more deeply institutionalized than the latter and provide, as a result, an important conduit through which human and social capital is transmitted (e.g., Grusky and Weeden 2001; Rytina 2000). We review this argument below, contrast it with more fundamental critiques of the class concept itself, and discuss how these various challenges of conventional mobility analysis might be evaluated empirically.

Within the discipline of economics, the study of mobility has not been equally prominent, at least not until a wave of mobility research was triggered by the increase in inequality in the 1980s and 1990s and the consequent interest in testing for an offsetting increase in mobility between economic categories (e.g., Gottschalk 2001; also see Bowles et al. 2005; Corak 2005). This motivation accounts in part for the characteristic focus among economists on economic rather than class mobility (cf. Kambourov and Manovskii 2004). Although the study of mobility within economics has been methodologically more diverse than its counterpart tradition in sociology, most economists proceed either by modeling the tabular arrays formed by discretizing the income (or earnings) distributions of parents and children or by analyzing correlations between continuous income (or earnings) measures for parents and children.

This focus on economic mobility becomes less defensible as multidimensionalist accounts of inequality grow increasingly popular within economics (e.g., Sen forthcoming). Indeed, just as big-class models have recently come under some criticism within sociology, so too has the measurement paradigm that underlies economic mobility research. These criticisms within economics have most frequently drawn on the argument that income-based measurement fails to "take cognizance of other aspects of the quality of life that are not well correlated with economic advantage" (Nussbaum forthcoming:4; also Bourguignon forthcoming). By implication, the conventional practice of focusing exclusively on economic mobility is no longer defensible, and multidimensional strategies for analyzing inequality, poverty, and mobility come to the fore (esp. Sen forthcoming). This reaction against the income paradigm has also taken the form of increasing sensitivity to the "lumpiness" of labor markets. By "lumpiness," we mean that income-based measures and arbitrary discretizations of those measures fail to capture the social organization of inequality, including the emergence of social networks, norms, and "adaptive preferences" (i.e., tastes, culture) within various social groupings (see Grusky and Kanbur forthcoming). We consider below whether such concerns might be usefully addressed with a new approach to studying mobility.

These developments in sociology and economics argue for a more comprehensive reevaluation of how mobility should be analyzed. We take on this task here by proposing a simple mobility model that is responsive to many of the concerns that have emerged in both disciplines. After introducing this model, we use it to show that sociologists have approached the study of mobility under the spell of three assumptions: (1) that the multidimensional space of inequality resolves into social classes, (2) that inequality is transmitted between generations via social classes, and (3) that these classes are small in number and big in size. To date, these assumptions have either gone unrecognized or been treated as a matter of faith, a state of affairs that we seek to rectify here. We show that these three assumptions can be examined empirically by taking advantage of new methodological developments in latent class analysis.

MULTIDIMENSIONALISM AND SOCIAL CLASS

It is useful to begin by reviewing the multidimensionalist critique because we draw so heavily on it in devising a new mobility model. As noted above, this critique levels two challenges at the income paradigm: first, that income does not exhaustively describe the quality of life; and, second, that it fails to capture the social organization of inequality as expressed in the tendency for groups at the "site of production" to develop distinctive cultures and adaptive tastes (e.g., Sen 1997). The latter criticism has not yet motivated new measurement strategies, but the former underlies the development of various scales that take into account noneconomic sources of inequality. The best-known "multidimensional" measure, the Human Development Index (HDI), is now closely monitored throughout the world, although it has been widely criticized as simplistic and under-theorized (e.g., Kanbur 2001) and hence has spurred much revisionist work.

Could multidimensional scales like HDI provide a useful foundation for a new round of mobility studies? We are skeptical for two reasons. First, any attempt to reduce the multidimensional space of inequality to a single scale, whether HDI, socioeconomic status, or some other index, can be misleading insofar as the underlying dimensions are only poorly correlated with one another. When these correlations are weak, much information is lost by replacing scores on each dimension with an aggregate score. The second reason for skepticism is that HDI, socioeconomic scales, and related indices are unresponsive to the "social organizational" critique of conventional measurement approaches. These scales are all highly abstract characterizations of inequality that smooth over the social groups within which norms, networks, and adaptive preferences emerge (Grusky and Kanbur forthcoming). For example, socioeconomic scales group together all occupations that have similar pay levels and educational requirements, even though these occupations may have quite distinct cultures and only rarely interact with one another.

How, then, should mobility analysts respond to the rise of multidimensionalism? We argue below that the multidimensionalist critique provides an unprecedented, and as yet unexploited, opening for sociological models of class. Indeed, multidimensionalism may breathe new life into the class-based mobility table, thereby quelling the growing tendency among sociologists to challenge class-based approaches (e.g., Pakulski 2005). In theory, class models can make multidimensional space tractable by characterizing it in terms of a relatively small number of classes, each comprising a distinctive combination of endowments (e.g., education, human capital), working conditions (e.g., level of authority, autonomy), and job rewards (e.g., income, wealth).

We are thus suggesting that classes should be understood as a set of institutionalized "solutions" in multidimensional space around which individual-level variability is relatively limited. The class of craft workers, for example, has historically comprised individuals with moderate educational investments (i.e., secondary school credentials), considerable occupation-specific investments in human capital (i.e., vocational training, on-the-job training), average income, relatively high job security, middling social honor and prestige, quite limited authority and autonomy, and comparatively good health outcomes (by virtue of union-sponsored health benefits and regulation of working conditions). By contrast, the underclass is characterized by a very different package of endowments, conditions, and rewards that combines minimal educational investments (i.e., secondary school dropouts), limited opportunities for on-the-job training, intermittent labor force participation, low income, virtually no opportunities for authority or autonomy on the job (during the characteristically brief bouts of employment), relatively poor health (by virtue of lifestyle choices and inadequate health care), and social denigration and exclusion. Similarly, other classes may be understood as particular combinations of scores on the fundamental endowments, working conditions, and job rewards of interest. The long-standing presumption, of course, is that social classes cannot be reduced to a unidimensional scale because the constituent endowments and rewards do not necessarily vary together, an inconvenience that makes it inadvisable to resort to socioeconomic scales or income-based measures of social standing (e.g., Jencks et al. 1988).

In short, class analysts presume that the space of rewards and capabilities has relatively low dimensionality, indeed a dimensionality no more nor less than the number of postulated classes. This assumption is a simplifying one because the social classes institutionalized in the labor market are presumed to represent only a small subset of the logically possible "packages" of endowments, working conditions, and rewards. If class models of this kind are on the mark, the task of reducing a potentially complicated multidimensional space to some manageable number of dimensions is solved institutionally and does not require any complex econometric machinations.

The obvious irony here is that economists have been searching for a measurement strategy that captures the multidimensional lumpiness of labor markets while sociologists have long been sitting on a solution (i.e., social class) without fully recognizing the problem (i.e., multidimensionality) to which it may be the answer. The great potential of class-based approaches has indeed gone largely unrecognized by sociologists. Even though the distinctive advantage of class categories is that they signal a complex of life conditions that are bound together in a package (i.e., a "lifestyle"), the typical sociologist will attempt to motivate a class categorization by singling out a particular variable (e.g., authority, employment relations) as analytically crucial and then claiming or demonstrating that the preferred categorization captures it. For example, Goldthorpe (2000) argues that the form of regulation of employment (e.g., salaried, short-term contract) is the analytically crucial variable, and he then demonstrates that the categories of the Erikson-Goldthorpe (EG) scheme differ in their characteristic forms of regulation (also see Evans 1992; Evans and Mills 1998; Rose and O'Reilly 1997, 1998).

This unidimensional approach to motivating class models fails to appreciate that their main selling point is their intrinsically synthetic character. If sociologists truly believe that a single variable, such as the "form of regulation of employment," is the fundamental source of interests and life chances, then they ought to measure that variable directly rather than operationalize it indirectly through conventional classes. The logic of current research practice among sociologists therefore eludes us. It is rather like an economist claiming that income is the master variable of interest, but then opting to measure income indirectly and imperfectly through a social class scheme. There is no good reason to resort to a proxy that is more costly and difficult to measure than the variable for which it is a proxy.

If the usual sociological motivation for class analysis is unconvincing, is there some alternative rationale that salvages the practice? We think so. Namely, we suspect that sociologists have been instinctively drawn to class schemes because they provide a synthetic measure of "life conditions" that broadly define the quality of our social lives, including the endowments we control, the organizational conditions under which we work, and the economic (e.g., wages) and noneconomic (e.g., health) implications of these endowments and organizational conditions. In textbook descriptions of class categories, a common rhetorical device is to contrast a "day in the life" of incumbents of different classes, precisely because the implications of class are presumed to be manifold and reliably revealed throughout the day in various ways (e.g., Kerbo 2002; Rossides 1990). Class schemes appear, then, to solve each of the two problems identified by multidimensionalist economists. The potential complexity of multidimensional space is resolved by resorting to prepackaged "bundles" of structural conditions, and the social organization that emerges within this space is captured by measuring institutionalized groupings rather than resorting to purely nominal statistical constructions.

To this point, our suggestion that class categories are prepackaged bundles of this sort is a mere assertion; and we of course do not advocate that analysts take the assertion on faith alone. Rather, one can examine empirically (1) whether the multidimensional space of inequality is indeed reducible to a relatively small number of characteristic combinations of endowments, working conditions, and job rewards, and (2) whether these prepackaged solutions are indeed rooted in the division of labor and thus correspond either to big classes or micro classes. As we noted above, some scholars (e.g., Evans 1992) have sought to validate their preferred class map against a few variables of interest, but such tests do not provide the comprehensive assessment that an omnibus measure of life conditions demands.

The first step in carrying out a more comprehensive test is to develop a list of life conditions that, taken together, adequately characterize the multidimensional space of inequality. The task of defining the variables of interest has itself generated much debate, not just among sociologists (e.g., Bourdieu 1984), but also more recently among economists and philosophers (e.g., Nussbaum forthcoming). If these literatures are compared, one nonetheless finds considerable agreement on the following three classes of variables: (1) *investments and endowments* refer to formal schooling, vocational schooling, literacy, occupation-specific experience, firm-specific experience, total experience, and IQ; (2) *working conditions* refer to the type of employment contract (e.g., salary, wage), unionization, labor market type (e.g., firm size), authority, autonomy, and substantive complexity; and (3) *job rewards* refer to income, health status, and wealth.[1] To be sure, this list omits some important variables that are not available in large-scale surveys, but it is surely comprehensive enough to shift the burden of proof to those skeptics who believe that adding more variables would lead to fundamental changes in the underlying multidimensional structure of inequality.

A MULTIDIMENSIONAL MODEL OF MOBILITY

With this understanding of the multidimensional space, the assumptions underlying conventional mobility research can then be represented with a latent class model that (1) characterizes the structure and dimensionality of inequality among parents as well as their offspring, and (2) allows for

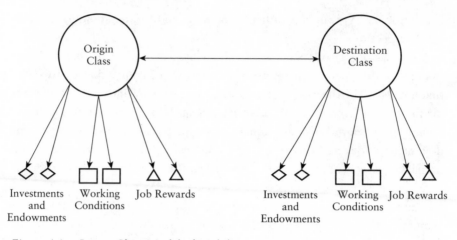

Figure 4.1.   Latent Class Model of Mobility

intergenerational reproduction in the context of this characterization. We offer our model principally as a heuristic that reveals the assumptions of conventional mobility research.[2] With a sufficiently large sample, a model of this
type could be estimated, but we leave that task for the (perhaps distant) future.

This heuristic model, which is diagrammed in Figure 4.1, has three
components: a measurement model specifying the structure of origin classes,
a measurement model specifying the structure of destination classes, and a
mobility model specifying the relationship between origin and destination
classes. The measurement model in each generation represents classes as
packages of investments and endowments, working conditions, and rewards.
Although we have simplified the presentation by allowing only six indicators
for the origin and destination models, an authentic multidimensional
specification would require a far better representation of the inequality space.[3]
It also bears noting that the class structure may take on a different form
when operating as a "background condition" (i.e., class origins) and as a
"contemporaneous condition" (i.e., class destinations). We could easily test
the claim that the class structure assumes a consistent form in each of these
two guises by imposing equality constraints on the respective conditional
probabilities.[4]

The structural part of the model, which grafts together the two measurement models, could be assumed to take on log-linear form (see Marsden
1985 for a related model). Although origin and destination classes may prove

to be latent rather than manifest, the usual array of log-linear models can still be applied (e.g., Hagenaars 2002). The measurement model for each generation is more complicated because some of the indicators will be continuous and others will be categorical. For such mixed-mode data, the following measurement model might be estimated:

$$f(\mathbf{y}_i|\theta) = \sum_{k=1}^{K} \pi_k \prod_{j=1}^{J} f_k(y_{ij}|\theta_{jk}), \tag{1}$$

where y_i denotes the parent's or offspring's scores on the manifest variables, K is the number of latent classes, π_k refers to the probability of belonging to the kth latent class (thus indexing latent class sizes), J denotes the total number of manifest variables, and j is a particular manifest variable. This equation states that the distribution of y_i, given the model parameters of θ (i.e., $f(y_i|\theta)$), is a mixture of class-specific densities (i.e., $f_k(y_{ij}|\theta_{jk})$).

We must also specify the appropriate univariate distribution for each element y_{ij} of y_i. The natural choice for continuous y_{ij} is the univariate normal, whereas the natural choice for discrete nominal or ordinal variables is the (restricted) multinomial. We assume that the manifest variables are independent within latent classes and that all of the observed association between manifest variables is therefore attributable to the particular patterning of latent class membership. That is, we don't assume that all class members have identical scores on the manifest variables, but we do assume that, whenever a class member has a score that deviates from the class profile, this deviation doesn't convey any information on the likelihood of deviating on any of the other variables. The assumption of local independence can be relaxed, but we insist on it because it captures a main constraint embodied in the class hypothesis.[5]

The resulting model, which we appreciate is ambitious, can be estimated because of three statistical advances: the recent development of latent class models for data that include continuous and categorical indicators (e.g., Vermunt and Magidson 2002), the development of increasingly sophisticated latent class models that fuse structural and measurement models (e.g., Hagenaars 2002), and new programming enhancements that make it possible to estimate models with more parameters than was before feasible (see Hagenaars and McCutcheon 2002, Appendix C). This approach is tractable, in particular, because models for mixed-mode data obviate the need to discretize continuous variables and thus allow them to be treated parsimoniously, an absolute necessity given the number of variables that multidimensionalists will likely wish to bring into the analysis.

We will not discuss issues of modeling or estimation in any further detail here. As we stressed above, our objective for this chapter is not to estimate a model of this sort, although doing so is, as we see it, a high priority for mobility researchers. For the purposes of this chapter, we wish merely to use the model to expose the assumptions of conventional mobility analysis, a task we begin in the next section.

ASSUMPTION #1: THE INEQUALITY SPACE RESOLVES INTO CLASSES

The claim that inequality takes on a "class form" (e.g., Wright 1997) is one of the few distinctively sociological contributions to inequality measurement. For all its popularity, the class concept nonetheless remains a largely metaphysical commitment, a conventional approach to constructing the mobility table that sociologists reflexively adopt with little substantiating evidence. With few exceptions, the discipline appears to have been quite satisfied to accept the class concept on faith alone, defending it either by referring to its long provenance in both the theoretical and empirical literatures or by rehearsing long-standing claims that social classes represent the underlying variables (e.g., authority, ownership) that define interests or life chances.[6] In recent years, a small contingent of postmodernists have begun to criticize class-based approaches (e.g., Pakulski 2005; also, Kingston 2000), yet these critics have for the most part simply asserted that class models are predicated on problematic assumptions; and such assertions are no more or less convincing than the equally unsubstantiated presumption in favor of the class concept. This impasse is, as we will show, altogether unnecessary, because the class model rests on assumptions that are testable.

It is useful to represent the class assumption graphically. In the graphs that follow, big-class membership will be signified by three symbols (i.e., square, triangle, circle), while micro-class membership within each big class will be signified by different shadings of these symbols (i.e., light, dark). That is, we are coveying the big-class hypothesis with the claim that the inequality space can be adequately represented with just three classes (e.g., nonmanual, manual, farm), while we are conveying the micro-class hypothesis with the claim that each of these big classes must be further divided into two subclasses. Also, we are assuming in all our graphs that the inequality space comprises only three individual-level variables (e.g., education, type of employment contract, income), a simplification that allows us to depict the various class and nonclass hypotheses in three-dimensional space. The resulting figures are clearly gross simplifications. If our model were to be estimated with real data, the inequality space would perforce be represented with many more variables, and the class schemes with which we would attempt to characterize that space would be the standard ones in the litera-ture, such as the 7-category Erikson-Goldthorpe scheme (Erikson and Goldthorpe 1992) or the 126-category Weeden-Grusky scheme (Weeden and Grusky 2005). We have simplified here merely to make the presentation tractable.

In considering the measurement portion of our latent class model (see Equation 1), the key question is whether the multidimensional space of in-equality resolves into classes of some kind, each characterized by a different constellation of scores on the underlying individual-level variables. We have depicted several ideal-typical solutions in Figure 4.2. Although class-based solutions may take on either a big- or micro-class form (see Assumption #3 below), the solution shown in Figure 4.2a is of course consistent with a big-class model. As shown here, the individual-level variables do not covary within each of the big classes, implying that there is no residual intra-class clustering into micro classes. The big classes of Figure 4.2a are termed "disorganized" because they do not overlap with functional groupings at the site of production (e.g., manual, nonmanual, farm). That is, incumbents of each latent class are diversely drawn from different positions in the division of labor, a solution that is inconsistent with the long-standing sociological presumption that inequality is generated at the site of production.

The class structure of Figure 4.2b takes on a more familiar sociological cast. Whereas the big classes of Figure 4.2a are formed outside the site of production and are therefore "postmodern" in composition (Hall 2001), the classes depicted in Figure 4.2b are rooted in the division of labor. Although most class analysts have simply assumed that classes are "sociological" in this way, one could instead test this assumption by forcing latent classes to be perfectly defined by big-class membership (thus making them manifest). The contrast between an unconstrained latent class model (Figure 4.2a) and a corresponding constrained model (Figure 4.2b) speaks to the extent of so-ciological organization in the class structure.

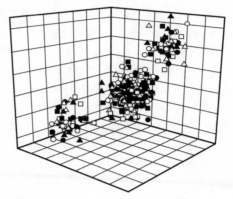

(a) Disorganized Big Classes

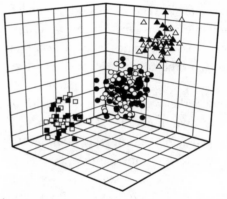

(b) Organized Big Classes

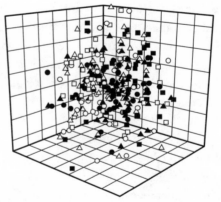

(c) Non-Class Solution

Figure 4.2. Big-Class and Non-Class Solutions of a Hypothetical Inequality Space

It is also possible that the inequality space will not resolve into classes of any kind. The one-class solution of Figure 4.2c, which is an extreme case of disorganization, represents an inequality regime in which there is no "crystallization" at all (see Landecker 1981). Under this specification, there is substantial inequality (as revealed by the variances on each of the univariate distributions), but it takes a peculiarly structureless form in which the independence assumption holds throughout multidimensional space, not just within a given latent class. Again, it is unlikely that such extreme disorganization will ever be realized, but the ideal type does represent a form of inequality that some postmodernists (e.g., Pakulski and Waters 2001) argue is emerging.

The measurement model in Figure 4.1 could of course take on many other forms. For now, there is no need to attempt any exhaustive accounting of the possibilities, because our point here is simply that the "class form" is a testable characterization of the inequality space. Although there is overwhelming evidence that the extent of inequality is increasing worldwide, we simply do not know whether equally revolutionary changes in the form and structure of inequality are also occurring. Is inequality increasingly taking on a class form? Or are social classes disappearing even as income inequality is increasing? Are particular social classes, such as the underclass, becoming more coherent even as other classes begin to fade? Is the class structure changing in similar ways in more developed (MDCs) and less developed countries (LDCs)? Are classes emerging in LDCs but disappearing elsewhere? These types of questions can only be answered by developing a multidimensionalist monitoring system that moves beyond simplistic measurements of the extent of inequality and additionally describes the form that such inequality takes.

ASSUMPTION #2: INEQUALITY IS TRANSMITTED THROUGH CLASSES

If an empirical case for class-based mobility analysis is to be made, it should be forged not only on the claim that classes provide a parsimonious account of the multidimensional space of inequality, but also on the claim that they have effects on life chances that are not reducible to the effects of endowments, working conditions, and job rewards. This second claim can be addressed by focusing on the transmission of inequality as represented by the structural component of our latent class model.

Although contemporary mobility analysts continue to routinely use class models, it seems that they increasingly do so out of tradition and habit rather than any strong conviction that inequality is truly transmitted through classes. This loss of faith in the class realist position is perhaps most striking in the work of Goldthorpe (2002, 2000) and Breen (2005b). For some time, Goldthorpe and Breen have sought to refashion class analysis on rational action foundations, yet their efforts have had the perverse and unintended effect of undermining all but a purely nominalist rationale for class analysis. The key assumption of rational action theorists is that classes are merely bundles of conditions and constraints that become the context within which decisions about human capital investments are made. In explaining, for example, the tendency for working class children to "underinvest" in schooling, Goldthorpe (2002, 2000) emphasizes that such decisions merely reflect the precarious economic situation within which such children are operating. This argument goes further than the standard claim that working class children cannot afford tuition, cannot forego wages while attending school, or cannot readily borrow money to finance an investment in schooling (because capital markets are imperfectly developed). Worse yet, whenever a working class experiment with higher education fails (i.e., working class children drop out), there are inadequate reserves to finance a fallback investment in vocational education or to otherwise salvage the situation and avoid downward mobility.

This line of reasoning implies that working class "underinvestments" in schooling are not underinvestments at all, but rather rational responses to the tenuous financial position of working class children. The important point for our purposes is that, under this rational action formulation, the real determinant of investment decisions (and hence outcomes) is wealth, not class. The class variable is accordingly reduced to nothing more than a proxy for wealth.

Obviously, wealth is unlikely to be the only variable that shapes investment decisions, but the nominalist critique of class analysis applies as long as there is a set of underlying variables (i.e., endowments, working conditions, and rewards) that define interests and determine decisions. These variables, whatever they may be, serve to "carry" the effects of class and hence obviate the need for a class concept. If this reductionist hypothesis is on the mark, it follows that the model of Figure 4.1 will not fit because some of the underlying variables, such as wealth, will have *direct* effects on outcomes.

Although such reductionist arguments are ubiquitous, they have not yet been tested with a plausibly comprehensive model that fits all the underlying variables in terms of which classes are defined (but see Halaby and Weakliem 1993).

It is also possible, however, that the model of Figure 4.1 will reveal that the class concept has merit. Why might net effects of class be detected even with rigorous controls for the underlying variables? There are two relevant arguments in this regard. First, insofar as classes are indeed organic "packages" of conditions, then the constituents of these packages may combine and interact in ways that lead to an *emergent* logic of the situation. The underclass, for instance, may be understood as a combination of negative conditions (e.g., intermittent labor force participation, limited education, poor health, low income) that, taken together, engender a sense of futility, despondency, or learned helplessness that is more profound than what would be expected from a model that simply allows for independent effects of each constituent class condition. Granted, a committed reductionist might counter that one need only include the appropriate set of interactions between the constituent variables, but insofar as classes define the interactions of interest (i.e., the relevant packages of interacting conditions) this approach becomes an unduly complicated way of sidestepping the reality of classes.

The second argument for a net class effect rests on the additional claim that such class-defined packages of conditions are associated with distinctive class cultures that take on a life of their own and thus independently shape behavior and attitudes. It is always possible that such class cultures are merely "rules of thumb" that encode best-practice behavioral responses to the working conditions that classes entail. These rules allow class members to forego optimizing calculations themselves and rely instead on cultural prescriptions that provide reliable and economical shortcuts to best practices (e.g., Goldthorpe 2000). At the same time, other theorists (e.g., Wilson forthcoming) allow for class cultures that are truly maladaptive, such as a "culture of poverty" that filters information in unduly cynical ways and that engenders an excessive sense of futility and despondency. In either case, classes will have net effects on aspirations and on decisions about human capital investments (especially schooling), effects that are not reducible to those of the individual-level variables in the measurement model.

We cannot, then, make a convincing realist case for classes without estimating models that include rigorous controls for endowments and investments, working conditions, and job rewards. If we find that classes have no net effects in the presence of such controls, we can conclude that the class concept is superfluous and that the variables constituting the inequality space should be used in quantitative modeling. This does not imply that a net class effect, were it to be found, would give license to the conventional sociological practice of using class alone as a measure of social origins. Rather, if the data reveal that both class and reductive measures have net effects, a hybrid model of inequality would be indicated. We can only defend an exclusively class-based approach if the underlying class indicators either have no effects or have such limited effects that conventional class schemes become a cost effective, albeit imperfect, approach to representing the transmission process.

ASSUMPTION #3: CLASSES ARE BIG

The third and final pillar on which conventional mobility research rests is the assumption that intergenerational reproduction occurs at the big-class level. That is, mobility scholars not only routinely assume that inequality is transmitted via classes (i.e., Assumption #2), but also that these classes are adequately described by Erikson-Goldthorpe categories or some other big-class scheme formed by aggregating detailed occupations or jobs (i.e., assumption #3). This preference for big classes rests on the assumption that (1) endowments, working conditions, and rewards come together to form a small number of coherent "packages," and that (2) intergenerational reproduction plays out identically for all members of each of these big class packages. The former assumption pertains to the measurement model of Figure 4.1, whereas the latter assumption pertains to the structural model of Figure 4.1. We will review each in turn.

We can again resort to graphs to depict the conditions under which our measurement model corresponds to a big- or micro-class account. In Figure 4.3a, for example, the individual-level variables are no longer independent of one another within each big class, thus implying that further subdivision into micro classes is necessary. Although these micro classes are assumed here to be "organized" (i.e., formed at the site of production), we could also represent the case of disorganized micro classes, an ideal type that would contradict the conventional sociological model both in terms of size of the classes and their composition.

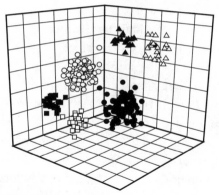

(a) Organized Micro-Classes

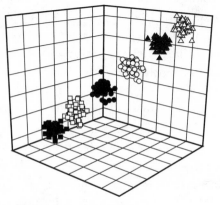

(b) Gradational Micro-Classes

Figure 4.3.   Micro-class Solutions of a Hypothetical Inequality Space

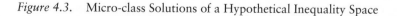

We can further distinguish between gradational and non-gradational variants of the micro-class solution (compare Figures 4.3a and 4.3b). In prior research, scholars have chosen between these two accounts on the basis of taste or "theory," and two parallel streams of research have therefore emerged. By contrast, our model makes it clear that the choice is best understood as an empirical choice, with the relevant test resting on the fit of a model that scales the latent classes or, less restrictively, imposes ordinality constraints on them (see Rost 1988; Croon 2002). We can also test whether this estimated scale (for the latent classes) is socioeconomic in structure. The socioeconomic index is merely a particular type of class model that (1) treats all occupations with the same socioeconomic score as a "micro class," and (2) presumes that such socioeconomic scores adequately index inequality along a host of dimensions, not just income and education. These various unidimensionalist solutions therefore provide precisely the simple index that economists have long sought in the context of multidimensional space. However, rather than simply imposing an arbitrary unidimensional solution on the data, a latent class approach lets us test existing scales, develop an alternative unconstrained scaling that may better account for the multidimensional structure of the data, and determine whether any scaling of the latent classes, even one that is freely estimated, can adequately characterize the structure of multidimensional space (see Hout and Hauser 1992).

We can likewise advance a micro-class hypothesis for the structural part of our latent class model. To be sure, the decline of farming has brought about a physical separation of home and workplace in most families, presumably making it more difficult for parents to provide specialized on-the-job training for their children. The separation of home and workplace underlies the emergence of reproduction theories (e.g., Bourdieu 1984) that focus on the intergenerational transmission of diffuse big-class capital (social, cultural, and human) rather than specialized micro-class capital. Although there is undoubtedly merit in such big-class theories, we suspect that the pendulum has swung too far in favor of them and that parents transmit not only generalized capital but also more specialized forms that generate substantial reproduction at the micro-class level (see Jonsson et al. 2005; Grusky and Weeden 2002; Sørensen and Grusky 1996).

These pockets of micro-class reproduction persist because many parents are deeply involved in their occupations and thus bring home much in the way of specialized human, social, and cultural capital. We are referring here to parents who work at home, who talk about their occupations at the dinner table and in other home settings, and who may even explicitly train their children in occupation-specific skills. For example, an actor may frequently practice lines at home, may bring her or his children to the set, and can provide instant access to specialized "Hollywood" networks. Likewise, professional baseball players provide ongoing expert instruction in the intricacies of hitting and fielding, deliver immediate "name recognition" in the fierce competition for access to the minor leagues and beyond, and transmit a taste for baseball as a vocation more profound than the usual childhood fantasies. At the bottom of the class structure, micro-level reproduction may emerge because parents can desensitize their children to tasks (e.g., embalming, plumbing) that outsiders would regard as unpleasant, unusual, or undesirable. The foregoing examples, which obviously are no more than suggestive, imply that much reproduction may occur at a more detailed level than has typically been appreciated.

In the context of our latent class model, the latter micro-class hypothesis can be tested by simultaneously fitting disaggregate and aggregate inheritance effects, where the former blank out the "thin" micro-diagonal and the latter blank out the "fat" macro-diagonal (corresponding to class inheritance in an aggregate array). By failing to fit the micro-diagonal, conventional analysts confound disaggregate and aggregate inheritance, thus upwardly biasing the effect of the latter and creating the impression of more aggregate closure than in fact there is. When a full model is estimated, we may find that micro-class reproduction is more pronounced than big-class reproduction, implying that decades of analysts have misunderstood where the rigidities in the mobility regime are principally found.

CONCLUSIONS

In sociology and economics alike, unidimensional approaches to representing inequality are increasingly unfashionable, with many economists questioning the long-standing "income paradigm" and many sociologists eschewing the equally venerable socioeconomic scale (e.g., Erikson and Goldthorpe 1992). Although there is, then, an emerging cross-disciplinary consensus on the importance of a multidimensional approach, this development has not yet affected how sociologists or economists study mobility.

We have elaborated a simple latent class model that can serve as a primitive framework for investigating the multidimensional structure of mobility. This model allows us to test for the class form by distinguishing between class-based, gradational, and disorganized forms of inequality and mobility. If a class form emerges, we can also determine how many classes are necessary to adequately characterize the space and whether those classes correspond to detailed occupations (i.e., the micro-class solution), aggregations of detailed occupations (i.e., the big-class solution), or more heterogeneous constellations of positions at the site of production (i.e., the "postmodern" solution). This framework could be used to characterize and compare the structure of mobility and inequality over time and across countries. We could use it to investigate whether the class principle is more developed in some countries (e.g., Sweden) than in others (e.g., United States), to examine whether high-inequality regimes (e.g., Brazil) tend to be organized in class terms, or to ask whether the worldwide rise in inequality has been coupled with a corresponding resurgence in class-based inequality.

We have paid particular attention to the class concept because of its potential to represent multidimensional space parsimoniously in terms of institutionalized packages of endowments, working conditions, and rewards. Ironically, economists have well appreciated the challenges of characterizing multidimensional space but have not yet provided satisfying solutions to this challenge, whereas sociologists have long held a possible solution (i.e., the class model) but have not fully appreciated the problem that it may very well solve. If these two literatures are brought together, the class model becomes nothing more than a particular hypothesis about the structure of multidimensional space (and mobility therein), and the sociological tendency to blithely default to it cannot be justified. Likewise, gradational scales (e.g., HDI, SES) are defensible only to the extent that they are consistent with the structure of mobility and inequality, meaning that decisions to default to such measurement approaches must again be empirically justified.

If the sociological approach to mobility is to survive, it must therefore be converted from a mere disciplinary predilection to an approach with real empirical standing. As best we can tell, sociology is slowly losing its once-privileged position in mobility studies, as scholars in other disciplines, especially economics, routinely default to income-based representations of mobility (e.g., Bowles et al. 2005; Corak 2005). It is unlikely that sociological models of mobility will survive this incursion because economists suddenly decide to mimic the research practices of sociologists or to read the famous treatises on class provided by Marx, Weber, and their followers. Rather, a compelling *empirical* defense of the payoff to class-based mobility models is required, without which we can expect economists and other social scientists to continue to apply income-based models and thereby dismiss or ignore the sociological legacy.

There is, to be sure, no guarantee that class models will pass the empirical test. If they fail, sociologists had best face up to this result now and jettison that part of our intellectual history that is an empirical dead end. Although the concept has survived a half-century without an empirical test, it is both dishonest and imprudent to duck the question any longer.

Notes

1. Some scholars, especially economists, might consider health as an endowment or capability rather than a "reward" or consequence of class. For our purposes, it suffices that health is recognized as a constituent of class, and the particular category under which it is subsumed is inconsequential.

2. The model of Figure 4.1 represents the "destination class" as a cause of investments (e.g., schooling) that were often made in advance of entering the labor force. Unlike the conventional status attainment model, our latent class model should not, then, be construed as a meaningful structural model of the life course. It is merely a specification that formalizes and tests the hypothesis that intergenerational association assumes a class form.

3. The latent class model graphed here does not include measures of big- and micro-class membership and thus does not allow us to assess whether latent and manifest classes overlap. It is straightforward to include such measures as additional observed variables and then fit a confirmatory model resting on the constraint that each "latent" class corresponds perfectly with a manifest class (see "Assumption #1: The Inequality Space Resolves into Classes").

4. We are glossing over additional complications that arise because the measurement and structural parts of the model can also imply a different form to the class structure (see Winship and Mare 1983 for relevant formulations). For example, the effects of origins on destinations might take on a simple gradational form (see, e.g., Hout and Hauser 1992), whereas the inequality space itself might not.

5. The well-read scholar of mobility will appreciate the resemblance between the model in Figure 4.1 and the multidimensional structural equation model posited long ago by Hauser (1973). In proposing such a model, Hauser was not only remarkably prescient in advancing a multidimensional conception of inequality, but also in attempting to characterize it parsimoniously through the device of latent variables. The model proposed here differs from Hauser's model by virtue of (1) including a wider array of endowments, investments, working conditions, and rewards, and (2) characterizing the resulting multidimensional space with the device of (latent) classes rather than (latent) continuous variables.

6. To be sure, some scholars have sought to examine the empirical standing of the class concept (e.g., Evans and Mills 1998, 2000), but they have not understood the inequality space to be multidimensional and hence have fallen short of carrying out the full test that we envision here.

References

Bourdieu, Pierre. 1984. *Distinction: A Social Critique of the Judgement of Taste.* Translated by R. Nice. New York: Cambridge University Press.

Bourguignon, François. Forthcoming. "From Income to Endowments: The Difficult Task of Expanding the Income Poverty Paradigm." In *Poverty and Inequality,* edited by D. B. Grusky and R. Kanbur. Stanford, CA: Stanford University Press.

Bowles, Samuel, Herbert Gintis, and Melissa Osborne, eds. 2005. *Unequal Chances: Family Background and Economic Success.* Princeton, NJ: Princeton University Press.

Breen, Richard, ed. 2005a. *Social Mobility in Europe.* Oxford: Oxford University Press.

Breen, Richard. 2005b. "Foundations of a Neo-Weberian Class Analysis." In *Approaches to Class Analysis,* edited by E. O. Wright. Oxford: Oxford University Press.

Corak, Miles, ed. 2005. *Generational Income Mobility in North America and Europe.* Cambridge: Cambridge University Press.

Croon, Marcel. 2002. "Ordering the Classes." Pp. 137–62 in *Applied Latent Class Analysis,* edited by J. A. Hagenaars and A. L. McCutcheon. Cambridge: Cambridge University Press.

Erikson, Robert, and John H. Goldthorpe. 1992. *The Constant Flux: A Study of Class Mobility in Industrial Societies.* New York: Clarendon.

Evans, Geoffrey. 1992. "Testing the Validity of the Goldthorpe Class Schema." *European Sociological Review* 8(3):211–32.

Evans, Geoffrey, and Colin Mills. 1998. "Identifying Class Structure: A Latent Class Analysis of the Criterion-Related and Construct Validity of the Goldthorpe Class Schema." *European Sociological Review* 14(1):87–106.

——— 2000. "In Search of the Wage Labour/Service Contract: New Evidence on the Validity of the Goldthorpe Class Scheme." *British Journal of Sociology* 51:641–61.

Goldthorpe, John H. 2000. *On Sociology: Numbers, Narrative, and the Integration of Research and Theory.* New York: Oxford University Press.

——— 2002. "Occupational Sociology, Yes: Class Analysis, No: Comment on Grusky and Weeden's Research Agenda." *Acta Sociologica* 45:211–17.

Gottschalk, Peter. 2001. "Inequality, Income Growth, and Mobility: The Basic Facts." In *Social Stratification: Class, Race, and Gender in Sociological Perspective,* 2nd ed., edited by D. B. Grusky. Boulder, CO: Westview.

Grusky, David B., and Ravi Kanbur. Forthcoming. "Conceptual Ferment in Poverty and Inequality Measurement: The View from Economics and Sociology." In *Poverty and Inequality,* edited by D. B. Grusky and R. Kanbur. Stanford, CA: Stanford University Press.

Grusky, David B., and Kim A. Weeden. 2001. "Decomposition without Death: A Research Agenda for the New Class Analysis." *Acta Sociologica* 44(3):203–18.

——— 2002. "Class Analysis and the Heavy Weight of Convention." *Acta Sociologica* 45:229–36.

Hagenaars, Jacques A., and Allan L. McCutcheon, eds. 2002. *Applied Latent Class Analysis.* Cambridge: Cambridge University Press.

Halaby, Charles, and David Weakliem. 1993. "Class and Authority in the Earnings Function." *American Sociological Review* 58:16–30.

Hall, Stuart. 2001. "The Meaning of New Times." In *Social Stratification: Class, Race, and Gender in Sociological Perspective*, 2nd ed., edited by D. B. Grusky. Boulder, CO: Westview.

Hauser, Robert M. 1973. "Disaggregating a Social Psychological Model of Educational Attainment." Pp. 255–84 in *Structural Equation Models in the Social Sciences*, edited by A. S. Goldberger and O. D. Duncan. New York: Seminar.

Hout, Michael, and Robert M. Hauser. 1992. "Symmetry and Hierarchy in Social Mobility: A Methodological Analysis of the CASMIN Model of Class Mobility." *European Sociological Review* 8:239–66.

Jencks, Christopher, Lauri Perman, and Lee Rainwater. 1988. "What Is a Good Job? A New Measure of Labor-Market Success." *American Journal of Sociology* 93:1322–57.

Jonsson, Janne, David B. Grusky, Reinhard Pollak, Mary C. Brinton, and Matt DiCarlo. 2005. "Will Our Children Become Professors or Professionals? A Critical Test of Class Reproduction." Working paper, Stanford University.

Kambourov, Gueorgui, and Iourii Manovskii. 2004. "Occupational Mobility and Wage Inequality." Institute for the Study of Labor (IZA), Discussion Paper 1189.

Kanbur, Ravi. 2001. "Economic Policy, Distribution and Poverty: The Nature of Disagreements." *World Development* 29:1083–94.

Kerbo, Harold. 2002. *Social Stratification and Inequality*. New York: McGraw-Hill.

Kingston, Paul W. 2000. *The Classless Society*. Stanford, CA: Stanford University Press.

Landecker, Werner S. 1981. *Class Crystallization*. New Brunswick, NJ: Rutgers University Press.

Marsden, Peter V. 1985. "Latent Structure Models for Relationally Defined Social Classes." *American Journal of Sociology* 90:1002–21.

Nussbaum, Martha. Forthcoming. "Poverty and Human Functioning: Capabilities as Fundamental Entitlements." In *Poverty and Inequality*, edited by D. B. Grusky and R. Kanbur. Stanford, CA: Stanford University Press.

Pakulski, Jan. 2005. "Foundations of a Post-Class Analysis." In *Approaches to Class Analysis*, edited by E. O. Wright. Oxford: Oxford University Press.

Pakulski, Jan, and Malcolm Waters. 2001. "The Death of Class." Pp. 866–74 in *Social Stratification: Class, Race, and Gender in Sociological Perspective*, 2nd ed., edited by D. B. Grusky. Boulder, CO: Westview.

Rose, David, and Karen O'Reilly, eds. 1997. *Constructing Classes: Towards a New Social Classification for the United Kingdom*. Swindon: ONS/ESRC.

Rose, David, and Karen O'Reilly. 1998. *Final Report of the ESRC Review of Government Social Classifications*. Swindon: ONS/ESRC.

Rossides, Daniel W. 1990. *Social Stratification: The American Class System in Comparative Perspective*. New York: Prentice Hall.

Rost, J. 1988. "Rating Scale Analysis with Latent Class Models." *Psychometrika* 53:327–48.

Rytina, S. 2000. "Is Occupational Mobility Declining in the United States?" *Social Forces* 78:1227–76.

Sen, Amartya. Forthcoming. "Concepts and Measures." In *Poverty and Inequality*, edited by D. B. Grusky and R. Kanbur. Stanford, CA: Stanford University Press.

Sen, Amartya. 1997. *On Economic Inequality.* Oxford: Oxford University Press.

Sørensen, Jesper B., and David B. Grusky. 1996. "The Structure of Career Mobility in Microscopic Perspective." Pp. 83–114 in *Social Differentiation and Social Inequality*, edited by J. N. Baron, D. B. Grusky, and D. J. Treiman. Boulder, CO: Westview.

Vermunt, Jeroen K., and Jay Magidson. 2002. "Latent Class Cluster Analysis." Pp. 89–106 in *Applied Latent Class Analysis*, edited by J. A. Hagenaars and A. L. McCutcheon. Cambridge: Cambridge University Press.

Weeden, Kim A., and David B. Grusky. 2005. "The Case for a New Class Map." *American Journal of Sociology* 111(1):141–212.

Wilson, William J. Forthcoming. "Social Theory and the Concept 'Underclass.'" In *Poverty and Inequality*, edited by D. B. Grusky and R. Kanbur. Stanford, CA: Stanford University Press.

Winship, Christopher, and Robert D. Mare. 1983. "Structural Equations and Path Analysis for Discrete Data." *American Journal of Sociology* 88:54–110.

Wright, Erik. 1997. *Class Counts: Comparative Studies in Class Analysis.* Cambridge: Cambridge University Press.

CHAPTER FIVE

The Economic Basis of Social Class

John H. Goldthorpe and Abigail McKnight

This chapter starts out from a theory of social class that has been presented more fully elsewhere (Goldthorpe 2000: ch. 10). The theory was developed together with a class schema for use in empirical research that has by now become quite widely adopted, especially in social mobility research, and is variously known as the Goldthorpe, Erikson-Goldthorpe-Portocarero or CASMIN schema. The new British National Statistics Socio-Economic Classification (NS-SEC), introduced in 2001, represents a further instantiation of the schema (Rose and O'Reilly 1997, 1998; Rose and Pevalin 2003). Table 5.1 shows the correspondence that exists between the classes of the original schema and those of the NS-SEC in its seven-class "analytical" version.[1] Both classifications will be applied in the course of this chapter.

Under the theory in question, class positions are seen as deriving from social relations in economic life or, more specifically, from employment relations. It is, therefore, in economic life that the implications for individuals of the class positions that they hold should be most immediately apparent. The main purpose of the chapter is to show that this is indeed the case, so far at least as contemporary British society is concerned, and, in particular, in regard to (1) economic security, (2) economic stability, and (3) economic prospects.

In this way, empirical support can be provided for the theory itself and also further confirmation of the validity of the social classifications that are

We are grateful to Tony Atkinson, Tak Wing Chan, Duncan Gallie, Eric Harrison, David Lockwood, Mark Tomlinson, and Michael White for helpful information and advice, and to Marina Shapira for assistance in the preparation of the graphs.

TABLE 5.1

Correspondence of the Classes of the Goldthorpe Schema
and of the NS-SEC Socioeconomic Classification and Common Descriptive Terms

Goldthorpe Schema	NS-SEC	Common Descriptive Term
I Professional, administrative, and managerial employees, higher grade*,**	1 Higher managerial and professional occupations*,**	Salariat (or service class)
II Professional, administrative, and managerial employees, lower grade;** technicians, higher grade	2 Lower managerial and professional occupations**	
IIIa Routine nonmanual employees, higher grade	3 Intermediate occupations	Intermediate white collar
IV Small employers and self-employed workers	4 Employers in small organisations, own account workers	Independents (or petty bourgeoisie)
V Supervisors of manual workers; technicians, lower grade	5 Lower supervisory and lower technical occupations	Intermediate blue collar
VI Skilled manual workers	6 Semiroutine occupations	
IIIb Routine nonmanual workers, lower grade	7 Routine occupations	Working class
VII Semi- and unskilled manual workers		

NOTES:

* Includes "large" employers (see Goldthorpe, 1997).

** Includes independent professionals (see Goldthorpe, 1997).

associated with it. At the same time, the findings reported serve to undermine currently fashionable arguments claiming the decline, or even death, of class in the context of the "postmodern" societies of the "global era" (see further Goldthorpe 2002).

THE THEORY AND THE SCHEMA

Since class positions are taken to derive from employment relations, the positions of employers, self-employed workers, and employees represent an initial level of differentiation. However, in modern societies major importance will attach to the further differentiation that is obviously required among employees who make up the large majority of the active population. This can be achieved, in a theoretically consistent way, by reference to the mode of regulation of their employment or, in other words, to the form of their employment contracts, due account being taken of both explicit and implicit features.[2]

Central to the theory in this respect is the following claim. Employers face contractual hazards in the labor market, ultimately on account of the essential "incompleteness" of all employment contracts but, more immediately, on account of the two problems of work monitoring and of human asset specificity. In consequence, contracts of differing form are offered to employees who are engaged to carry out different kinds of work in which these problems arise to a greater or lesser extent. The situation thus envisaged can be represented schematically as in Figure 5.1 (adapted from Goldthorpe 2000: Figure 10.2).

The detailed arguments underlying Figure 5.1 cannot here be rehearsed, although some will be introduced, as relevant, in interpreting the empirical findings that are later reported. For the moment, it will be sufficient to note three salient points.

    1. Those classes of the Goldthorpe schema and likewise of NS-SEC that fall in bottom-left quadrant of Figure 5.1 and that could together be taken as representing the working class (see Table 5.1) are associated with the regulation of employment via a 'labor contract' ": that is, an approximation to a simple if recurrent spot contract for the purchase of a quantity of labor on a piece- or time-rate basis. This approximation will be closest in the case of non-skilled, entirely routine workers (Classes IIIb and VII/7), with modifications being most likely in the case of skilled manual and semi-routine workers (Classes VI/6).

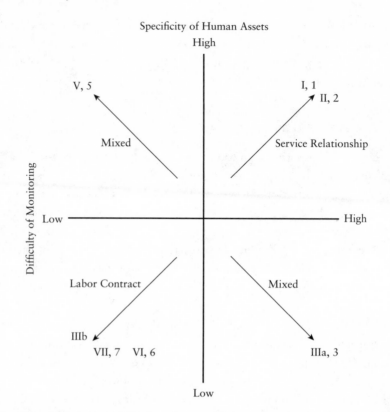

Figure 5.1. Dimensions of Work as Sources of Contractual Hazard, Forms of Employment Contract and Location of Classes

2. Those classes that fall into the upper-right quadrant of Figure 5.1 and that together represent the salariat of professional and managerial employees are associated with the regulation of employment via a "service relationship": that is, a contractual exchange of a relatively long-term and diffuse kind in which compensation for service to the employing organization comprises a salary and various perquisites and also important *prospective* elements—salary increments, expectations of continuity of employment (or at least of employability), and promotion and career opportunities. The service relationship will be most fully realized with higher-level professionals and managers (Classes I/1), while modified forms will be most common with lower-level professionals and managers (Classes II/2).

3. Those (employee) classes that fall into the two "reverse" quadrants of Figure 5.1 and that are characterized as "intermediate" between the working class and salariat (i.e., Classes IIIa and V/3 and 5) are associated with the

regulation of employment via "mixed" forms of contract in which elements of both the labor contract and service relationship will be found.[3]

In the next three sections of the chapter, versions of either the class schema or the NS-SEC are used as the basis for examining, in turn, class differences in economic security, economic stability and economic prospects in Britain over the last twenty-five years or so. In some instances, already published research findings are adapted to present purposes; in others, original analyses are made of standard data sets.

ECONOMIC SECURITY

The most obvious way in which individuals' class positions are likely to influence their economic security is through the associated risks of job loss and unemployment. In order to investigate the extent and pattern of such risks, longitudinal data in the form of individuals' complete work histories, including information on any episodes of unemployment, are desirable. One major study based on such data is that by Gallie et al. (1998).

Using work histories from representative samples of both employed and unemployed individuals in Great Britain in 1992, Gallie and his colleagues document a general increase in job insecurity from the 1970s onward—as might indeed be expected in view of the return of recessions in which rates of unemployment reached "double-digit" levels. However, they also find that throughout the period in question the risks of unemployment remained clearly linked with class position (using the Goldthorpe schema), and even when various individual characteristics, including level of education, were introduced into the analysis. Furthermore, no general tendency for this association to weaken was apparent (Gallie et al. 1998:143, Table 5.7).

The findings of this research can then be complemented by those more recently reported by Elias and McKnight (2003). These authors use the data set of the British Household Panel Survey in order to analyze the relationship between class position and the risk of unemployment in two different ways: first, according to whether an individual in the active labor force had or had not been unemployed at any time between September 1991 and August 1999; and second, according to whether over this same period an individual had or had not spent a total of more than twelve months in unemployment. Elias and McKnight estimate logistic regressions in which these two binary

(a) Experience of any unemployment

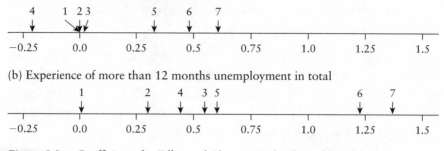

(b) Experience of more than 12 months unemployment in total

Figure 5.2.   Coefficients for Effects of Class on Risks (log odds) of Experiencing Unemployment 1991–1999 (controlling for age, sex, marital status and family composition).

SOURCE: British Household Panel Study (figures derived from Elias and McKnight, 2003)

measures are the dependent variables and class (NS-SEC) is the explanatory variable of interest, but with age, sex, marital status, and family composition also being included as control variables. Figure 5.2 graphs their main results.

As regards the experience of any episode of unemployment, the influence of class is readily apparent, with the main contrast shown in graph (a) being that between the risks run by "blue collar" employees (Classes 5, 6, and 7) and "white collar" employees (Classes 1, 2, and 3).[4] It is in fact among independents or the petty bourgeoisie (Class 4) that the risk appears lowest but it should be recognized that in their case underemployment may be another source of economic insecurity.

As regards the experience of recurrent or long-term unemployment, amounting to more than twelve months in total, a still stronger class effect is apparent, with the main contrast evident from graph (b) now being that between the risk to those in the working class, especially its lower division, and to those in the salariat, especially its higher division. In multiplicative terms, being a routine wage worker (Class 7) increases the odds of recurrent or long-term unemployment almost fourfold relative to the odds for a higher-level professional or managerial employee (Class 1). It may also be noted that on graph (b) independents (Class 4) fall, along with the two intermediate employee classes, in-between the working class and the salariat; and in the case of independents lengthy unemployment is indicative, one would suppose, of some form of business failure.

Taking both graphs of Figure 5.2 together, one can then say that over the last decade of the twentieth century, just as previously, class position remained very clearly linked to both the incidence and severity of unemployment. Thus, the Beck's argument (2000:153) that in the global era the risks of unemployment become less and less class related is, for Britain at least, quite unfounded. And the claims of other globalization theorists such as Castells (1996/2000:290) or Gray (1998:29, 71–2, 111) to the effect that, in consequence of a "generalization" of insecurity, the "bourgeois" institution of the career is now being undermined have to be seen as, at all events, highly exaggerated. Jobs are still far more likely to be lost than are careers to be disrupted.

Moreover, not only is the *association* between class position and the risk of unemployment a robust one, but from the theoretical standpoint earlier outlined, class position is itself to be regarded as having *causal* significance. That is to say, members of the working class, and nonskilled, routine workers especially, must be seen as facing relatively high risks of job loss and unemployment *as a direct result of* the typical form that their employment contracts take.

In the case of such workers, where problems of work monitoring or human asset specificity are relatively slight (cf. Figure 5.1), employers have little reason to offer more than the basic labor contract—in effect, an approximation to a spot contract for the purchase of a quantity of labor, which, even if recurrent, carries with it no expectations of long-term continuity of employment. It is indeed in employers' interests to "commodify" labor to the greatest degree possible, so that when they need less of this commodity they will have maximum freedom simply to stop buying it. Thus, routine wage workers tend to be employed on only short periods of notice, whether formally or by "custom and practice"; and not only is it then generally easier for employers to dismiss or lay off such workers (cf. Gallie et al. 1998:139–41) but, further, if they do lose their jobs, for whatever reason, there is a relatively high probability that they will become unemployed for some period simply because they will have only quite limited time in which to find alternative work. In contrast, in the case of professional and managerial staff, where employers have more to lose from "hasty quits" and a thus a greater incentive to establish expectations of continuity of employment, longer periods of notice—usually at least a month—are the norm; and these employees have therefore much better chances, should they in fact lose their jobs, of still avoiding unemployment other than perhaps of a "transitional" kind.[5]

It should in addition be noted that wage workers are generally less well protected than are salaried staff against employment insecurity arising from ill health, which has been shown to be an especially important factor in long-term unemployment (White 1983). The superior fringe benefits that members of the salariat typically enjoy mean that they are better able to maintain continuity of employment on the basis of extended sick leave or, in the case of older workers, to avoid entering unemployment by taking early retirement pensions.

Although, then, vulnerability to job loss and unemployment will in various ways be affected by individual as well as structural factors—as indeed by other structural factors apart from class—the persisting centrality of class in creating differentials in this respect is apparent enough.[6] In turn, there would seem little reason to modify White's view (1991:110) that a relatively high risk of unemployment, and thus of economic insecurity, is "inherent to the condition" of those individuals holding working class positions, as these positions are here understood.

ECONOMIC STABILITY

As well as being a major determinant of their longer-term economic security, the class positions that individuals hold, as determined by the form of their employment contracts, can also be expected to influence their economic lives in the shorter term—that is, from week to week and month to month—through the consequences that follow for the degree of stability or fluctuation of their earnings.

Earnings data that would allow this matter to be examined directly are not, unfortunately, available in the British case. However one data set, that of the New Earnings Survey (NES), does provide information of value. The NES data are obtained each year directly from employers' payrolls for a sample of employees randomly selected on the basis of their National Insurance numbers, and can thus claim higher quality than earnings data collected through individuals' responses in interviews or to questionnaires. Information is available that allows the "makeup" of gross earnings in different occupations to be analyzed according to four categories: that is, three categories of variable pay—all forms of "payment by results," overtime earnings, and shift and other premiums—and a fourth, residual category, "all other pay." This latter category cannot be entirely equated with fixed or "basic" pay, chiefly because it includes the pay of workers on time rates that is variable in the sense that their contracts do not specify any normal or standard hours. Nonetheless, it would seem possible to treat "all other pay" as in general giving a good indication of basic pay, and it thus becomes possible to make comparisons of the relative importance of variable forms of pay in the total earnings of different categories of worker, even if the actual amount of variation that is produced at the individual level remains unknown.[7]

By recoding the occupational unit groups used in the NES to the six employee classes of NS-SEC (see Table 5.1), we can produce results of the kind reported in Table 5.2. This shows the relative importance of different components of gross weekly earnings, in 1975 and 1998, for men in each of these six classes who were in full-time employment.

Two major points emerge. First, the relative importance of variable forms of pay clearly differs across classes. In particular, such pay accounts for, if not a negligible, still only a very slight proportion of the total earnings of men in the salariat—that is, in Classes 1 and 2—but for a far more significant proportion, upward of 20 percent, of the earnings of men in working class positions—that is, in Classes 6 and 7. It is, moreover, with men in these classes that variable pay is most likely to be underestimated through the inclusion in the "other" category of the time-rate earnings of employees who have no standard hours of work.

Second, such class differences do not show any very dramatic alteration over the period covered. The most notable change is the decline in importance of payment by results (PBR) for men in Classes 6 and 7, reflecting, one may suppose, the decreasing use of piece rates in modern industry; and, chiefly on this account, the proportion of the total earnings of these workers that falls into the "other" pay category increases. It is also the case that among men in Classes 1 and 2 some evidence of a reverse tendency is apparent. Indeed, if attention is focused on the proportion of men receiving some part of their earnings in the form of PBR, then a marked narrowing in differences between the working class and the salariat might be claimed. Nonetheless, it is important not to lose sight of the fact that still in 1998 PBR accounted for under 5 percent of the total earnings of men in Classes I and 2 and that the "other" pay category—which in their case can be rather safely equated with basic

TABLE 5.2

Components of Average Gross Weekly Earnings, Men in Full-time Employment, 1975 and 1998

NS-SEC Class		PERCENT TOTAL EARNINGS				PERCENT RECEIVING		
		PBR*	Overtime Pay**	Shift etc Premiums***	Other	PBR*	Overtime Pay**	Shift Premiums***
1 Higher managerial and professional	1975	0.9	1.5	0.4	97.2	3.9	9.9	3.2
	1998****	4.3	1.8	0.4	92.5	12.2	11.3	3.2
2 Lower managerial and professional	1975	1.8	2.3	0.5	95.3	6.9	14.6	5.1
	1998****	3.4	1.9	0.6	93.1	12.6	12.6	5.5
3 Intermediate	1975	3.4	6.6	0.8	89.1	9.7	35.5	7.4
	1998****	2.7	5.7	0.8	89.7	11.9	32.5	6.0
5 Lower supervisory and technical	1975	5.2	13.4	2.6	78.7	30.8	54.3	19.4
	1998****	3.0	13.9	3.3	78.5	20.5	54.6	20.1
6 Semiroutine	1975	9.9	13.7	4.2	72.3	38.3	53.2	28.4
	1998****	3.9	13.1	4.3	77.7	26.9	49.2	28.9
7 Routine	1975	10.1	14.7	2.3	72.9	49.6	57.3	19.1
	1998****	4.4	14.1	2.2	78.1	22.7	52.5	15.3

NOTES:

* Includes piecework, bonuses, and profit-related commissions and all other incentive payments not related to overtime.

** Relates to all pay for overtime hours, not just to premium elements.

*** Includes pay for night or weekend work not treated as overtime.

**** Because of deficiencies in the current version of the 1998 NES data set, percentages in left-hand panel of the table sum to 98–99 rather than to 100.

SOURCE: New Earnings Survey Dataset

pay—was little less dominant than in 1975. In other words, the salariat clearly remains the salariat.[8]

Comparable data to those of Table 5.2 can be produced for women but interpretation is more difficult in that the restriction of coverage to full-time employees is likely to be far more consequential than with men. In particular, this restriction would seem the most probable explanation for two results of note: first, in all classes alike, variable forms of pay are less important than for men and, second, class differences are less marked overall. At the same time, though, the differences that do show up are on essentially the same pattern as those for men and, also as for men, changes over time are quite limited, with the declining importance of PBR for employees in Classes 6 and 7 again emerging most strongly.[9]

These findings on variable pay do then provide further grounds for skepticism over claims of the decline of class and, more specifically, of the erosion of distinctive features of the "service relationship." Several authors have argued (e.g. Brown 1995; Savage 2000: ch. 6) that, as a result of the intensified competition of the global economy, remuneration on the basis of fixed salaries has to be modified. Pay must, to an increasing degree, be linked to performance and for professional and managerial staff no less than for rank-and-file employees. From this point of view, the service relationship is seen not as expressing an employment contract with a rather sophisticated underlying rationale but simply as a conventional status distinction that could be sustained during the long boom of the postwar years but that is now being swept aside as a new individualistic and entrepreneurial culture undermines that of old bureaucratic hierarchies.

It is, however, surprising that, if such a development is in train, there are not more signs of it in the findings presented above. Of course, if the data would allow a yet closer focus on, say, CEOs and others in very senior managerial positions, it is likely that in this case profit-related pay in particular would take on a greater significance. But for professional and managerial employees at large, one can only conclude that evidence to suggest that their mode of payment is now increasingly influenced by a new business ethos is scarcely compelling.

In sum, although class differences in the stability of earnings may not be quite so marked as in the past, clear enough indications show that they still persist. For most members of the salariat, variation in earnings on a relatively short-term basis is unlikely to be a matter of much importance: the monthly pay slip will be fairly predictable. In contrast, for most blue collar workers and, one may suppose, for members of the working class especially, at least the potential instability of pay remains a feature of their economic lives. The possibility, if not the actuality, of week-to-week fluctuation in earnings, even if now more related to hours worked and in particular to overtime working than to piece-rate payment, is still widely present. Weekly income depends in some significant part both on the readiness of individuals to do overtime and, of course, on its availability. And it should also be kept in mind that the earnings of non-salaried workers are also liable to fluctuate in another way that the available data do not allow us to explore at all. That is, as a result of pay being lost through hours or days taken off on account of (at least uncertified) sickness, domestic or family problems, and so on—a situation that would seem especially likely to arise in the case of women who work part time on account of their family responsibilities.

These differences in earnings stability—just as those in the risks of unemployment—can then be seen as stemming directly from the differences in employment relations in terms of which class is here defined. The basic labor contract, as an approximation to a spot contract for the purchase of a quantity of labor, requires that the work involved is such that it can be adequately measured and controlled—typically, that it entails physical rather than symbolic activity and that worker autonomy is low. If measurement is by output, piece rates with checks for quality are the obvious form of payment, while if measurement is by input, usually as indexed by time spent on the job, time rates with checks for effort will apply. But, in either case, the underlying logic is that pay will indeed vary with the amount of work done.

In contrast, the service relationship, implying a less specific, more diffuse exchange than a simple "money-for-effort" bargain, is well adapted to circumstances where work is not easily measured or otherwise monitored— typically, where it entails symbolic rather than physical activity and worker autonomy is high. The logic of the service relationship is that the commitment of employees to organizational goals is gained and appropriate incentives are created through payment by salary that is not subject to short-term fluctuation, but that can be expected steadily to increase in its level, conditional on satisfactory appraisal of a relatively long-term kind, over most of the individual's working life.[10]

Finally, here, it should be noted that the foregoing relates entirely to earnings stability among members of employee classes, to whom the coverage of NES is restricted. There is in fact little information of any kind on the stability of earnings of small employers or the self-employed. If, however, any supposition were to be made in this regard, it could only be that among such independents—as comprised by Class IV of the Goldthorpe schema or Class 4 of NS-SEC—fluctuations in earnings will be significantly greater than among employees in general, and again as a direct consequence of the relations that characterize their class position (cf. Boden and Corden 1994). Rather than receiving salaries or wages from an employer, independents generate their own earnings through their market transactions with customers or clients, and also with suppliers, creditors, and their own employees, under economic conditions that are subject to a wide range of variation. Qualitative studies of small entrepreneurs, shopkeepers, self-employed artisans, and the like have indicated that maintaining custom or "the flow of work" is a frequent preoccupation, and that the uncertainty of earnings tends to create problems in both business planning and family budgeting (see, e.g., Scase and Goffee 1980, 1982).

ECONOMIC PROSPECTS

In considering the consequences of class for economic security and economic stability, the risks of unemployment and the likelihood of short-term fluctuation in earnings, respectively, have served as empirical referents. As regards economic prospects, these will be indexed by the relationship that exists between earnings and age. Economists have for long recognized that earnings tend to follow a parabolic curve with age, first rising and then later leveling out and falling off somewhat. However, far less attention has been given (a notable exception is Phelps Brown 1977: ch. 8) to the fact that the particular shapes of age-earnings curves vary across different groups of employees. What, for present purposes, is of chief interest is the extent and persistence of such variation as it occurs across classes. NES data, recoded as in the previous section, again allow relevant analyses to be made, and in this case a comparison is possible between 1975 and 1999.

Figure 5.3 graphs 1975 median gross weekly earnings for three-year age groups of men in full-time employment in each of the six employee classes of

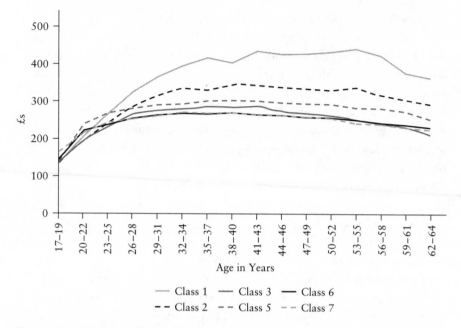

Figure 5.3.   Men in Full-time Employment in 1975—Median Gross Weekly Earnings in 1999 Prices

SOURCE: New Earnings Survey Dataset

NS-SEC. As is indicated, these earnings are expressed in 1999 prices so that comparisons with that year can be made in real terms.[11]

It is important that this and subsequent similar figures are carefully interpreted. The graphs derive from cross-sectional data. Thus, they should be understood as showing what in a certain year employees within a certain class and of a certain age were, on average, earning. Given our primary concern with the structural effects of class position, it is in fact this information that is of chief relevance. By the same token, the graphs should not be read as tracing out the lifetime earnings of particular individuals. Apart from anything else, mobility between classes does of course occur during working life, and any analysis of the course of lifetime earnings of individuals would have to take such mobility into account.[12] Furthermore, at the same time as they show age effects, the graphs will also reflect birth-cohort effects (which could be important if members of successive cohorts have experienced contrasting economic fortunes) and also—and especially toward their tails—various selection effects. Such complicating factors have always to be kept in

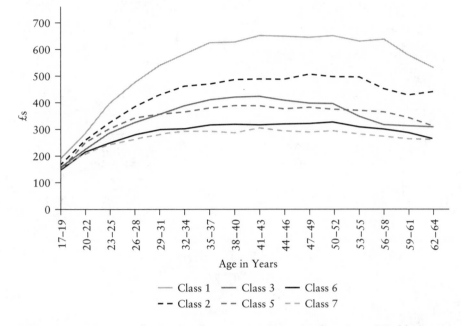

Figure 5.4. Men in Full-time Employment in 1999—Median Gross Weekly Earnings in 1999 Prices.

SOURCE: New Earnings Survey Dataset

mind, and attention should focus on the larger features of the different curves that are depicted.

From Figure 5.3 the following points most clearly emerge. First, up to around age 25 class differences in earnings are rather slight. Young professionals and managers earn little more than young wage workers in routine jobs, and rates of increase in earnings are also similar. Second, though, from the mid-twenties onward the curves begin to diverge. Those for Classes 6 and 7 rise only up to around age 30 and then remain more or less flat before tending to slope downward somewhat as men pass 50. However, the curves for both intermediate classes, Class 3 and Class 5, and also that for the lower-level salariat, Class 2, show a rise that continues well into the thirties before leveling out. And, in most marked contrast, the curve for the higher-level salariat, Class 1, rises quite sharply up the late thirties and then more slowly and irregularly into the fifties before declining after age 55.[13]

In Figure 5.4 corresponding results to those of Figure 5.3 are shown for 1999. It is apparent (note the changed vertical scale) that real earnings have

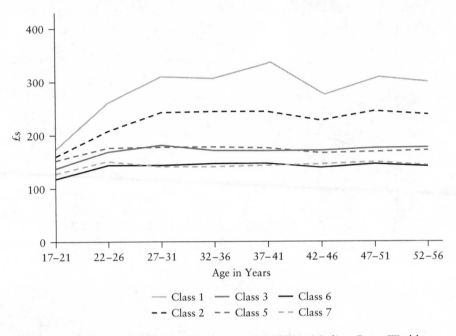

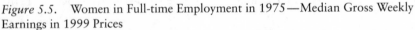

Figure 5.5.   Women in Full-time Employment in 1975—Median Gross Weekly Earnings in 1999 Prices

SOURCE: New Earnings Survey Dataset

increased and also that class inequalities have at the same time widened—as one would expect to find in the light of other analyses of earnings over the period covered (e.g. Gosling, Machin, and Meghir 1994; Johnson and Makepeace 1997; McKnight 2000). However, of chief concern here is what has happened to the shapes of the class curves.

The curves for Classes 6 and 7, the two divisions of the working class, reveal rather little change. They rise for slightly longer than in 1975—that is, now up to the mid-thirties—but then remain essentially flat until their eventual decline for older age groups, essentially as before. Similarly, the curve for Class 1 is not greatly altered. It again shows a sharp rise up to the late thirties followed by a slower increase—possibly less sustained than in the earlier graph—before turning down from the mid-fifties. Changes of greater consequence are in fact restricted to the curves lying between those for Classes 6 and 7 and that for Class 1. Thus, the curves for Classes 3 and 5 show somewhat longer periods of increase in 1999 than in 1975—that is, ones continuing up to around age 40—and that for Class 3 does in fact rise

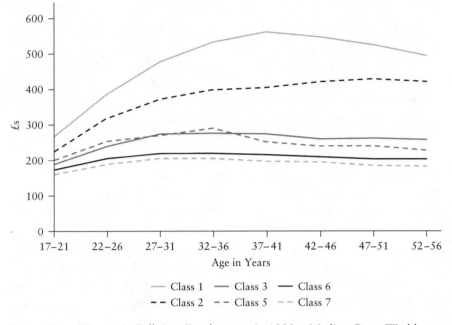

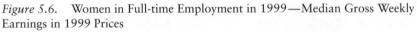

Figure 5.6.   Women in Full-time Employment in 1999—Median Gross Weekly Earnings in 1999 Prices

SOURCE: New Earnings Survey Dataset

above that for Class 5 between the ages of 30 and 50 while in 1975 it remained always below.[14] However, it is the change in shape of the curve for Class 2 that is most significant. In 1999 this curve is much more similar to that for Class 1 than it was in 1975. It too now rises sharply into the thirties and then more slowly into the fifties. In other words, so far as economic prospects are concerned, there is here evidence of some "consolidation" of the salariat.

Figures 5.5 and 5.6 then present comparable graphs to those of Figures 5.3 and 5.4 for women in full-time employment. Two minor differences in format are that five-year rather than three-year age groups are used, because of the smaller numbers involved, and that the age range covered extends only to 52–56 because of the tendency of women to retire earlier than men.

If Figure 5.5 is compared, first of all, with Figure 5.3, it can be seen that in 1975 age-earnings curves for women were less differentiated by class than were those for men. The curves for women in Classes 3 and 5, as well as those for women in Classes 6 and 7, are essentially flat after a slight rise up to the mid-twenties. And further the curves for women in Classes 1 and 2 are distinctive only in that earnings increase, and rather more sharply, up to around age 30.

However, if Figure 5.5 is then compared with Figure 5.6, it is apparent that by 1999 not only had class inequalities in earnings widened among women, as among men, but that at the same time greater differences in the shapes of class curves had developed. And in turn the comparison of Figure 5.6 with Figure 5.4 then serves to show that this differentiation is for the most part on similar lines to that found among men. In particular, there is now the same marked contrast between the working class and the salariat: that is, between, on the one hand, the curves for Classes 6 and 7 that remain largely flat after the twenties and, on the other, the curve for Class 1 that now rises steeply up to around age 40 and that for Class 2 that shows a slower though apparently more sustained rise.

The only gender difference of note occurs with Class 3, that of intermediate white collar workers, in which a high proportion of women employees are of course found. For men, the Class 3 curve, as earlier observed, moved somewhat closer between 1975 and 1999 to that for Classes 1 and 2, at least in rising quite sharply up to age 40. But for women no such change is revealed: in 1999 as in 1975 the Class 3 curve essentially follows the Class 6 and 7, or working class, trajectory.[15]

In sum, it can be shown that clear class differences in age-earnings curves exist and, further, that, in so far as changes have occurred over the last quarter of the twentieth century, these changes have tended to make such differences more rather than less apparent. In 1975 the most marked contrast was that found, in the case of men, between earnings within the working class, which did not increase with age after the twenties, and earnings within the higher salariat, which increased until a quite late stage in working life. In 1999 this contrast remains and has also become evident among women as well as men. Furthermore, for men and women alike, the lower salariat is now clearly differentiated from the working class on much the same lines as the higher salariat.[16]

What this means in terms of the economic prospects of particular individuals will, to repeat, depend in part on their chances of mobility. However, it is known that rates of work-life class mobility do fall off rather sharply for individuals in their thirties (Goldthorpe 1987: ch. 6; Gershuny 1993), and thus, for individuals who have reached this age, some fairly clear implications can be spelled out. In particular, for men who are still at this stage in their lives in working class positions or for women in working class or intermediate class positions, their expectations of any further improvement in the level of their real earnings must be regarded as poor, apart from that which may result from general economic growth. In contrast, for those individuals who have achieved positions in the salariat—from which downward mobility in the course of working life is infrequent—there are good expectations that their real earnings will steadily increase at least up to some time in their fifties.

Once more, then, the empirical evidence produced is scarcely consistent with the claim of declining class differences and, in particular, of the demise of the service relationship as the basis of professional or managerial careers.[17] Rather, the relevant curves of Figures 5.3 to 5.6 can be taken as well illustrating the consequences for earnings that follow from its operation. As earlier argued, the service relationship can be understood as a response by employers to problems of work monitoring and human asset specificity, through which is created an expectation of continuity of employment and also appropriate incentives for employees to act consistently in the pursuit of organizational goals. An age-earnings curve that moves upward over much of working life is an important element in the logic of this relationship. On the one hand, employees know that the better they perform, the quicker and further their promotion is likely to be into the better-paid levels of the hierarchy. On the other hand, because for most employees higher rewards will still lie ahead, "hasty quits" are discouraged and, further, the threat of dismissal, as, say, for manifest underperformance or malfeasance, is made more potent. Thus, for so long as the service relationship remains an effective response to problems widely associated with the employment of professional and managerial staff, class differences in economic prospects, and ones especially marked as between the salariat and the body of wage workers, can be expected to persist.

Finally, separate attention needs once more to be given to small employers and the self-employed whose economic prospects, as indexed through age-earnings curves, cannot be treated on the basis of the NES; and, again, the British Household Panel Study would appear the best alternative, despite offering no opportunity to examine long-run trends and having a response rate for the earnings of independents of only around 50 percent (cf. Meager, Court, and Moralee 1996).

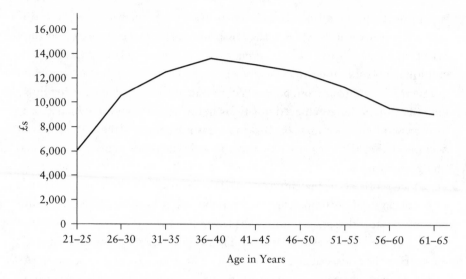

Figure 5.7.   Men in Class IV—Median Reported Annual Labor Income –
1999–2000

SOURCE: British Household Panel Study

Drawing on the BHPS data set, it is possible to show, as in Figure 5.7, the median reported annual "labor incomes" (1999–2000) for five-year age-groups of men falling into Goldthorpe Class IV (similar analyses for women could not usefully be undertaken because of inadequate numbers).[18] Because it is annual rather than weekly earnings that are here plotted, the curve with age appears more pronounced than in the figures previously presented. But if derived weekly earnings were to be shown on Figure 5.4 above—that is, that for male employees in 1999—the curve would in fact rather closely follow those for Classes 6 and 7 over the age-range 32–49, although falling below for both the earlier and later ranges.

That the earnings of members of Class IV would thus appear as being, at best, only at the same level as those of primarily manual wage workers suggests some significant degree of underreporting, as indeed has been found in studies that have focused on this issue (e.g. Meager and Bates 2001); and any reasonable correction made in the light of these studies would in fact lead to Class IV earnings being placed somewhere in-between those for Class 5 and Class 6 for all except the youngest and oldest age groups.[19] However, for present purposes, it is the general shape of the curve of Figure 5.7 that is of chief significance. While this shows a rate of increase over younger age groups similar to that for intermediate white collar employees or even the lower salariat, it is more distinctive in the rate and extent of its subsequent decline. Selection effects are very likely to be involved here. The probability of self-employment in relation to age has been shown to be nonlinear, first rising then falling in later life (Rees and Shah 1986), and self-employed craftsmen in particular would seem inclined to opt for wage work as middle age approaches (Scase and Goffee 1982: ch. 4). But what is more generally reflected, one may suppose, is a tendency for older independents, whether out of choice or constraint, to take on less business and to work shorter hours than they did when of prime age: that is to say, either because they can afford to enjoy more leisure or because of diminishing powers. In this respect, both the advantages and disadvantages of the economic position of independents are well brought out.

CONCLUSIONS

It has been shown that if class positions are defined by reference to employment relations, then the experience of individuals in terms of economic security, stability, and prospects will typically differ with the class positions that they hold. At least with some of the more marked contrasts that in this way arise, individuals in different class positions could in fact be seen as living in quite different economic worlds, not just as regards their levels of material welfare but, further, as regards the whole range of economic life chances—of risks and opportunities—that they face.

From a methodological standpoint, the findings presented above thus provide additional confirmation of the validity and utility of conceptualizing class in the way in question (cf. also Rose and Pevalin 2003). More substantively, they throw further doubt on claims of the decline or death of class in modern—or, supposedly, "postmodern"—societies such as that of contemporary Britain. What is rather indicated is the general persistence, and in some respects even the heightening, of inequalities that can be shown to derive directly from the incumbency of different class positions: that is, not from the attributes of individuals per se but from their location within the social relations of labor markets and production units that form the class structure as here understood.

Finally, then, and from the standpoint of the present volume in particular, the value of taking a class structural context for the study of economic and social mobility may be underlined. A clear distinction can in this way be established between "positions" and "persons": class positions represent the "empty places" (cf. Sørensen 1991) among which the mobility of individuals (or families) occurs. But further, as well as thus providing a framework within which rates and patterns of mobility can be observed and measured, a class structural perspective also provides a natural starting point for the explanation of these rates and patterns.

In so far as individuals in different classes do inhabit different economic worlds, as characterized by security, stability, and prospects, then not only can their class positions be seen as constraining their life chances in regard to mobility—as in a range of other respects—but, further, as shaping the life choices that they make within such constraints, as, for example, their educational and occupational choices. What has of late become increasingly apparent is that where fairly systematic class differences in patterns of such choice are empirically demonstrable, it is possible to provide causally adequate accounts in terms of individuals' rationally adaptive responses to features of the class situations that they typically face—or, more specifically, in terms of their attitudes to risk, their propensity to discount the future, their sense of personal adequacy and so on (e.g. Goldthorpe 2000: chs. 8, 9, 11; Jonsson and Erikson 2000; Breen 2001; Bowles and Gintis 2002).

Explanations on these lines often help in understanding why class-linked patterns of choice should persist over time and, in turn, the marked self-maintaining properties that inequalities of opportunity and social mobility regimes often appear to possess. Such explanations can, moreover, claim to be ones given at a more fundamental level than those that rely merely on the invocation of class cultures or subcultures. Explanations of this latter kind often struggle to avoid tautology—that is, through inferring cultural values and derived social norms from the very patterns of action to which they are addressed; and in any event they leave unanswered the question of just why individuals should tend to act in accordance with such values and norms rather than deviating from them. In contrast, explanations that are able to show at least the subjective rationality of individuals' actions, given their class situations, come closer to what Boudon (2003) has called "final" explanations or "explanations without black boxes." They offer accounts both of typical patterns of action and at the same time—by revealing their adaptive qualities—of the particular values and norms by which such action would appear to be informed.

Notes

1. As shown, the corresponding classes of the Goldthorpe schema and of the NS-SEC in this version carry the same number, roman in the former case, arabic in the latter. This distinction will serve to make it clear in the text which classification is at any point being used. At the five-class level, to which the common descriptive terms are applied, the class allocation of individuals shows almost 90 percent continuity between the two systems.

2. The implicit provisions of employment contracts can be defined as informal but shared understandings between employers and employees, usually concerning how each will respond to contingencies, that are backed not by law but rather by the parties' reputations.

3. As can be seen from Figure 5.1, the class of intermediate white collar workers (III/3) is located, somewhat speculatively, in the lower-right quadrant, where work monitoring problems dominate over asset specificity problems, while the class of intermediate blue collar occupations (V/5) is located in the upper-left quadrant, where the reverse applies. The former situation could be expected to lead to a form of contract in which some departure from the exchange of discrete amounts of money and effort, characteristic of the basic labor contract, would be more apparent than features directed toward furthering a long-term relationship, while the latter situation would be expected to lead to a still fairly specific money-for-effort bargain but combined with understandings, if only implicit, about the desirability of continuity (see further Goldthorpe 2000:221–23).

4. The lower risks of unemployment of intermediate white collar employees as compared with intermediate blue collar employees might appear to go contrary to the expectation indicated in the previous note that the latter would be the more likely to have contracts in which understandings on continuity of employment would figure. However, unpublished results from the study by Gallie et al. (1998), previously referred to, show that over the earlier period that this study covered the risks for Class III did tend on the whole to be higher. Further investigation of this issue is required.

5. Data from the British Labour Force Survey, collected in the course of research aimed at the validation of NS-SEC, are revealing in this regard. The proportion of individuals working to one month's notice or more falls steadily across the employee classes as follows: Class 1, 89 percent; Class 2, 78 percent; Class 3, 69 percent; Class 5, 38 percent; Class 6, 29 percent; Class 7, 17 percent (ESRC Validation Group 1997).

6. For example, level of qualification may be regarded as affecting the risk of unemployment largely *via* its influence on the type of employment, and thus the class positions, to which individuals gain access; and structural factors such as industry or organizational size would appear chiefly of significance in determining the incidence of unemployment *within* classes.

7. The only other variable element included in total gross earnings would appear to be that of "tips and gratuities," in so far as these are shown in employers' pay records.

8. It should be noted that the results here reported from the NES—and likewise those reported in the next section of the chapter—do of course refer only to employees and thus do not cover the small numbers of employers and self-employed professionals who, as indicated in Table 5.1, are also included in Classes 1 and 2.

9. These findings for women are available on request.

10. See further Goldthorpe (2000: ch. 10). The issues that arise here have been extensively discussed in the literature of the "new" institutional and managerial economics under the rubric of "principal-agent" problems (see e.g. Eggertsson 1990; Holmström and Milgrom 1991; Milgrom and Roberts 1992; and Gibbons 1997).

11. Data are also available on gross hourly earnings. For our present purposes, we have opted for weekly earnings. This is because hours of work reported are contractual rather than actual hours, and because for professionals and managers the latter may much exceed the former, which might be thought to lead to some exaggeration of class differences. However, we have repeated the analyses reported in the text using hourly earnings, and no major differences in the pattern of results emerge. We did, however, note that male employees in Class 3 have higher relative weekly earnings than hourly wages, reflecting relatively longer contracted weekly hours of work.

12. Data linkage procedures do in principle allow the earnings and employment histories of individuals covered by the NES to be constructed. Preliminary investigations by Elias and Gregory (1994) point to various technical problems but also suggest, interestingly, that the main features of cross-sectional analyses tend in fact to be replicated by longitudinal analyses.

13. It should be recognized that the very small class differences in earnings in the youngest age groups will be subject to selection effects in regard to education and that selection effects in relation to early retirement may also play a part where curves turn down for older age groups. The latter tendency could also illustrate birth cohort effects: that is, where members of a particular class and cohort "carry with them" a certain historic level of earnings that, in a context of, say, generally rising earnings, individuals in similar class positions in following cohorts will exceed.

14. In the case of the curve for Class 3, which in 1999 declines rather more sharply from around age 40 than in 1975, one may suspect the rather strong operation of selection effects associated with work-life mobility. For men, the intermediate white collar positions comprised by this class are known to have relatively low "holding power" (Erikson and Goldthorpe 1992: ch. 6), often in fact serving as stepping-stones for upward mobility into managerial positions in Classes 1 and 2. In turn, men who are found in Class 3 in later life would seem likely to be in

relatively inferior positions in terms of pay (perhaps ones to which they were promoted after spending most of their lives in manual wage-earning jobs) or to have themselves rather low earning potential.

15. In contrast to the situation for men as described in the previous note, in the case of women Class 3 positions appear to have quite high "holding power."

16. For all the graphs presented we have calculated 95 percent confidence intervals that turn out to be generally very narrow. We have also examined in the case of the salariat whether differences in age-wage curves show up as between professional and managerial groupings, since some authors (e.g., Savage et al. 1992) have argued that professionals and managers typically dispose of different kinds of "assets" in labor markets and should therefore be regarded as holding different class positions. It emerges that with Classes 1 and 2 alike the curves for the two groupings follow each other very closely—although while in 1975 those for professionals tend at most ages to be slightly above those for managers, the reverse holds in 1999. All results referred to in this note are available from the authors on request.

17. In this regard, particular comment must be made on Savage's attempt (2000: ch. 3) to use NES data as a basis for furthering his argument of the erosion of the service relationship—an attempt that is not in fact at all convincing. Savage computes for 1976 and 1990 (using the published, not original data for these years) the extent to which men aged 40–49 earn more than the average for their occupational group (not class), and then takes this "age premium" as an indicator of how far a service relationship, implying rising earnings over most of working life, is in operation. He finds that the age premium that professionals and managers enjoy over most manual workers is rather small and tends to fall over the period covered. However, calculating summary measures of this kind is a poor substitute for looking at age-earnings curves per se, and Savage fails to provide a clear rationale for the particular measure that he adopts—various alternatives to which could be suggested. For example, it would seem more direct to calculate the ratio of the earnings of employees aged, say, 50–55 to the earnings of those aged 23–28. And if this is done for each NS-SEC class for the period 1975 to 1999, then conclusions generally in line with those set out above, and at variance with Savage's own, are indicated. Examples are available on request.

18. Tak Wing Chan provided generous assistance in extracting the data on which Figure 5.7 is based.

19. In the light of existing research, Meager and Bates (2001) suggest that the extent of underreporting lies between a third and a sixth. It should also be noted that there is general agreement that the earnings of the self-employed show greater dispersion than those of employees (see e.g. Meager, Court, and Moralee 1996), although this dispersion will be heightened if, as in the work of Meager and his colleagues, self-employed professionals are considered together with the small employers and self-employed workers who constitute Class IV.

References

Beck, Ulrich. 2000. *What Is Globalization?* Cambridge: Polity Press.

Boden Rebecca, and Anne Corden. 1994. *Measuring Low Incomes: Self-Employment and Family Credit.* London: HMSO.

Boudon, Raymond. 2003. *Raison, bonnes raisons.* Paris: Presses Universitaires de France.

Bowles, Samuel, and Herbert Gintis. 2002. "The Inheritance of Inequality." *Journal of Economic Perspectives* 16:3–30.

Breen, Richard. 2001. "A Rational Choice Model of Educational Inequality." Istituto Juan March, Madrid. Working Paper 2001/166.

Brown, Philip. 1995. "Cultural Capital and Social Exclusion: Some Observations on Recent Trends in Education, Employment and the Labour Market." *Work, Employment and Society* 9:29–51.

Castells, Manuel. 1996/2000. *The Rise of the Network Society.* Oxford: Blackwells.

Eggertsson, Thráinn. 1990. *Economic Behaviour and Institutions.* Cambridge: Cambridge University Press.

Elias, Peter, and Mary Gregory. 1994. *The Changing Structure of Occupations and Earnings in Great Britain, 1975–1990.* Sheffield: Department of Employment Research Series, no. 27.

Elias, Peter, and Abigail McKnight. 2003. "Earnings, Unemployment and the NS-SEC." Pp.151–72 in *A Researcher's Guide to the National Statistics Socio-economic Classification,* edited by David Rose and David J. Pevalin. London: Sage.

Erikson, Robert, and John H. Goldthorpe. 1992. *The Constant Flux: A Study of Class Mobility in Industrial Societies.* Oxford: Clarendon.

ESRC Validation Group.1997. *Report on LFS Analyses.* London: Economic and Social Research Council.

Gallie, Duncan, Michael White, Yuan Cheng, and Mark Tomlinson. 1998. *Restructuring the Employment Relationship.* Oxford: Oxford University Press.

Gershuny, Jonathan. 1993. "Post-Industrial Career Structures in Britain." Pp.136–70 in *Changing Classes: Stratication and Mobility in Post-Industrial Societies,* edited by Gösta Esping-Andersen. London: Sage.

Gibbons, Robert. 1997. "Incentives and Careers in Organisations." Pp.1–37 in *Advances in Economics and Econometrics: Theory and Application,* edited by D. M. Kreps and K. F. Wallis. Cambridge: Cambridge University Press.

Goldthorpe, John H. 1987. *Social Mobility and Class Structure in Modern Britain,* 2nd ed. Oxford: Clarendon.

Goldthorpe, John H. 1997. "The 'Goldthorpe' Class Schema: Some Observations on Conceptual and Operational Issues in Relation to the ESRC Review of Government Social Classifications." Pp.40–48 in *Constructing Classes: Towards a New Social Classification for the UK,* edited by David Rose and

Karen O'Reilly. London: Economic and Social Research Council and Office of National Statistics.

Goldthorpe, John H. 2000. *On Sociology: Numbers, Narratives and the Integration of Research and Theory.* Oxford: Oxford University Press.

Goldthorpe, John H. 2002. "Globalisation and Social Class." *West European Politics* 25:1–28.

Gosling, Amanda, Stephen Machin, and Costas Meghir. 1994. "What Has Happened to Men's Wages Since the Mid-1960s?" *Fiscal Studies* 15:63–87.

Gray, John. 1998. *False Dawn: The Delusions of Global Capitalism.* London: Granta.

Holmström, Bengt, and Paul Milgrom. 1991. "Multitask Principal-Agent Analyses: Incentive Contracts, Asset Ownership, and Job Design." *Journal of Law, Economics and Organisation* 7:25–51.

Johnson, Daniel, and Gerald H. Makepeace. 1997. "Occupational Advantage in the Eighties: An Analysis of the Lifetime Earnings of Men." *Work, Employment and Society* 11:401–11.

Jonsson, Janne O., and Robert Erikson. 2000. "Understanding Educational Inequality." *L'année sociologique* 50:345–82.

McKnight, Abigail. 2000. *Trends in Earnings Inequality and Earnings Mobility, 1977–1997: The Impact of Mobility on Long-term Inequality.* Department of Trade and Industry, Employment Relations Research Report Series No. 8.

Meager, Nigel, Gill Court, and Janet Moralee. 1996. "Self-Employment and the Distribution of Income." Pp.208–35 in *New Inequalities: The Changing Distribution of Income and Wealth in the United Kingdom,* edited by John Hills. Cambridge: Cambridge University Press.

Meager, Nigel, and Peter Bates. 2001. "The Self-Employed and Lifetime Income." *International Journal of Sociology* 31:27–58.

Milgrom, Paul, and John Roberts. 1992. *Economics, Organization and Management.* London: Prentice Hall.

Phelps Brown, Henry. 1977. *The Inequality of Pay.* Oxford: Oxford University Press.

Rees, Hedley, and Anup Shah. 1986. "An Empirical Analysis of Self-Employment in the U.K." *Journal of Applied Econometrics* 1:95–108.

Rose, David and Karen O'Reilly, eds. 1997. *Constructing Classes: Towards a New Social Classification for the U.K.* London: Economic and Social Research Council and Office for National Statistics.

Rose, David, and Karen O'Reilly, eds. 1998. *The ESRC Review of Government Social Classifications.* London: Economic and Social Research Council and Office for National Statistics.

Rose, David, and David J. Pevalin, eds. 2003. *A Researcher's Guide to the National Statistics Socio-Economic Classification.* London: Sage.

Savage, Mike. 2000. *Class Analysis and Social Transformation.* Buckingham: Open University Press. Savage, Mike, James Barlow, Peter Dickens, and Toby Fielding. 1992. *Property, Bureaucracy and Culture.* London: Routledge.

Scase, Richard, and Richard Goffee. 1980. *The Real World of the Small Business Owner.* London: Croom Helm.

Scase, Richard, and Richard Goffee. 1982. *The Entrepreneurial Middle Class.* London: Croom Helm.

Sørensen, Aage B. 1991. "On the Usefulness of Class Analysis in Research on Social Mobility and Socioeconomic Inequality." *Acta Sociologica* 34:71–87.

White, Michael. 1983. *Long-Term Unemployment and Labour Markets.* London: Policy Studies Institute.

White, Michael. 1991. *Against Unemployment.* London: Policy Studies Institute.

CHAPTER SIX

Mobility: What? When? How?

Andrew Abbott

The intersection of individual careers, intergenerational transmission, and the division of labor seems an especially puzzling problem. On the one hand, life courses have various regular and determinative properties, one of which is a certain rhythm and pacing. On the other, the structures through which those life courses flow have themselves considerable solidity, as well as their own quite different historical pacing. When we study mobility, our challenge is to theorize the intersection of two such temporal structures. Yet at the same time we must also theorize the way each separate structure—careers and divisions of labor—endures through time, since that too is not self-evident.

THE OCCUPATIONAL PROCESS AND THE MOBILITY CONCEPT

Mobility is not itself a primitive concept, but a higher-level one. It focuses on specific aspects of a much more general thing, a thing I shall here call "the occupational process." Although everyone who writes about mobility has this more general process in mind most of the time, it is helpful to make it visible. We can begin by imagining it in terms of the Lexis diagram, with time running to the right and age rising along the vertical. Individual lives are diagonals rising to the right with a slope of 1. To this array we need to add a social structural "dimension"—which I will name occupations here,

I thank David B. Grusky and his colleagues for the original invitation that led to this paper. All unreferenced statistics and calculations relative to the American labor force are taken from Abbott (2005).

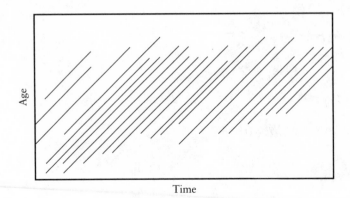

Figure 6.1.   Age/Time

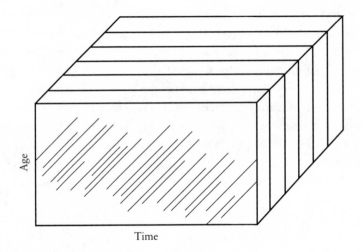

Figure 6.2.   Age/Time

although it could just as easily be classes as in John Goldthorpe's formulation, or a linear prestige dimension as in Blau and Duncan, or something else. This constitutes a third dimension, perpendicular to the page.

Figures 6.1 and 6.2 suggest this occupational dimension. Figure 6.1 shows a standard Lexis diagram, with period time advancing to the right and age advancing upward. Unlike the normal Lexis diagram, this one has as its x axis the conventional age of labor force entry—sixteen. Each diagonal line represents an individual (or individuals, as we shall see below) who enters the occupation at a given age. Since that age need not be sixteen, many of these lines begin above the x axis. Lines terminate when an individual (or

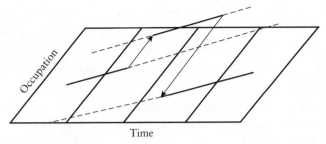

Figure 6.3. Occupation / Time

individuals) leaves the occupation either by death, retirement, or removal to another occupation. Lines thus represent segments of an individual's career trajectory that lie within a particular occupation, showing the relation of age and period. The occupation shown has been getting older with time, but only in terms of entry age.

Figure 6.2 shows a lamination of such planes, each one representing a different occupation. Obviously, the pattern of trajectory segments within each plane will be quite different, depending on the age structure of occupational entry and departure. Unlike the occupation shown in Figure 6.1, the visible occupation in this figure has been growing younger, both in terms of entry age and of departure age.

Because individuals change occupations in their work lives, an individual's occupational Lexis line is not necessarily continuous. But we will imagine some way of identifying an individual's trajectory as a linked sequence of the trajectory segments that capture an individual's spells in his or her several occupations. This linkage is shown in Figure 6.3 as arrow segments, which are perpendicular to the occupation plane and hence involve no change in age or period but simply in occupation. The dotted lines in Figure 6.3 represent the implicit careers that would have been realized had the individual spent his or her entire career in a single occupation.

We must also imagine a way of conceiving of multiple individuals on the same trajectory or trajectory segment. If we want to stay in relatively comprehensible three-dimensional space, this can be imagined as a kind of density or mass of any given trajectory segment. (Alternatively, we can imagine yet a fourth orthogonal dimension, that of individuals.)

This image captures much of what interests us in the occupational process. The careers of individuals are the trajectory segments of a given person, linked across time periods and occupations into a single, individual trajectory as in Figure 6.3. The (demographic) careers of occupations are the ensembles of trajectory segments lying in particular planes perpendicular to the occupational axis. Thus we have easy ways to envision the "careers" of both individuals and of occupations.

If we consider by contrast the plane perpendicular to the time axis at some moment, the individual inter-occupational transitions in a given moment are represented by the ensemble of all arrow segments in such a plane, augmented by point masses for those who remain in place. This is the conceptual foundation of the classic mobility matrix. Once we refer each arrow conventionally to either the origin or target occupation (it doesn't matter which as long as we do the same with all of them), the intersection of all trajectory segments with that plane is a particular period's demographic/occupational structure (PDOS); this structure captures "who is where now at what age." We can think of this PDOS as an empirical realization of the division of labor itself, since a given system of technical production can be divided among occupations in many different ways (so there is no warrant for assuming a constant structure to this dimension). The division of labor is itself thus a largely conceptual entity, given empirical shape in actual occupational conflicts (which I have not represented here) and demographic structurings (which I have). Note that there is nothing particularly "occupational" about the social structural dimension up to this point. This entire analysis, in different terms, still applies if we take the social structural dimension to be class or indeed even region.

So far we have considered two of the basic planes in Figure 6.2. The first is that perpendicular to the occupational axis (the page plane), which captures given occupations' demographic structure over time (ODST). The second is the plane perpendicular to the time dimension. This is the PDOS, the demographic realization of the division of labor at a moment. Consider now the third plane and its associated dimensional structure: the intersection of trajectory segments with a plane perpendicular to the age dimension. This plane captures the changing occupational structure of an age grade over time (AGOST). The AGOST is of considerable importance. In part, this is because many occupations are characterized by particular age structures that endure over time. In the current labor force, for example, a survey of employment at age 20 will find it very heavily concentrated in a number of occupations—about half of it in busboys and food-service assistants, private

household child-care workers, short-order cooks, and food counter and related workers, in fact. These occupations have however little connection
with incumbents' later occupations. This pattern has endured over time and
indeed represents a kind of permanent age structuring of certain "occupations." (I shall explain these scare quotes later.) But the more important fact
is that a given AGOST is very much a function of both period changes in the
division of labor and of the "mass pattern" of other AGOSTs. If we think of
a division of labor as having a kind of natural age structure, then variations
in entering cohort size will have enormous age-grade effects on waiting times
for promotion and the like, as the post-baby-boom generation knows well.

Most of the crucial structures of the labor force are thus represented here:
occupations over time and age, age grades over time and occupation, and successive demographic/occupational structures. We also have individual careers, their segments, and the lines hooking these segments together. This array also allows us to begin to see how these things relate to one another. Note,
incidentally, that there is no necessity to decide ahead of time how we think
determination flows through this array—whether or when or how careers
shape occupations or the division of labor, or the division of labor governs
occupations or careers, or some careers determine other careers, and so on.
One has only to recite this list to think of distinguished exponents of all of
these possibilities.

Note too that in temporal terms we have to think of this system as generated by a sequence of DOS planes, marching along to the right, perpendicular to the time axis. However we may want to think about causality—
whether we think it flows through individual lives or through occupational
histories or in the synchronic relations of the divisions of labor in their suc-
cession—it has to exercise itself through the progression of these adjacent
planes on their inexorable march into the future. The deep past cannot reach
out and cause things in the current present. To act in the present, it has to
have encoded its influence into the present that immediately followed it,
which then encoded itself into *its* immediate future, and so on and on until
that influence reaches the current present. Of course there are certain kinds
of historical action-at-a-distance: through memory, for example, or through
forms that are culturally constructed for this express purpose, like credentials. But the assumption that determination happens in the immediate pass-
ing of past into present is a good place to start. It has also been generally
characteristic of the recent mobility literature.

What then is intergenerational mobility in the context of this simple diagram? It concerns a particular association between the career trajectories of different individuals, comparing the occupational location of parent and child. The parental occupation is sampled at a particular point (when the child is 16, in the famous 1962 OCG data, for example) or by a general question such as "what was your father's occupation?" (The two are likely to produce different answers, to some extent.) Data exigencies often mean that the elapsed time of the generational link in this design can vary quite widely in a sample. But most often, our mobility questions simply arise from wondering whether children are better off than parents in some sense and measures this difference by comparing parent's occupation (or class location) at some point with child's occupation (or class location) at some other point. As with many such measures there is a delicate balance between indicator and concept, the former sometimes being mistaken for the latter, as is often the case with income measures and satisfaction concepts.

By presenting mobility in this larger context, I wish to underscore that the mobility question is only one of many questions that can be asked about the occupational process. The importance of mobility investigation in social science flows from the political importance of the question of equal opportunity in liberal societies, not from the intellectual centrality of mobility in understanding the occupational process. There is little reason to think that the mobility question is the right question to start with if our goal is to understand the evolution of the entire system over time, nor even that mobility is the principal system outcome to be explained. As my diagram makes quite explicit, many aspects of the mobility process are overshadowed by structural changes that flow into this system more or less from outside it: demographic changes, technological changes, autonomous reorganizations of the division of labor. Certain levels of intergenerational mobility are likely to emerge from various combinations of exogenous change, and indeed may feed back onto those changes.

THREE QUESTIONS ABOUT MOBILITY

A variety of detailed questions can be asked about our mobility concept. I shall mention three, the first briefly, the other two more extensively.

I mention only briefly my first issue, which is well known on the "class" side of the mobility literature. There is a real question about the reality and endurance of the "planes" of my social structural dimension. Most important, it is not the case that the occupational version of this dimension defines a "more solid" set of social structures, available as a fallback if class categories prove unstable or artifactual. The history of occupations shows that linking detailed occupations across periods of even thirty years—a necessity within our conception of mobility—is quite suspect. Linking over fifty years is in many cases next to impossible, as is well shown by the work of Margo Anderson (Conk 1980), Alain Desrosières (Desrosières and Thévenot 1988), and others. Not only is the continuity of naming and classification at issue, so also is the task identity of occupations, which is established relationally within a contested or bureaucratic division of labor, not abstractly or functionally in some dictionary of occupations. As that division of labor changes, the very meaning of occupations located in it changes, even if their names remain the same. (For example, "secretary" meant quite different things in 1895 and 1925. Hence van Leeuwen et al.'s [2002] "historical" occupation codes have merely nominal continuity, a fact that unfortunately will not prevent their being widely used.) Finally, for all occupations but the professions, there is almost no evidence of their demographic continuity, their "reality" as groups made up of the same people over time. Demographically, doctors are an occupation; food counter workers by contrast are not an occupation, but a life stage.

In short, a preliminary question about how we frame the problem of mobility concerns the enduring character of the structures in terms of which we locate parents and children. It is not at all clear how to theorize mobility in the face of constituent change in these structures. The traditional solution (with PUMS, for example) is aggregation to more stable units. But this more or less dodges the issue.

MOBILITY AND CAREER

A second, less familiar question about mobility involves careers. Why should we evaluate mobility in terms of a point in the parent's career and a point in the child's? Particularly because this forces us to decide which points to use, whether to insist on the same (whatever that means) point in each career, and so on? Why not use the whole career to conceptualize mobility?

For those of us who study internal labor markets (ILMs), the career seems a natural unit of analysis. Unlike the classical mobility literature with its implicit ideal of perfect freedom of motion, the ILM literature addresses systems with structures. Structure makes us expect patterns. A focus on careers thus reflects the importance of direct constraint and formal structure in ILMs and ILM-like systems.

To be sure, in the extreme case mobility can be dictated simply by the structure of vacancies. For example, college coaches (Smith and Abbott 1983; Abbott and Smith 1984) work in tightly structured markets, with identifiable positions held by unique individuals. Here, mobility is completely contingent on vacancies; to model it with individual attributes is to ignore the central fact of the system. And indeed, even to approach it in career terms is probably a mistake. Such a system is best characterized through its vacancy chains.

In slightly less-constrained systems, vacancies come in small handfuls: not in huge free strata as in the usual society-wide mobility model, but in small numbers. Among nineteenth- and twentieth-century mental hospital superintendents, for example (Abbott 1990), there obtains a looser structure, rather like Shelby Stewman's venturi systems (Stewman and Konda 1983). Here one can only estimate a variety of demographic parameters and from them extrapolate, for each period, waiting times for status transitions. This is a typical example of an occupational system largely driven by exogenous factors. For the central fact of assistant physicians' lives was the rapid decline in promotion rates over time as the states chose to expand existing hospitals (making room for more assistants) rather than to build new ones (creating more positions for superintendents). If one had tried to estimate the ability of a given superintendent to find superintendent positions (elsewhere) for "his assistants"—the classic sponsored intergenerational mobility question—one would have found that while such effects existed (as the individual level data for New York and Massachusetts show), they would be completely overshadowed by the massive structural change.

In more loosely structured ILMS, the relative lack of structural constraint makes it natural to ask questions about typical career patterns. Often ILMs are designed to embody career patterns, but equally often, individuals prefer interorganizational mobility. As a result, the degree to which careers actually take the "designed" form becomes a natural empirical question. Do there really exist ladders of promotion and advance or characteristic patterns of career development? This is a logical question not only for individuals (e.g., Abbott and Hrycak 1990) but also for occupations evolving in local competition with other occupations (e.g., Abbott 1991). Within constrained systems like ILMs, then, the career or trajectory seems the natural unit of analysis for thinking about mobility. And the methods chosen reflect that natural unit. If we think in terms of trajectories built by individual units but possibly constrained by occupational and labor market structures, we will choose methods seeking overall sequential patterns in these careers. And sequence analysis and multidimensional scaling (used in the studies just cited) are both techniques frankly aimed at finding ordered regularities rather than theorized causal structures. To be sure, Leo Goodman (1996) has elegantly shown that there is a deep relation between the mathematics of some forms of scaling and log-linear models—that is, that some types of pattern-recognition methods are closely related to his type of association model, a connection also well shown by the historical fact that among the earliest applications of the proportional adjustment algorithms used to estimate log-linear models were attempts to make regularities more visible by fitting table-internal interactions to fixed marginals (Mosteller 1968, as cited in Bishop, Fienberg, and Holland 1975:100.) But sequence analysis draws on a quite different technical vocabulary. Levenshteinian alignment algorithms (as in Abbott and Hrycak 1990) are dynamic programs for producing distance data. Monte Carlo Markov Chain sequence algorithms (e.g., Abbott and Barman 1997) are iterative structures maximizing selected aspects of local resemblance. Neither of these involves the kind of cross-classified data subject to the Goodman approach.

The literature on ILMs thus evinces both a theoretical and a methodological interest in careers. By contrast, in the fields of intergenerational mobility and general intragenerational mobility as well, the study of whole careers as larger patterns in and of themselves basically vanished from sociology in the mid-1960s. Throughout the earlier period, studies of mobility generally considered both individual transitions and whole careers. Examples are Davidson and Anderson (1937), Form and Miller (1949), Palmer (1954), Parnes (1954), and Wilensky (1960, 1961). In all of this work, not only was there analysis of individual transitions and turnover of jobs but also of individuals' employer and occupation tenures (in Palmer's case even joint data on these), as well as of patterns of job and occupation tenure over the life course. After 1965, however, this attention to whole careers disappeared. Rachel Rosenfeld's splendid 1992 review on job shifts and careers in the *Annual Review* considered dozens and dozens of studies from the late 1960s to the early 1990s. But only a handful looked at whole careers. The vast majority studied the effects of particular variables on rates of various types of job shift—particular transitions or hazards at a point in time. In terms of Figure 6.3, this is focusing on the arrow segments and the point masses that represent those who do not move.

Why should it have happened that we analyze intergenerational mobility in terms of point to point association rather than by comparison of some aspect of whole careers? Reflection suggests that there are both some contingent historical reasons for the choice of point to point measure and some enduring problems with career conceptions that made this alternative less attractive. Together, they add up to a path dependence argument for where we are today.

The most obvious contingent argument has to do with methods. As many people have pointed out, the last quarter century of mobility studies were built on new methods. Raymond Boudon's 1973 book on mathematical structures of social mobility—reporting the state of the art of the Markovian approach, which at least implicitly considered both whole careers and transitions—described a literature in decline even as Boudon wrote, although it was to some extent continued in the work of Aage Sørensen (1974, 1984). Even Spilerman's famous 1977 careers paper was really less about overall career structures than about income trajectories, a topic economists would give a thorough going-over in the guise of lifetime income studies. But the major new sociological literature on mobility took as its problem the father-son point to point transition, which it examined using the Goodman log-linear model brought into mobility studies by Hauser and colleagues at Wisconsin (Hauser et al. 1975) and later amended to include various scaled variables by Breiger (1981), Hout (1984), and others who applied the Duncan (1979) uniform association model. In later years came event history methods and a detailed focus on hazard rates for various particular changes of state. All of this meant a focus on moments in careers: on point to point transition probabilities between fathers and sons in the intergenerational case or on hazard functions at particular points in the individual career case. Sequencing algorithms that might have kept whole careers in view as a research interest were unknown outside biology and computer science, the first general overview not being published until 1983 (by Sankoff and Kruskal).

So the first reason for the move away from whole career studies was probably the availability of new methods. A second body of reasons has to do with data. Concern for careers as a whole remained, at least implicitly, in the design of the PSID and NLS data sets, although neither of these was really designed explicitly around the problem of understanding careers in toto. The original NLS studies (of mature men and women) did not get full retrospective career data, the young men's study stopped after 15 years, and NLSY 1979 has to this point only covered part of the work life course of its subjects. Only the original young women's study covers most of the work life course. By contrast, PSID has the data, but problems with PSID's job, employer, and occupation data are well known. At the same time, there are inherent practical problems with career data that cannot be ignored. Whole career data is either retrospective (and hence subject to memory errors, heaping, and the like) or takes an enormous elapsed time to create. Nor is it clear what the proper sampling frame is for extended processes that face so many types of censoring. Career data is also vulnerable to my earlier problem—change in categories of classification—to an even greater extent than is point to point data on parents and children.

Another enduring pressure against whole career approaches to mobility is political. One of the numbers a liberal democracy requires from its social scientists is a rating of "whether we really do have equality of opportunity," a rating on the basis of which the civil society and the state can take action, if they wish, to produce (or reduce) social and economic democracy. An answer that "we have to wait and see how people's lives turn out" is not acceptable. The political system wants a number about "now" that can be debated and in some way changed by policy. Hence the academic literature discusses careers by means of piled-up synthetic cohorts, as did Blau and Duncan (1967) for example, in order to have some image to present to the politicians who fund their research. Even though it is known with certainty that no individual will ever have a career like those implied by synthetic cohorts, the synthetic career at least provides the political system with a basis for discussion and policy.

The result of these forces—some of them historical accidents, some of them enduring practical and political difficulties with studying whole careers—has been to largely remove study of full careers from the mobility agenda. The consequence of that in turn is that we know an enormous amount about how various job shifts (less often occupational shifts) are affected by many variables, at particular times. We have an extraordinary degree of detail on these effects, even over periods of a decade or more in some studies. But we don't really have much sense of how these effects are modified when they are assembled into an idiosyncratic work life course, nor do we know much about the cumulative impacts of them over the career and life course.

For example, we don't actually even know how long the typical work life course lasts. We haven't really tried to gather such data. But here is another conceptual difficulty. In part we lack this figure because the beginnings and ends of employment careers have become extremely fuzzy in a world where almost half of high school seniors are in the labor force and averaging twenty hours work per week while in school, where elite college graduates routinely undertake a year or two of more or less random full-time work before leaving the labor force for full-time postgraduate study, and where retirement is a gradual slide from a primary labor-force, long-duration job through various smaller jobs to eventual permanent removal from the labor force. There really is no school to work transition and there really is no point of retirement, so it is not clear at this point how to think about the length of a typical work career.[1]

We also have little sense of the arrangement of transitions in lives. Older studies like those of Palmer (1954) and Wilensky (1960) show that once we eschew the aggregation of occupations into larger groupings or classes or the mapping of occupations onto a simple prestige scale, there is an enormous amount of small-scale job shifting in the labor force—between employers, occupations, or both. Nearly all of Wilensky's (1960) interviewees (a focused sample of blue collar and lower white collar employees) had at least fourteen years with one employer, but many of them had had several different jobs (occupations) for that one employer. Palmer (1954) had a more representative (although purely urban) sample, but still found that over 10 percent of men who had not changed employers in a ten-year period had changed occupation for that employer.

Now this matters because when we study mobility by cross-classifying a point measure of parent's occupation and a point measure of child's occupation, we are taking a sample of each career at a particular point. And we are expecting that sample to capture the important parts of the mobility process. But the image of relative stability in work histories that permits us to have confidence in this procedure—the idea that a parent "has" an occupation and that a child "has" an occupation—rests on our ignoring much low-level change. And it is striking, too, that while there have been many serious attempts to investigate "job tenure" figures (which refer to spells with a single employer), very few studies (Carey 1988 and Maguire 1993 are rare exceptions) have tried to discuss occupational tenures, with or without employer changes. For example, the discussion about potential declines in job tenure in the current period (see Neumark 2000, for a review) is completely conducted in terms of employer spells, not occupational ones, in part precisely because employer change data are more solid than occupational change data in both CPS and PSID, the major data sets used in this literature.

Thus we see that there are some pretty simple questions—how many job and occupation changes will an individual actually have in a career, how do job and occupation changes build on each other over actual work life courses, how long does a work life course typically last—to whose answers we are not much closer than we were a quarter century ago. We have lost sight of these questions because we do not think in careers. At the same time, we have also seen that there are some deep practical difficulties in answering these questions even if we did focus on careers.

Yet there are not only these practical, but also some very deep theoretical difficulties with conceptions of mobility in terms of career, difficulties which have to do with the temporal architecture of careers and measurement of them. It turns out, to be sure, that these problems are just as pressing (albeit in a different way) for point to point framings of the mobility question, but they are easier to see with careers. There are two such problems.

The first concerns the relative pacing of careers and what we might call labor market regimes. Most of us think that the processes ultimately driving mobility across work lives are forces exogenous to those lives: things on the demand side like technological changes and labor process changes, things on the supply side like immigration and educational change. We can think of these as making up, in toto, something called a labor market regime: a state of technology, a division of labor, an educational level, levels of labor availability, and so on. As we usually imagine the situation, careers are largely shaped by the forces in this regime.

Note that we take these forces to be "faster," in some sense, than careers. The typical employment career lasts about forty years (probably closer to fifty if we add in the fuzzy edges noted above). A forty-year career will traverse not only some transitions in occupational definitions, but also at least one transition in the overall labor market regime of a society, not to mention numerous smaller transitions in things like technology or labor process that can easily change over the course of a decade. All careers, that is, traverse temporal boundaries that see fundamental shifts in the kinds of social forces shaping them. Because of this, it is not clear why we should or how we could conceptualize mobility in terms of careers.

In the United States, for example, a major transition in employment regimes took place in the 1920s with the end of mass immigration, the taming of hyper-rapid employee turnover, and the coming of the mass clerical labor force. The 1930s and 1940s were a long transition between this and the postwar regime; massive labor unrest culminated in a new regularization of labor relations, which was followed by the mobilization of nearly a quarter of the labor force into the military in the 1940s. After the war, things were more or less stable for about thirty years; it was an era of large employers and pattern bargaining, an era that saw a vast extension of the "wealth franchise" through home ownership and private pensions, the emergence of modern retirement, and the lowest levels of job turnover in American history. But from 1975 onward came yet another labor regime: the destruction of private sector collective bargaining, the resumption of mass immigration, the resumption of subcontracting both between and within firms, and the rise of the nimble small organization with its evanescent labor policies.

We have only to rehearse these facts to see the issues they raise about the career as a theoretical basis for the conceptualization and measurement of mobility. No American worker in the twentieth century finished his or her career in a labor force that looked much like the one in which he or she began; a very narrow slice of the war generation is perhaps the only exception. As a result much of the actual "outcome"—in the sense of the level at retirement of such measures as total wealth—has more to do with the timing of a work life course relative to the regime changes than with anything else. It is little wonder, then, that we have some difficulties with imagining that people really have comprehensible careers outside the formal fancies of synthetic cohorts.

I shall have more to say about the issue of exogenous shocks to careers below. But here I wish to turn to a second theoretical complication in thinking about careers, indeed in any thinking about mobility. That has to do with how we think about outcome. The paradigm of the mobility literature is to ask the simple question "given how the parent did, how does the child do?" The normative framework behind this question, as many people have argued, is the idea of equality of opportunity through which citizens of liberal states attempt to square the circle of simultaneously believing in meritocracy and equality. (For an excellent elaboration of this dilemma, together with an interesting analysis of American as opposed to French stratification research, see Cuin 1993.) But my concern here is not so much with the compromised theoretical structure of our mobility ideologies, but rather with their simple-minded temporal structure. When, exactly, do we think that the achievement of the parent or the child occurs? It has been the tradition in mobility research to choose particular instants in both lives to represent that achievement. But why not choose intervals? Why not choose whole careers? If we do choose moments, why choose the moments we choose?

The simple answer says that we measure the parent's resources at a point because it is easier and more stable than measuring them over a time period. And we measure the parent's resources around the time of the child's birth or transition into the labor force (rather than, say, at the end of life) because that is "when the causal effects happen," when we think it matters whether parents have resources. Also, we can argue that if we measure parents' resources when the children enter the labor force, parental resources are likely to be pretty stable, at least in terms of relative position on an overall societal scale, from that point (typically the late thirties) onward.[2]

But if we were thinking of the protagonists in the mobility story as purely rational actors, parents' investments in their children's achievements would in fact involve projections of future income on the parents' part, because their calculations about the allocation of current resources have to do with their own future utility streams under alternative scenarios of current allocation. Under such a view, we do not imagine mobility as a kind of precious substance (Yamaguchi's [1983] "generalized resource") handed on because parents are assumed always to intend their children to succeed, but rather as a consequence of decisions within a parent's own utility calculus.[3] My purpose in raising this example is not to propose an alternative conception of mobility but simply to suggest that there are conceptions of mobility under which measuring a parent's status by a single-valued function referring to one point in current time does not suffice. The parents in my example conceive of their status at any given moment as an integral of their predicted statuses in the future, suitably discounted to produce a present value. Indeed, there are several economic literatures rooted in such lifetime earnings predictions, the most familiar having to do with choices of occupation and of educational plans under uncertainty about future scenarios (e.g., Altonji 1993; Makepeace 1996). It is no surprise, then, that there is a literature on intergenerational earnings mobility, some of it relatively descriptive, as in Atkinson, Maynard, and Trinder (1983), some a little more formal as in Creedy (1988). Creedy's classic paper (1991) on lifetime earnings and inequality raises a host of difficulties with the lifetime earnings concept, yet remarks that:

> it must be recognized that for many purposes a short-period measure is of very little, if any, value and that quite spurious comparisons may be made unless a longer time period framework is adopted. (Creedy 1991:57)

All this suggests that we should think about mobility in lifetime, career-type terms, say in terms of realized income over parents' life courses as compared with realized income over their children's. But at the same time, Creedy despairs of extended period measures because of technical problems cognate with the issues discussed above.

This problem of thinking about mobility in point to point terms is underscored by the small but tantalizing literature on job tenures and their duration in the life course, which implies that point to point measures may involve some complex sampling biases. The classic paper in this literature (Hall 1982, discussing 1978 data) showed that by age 60, about 40 percent of men will have held at some point a job lasting at least twenty years. Men are likely to hold eleven jobs in a lifetime, seven of them by age 30. For all ages over 40, about 40 percent of all workers will eventually have twenty years of tenure in the job they currently hold. These figures may have changed in the neoliberal economy.[4] But they underline the longstanding reality that job shifts are very unevenly distributed in the life course, and that while most workers will eventually have some job that they retain for a long time, they are most likely to be in that job late in the work life course. These facts mean that ideally we would prefer, if we have to test mobility with a point to point measure, to sample both parent and child during their long-stay jobs; it is where the younger generation ends up, not where it starts, that matters from the political point of view. But in practice we have little ability to assure sampling in the long-stay jobs, and in practice we often sample relatively early in both work histories, probably somewhat earlier in the children's. Because it is probable that the structure of work histories varies systematically from region to region in the division of labor (many occupations with high lifetime incomes start with a long initial period of low income because of required education), such a measurement approach is likely to induce biases.

All of this suggests that there are quite complex issues involved in our decisions about when and how we measure mobility: at a point or over an interval, at the beginning or at the end, with discounting or without (as was originally done in the health evaluation literature), and so on. This is not the place to attempt a general analysis of the temporality of all our mobility measures. But by raising some of the temporal problems involved in both the point conception and the career conception, I hope to sensitize us to the extent of the difficulties involved. (A more general discussion of the temporality of outcome measures can be found in Abbott [2005].) Note however that at least at present, we are damned if we do, damned if we don't. If we don't look at extended rather than point measures, we introduce all sorts of arbitrary effects having to do with the structure of work life courses, the change of occupational categories, and so on. If we do look at extended measures, then we have to directly theorize the change in categories (or move to a measure like income that has more stability) and to come up with notions of "mobility" between complex structures (the whole careers) or choose some simpler but extended measure like the longest duration occupation. Each alternative has its own problems.

EXOGENEITY

One of the central assumptions of the intergenerational mobility paradigm, as I said earlier, is that the outcomes of individual work lives—however or whenever they are measured—generally occur within an exogenous framework of what we usually think of as "larger historical forces." These are things like technology and the shop-floor division of labor about which, as I noted, we assume two things: that they are exogenous and that they change, in some sense, faster than individual careers do. It is these two assumptions that give rise to the general feeling, as one reads the sociology of work, that the work world consists of a set of largely atomized individuals being pushed around by various historical forces over which they have no control.

Having just raised some questions about the temporality of careers and "larger forces," let me continue by arguing that these "larger historical forces" are not as exogenous as they look. Put another way, while the individual career appears to be a weak reed blowing in the winds of change, when taken as a whole, the mass of labor force careers actually takes on the character of a "larger historical force" itself. At any given time the labor force presents an inscribed or encoded mass of characteristics: of ages, genders, education, occupational training, and so on. This mass of qualities does not change very fast. Technology and other such forces must come to terms with it—a fact we see, for example, in the capture of the community colleges in the mid-1960s by a business community starved for certain kinds of skilled labor.

The idea that the labor force taken as a whole should be viewed as itself a "large historical force" follows in the first instance from its historical demography. Since the typical work career lasts forty to fifty years, in stable state the labor force replaces itself once over that period, which means that its annual rate of replacement is about 2 to 2.5 percent. In reality, of course, the twentieth-century American labor force saw steady changes in age-specific labor force participation rates as well as fertility and migration shifts that irregularized the sizes of cohorts facing those rates. As a result, the actual annual change in the labor force only approximates this stable population guesstimate. Calculations on census figures from 1940 to 1960 (U.S. Census 1963, Table 2), a period with minimal immigration, show that 25.5 percent of those working in 1950 were new to the labor force since 1940. A little less than half of the new workers (43 percent) represented net growth; the other 57 percent replaced retiring or dying workers. In 1960 27 percent of the workers were new since 1950, 51 percent of those representing net growth, 49 percent representing replacement. Looking at the twenty year figures, in 1960 47 percent of the labor force was new since 1940, split fifty-fifty between net growth and replacement. Looked at the other way, however, 70 percent of the workers in the labor force in 1940 were still in it in 1960. Roughly speaking then, if we ignore immigration (with its relative concentration of working people), the labor force gains about 2.5 percent new workers each year, equally divided between net growth and replacement. The majority of these new entrants are entering the high turnover youth labor force.[5]

This is a slower replacement process than it looks. As I noted earlier, we know from tenure distributions over the work life course that employment in the twenties is extremely unstable. Individuals are likely to have ten to eleven jobs in a lifetime and to have had 6 or more of them by age 30. The vast majority of labor force entry (even given the rapidly rising labor force participation rates for women at nearly all ages in the twentieth century) comes in the early years, when most workers are in relatively less skilled, high turnover jobs. Workers in relatively skilled jobs tend to be older. Even in high technology employment, design and architecture functions are in the hands of employees in their stable mid- and late-career periods, even if young workers know the latest coding wrinkles and technological fixes.

Thus, the labor force is in many ways a huge, unchanging flywheel; its mix of skills, educational credentials, and occupational experience changes much more slowly than we imagine. In the early 1960s, when Daniel Bell (1973) was proclaiming the arrival of postindustrial society, the generation just retiring had a median education of about eight years. Not until 1970 did the total population over age 25 have a median education of twelve years. Because of this demographic inertia, technology and the other forces normally thought to determine the actual division of labor are not free to do so just as they please. They must create a labor force out of the labor offer, which has itself resulted from past policies, past divisions of labor, and past choices by workers and their children. Under the conditions obtaining from the 1920s to the 1980s, immigration and off-shoring were not available as ways of escaping this determination. In such a relatively closed economy, a certain kind of Say's law obtains; the labor hired must more or less be the labor offered. That constrains the division of labor in important ways.[6]

This still does not mean that the occupational distribution remains completely exogenous, however. Endogenous change in the quality of the labor offer can sharply affect the scenarios possible for the division of labor. A simple example involves college education. About two-thirds of a cohort of eighteen-year-olds begins college. As of 2000, 29.1 percent of the American population age 25–29 had four years of college education or more (U.S. Department of Education, 2002:17; all education figures in this paragraph are from this source). At the same time, 21.8 percent of the American occupational system will consist, in 2010, of jobs requiring a college degree (the figure is 20.7 percent today; see Hecker 2001 for all labor force figures in this paragraph). To be sure, 29 percent of the total growth will come in occupations requiring a college degree, but the newly educated people entering the labor force have to occupy overall growth, not relative growth. And by 2010, the proportion of 25–29 year olds with college degrees will not be the 29 percent it is today, but probably around 35 percent (it has grown a steady 6 percent per decade since 1960). And only 20.9 percent of the net job growth occurring in the next ten years will occur in occupations requiring a college degree (69.8 percent will occur in occupations requiring only work-related training, most of that the

42.7 percent in occupations requiring only a month or less of on-the-job train-ing [OJT]. So much for the skilled labor force of the future!)

This draconian oversupply arises because parents and children make their decisions about training on the margin, employing existing informa-tion about returns to a college degree. They don't know that those returns must fall sharply over the next ten years because of oversupply. Thus, the level of education in the labor force is governed by an endogenous, lagged process. As a result, returns to education—which are after all an important part of our conception of mobility both as an outcome measure and as part of the rational calculus mechanism that we think governs behavior—turn out themselves to be endogenous, in the sense that judgments made by par-ents and children in the interest of producing mobility will give us a labor force far too educated for the jobs offered and hence will drastically reshape the rewards of education. And this will take place in much less than the length of a typical work career.[7]

Note however, that this situation could also be seen as a huge opportu-nity for the skill upgrading of the occupational mix itself. That is, with so much skilled labor on offer, technological and managerial forces could choose to reorganize the division of labor to take advantage of it. Note again that this suggests ways in which these supposedly "larger historical forces" like technology and managerial choice rest on factors endogenous to the oc-cupational process itself.

What are the consequences for our approach to mobility if the occupa-tional distribution of the future—the destination marginal—is in some im-portant sense endogenous? They seem to me to be quite important. The log-linear approach to mobility generally fits both prior and posterior marginals as a baseline matter. And this has important theoretical implications, as John Goldthorpe reminds us in his "Outline of a Theory of Mobility":

> if variation in absolute mobility rates and patterns was to be explained this
> would have to be primarily by reference to factors that were exogenous rather
> than endogenous with respect to processes of class stratification themselves:
> that is, to factors that determine the "shapes" of class structures, in the sense of
> the proportionate sizes and the rates of growth and decline of different classes,
> rather than to factors that determine the propensities of individuals actually to
> retain or change their positions within those structures. . . . most mobility re-
> searchers came to accept the view, implicitly if not explicitly, that variation in
> absolute rates cannot in fact usefully be regarded as systematic, and that expla-
> nations of such variation, whether over time or cross-nationally, will need to be

provided far more in specific historical, than in general theoretical, terms. (Goldthorpe 2000:232)

But if we feel that we cannot justifiably assume that the posterior marginal is exogenous, we are in trouble. The hierarchical nature of log-linear modeling compels us to fit the posterior marginal whether we like it or not. Once Goldthorpe's "specific historical terms" are inside the mobility process, we can no longer do this. As a result, we are back, once again, in the kind of Markovian, iterative approach to mobility characteristic of the pre-1975 years and continued in the work of scholars like Aage Sørensen (1984).

Again, it is not clear what the solution to the problem is. But once we believe that the mechanisms that produce mobility involve predictions about future returns to various current choices we have produced an endogeneity that seriously challenges the current methodological stance characteristic of mobility analysis.

In this chapter I have raised a number of concerns about our current strategies for thinking about mobility. Together, they seem to suggest that mobility studies are poised at a moment of renewal. In particular, embedding mobility analysis within the comprehensive framework of an "occupational process" would enable us to move toward a full model of the allocation of individuals into occupational positions. For that model, my three issues are less problems than they are opportunities, in particular for renewed mathematical modeling of the system and for simulational analysis. That occupations change, absorb, and lose tasks, that they merge and redivide, all over a time scale commensurate with the length of an average career, is simply a fact. It constitutes a crucial, "corporate" aspect of mobility, one that demands direct study. It is the same with the problems of the temporal assumptions of both career and point conceptions of mobility measures and of the general endogeneity of the occupational structure to the mobility process. These too present difficulties whose resolution can only come by serious deepening of our analytic tools and our theoretical concepts. With so rich a body of problems ahead, mobility studies will be sure to flourish in the future.

Notes

1. In fact, we also know little about this duration in the past, although we do know that it is only as recently as the late 1950s or early 1960s that a young person entering the labor force knew he or she was more likely leave it by retiring than by dying.

2. John Goldthorpe made this point in commenting on the original paper.

3. One of the reasons for wanting to think about mobility in terms of careers is that people themselves do, at least at the outset of their lives, probably because it is a widespread cultural model for thinking about occupational life. Whether they conclude, at the other end, that "a career" is what has really happened to them is unclear.

4. Actually, the current figures look surprisingly close to these. A BLS *News* release of 25 April 2000 (USDL 00-119) using NLSY79 data found that the overall average number of jobs held by men from 18 to 34 was 9.6. This may be an increase (over seven jobs by age 30), but is not a major one, since 2.6 jobs were held in the ages 30 to 34 (one of which might, of course, have endured from before age 30, so the figures do not subtract exactly).

5. These figures are calculated by quinquennial labor force figures on the standard assumption that those in the labor force at age x in year y are the same as those in the labor force age x + 10 in year y + 10. The calculation thus assumes no immigration and also cannot detect exchanges within a single cohort (where one person of the cohort leaves the labor force and another enters).

These figures are thus *minimum* estimates of labor force turnover. However, because the lion's share of the labor force in this period came from men in age brackets with extremely high labor force participation rates, the room for underestimate from the second factor is not large. The quinquennial turnovers are monotonic (from highly positive to highly negative as age gets higher) for men; the figures turn negative by age 40–44. For women there is a short negative peak at 30–34, but the move of women into the labor force over this period kept female figures positive up to the 55–59 quinquennium.

6. Under neoliberal conditions, this constraint is considerably relaxed, since the effective labor force is international (the total number of foreign workers worldwide is about two-thirds the size of the entire American labor force [Stalker 1994]) and since off-shoring has taken large shares of formerly "American" work elsewhere. Since the labor offer is thus much larger, one can believe that, for the United States at least, the technological and managerial sources for the division of labor are far less constrained than they had been in the past.

7. Some might argue that while the *models* of labor economists assume that actors are marginal rationalizers, in practice people typically are not. But maybe this restraint betrays the cunning of reason; maybe people suspect (correctly) that the skilled labor force of the future is a mirage. (Since this paper was originally delivered, the export of highly skilled work has become common knowledge.) The Bureau of Labor Statistics biennial projections show with monotonous regularity that the notion of "explosive demand for high-skilled workers" results from mistaking marginal rates of growth in highly skilled but hitherto small occupations for predictors of general job growth, which is by contrast concentrated in relatively unskilled work. (See Hecker 2004, for the latest such report.) Of the top twenty occupations in total predicted job growth by 2012, one requires a doctorate (postsecondary

teaching), one requires a bachelor's degree (general managers), one an associate's degree (nursing), three require moderate on-the-job training (1 to 12 months), and fourteen require short-term (1 month or less) on-the-job training (Hecker 2004:101).

References

Abbott, A. 1990. "Vacancy Methods for Historical Data." Pp. 80–102 in *Social Mobility and Social Structure*, edited by R. Breiger. Cambridge: Cambridge University Press.

———. 1991. "The Order of Professionalization." *Work and Occupations* 18:355–84.

———. 2005a. "The Idea of Outcome." Pp. 393–426 in *The Positivist Unconscious*, edited by G. Steinmetz. Durham, NC: Duke University Press.

———. 2005b. "Sociology of Work and Occupations." Pp. 307–330 in N. J. Smelser and R. Swedberg, eds., *The Handbook of Economic Sociology*. Princeton and New York: Princeton University Press and Russell Sage Foundation.

Abbott, A., and E. Barman. 1997. "Sequence Comparison via Alignment and Gibbs Sampling." *Sociological Methodology* 27:47–87.

Abbott, A., and A. Hrycak. 1990. "Measuring Resemblance in Social Sequences." *American Journal of Sociology* 96:144–85.

Abbott, A., and D. R. Smith. 1984. "Governmental Constraints and Labor Market Mobility." *Work and Occupations* 11:29–53.

Altonji, J. G. 1993. "The Demand for and Return to Education When Education Outcomes Are Uncertain." *Journal of Labor Economics* 11:48–83.

Atkinson, A. B., A. K. Maynard, and C. G. Trinder. 1983. *Parents and Children*. London: Heinemann.

Bishop, Y. M. M., S. E. Fienberg, and P. W. Holland. 1975. *Discrete Multivariate Analysis*. Cambridge, MA: MIT Press.

Blau, P. M., and O. D. Duncan. 1967. *The American Occupational Structure*. New York: The Free Press.

Boudon, R. 1973. *Mathematical Structures of Social Mobility*. San Francisco: Jossey-Bass.

Breiger, R. L. 1978. "The Social Class Structure of Occupational Mobility." *American Journal of Sociology* 87:578–611.

Carey, M. L. 1988. "Occupational Tenure in 1987." *Monthly Labor Review* 111:10:3–12.

Conk, M. A. 1980. *The United States Census and Labor Force Change*. Ann Arbor, MI: UMI Research Press.

Creedy, J. 1988. "Earnings Comparisons between Generations." *The Manchester School* 56:268–81.

———. 1991. "Lifetime Earnings and Inequality." *Economic Record* 67:46–58.

Cuin, C. -H. 1993. *Les sociologues et la mobilité sociale*. Paris: PUF.

Davidson, P. E., and H. D. Anderson. 1937. *Occupational Mobility in an American Community*. Stanford, CA: Stanford University Press.

Desrosières, A., and L. Thévenot. 1988. *Les catégories socioprofessionelles*. Paris: Editions La Découverte.

Duncan, O. D. 1979. "How Destination Depends upon Origin in the Occupational Mobility Table." *American Journal of Sociology* 84:793–803.

Form, W. H., and D. C. Miller. 1949. "Occupational Career Pattern as a Sociological Instrument." *American Journal of Sociology* 54:317–29.

Goldthorpe, J. H. 2000. "Outline of a Theory of Social Mobility." Pp. 230–258 in *On Sociology*. Oxford: Oxford University Press.

Goodman, L. A. 1996. "A Single General Method for the Analysis of Cross-Classified Data." *Journal of the American Statistical Association* 91:408–28.

Hall, R. E. 1982. "The Importance of Lifetime Jobs in the U.S. Economy." *American Economic Review* 72:716–24.

Hauser, R. M., J. N. Koffel, H. P. Travis, and P. J. Dickinson. 1975. "Temporal Change in Occupational Mobility." *American Sociological Review* 40:279–97.

Hecker, D. E. 2001. "Occupational Employment Projections to 2010." *Monthly Labor Review* 124:11:57–84.

———. 2004. "Occupational Employment Projections to 2012." *Monthly Labor Review* 127:2:80–105.

Hout, M. 1984. "Status, Autonomy, and Training in Occupational Mobility." *American Journal of Sociology* 89:1379–1409.

Maguire, S. R. 1993. "Employer and Occupational Tenure." *Monthly Labor Review* 116:6:45–56.

Makepeace, G. H. 1996. "Lifetime Earnings and the Training of Young Men in Britain." *Applied Economics* 28:725–35.

Mosteller, F. 1968. "Association and Estimation in Contingency Tables." *Journal of the American Statistical Association* 63:1–28.

Neumark, D., ed. 2000. *On the Job*. New York: Russell Sage Foundation.

Palmer, G. L. 1954. *Labor Mobility in Six Cities*. New York: Social Science Research Council.

Parnes, H. S. 1954. Research on Labor Mobility. *Social Science Research Council, Bulletin #65*. New York: Social Science Research Council.

Sankoff, D., and J. B. Kruskal. 1983. *Time Warps, String Edits, and Macromolecules*. Reading, MA: Addison Wesley.

Smith, D. R., and A. Abbott. 1983. "A Labor Market Perspective on the Mobility of College Football Coaches." *Social Forces* 61:1147–67.

Sørensen, A. 1974. "A Model for Occupational Careers." *American Journal of Sociology* 80:44–57.

———. 1984. "The Organizational Differentiation of Students in Schools." Pp. 25–43 in *Education from a Multilevel Perspective*, edited by H. Oosthoek and P. Van den Eeden. New York: Gordon and Breach.

Spilerman, S. 1977. "Careers, Labor Market Structure, and Socioeconomic Achievement." *American Journal of Sociology* 83:551–93.

Stalker, P. 1994. *The Work of Strangers.* Geneva: ILO.

Stewman, S., and S. L. Konda. 1983. "Careers and Organizational Labor Markets." *American Journal of Sociology* 88:637–85.

U.S. Census. 1963. "Employment Status and Work Experience." *U.S. Census of Population, Final Report PC(2)-6A.* Washington: Government Printing Office.

U.S. Department of Education. 2002. *Digest of Educational Statistics, 2001.* NCES 2002-130. Washington: Government Printing Office.

van Leeuwen, M. H. D., I. Maas, and A. Miles. MMII. *HISCO: Historical International Standard Classification of Occupations.* Leuven: Leuven University Press.

Wilensky, H. L. 1960. "Work, Careers, and Social Integration." *International Social Science Journal* 12:543–60.

———. 1961. "Orderly Careers and Social Participation." *American Sociological Review* 26:521–39.

Yamaguchi, K. 1983. "The Structure of Intergenerational Occupational Mobility." *American Journal of Sociology* 88:718–45.

PART FOUR

MECHANISMS OF
MOBILITY: EDUCATION
AND THE PROCESS OF
INTERGENERATIONAL
MOBILITY

CHAPTER SEVEN

Inequality of Conditions and Intergenerational Mobility: Changing Patterns of Educational Attainment in the United States

Stephen L. Morgan and Young-Mi Kim

In the 1980s and 1990s, most advanced industrialized countries experienced substantial increases in inequality, as measured by labor market earnings, total family income, and wealth (see Blau and Kahn 2002; Freeman and Katz 1995). In some countries, such as the United States, absolute levels of labor market inequality are now as high as they were prior to World War II (see Katz and Autor 1999). For the study of intergenerational mobility, these increases represent an unexpected reversal of the postwar trend toward greater equality of conditions. As such, they directly challenge a basic presupposition of the industrialization theories that predict a decline in inequality of conditions alongside a moderation in the total effects of social origins on occupational destinations. The presupposed causal variable – equality of conditions – has failed to exhibit its expected time trend, and as a result these theories appear less relevant as we move toward the study of social mobility in ostensibly postindustrial societies.[1]

Somewhat ironically, these increases in inequality of conditions evolved just as sociologists were developing their strongest case yet for the invariance of core social mobility patterns over time and across industrialized countries. At the conclusion of their definitive cross-national study, Erikson and Goldthorpe (1992:367) wrote: "Over the years covered by our data, total

We thank Christopher Jencks for helpful comments on a prior version of this chapter. This research was supported by a seed grant from the Center for the Study of Inequality at Cornell University and by NSF Grant #0213642 for a project entitled "Rent and Social Class, 1982–2000."

mobility rates move in what would appear to be an essentially directionless fashion." Accordingly, the thesis of mobility-spawning industrialization was dismissed by Erikson and Goldthorpe in favor of a model of trendless fluctuation in mobility rates, a return in spirit to Pitirim Sorokin's (1927) conclusions in his pioneering study of social mobility.

It will take a decade or more to develop sufficiently deep explanations for the consequences of the recent growth in inequality of conditions, and research on changes in patterns of intergenerational mobility will be central to the endeavor (see Neckerman 2004). And herein lies the departure point of our study, one that is consistent with the closing appeal of Erikson and Goldthorpe (1992:396) that more effort be directed at evaluating and elaborating the "hypothesis that, within the class structures of industrial societies, inequality of opportunity will be the greater, the greater inequality of condition – as a derivative, that is, of the argument that members of more advantaged and powerful classes will seek to use their superior resources to preserve their own and their families' positions."

The data analyzed for the Erikson and Goldthorpe study were drawn from cross-sectional surveys between 1970 and 1978 (see Erikson and Goldthorpe 1992:50, Table 2.3). As with other classic studies of social mobility, their results captured intergenerational mobility patterns prior to the 1980s, and hence before the recent growth in inequality was evident. The primary question that motivates our chapter is therefore quite simple: Is there reason to expect a decline in intergenerational mobility that will be revealed in the decades to come, one that is attributable to the recent growth in inequality of family wealth and income? If so, it is reasonable to expect changes in patterns of educational attainment now for those birth cohorts whose relative life chances have been affected by recent changes in inequality of conditions.[2]

In this chapter, we will engage this primary question by investigating the educational attainment patterns of two recent cohorts of young adults, those between the ages of 17 and 21 in 1986 and in 1996. If we are to observe in the future substantial changes in mobility patterns that commenced with the increase in inequality in the 1980s and 1990s (perhaps using comparative retrospective data after 2010), then we should see changes in patterns of educational attainment for these two cohorts.

EDUCATIONAL ATTAINMENT AND
THE COLLEGE ENROLLMENT DECISION

Social mobility research in the 1990s embraced a core implication of the results of Blau and Duncan (1967), seeking to model the educational attainment process as an intervening mechanism for intergenerational mobility (see
also Sewell, Haller, and Portes 1969). Carrying the log-linear tradition into
empirical work on education and invoking rational choice theory (see Breen
and Goldthorpe 1997; Goldthorpe 1996; Raftery and Hout 1993), studies of
educational attainment returned to the research frontier, but now more commonly with reference to continuation decisions for discrete educational transitions (Mare 1980, 1981). The collection of papers published in Shavit and
Blossfeld (1993) reaffirmed the basic invariance of core mobility processes
across countries, noting (with only a few exceptions) a robust pattern across
national datasets of logit coefficients for the effects of social origins on progression through common educational transitions.[3]

In the United States, on which our empirical analysis will focus, a number of pointed debates emerged around specific questions on educational
attainment, mostly without direct reference to the cross-national mobility
literature. The customary practice of measuring family advantage with
socioeconomic status (i.e., parents' education and labor force characteristics) was challenged by those who wished to focus more directly on the availability of resources. Dalton Conley (1999, 2001), for example, attempted to
estimate the causal effect of family wealth on college entry (independent of
effects for parental education, occupational prestige, and family income). He
concluded that wealth effects are large, especially in proportion to the lack
of attention that they were given in the extant literature.[4] Extending the
work of Oliver and Shapiro (1995), he also stressed the power of wealth differentials to explain residual race differences in levels of educational attainment. This sociological attention to the effects of wealth on educational attainment was preceded in the economics literature by Mulligan (1997; see
also citations therein and the subsequent work of Bowles and Gintis 2002).
In the economics literature, however, wealth differences across families are
interpreted more broadly, either as indicators of differential behavioral orientations correlated with savings behavior and lifetime success or reasons
for families to pursue alternative strategies for human capital investment in
their offspring.

While these arguments were being developed, labor economists also confronted an important policy-relevant issue arising from the growth in inequality. How would prospective college students respond in the 1990s to the substantial increase in labor market incentives to obtain college degrees? Most decision-theoretic models predict that gross rates of college entry should increase substantially in response to relative increases in the labor market payoff to college degrees. However, because incentive-based policies targeted at increasing college enrollments changed only modestly between the 1980s and 1990s in the United States (see Kane 1999a, 1999b), the same models predict that increases in inequality may have variable effects on different groups of prospective college students. In particular, increases in college enrollment should be smaller for prospective students from resource-poor families (or, at least, no larger), as these students' relative access to liquid funds to finance a college education has declined.

Mayer (2001) developed evidence for both hypotheses, using aggregate state-level data to identify the total effects of inequality on patterns of educational attainment. Ellwood and Kane (2000) offered similar results, using NELS and HS&B data (even though these data have rather coarse information on family income). But, Cameron and Heckman (1999) and Carneiro and Heckman (2002) challenged their interpretations, arguing that long-run deprivation is a much more important determinant of college entry and completion than short-run credit constraints, which is an argument consistent with the classic status attainment literature in sociology (e.g., Sewell et al. 1969 and Hauser, Tsai, and Sewell 1983; see Morgan 2005 for a review). Heckman and his colleagues argue that few students are credit-constrained (i.e., considerably less than 10 percent). Furthermore, the evidence that adolescents from high income families are more likely to have responded to the greater incentives to acquire college degrees is not necessarily supportive of the credit-constraint hypothesis (see Kosters 1999 and Heckman and Krueger 2003 for further debate).

No consensus has since emerged in the empirical literature in labor economics on the size or meaning of the effect of family income on college enrollment and completion, and understanding this effect seems necessary before an estimate of the incentive-effect of recent increasing returns can be constructed (see also Mayer 1997). As sociologists have long contemplated the consequences and meaning of long-run social disadvantage, perhaps at the cost of ignoring other factors that also explain patterns of social mobility,

it is nonetheless somewhat heartening for sociology to see long-run deprivation effects at the core of some of the best recent work in the economics
of education. To this convergent literature, we offer the following empirical
analysis.

EMPIRICAL ANALYSIS

In order to investigate changes in patterns of educational attainment, we
need a dataset that includes good measures of family income and wealth,
spanning some portion of the time period in which inequality of income and
wealth has increased. The standard datasets on which models of educational
attainment are usually estimated are not ideal. The NLS-72, HS&B, and
NELS data have large samples of high school students, but they have coarse
family income measures and no direct wealth measures. The NLSY data
have better income and wealth measures, but they represent cohorts of students who contemplated college enrollment primarily in the early to mid-
1980s before much of the increase in inequality of conditions unfolded. Instead, we will analyze the 1986 and 1996 rounds of the Survey of Income
and Program Participation (SIPP; see U.S. Department of Commerce, Bureau
of the Census 2001), focusing on those age 17 to 21 in the spring of 1986
and 1996. We describe the construction of our analytic sample in a supplementary appendix (available by request and on the website for the volume:
http://www.inequality.com/publications/symposia_books.shtml).

The primary strength of the SIPP data is the carefully and consistently
defined income and wealth variables for two separate cohorts of students.
And yet, as we detail in the supplementary appendix, the data are not without limitations, which may explain why we have been unable to find any
other research reports using these data for the modeling of college entry patterns. The SIPP design, because of its focus on a nationally representative
sample of households, yields a relatively small sample of college-age students.
This limitation makes detailed subgroup comparisons nearly impossible because of sampling noise. Furthermore, there are substantial limitations in the
available data for both college-age students and their parents. The SIPP provides no measures of cognitive skills, and hence we cannot enter the vigorous
debate on the relationships between mental ability, measures of cognitive
skill, and educational attainment (see Epstein and Winship, Chapter 10 of
this volume).[5]

Finally, the sampling design rendered some 17- to 21-year-olds in the SIPP as members of households other than those of their parents, although the problem is not as severe as one might fear. Consider the procedures by which interviews are initiated for the SIPP. When a SIPP interviewer approaches a sampled household to develop a roster of all household members, individuals who are not currently living in the household but enrolled in college are retained on the household roster. Likewise, when a SIPP interviewer approaches a household of college students living together, students are eliminated from the household roster for that household if they could be listed as permanent members of their parents' households (which could thereby reduce the number of individuals in the sampled household to zero, thereby ending the interview). These two procedures ensure that the vast majority of enrolled students between the ages of 17 and 21 are listed as members of their parents' households for the SIPP.

Patterns are not as clean for nonstudents. In particular, 17- to 21-year-olds not enrolled in school and living in households without their parents are considered independent members of their own households for the SIPP. And thus, because we are interested primarily in the relationship between parental resources and college enrollments, we had to develop an imputation scheme for the parents' characteristics of these nondependent, nonenrolled, 17- to 21-year-olds, which we detail in the supplementary appendix. As we describe there, it is quite likely that our imputation scheme is too conservative, yielding estimated parental resources for nondependent, nonenrolled, 17- to 21-year-olds that are too close on average to the levels of resources typical of nonenrolled 17- to 21-year-olds still living with their parents. Mindful that our imputation scheme was necessarily limited, we carried on to analysis because we judged that this limitation, like others, does not vary meaningfully across the 1986 and 1996 surveys, thereby allowing for reliable analysis of the cohort comparisons that are our central focus.

Evolving Wealth and Income Differentials

We begin our empirical analysis by documenting the substantial increase in inequality between 1986 and 1996 using the SIPP data. Table 7.1 presents selected measures of the distribution of wealth and income for the entire SIPP sample, including (for now) all households with and without college-age students. Table 7.2 presents descriptions of the component SIPP variables used for the composite wealth and income variables analyzed for Table 7.1.

TABLE 7.1
Changes in Family Income and Household Wealth by Racial Group

		1986	1996	Change
Family Income (Monthly)				
Median	All	2,493.12	2,619.00	5.1%
	White	2,700.77	2,845.00	5.3%
	Black	1,522.27	1,791.00	17.6%
	B/W ratio	.56	.63	
Mean	All	3,189.91	3,545.10	11.1%
	White	3,384.50	3,775.03	11.5%
	Black	1,988.11	2,484.51	25.0%
	B/W ratio	.59	.66	
95th percentile	All	8,006.05	9,156.00	14.4%
	White	8,275.58	9,591.00	15.9%
	Black	5,167.76	6,722.00	30.1%
	B/W ratio	.62	.70	
Gini coefficient	All	.43	.45	
	White	.41	.45	
	Black	.44	.47	
Net worth				
Median	All	50,364.41	43,560.00	−13.5%
	White	64,286.30	61,632.00	−4.1%
	Black	4,290.43	5,667.00	32.1%
	B/W ratio	.07	.09	
Mean	All	111,786.30	147,575.10	32.0%
	White	126,808.00	175,300.20	38.0%
	Black	28,885.68	29,329.08	1.5%
	B/W ratio	.23	.17	
90th percentile	All	270,627.10	305,092.00	12.7%
	White	293,184.80	353,460.00	20.6%
	Black	87,733.77	83,500.00	−4.8%
	B/W ratio	.30	.24	
Gini coefficient	All	.63	.71	
	White	.61	.69	
	Black	.65	.65	

NOTES: Nominal dollars have been converted to 1996 dollars using the PCED deflator. The 1986 panel includes 30,577 respondents from 11,454 households; 5.6% of the heads of households did not provide answers to the wealth questions. The resulting N for this table equals 10,139 households. The 1996 panel includes 95,141 respondents from 36,730 households; 11.5% of the heads of households did not provide answers to the wealth questions. The resulting N for this table equals 32,519.

TABLE 7.2

Components of the Composite Income and Wealth Variables

Composite Variable	Component Raw Variables	Level
Monthly family income	Total family earned income Total family property income Total family means-tested cash transfers Total family "other" income	Family
Total net worth	Total wealth − total unsecured debt	Household
Total wealth	Home equity Net equity in vehicles Business equity Interest earning assets held at banking institutions Interest earning assets held at other institutions Equity in stock and mutual funds shares, real estate Other assets IRA and KEOGH accounts	Household
Total home equity	Market value of the resident property − total debt owed on home	Household

To enable direct cohort comparisons, nominal dollars in 1986 were converted to inflation-adjusted 1996 dollars using the personal consumption expenditures deflator of the Bureau of Labor Statistics.

The first panel of Table 7.1 presents patterns of income inequality for all SIPP households and then separately for those with white and black household heads. For economy of space, but also in recognition of the careful focus usually given to black-white differences in educational attainment (e.g., Conley 1999; Hallinan 2001), we do not present separate tabulations for Hispanics and Asians. However, these racial groups (and a catchall "other" category) are included in the full sample results and in our subsequent models of educational attainment.

As shown in Table 7.1, income inequality increased, which can be seen most clearly in an examination of comparable quantiles of the income distribution. For example, median family income increased by 5.1 percent while the 95th percentile of family income increased by a much larger 14.4 percent. Alongside this overall increase in income inequality, the black-white gap narrowed. Although black family income remained low, the black-to-white ratio for the mean, median, and 95th percentile of family income increased substantially between 1986 and 1996.

The second panel of Table 7.1 presents similar findings for the net worth of SIPP families. Consistent with other research using similar data (e.g., Wolff 1998), median household net worth fell slightly between the mid-1980s and mid-1990s while at the same time mean household net worth increased. This growth in the inequality of wealth is evident in the Gini coefficient for net worth, which increased from 0.63 to 0.71. Similar to race differences in family income, the black-white gap in wealth is large. But, the magnitude of the racial difference is much more dramatic for wealth, with the black-white ratio of median net worth less than 0.1 in both 1986 and 1996. Moreover, there were few signs of improvement in these differences. Whereas the black-to-white ratio for the median of net worth increased from 0.07 to 0.09, the same ratio for the mean of net worth decreased from 0.23 to 0.17. In tandem, the growth in wealth inequality disproportionately benefited whites relative to blacks.

Table 7.3 presents the same measures of wealth and income as Table 7.1, but now only for families with young adults in our restricted college-entry sample. For these results, we drop more than 85 percent of the SIPP sample and then recalculate the same measures of family and household resources. The general pattern matches the results for the full sample, as reported earlier in Table 7.1. To the extent that resource differentials of wealth and income represent the crucial dimensions of the inequality of conditions that are relevant for entry into postsecondary education, we conclude that a comparison of the 1986 and 1996 SIPP panels is well suited to an examination of changes in the relationship between inequality of conditions and educational attainment.

Income and Wealth as Predictors of College Enrollment

To test for variation in the associations between family resources and college enrollment, many modeling strategies can be adopted. Before directly examining college enrollment rates for separate social classes, in Tables 7.4 and 7.5 we present coefficients from five variants of a basic specification of resource and demographic variables. For these models, the probability of college enrollment in November of each year is predicted using a logit model, with adjustments for associations with gender, race, age, and prior enrollment status in March. In models I through V, alternative combinations of family resource variables are specified.[6]

TABLE 7.3

Changes in Family Income and Household Wealth by Racial Group,
Restricted to Families with College Eligible Children
Between the Ages of 17 and 21

		1986	1996	Change
Family Income (Monthly)				
Median	All	3,411.72	3,519.00	3%
	White	3,926.02	4,151.00	6%
	Black	2,013.20	2,209.00	10%
	B/W ratio	.51	.53	
Mean	All	4,130.13	4,408.45	7%
	White	4,564.83	5,040.27	10%
	Black	2,404.01	2,973.05	24%
	B/W ratio	.53	.59	
90th percentile	All	7,660.89	8,464.00	10%
	White	8,102.00	9,130.00	13%
	Black	4,165.00	6,021.00	45%
	B/W ratio	.58	.65	
Gini coefficient	All	.40	.44	
	White	.37	.41	
	Black	.45	.45	
Net worth				
Median	All	55,294.28	36,541,00	−34%
	White	74,049.78	62,400.00	−15%
	Black	5,088.01	5,847.00	15%
	B/W ratio	.07	.09	
Mean	All	116,996.70	129,899.60	11%
	White	142,159.70	170,919.80	20%
	Black	27,933.36	31,087.63	11%
	B/W ratio	.20	.18	
90th percentile	All	282,563.30	274,288.00	3%
	White	320,123.80	339,375.00	6%
	Black	89,183.10	85,039.50	−5%
	B/W ratio	.28	.25	
Gini coefficient	All	.61	.71	
	White	.59	.68	
	Black	.61	.69	

NOTES: Nominal dollars have been converted to 1996 dollars using the PCED deflator.

TABLE 7.4
Estimated Logit Coefficients for the Effects of Income
and Wealth on College Enrollment in November of 1986
and 1996 for SIPP Respondents Ages 17 to 21

	I		II		III	
	1986	*1996*	*1986*	*1996*	*1986*	*1996*
Female	.214	.248	.260	.233	.276	.239
	(.136)	(.086)	(.140)	(.086)	(.139)	(.086)
Black	−.658	−.109	−.402	−.054	−.538	−.132
	(.224)	(.130)	(.228)	(.132)	(.224)	(.130)
Hispanic	−.309	−.413	−.089	−.379	−.230	−.476
	(.273)	(.137)	(.273)	(.138)	(.271)	(.137)
Asian	−.031	.608	−.005	.649	.090	.656
	(.429)	(.220)	(.427)	(.222)	(.439)	(.225)
Income	.121	.141				
	(.031)	(.018)				
Zero income	.889	<−.001				
	(.728)	(.539)				
Net worth			.039	.035		
			(.007)	(.004)		
Zero net worth			−.968	−.567		
			(.370)	(.290)		
Negative net worth			−.888	.325		
			(.286)	(.152)		
Home equity					.087	.075
					(.016)	(.011)
Zero home equity					−.132	.014
					(.202)	(.125)
Negative home equity					−.327	1.160
					(.434)	(.291)
Covariates:						
Other race	✓	✓	✓	✓	✓	✓
Age	✓	✓	✓	✓	✓	✓
March enrollment	✓	✓	✓	✓	✓	✓
N	1,900	4,994	1,900	4,994	1,900	4,994

TABLE 7.5

Estimated Logit Coefficients for the Effects of Income and Wealth
on College Enrollment in November of 1986 and 1996 for SIPP
Respondents Ages 17 to 21 with Covariates for Parental Education

	IV		V	
	1986	*1996*	*1986*	*1996*
Female	.261	.255	.274	.266
	(.141)	(.088)	(.141)	(.088)
Black	−.262	.079	−.377	.073
	(.237)	(.136)	(.234)	(.135)
Hispanic	.175	.202	.032	.193
	(.285)	(.152)	(.284)	(.153)
Asian	−.022	.815	.067	.845
	(.427)	(.227)	(.441)	(.230)
Father's education	.040	.126	.033	.128
	(.033)	(.028)	(.033)	(.028)
Mother's education	.107	.103	.109	.109
	(.040)	(.029)	(.040)	(.029)
Income	.009	.049	.017	.046
	(.036)	(.020)	(.035)	(.020)
Zero income	.034	.043	.271	.073
	(.713)	(.552)	(.699)	(.549)
Net worth	.032	.018		
	(.008)	(.005)		
Zero net worth	−1.069	−.346		
	(.375)	(.295)		
Negative net worth	−.872	.225		
	(.290)	(.156)		
Home equity			.076	.051
			(.016)	(.011)
Zero home equity			−.124	.048
			(.205)	(.128)
Negative home equity			−.205	.852
			(.430)	(.302)
Covariates:				
Other race	✓	✓	✓	✓
Age	✓	✓	✓	✓
March enrollment	✓	✓	✓	✓
N	1,900	4,994	1,900	4,994

For model I, which is estimated separately by cohort, college enrollment is predicted from family income and a dummy variable for zero income (and the other covariates listed earlier).[7] For both 1986 and 1996, the logit coefficients are similar. In a pooled model, the increase of 0.020 has a standard error of 0.035, a ratio that suggests the cohort difference in coefficients is consistent with the fluctuation produced by sampling error. In magnitude, the coefficients imply that an increase of $500 in monthly family income is associated with an increased probability of enrolling in college of between 0.006 and 0.010 (depending on the values at which other variables are set). Were we prepared to regard this coefficient as a warranted causal effect (see the discussion section for an explanation of why we will not), this small but substantial association would suggest that giving the average family $6,000 per year in family income would increase the college enrollment rate among their adolescents by an additional two-thirds to 1 full percent.

The size of this association is somewhat artificial, because the estimate is conditional on the prior spring enrollment coefficients parameterized with four dummy variables for (1) not enrolled in school, (2) enrolled in college, (3) enrolled as a high school junior, and (4) enrolled as a high school freshman or sophomore (and thereby leaving high school seniors as the reference category). Models removing these dummy variables for types of spring enrollment yield larger logit coefficients for family income (i.e., from 0.121 and 0.141 to 0.161 and 0.194, respectively), but no pattern of alternative cohort differences is revealed in such models.

Other variants of this model also reproduced our basic claim of no-cohort differences. For example, when we ignored shifts in the distribution of family income, we obtained similar results. The difference in the odds of enrolling in college for those in the highest quintile in family income in comparison with those in the lowest quintile was virtually the same for both cohorts. Models using the natural logarithm of income yielded coefficients of 0.275 and 0.239.[8]

Model II substitutes household net worth for family income and model III substitutes home equity for family income, both right-censored at the 95th percentile. For model II, the cohort-specific coefficients for net worth are within sampling error of each other. And, for model III, the analogous coefficients for home equity are also similar and within sampling error.[9]

Models IV and V present slightly more elaborate specifications, in order to demonstrate that no cohort differences are masked by movements in other family resource variables. For both models, measures of parental education and family income are included along with net worth for model IV and home equity for model V. The magnitudes of the coefficients for all dimensions of resources decline, which is entirely unsurprising given the positive correlations between them and with parental education. But all of the between-cohort fluctuations in coefficients remain erratic, and small enough to be reasonably attributed to sampling error. In sum, based on the results reported in Tables 7.4 and 7.5, we conclude that (1) family resources exhibit substantial associations with college enrollment for both cohorts and that (2) the relatively stable but erratic pattern of coefficients across specifications suggests that little has changed between cohorts.[10]

Social Class as a Predictor of College Enrollment

Against this backdrop of relatively constant (though noisy) associations between family resources and college enrollment, we now ask whether social class of origin predicts college enrollment in the same pattern for both cohorts. To the extent that between-class inequality of conditions has increased, and yet the predictive power of direct measures of resources has not changed, then one might expect to see a larger social class advantage in 1996 for those at the top of the class hierarchy.

Table 7.6 presents four sets of logit models, predicting college enrollment from dummy variables for a variant of the class schema developed for Erikson and Goldthorpe (1992) and its predecessors. The reference category for the social class dummy variables is class VIIa, which is comprised of semi-skilled and unskilled workers not employed in agriculture. Class effects are parameterized with reference to this class, which has the lowest mean levels of resources in income and wealth. Classes I and II are comprised primarily of higher-level and lower-level professional and managerial workers, respectively. Class III represents routine, nonmanual workers, and class IV represents self-employed small proprietors and landholding farmers. Class V primarily consists of the supervisors of manual workers and some higher-grade technicians, while class VI is composed of skilled manual workers. Finally, class VIIb is the smallest of the eight social classes, as it includes only agricultural laborers and others in primary production who are not proprietors.

The point estimates for social class in model VI suggest that adolescents whose parents are members of class VIIa are the least likely to enroll in college between the ages of 17 and 21 (with the possible exception of class VIIb

TABLE 7.6

Estimated Logit Coefficients for the Effects of Social Class on College Enrollment in November of 1986 and 1996 for SIPP Respondents Ages 17 to 21

	VI		VII		VIII		IX	
	1986	1996	1986	1996	1986	1996	1986	1996
Female	.294	.240	.283	.259	.282	.241	.277	.264
	(.165)	(.101)	(.166)	(.102)	(.167)	(.103)	(.170)	(.102)
Black	−.573	−.052	−.446	.069	−.468	.029	−.276	.143
	(.279)	(.153)	(.284)	(.156)	(.284)	(.157)	(.290)	(.159)
Hispanic	−.296	−.287	−.201	−.195	−.141	.158	.014	−.166
	(.360)	(.169)	(.364)	(.170)	(.371)	(.180)	(.369)	(.170)
Asian	−.231	.704	−.323	.719	−.302	.811	−.369	.807
	(.478)	(.273)	(.491)	(.273)	(.486)	(.277)	(.492)	(.275)
Class I	.876	1.353	.651	1.100	.490	.787	.625	1.144
	(.262)	(.164)	(.279)	(.173)	(.293)	(.184)	(.272)	(.168)
Class II	.815	.795	.669	.639	.462	.325	.731	.670
	(.270)	(.150)	(.276)	(.155)	(.290)	(.165)	(.277)	(.153)
Class III	.318	.486	.254	.471	.176	.290	.292	.426
	(.259)	(.159)	(.262)	(.160)	(.265)	(.163)	(.269)	(.161)

(continued)

TABLE 7.6
(continued)

	VI		VII		VIII		IX	
	1986	1996	1986	1996	1986	1996	1986	1996
Class IV	1.231	.812	1.109	.626	.900	.633	.950	.517
	(.611)	(.774)	(.626)	(.801)	(.646)	(.790)	(.619)	(.786)
Class V	.092	.274	-.032	.153	-.008	.158	-.033	.216
	(.357)	(.236)	(.363)	(.238)	(.360)	(.240)	(.362)	(.237)
Class VI	.243	.309	.162	.228	.240	.263	.141	.285
	(.287)	(.177)	(.291)	(.178)	(.290)	(.177)	(.295)	(.177)
Class VIIa (reference)								
Class VIIb	-.223	.616	-.365	.547	-.195	.640	-.261	.506
	(.991)	(.435)	(1.016)	(.441)	(.995)	(.463)	(1.027)	(.444)
Covariates:								
Other race	✓	✓	✓	✓	✓	✓	✓	✓
Age	✓	✓	✓	✓	✓	✓	✓	✓
March enrollment	✓	✓	✓	✓	✓	✓	✓	✓
Income			✓	✓	✓	✓		
Parental education								
Net worth					✓	✓	✓	✓
N	1,331	3,563	1,331	3,563	1,331	3,563	1,331	3,563

in 1986). All other classes have positive logit coefficients, with those from classes I, II, and IV somewhat more likely than those from classes III, V, and VI to enroll in college. These results are entirely consistent with the literature, demonstrating (once again) the predictive power of this sort of class schema.

Moreover, for model VI, the only noticeable change between cohorts is the increase in the relative odds of college enrollment for those from class I. The increase from 0.876 to 1.353 is substantial, and in a pooled model for both cohorts the difference of 0.478 has a standard error of 0.309. Although not statistically significant by conventional standards, the increase is consistent with our prior beliefs, which are grounded in the received wisdom about the increasing resources of class I and the importance of resources in explaining college enrollment. Thus, we are inclined to view the increase as genuine, even though we recognize that substantial caution is in order. The increase suggests that prospective students from the most advantaged social origins were more likely to be enrolled in college in 1996 than in 1986. This result, when paired with the apparent stability of the associations between resources and college entry, suggests that the increase in inequality of conditions between classes may be responsible for the increased odds of college entry for class I.

We evaluate this inductive conjecture in the last three models of Table 7.6, where parental education, income, and net worth are added to the model successively (and exclusively). Our conjecture that increased resources can account for the increased odds of class I is, however, disconfirmed by these results. Although adjusting for each of these additional measures of family advantage attenuates social class as a predictor of college enrollment, the increase in the odds of college enrollment for class I is only slightly altered in these models. To the extent that there has been a relative increase in the enrollment rate for those from the most advantaged social class origins, our results suggest that (1) this increased enrollment rate is attributable to a change between 1986 and 1996 other than increasing relative resources or (2) our specification of resource effects does not capture the relevant levers relating social mobility to inequality of conditions. We reserve discussion of the latter for the end of the chapter.

Summary of Empirical Conclusions

Our results from Tables 7.4 and 7.5 reveal little or no change in the associations between family resources and college enrollment. Given this apparent invariance across cohorts, it would be reasonable to expect that the particular distributional shift in resources revealed in Tables 7.1 and 7.3 (i.e., where the increases in inequality represent a relative redistribution of resources away from those in the middle toward those in the tails) to generate greater inequality of college enrollment. Adolescents from the top of the resource distribution might be expected to attend college more frequently in 1996 than in 1986, as their relative resources increased while the apparent effect of each increment of resources remained the same.

Our results from Table 7.6 are consistent with this baseline expectation. We found a small increase in the relative odds of college entry for those from the most advantaged social class I, comprised primarily of the children of professionals and higher-level managers. However, we could not attribute the relatively large logit coefficient predicting college enrollment for class I in 1996 to any of the resource or family background variables, thereby undermining the main rationale for the expectation that a greater relative enrollment rate would emerge at the top of the class hierarchy in 1996. This inconsistency represents a puzzle that awaits resolution, as we will discuss later. It could, for example, reflect a greater relative recognition among adolescents and parents from class I that college is ever more essential for labor market success.

In total, we have not found any evidence that recent increases in inequality will generate dramatic changes in patterns of social mobility. At best, quite modest changes are unfolding, with the advantages of class I escalating slightly for unknown reasons. Two qualifications to these conclusions are in order.

First, this judgment of relatively little change in the social mobility arising from inequality of conditions is based on the assumption that future changes in social mobility patterns would necessarily be revealed to some degree in patterns of educational attainment in the 1980s and 1990s (and, furthermore, rather narrowly in basic college enrollment patterns, as opposed to college graduation, and so on). We are well aware that change could result from other mechanisms relating social origins to occupational destinations, and if so, we may nonetheless see a change in patterns of social mobility that is a consequence of changes in inequality of conditions. But, were this to be the case, the consensus position of the literature – that inequality of conditions regulates levels of social mobility primarily via selection and allocation mechanisms of the educational system – would be open to revision. We doubt that the literature would be proven so far off the mark, even though we agree that investigation of change in other mechanisms is surely in order.

Second, total mobility rates could change in the future for reasons entirely unrelated to the recent increase in inequality of conditions. In particular, entry rates into class I may increase substantially in the United States in the future if the narrative of the evolving global economy is substantiated. But this increase would then be duly labeled as structural mobility, rather than that which would be attributed directly to the mechanisms regulated by inequality of conditions. Uncovering such a pattern of structural mobility would be an important contribution to the empirical literature, but it would not have much relevance for the direct question we have addressed in our empirical analysis in this chapter.

DISCUSSION

Within the social sciences, standards by which coefficients of statistical models are judged relevant for theoretical propositions and policy prescriptions are in the process of revision. Our chapter is rather old-fashioned in this regard, as we merely attempt to assess whether or not the predicted relationships suggested by theoretical propositions are realized in the available data (using the accepted model specifications that prevail in sociological research on social mobility). And yet, there are two distinct types of inquiry embedded within our analysis: (1) an assessment of the effects of family resources on college enrollment and (2) an assessment of the consequences of changes in estimated associations for subsequent patterns of social mobility and the industrialization theories that have been constructed to explain them. Whereas the first type of inquiry is carefully defined and precise answers should be expected, the latter is more deeply a matter of judgment, given the limitations of available data, the potential for entirely unforeseeable shocks to the economy, and the rather informal nature of the predictions set forth in the social mobility literature from the 1950s through the 1980s. In this section, we first draw this distinction more clearly, indicating where in the methodological and epistemological terrain we would wish our study to be placed. We then conclude by laying out a more encompassing set of issues that relate our findings to some of the core themes of this volume.

Causal Inference for the Effects of Family Resources

Focus on a single dimension of family resources – such as family income – and suppose that (1) our primary subject of investigation is the causal effect of family income on college enrollment and (2) our secondary subject of investigation is whether this causal effect has changed between 1986 and 1996. In this scenario, we are interested in more than just the degree to which observed family income predicts the observed odds of college enrollment, as we are interested in the underlying causal effect. And, our position is that one cannot be interested in this causal effect without wishing to know the answer to counterfactual questions, such as "What would the college enrollment rate of students with family income equal to X have been if instead these same students had family income equal to Y?" Indeed, ideally we would wish to know the equation:

$$Pr\,(ENROLL)_i = f_i\,(FAMINC) + e_i \qquad (1)$$

where *FAMINC* is a deterministic "what if" family income, $f_i(\cdot)$ is an individually varying function of potential family income, and the final term is a random shock.[11]

Our logit coefficients for family income, such as for model I in Table 7.4, do not reveal very much about the fundamental causal relationship that Equation 1 represents. Thus, we make no claims that our logit coefficients are informative about the true counterfactual causal effects of family resources on college enrollment.[12] In fact, as causal effect estimates, the literature suggests that our coefficients for family resources are almost certainly too large because of the absence of covariates such as cognitive skill (see Heckman and Krueger 2003 along with Cunha, Heckman, and Navarro, Chapter 11 of this volume and also Epstein and Winship, Chapter 10 of this volume). Given our recognition of this limitation of our models, why were they worth estimating?

Before answering this question, we should make clear that we do not share the position of others that counterfactual causality is an improper conceptual foundation for the methodology of sociological research, even if one's results fall far short of its standards.[13] We most certainly should attempt to generate results that can warrant counterfactual conditional statements (i.e., if we wish our causal models to be portable across time and space to at least some degree, if we wish our conclusions to have some relevance to the design of policy interventions, and so forth). Accordingly, we would very much encourage efforts to find natural experiments that produce more direct information about Equation 7.1, including the pursuit of the sort of social experiments advocated by Hanushek (2003). And, net of the causal effect of income on college enrollment, it would surely be fruitful to learn whether wealth does indeed have a meaningful causal effect on educational attainment. Part and parcel of pursuing such a conclusion would be the determination of whether wealth has as an effect by eliminating credit constraints on college entry or instead by enabling the purchase of an environment early in a child's life that is conducive to learning and more general features of child development.[14]

Given that we cannot warrant strong counterfactual conditionals, why then are our models useful? Note that the existence of meaningful omitted variables such as cognitive skill does not necessarily invalidate our "no-change in the association" conclusions for family resources. In order for the absence of a measure of cognitive skills to have suppressed a genuine cohort difference in the effects of social class or family resources, the relationship between these variables and the cognitive skills of adolescents would have to have changed between 1986 and 1996. Although some scholars have claimed that there are trends in these relationships, none of these claims has been substantiated in the literature (see Devlin, Fienberg, Resnick, and Roeder 1997). Thus, even though we are willing to concede that we cannot offer reasonable estimates of causal effects in the potential outcome framework for income, wealth, or social class, we still regard our models as worthwhile, for they succeed in addressing some of the key change-over-time propositions at the heart of sociological writing on social mobility, as we discuss next.

Implications for the Mobility and Education Literature

As discussed in the introduction, in the 1980s and 1990s the simple narrative of equality-spawning industrial development fell apart. Along with the evolution of an economy often characterized as postindustrial, we have seen an increase in inequality of conditions. Our contribution to this volume is motivated by our prediction that a new wave of studies will be forthcoming on the connections between the logic of postindustrialism and rates of social mobility. We have offered results bearing on a classic proposition of the social mobility literature—inequality of conditions regulates the level of social mobility in a society. And we have used the customary model specifications employed in sociological research on mobility. Our results lead us to the conclusion that post-1980 trends in educational attainment are less supportive of this classic proposition than one might have expected.

Our findings are also relevant (in an analogous way) to the conjecture of American exceptionalism in mobility patterns. Commencing with Tocqueville, and carried forward by Parsons, Duncan, Treiman, and others, many scholars have put forth the conjecture that rates of social mobility are comparatively high in the United States because of (1) its unique historical legacy as a new state without a titled nobility, (2) its supposed status as the vanguard nation of industrialization, and (3) its greater reliance on universalistic criteria for educational and occupational placements. An equally impressive group of scholars has sought to disconfirm the same conjecture, most prominently Lipset and Bendix (1959) and Erikson and Goldthorpe (1985).

The conjecture of American exceptionalism survives because a modest amount of empirical evidence seems to support it. Indeed, Erikson and Goldthorpe (1992) demonstrate the endurance of the conjecture. Their primary goal was to parsimoniously account for the pattern of intergenerational mobility characteristic of the industrialized nations in Europe, which they fulfilled admirably with their model of core social fluidity for nine European nations. When separate attention was then given to the United States, they concede that some evidence for higher rates of social mobility in the United States was found (even though it is less, in their estimation, than an exceptional amount).[15]

How do our results relate to the thesis of American exceptionalism? Erikson and Goldthorpe (1992:369) noted, with reference to Treiman and Yip (1989), that industrialization theories had identified declining inequality of conditions as the primary proximate cause of increasing rates of mobility in countries such as the United States. If we had seen the influence of social origins strengthening between the two cohorts and could have attributed this increase to widening resource differentials, then this result would have been consistent with a particular narrative of American exceptionalism, wherein the United States is seen as the vanguard nation of industrialization and, by virtue of this status, has levels of social mobility that respond to changes in levels of inequality of conditions more immediately and consequentially than other nations. That is, one could have argued that the moderation of differences in initial conditions generated openness of entry at the top of the occupational structure in the United States between 1950 and 1980, but then that the accentuation of inequality has led to (or will lead to in the next two decades) a general decline in exchange mobility. But, we did not find this pattern, and as a result we are left with alternative implications for the thesis of American exceptionalism. Our findings may suggest that the discounted ideas of historical contingency and cultural differences will yet be revealed as more than just ideas that serve the "cause of national mythologies" (Erikson and Goldthorpe 1992:372).[16]

Finally, while we await the discovery of natural experiments that can help tease out the genuine causal effects of family resources (and government transfers to meet resource shortfalls), and as we await descriptive patterns relevant to a new engagement of postindustrialization theories of mobility and the thesis of American exceptionalism, we should, in the meantime, attempt to build a better model of educational attainment. As discussed in the introduction, a promising mixture of perspectives is emerging in sociology and economics, one that seeks to link these two traditions together. For example, in sociology, the first author (see Morgan 2002, 2005) has used this convergent literature to develop a stochastic decision tree model for determining intermediate levels of preparatory commitment and then the educational attainment that follows from it. If this type of modeling more effectively captures the genuine process of educational attainment, then the increased odds of enrollment for those from class I would reflect (1) the more certain recognition of those from class I that higher education pays off and (2) that this differential recognition causes more adolescents from class I to prepare themselves for college entry by engaging more deeply in the pursuit of academic success while still in high school.

New theoretical work will only have a substantial payoff if it generates a fruitful agenda for new empirical research. And, in this regard, there already has been some progress by other sociologists, as the results of Breen and Yaish in this volume build directly on the work of Breen and Goldthorpe (1997) and then Breen (1999). The next goal for those following in this tradition (that is, if our finding of increased relative odds of college enrollment for class I begins to appear elsewhere) would be to show that students from class I are responding differently to changing incentives as well, with perhaps a deeper change in the decision rules on which their continuation choices are based.

Notes

1. As eloquently discussed by Erikson and Goldthorpe (1992), these "logic of industrialism" theories were championed by Talcott Parsons (although they may have originated in the convergence theory of Clark Kerr) and were then further developed by Blau and Duncan (1967) and Treiman (1970). For the last of these, see Treiman's (1970) proposition I.A.6 of increases in equality of income, which he argues is supported by evidence available at the time of his writing. Then, see his predictions I.B.1 through I.B.7 on increases in mobility, which he argues follow from proposition I.A.6 (and other propositions). As indicated by Erikson and Goldthorpe (1992) with reference to Treiman and Yip (1989), the link between increasing equality of conditions and slightly increasing mobility remains the most robust piece of the thesis.

2. As we discuss later, this expectation rests on assumptions about the existence of a relatively invariant model for educational attainment and the continued importance of educational attainment for mobility patterns, following on the classic argument of Blau and Duncan (1967) and as elaborated and qualified by Raftery and Hout (1993).

3. Cameron and Heckman (1998) challenge the interpretation of these coefficients across transitions but do not challenge the claim that the same pattern prevails across countries. If the common pattern is a result of modeling assumptions encoded in sequential logits, then some of the similarity may reflect common methodology across national studies rather than common substantive findings. The jury is still out on this larger issue.

4. This is not necessarily a fair interpretation of the evidence. Conley (1999), for example, gives rather little consideration to the impact of basic multicollinearity. He relies on statistical significance as his measure of "strength" and "predictive importance" but ignores how hard it is to precisely estimate the unique contribution of family income to college enrollment and completion in the presence of other variables for parental education, occupational prestige, and levels of wealth (see especially Conley 1999, Tables 3.2 and A3.2). See also Orr (2003) for a similar set of interpretations.

5. Even constructing a college entry measure was challenging. As discussed later (and in the supplementary appendix), we pooled those aged 17 to 21 and then estimated the logit models conditional on dummies for age and spring enrollment status. Both sets of dummies partial out common age and grade-of-origin effects across cohorts, enabling comparisons of the adjusted coefficients. The modeling strategy represents our attempt to get as close as possible to the usual practice of estimating college entry rates for graduating high school seniors. Of course, our coefficients represent unknowable mixtures of enrollment probabilities across our mixed-age samples, further conditioned on prior spring enrollments. Our assumption is that these unknowable mixtures are invariant across the two cohorts, thereby enabling meaningful comparisons of coefficients across cohorts.

6. As we hint throughout, many other variants on this basic specification were estimated, and no substantively important differences were detected. In particular, we used alternative specifications of family and household resources (both quantile dummy specifications and monotonic transformations). We estimated the models ignoring March enrollment status. And, we estimated the models on the subset of respondents (approximately 86 percent of respondents) who were still dependent on their parents (i.e., excluding those "living alone," who by SIPP design were, by definition, independent adults). Results for these alternative models are available from the authors, but we assure the reader that they differ little from what we present in this chapter. See also the details in the appendix.

7. As is shown in the appendix, and discussed later in the text, we chose a specification of resource variables that matches the sort of censored resource variables available in other datasets on which models of educational attainment are usually estimated (such as the NELS or HS&B). We therefore censored the original income and wealth variables, coding all those above the 95th percentile as if they were at the 95th percentile. For monthly income, those above the 95th percentiles were recoded to values of 9,526 and 10,698 for 1986 and 1996, respectively. For total net worth, the equivalent values are 392,808 and 425,926, and for home equity they are 198,019 and 170,000. This specification also makes sense to us for deeper theoretical reasons: (1) With regard to a coarse college enrollment variable, we do not expect differences between the very rich and the very, very rich; (2) other transformation of resources which would shrink the very, very rich toward the very rich (such as the log of resources) transform the entire resource scale, which seems inappropriate to us. Nonetheless, we did estimate these alternative models, and the same non-trends were evident. For the income variable in model I, the numbers in the table – 0.121 and 0.141 would have been 0.098 and 0.069 for the original income variable and 0.275 and 0.249 for the log of the original income variable. For both of these alternative specifications, the cohort difference was nonsignificant.

8. The zero income coefficients appear somewhat puzzling, but further inspection convinced us that they are not. The income variable is monthly income from the prior March, when we measured spring enrollment status at our chosen baseline reference point for the study. Only 1.1 percent and 0.8 percent of respondents were from families with zero income in March of 1986 and 1996, respectively. Thus, this is a small group of unusual respondents, susceptible to both model specification issues and sampling error. Why was the zero-income coefficient larger in 1986? The zero-income families had relatively high wealth in 1986. The mean net worth of the students who were from zero-income families in 1986 was $194,161, in contrast to $107,850 for all other families. In 1996, the mean net worth of zero-income families was only $21,675 in comparison to $103,353 for all other families. We therefore expect that some of the zero-income families are a type of temporary zero-income families, and that this was more likely to be the case in 1986. We suspect that many of these families have heads of household who were between jobs but who also had levels of family resources that allowed them to remain in active job

search mode rather than accepting a job at a rather low wage or taking public assistance. This was perhaps more likely to be the case in 1986, either because of sampling error or because of the higher rate of unemployment in 1986 (that is, accordingly to the Bureau of Labor Statistics, 7.2 percent versus 5.5 percent in March 1986 versus March 1996).

9. Again, the point estimates for the zero wealth and negative wealth estimates deserve some attention. There is a literature on how negative net worth is a misleading indicator of wealth (see Kennickell 2003), and our results confirm that some of the families with negative net worth are generally quite resource rich, to the extent that banks are willing to lend them money against their assets because of their relatively high income. But, the group is nonetheless rather heterogeneous, and in view of this heterogeneity, it is not surprising that the point estimates jump around from model to model.

10. Nonetheless, it should be recognized that the sample sizes of the SIPP are relatively small. Rejecting a no-change null hypothesis based on statistical significance tests would require a fairly substantial change between cohorts. Accordingly, it is possible that the small increase in the point estimate for the effect of family income in model I, when coupled with prior knowledge of the results of Ellwood and Kane (2000), would be regarded by a Bayesian as confirmatory evidence that the association between family income and college entry has increased between the 1980s and the 1990s. Of course, an alternative Bayesian could come to the opposite conclusion, after taking note of the slight decline in point estimates for family income when it is specified in logarithmic form, as reported in the main text.

11. See Angrist and Krueger (1999) for a similar setup. See Winship and Morgan (1999) for a sociological account of the counterfactual model of causality. See Sobel (1998) for methodological discussion that prosecutes the literature in social stratification.

12. Indeed, we agree with Sobel (2004:418) that "virtually all of the so-called 'effects' estimated in the [sociological] literature over the past 35 to 40 years are at best fancy associations that have little to do with causation." We will even admit that our coefficients are not fancy.

13. See Goldthorpe (2000: ch. 7) for a cogent presentation of an alternative position.

14. In judging the wisdom of recommending research on natural disasters to find wealth destruction natural experiments, we ultimately decided not to do so. Aside from having to model insurance effects and so forth, such efforts would have to partial out all of the consequences of disasters other than wealth destruction (see Norris et al. 2002), and this seems beyond our current capacities.

15. Erikson and Goldthorpe (1992) offer a somewhat different interpretation than we have just claimed. In their main text, the departure of the United States from the core social fluidity model is downplayed, as attention is focused instead on the comparable global measures of model fit. But tucked within footnote 7 (p. 318)

are hints of the substantial differences. They reach two alternative conclusions (p. 320): "One is that some further support is here provided for Blau's and Duncan's view that the American mobility regime is distinctive at least in the greater openness of more advantaged class positions that it affords; the other is that the deviation from core fluidity that our model captures reflects not so much American social reality as the difficulties we faced in recoding the American data. Our own preference is strongly for the second of these interpretations."

16. The economics literature has also begun to engage the thesis of American exceptionalism in two ways. Bowels and Gintis (2002) further challenge the notion that the United States is properly described as a land of opportunity, and Corak and Heisz (1999) and Solon (2002) note that countries such as Canada and Sweden may have higher rates of intergenerational income mobility, which they surmise may reflect alternative levels of subsidies for human capital accumulation.

References

Angrist, Joshua D., and Alan B. Krueger. 1999. "Empirical Strategies in Labor Economics." Pp. 1277–366 in *Handbook of Labor Economics*, vol. 3, edited by O. C. Ashenfelter and D. Card. Amsterdam: Elsevier.

Blau, Francine D., and Lawrence M. Kahn. 2002. *At Home and Abroad: U.S. Labor-Market Performance in International Perspective*. New York: Russell Sage Foundation.

Blau, Peter M., and Otis Dudley Duncan. 1967. *The American Occupational Structure*. New York: Wiley.

Bowles, Samuel, and Herbert Gintis. 2002. "The Inheritance of Inequality." *Journal of Economic Perspectives* 16:3–30.

Breen, Richard. 1999. "Beliefs, Rational Choice, and Bayesian Learning." *Rationality and Society* 11:463–79.

Breen, Richard, and John H. Goldthorpe. 1997. "Explaining Educational Differentials: Towards a Formal Rational Action Theory." *Rationality and Society* 9:275–305.

Cameron, Stephen V., and James J. Heckman. 1998. "Life Cycle Schooling and Dynamic Selection Bias: Models and Evidence for Five Cohorts of American Males." *Journal of Political Economy* 106:262–333.

———. 1999. "Can Tuition Combat Rising Wage Inequality?" Pp. 76–124 in *Financing College Tuition: Government Policies and Educational Priorities*, edited by M. H. Kosters. Washington, DC: AEI Press.

Carneiro, Pedro, and James J. Heckman. 2002. "The Evidence on Credit Constraints in Post-Secondary Schooling." *The Economic Journal* 112:705–34.

Conley, Dalton. 1999. *Being Black, Living in the Red: Race, Wealth, and Social Policy in America*. Berkeley: University of California Press.

Conley, Dalton. 2001. "Capital for College: Parental Assets and Postsecondary Schooling." *Sociology of Education* 74:59–72.

Corak, Miles, and Andrew Heisz. 1999. "The Intergenerational Earnings and In-
    come Mobility of Canadian Men: Evidence from Longitudinal Income Tax
    Data." *Journal of Human Resources* 34.

Devlin, Bernie, Stephen E. Fienberg, Daniel P. Resnick, and Kathryn Roeder, eds.
    1997. *Intelligence, Genes, and Success: Scientists Respond to the Bell Curve.*
    New York: Springer.

Ellwood, David T., and Thomas J. Kane. 2000. "Who Is Getting a College Educa-
    tion: Family Background and the Growing Gaps in Enrollment." Pp. 283–325
    in *Securing the Future: Investing in Children from Birth to College*, edited by
    S. Danziger and J. Waldfogel. New York: Russell Sage Foundation.

Erikson, Robert, and John H. Goldthorpe. 1985. "Are American Rates of Social
    Mobility Exceptionally High? New Evidence on an Old Issue." *European So-
    ciological Review* 1:1–22.

———. 1992. *The Constant Flux: A Study of Class Mobility in Industrial Societies.*
    Oxford: Oxford University Press.

Freeman, Richard B. and Lawrence F. Katz, eds. 1995. *Differences and Changes in
    Wage Structures.* Chicago: University of Chicago Press.

Goldthorpe, John H. 1996. "Class Analysis and the Reorientation of Class Theory:
    The Case of Persisting Differentials in Educational Attainment." *The British
    Journal of Sociology* 47:481–505.

———. 2000. *On Sociology: Numbers, Narratives, and the Integration of Research
    and Theory.* Oxford: Oxford University Press.

Hallinan, Maureen T. 2001. "Sociological Perspectives on Black-White Inequalities
    in American Schooling." *Sociology of Education* Extra Issue 2001:50–70.

Hanushek, Eric A. 2003. "Comment." Pp. 252–68 in *Inequality in America: What
    Role for Human Capital Policies?*, edited by J. J. Heckman and A. B. Krueger.
    Cambridge: MIT Press.

Hauser, Robert M., Shu-Ling Tsai, and William H. Sewell. 1983. "A Model of
    Stratification with Response Error in Social and Psychological Variables." *So-
    ciology of Education* 56:20–46.

Heckman, James J. and Alan B. Krueger. 2003. *Inequality in America: What Role
    for Human Capital Policies?* Cambridge: MIT Press.

Kane, Thomas J. 1999. "Reforming Subsidies for Higher Education." Pp. 53–75 in
    Financing College Tuition: Government Policies and Educational Priorities,
    edited by M. H. Kosters. Washington, DC: AEI Press.

———. 1999. *The Price of Admission: Rethinking How Americans Pay for College.*
    Washington, DC: Brookings.

Katz, Lawrence F., and David H. Autor. 1999. "Changes in the Wage Structure
    and Earnings Inequality." Pp. 1463–555 in *Handbook of Labor Economics*,
    vol. 3, edited by O. C. Ashenfelter and D. Card. Amsterdam: Elsevier.

Kennickell, Arthur B. 2003. "A Rolling Tide: Changes in the Distribution of Wealth
    in the United States." Survey of Consumer Finances Working Paper, Federal
    Reserve Board, Washington, DC.

Kosters, Marvin H., eds. 1999. *Financing College Tuition: Government Policies and Educational Priorities.* Washington, DC: AEI Press.

Lipset, Seymour Martin, and Reinhard Bendix. 1959. *Social Mobility in Industrial Society.* Berkeley: University of California Press.

Mare, Robert D. 1980. "Social Background and School Continuation Decisions." *Journal of the American Statistical Association* 75:295–305.

———. 1981. "Change and Stability in Educational Stratification." *American Sociological Review* 46:72–87.

Mayer, Susan E. 1997. *What Money Can't Buy: Family Income and Children's Life Chances.* Cambridge: Harvard University Press.

———. 2001. "How Did the Increase in Economic Inequality between 1970 and 1990 Affect Children's Educational Attainment?" *American Journal of Sociology* 107:1–32.

Morgan, Stephen L. 2002. "Modeling Preparatory Commitment and Non-Repeatable Decisions: Information-Processing, Preference Formation and Educational Attainment." *Rationality and Society* 14:387–429.

———. 2005. *On the Edge of Commitment: Educational Attainment and Race in the United States.* Stanford, CA: Stanford University Press.

Mulligan, Casey B. 1997. *Parental Priorities and Economic Inequality.* Chicago: University of Chicago Press.

Neckerman, Kathryn M., ed. 2004. *Social Inequality.* New York: Russell Sage.

Norris, Fran H., Matthew J. Friedman, Patricia J. Watson, Christopher M. Byrne, Eolia Diaz, and Krzysztof Kaniasty. 2002. "60,000 Disaster Victims Speak: Part I. An Empirical Review of the Empirical Literature, 1981–2001." *Psychiatry* 65:207–39.

Oliver, Melvin L., and Thomas M. Shapiro. 1995. *Black Wealth / White Wealth: A New Perspective on Racial Inequality.* New York: Routledge.

Orr, Amy J. 2003. "Black-White Differences in Achievement: The Importance of Wealth." *Sociology of Education* 76:281–304.

Raftery, Adrian E., and Michael Hout. 1993. "Maximally Maintained Inequality: Expansion, Reform, and Opportunity in Irish Education, 1921–75." *Sociology of Education* 66:41–62.

Sewell, William H., Archibald O. Haller, and Alejandro Portes. 1969. "The Educational and Early Occupational Attainment Process." *American Sociological Review* 34:82–92.

Shavit, Yossi, and Hans-Peter Blossfeld, eds. 1993. *Persistent Inequality: Changing Educational Attainment in Thirteen Countries.* Boulder, CO: Westview.

Sobel, Michael E. 1998. "Causal Inference in Statistical Models of the Process of Socioeconomic Achievement: A Case Study." *Sociological Methods and Research* 27:318–48.

———. 2004. "Review of 'The Theory of the Design of Experiments' by D. R. Cox and N. Reid." *Sociological Methods and Research* 32:416–18.

Solon, Gary. 2002. "Cross-Country Differences in Intergenerational Earnings Mobility." *Journal of Economic Perspectives* 16:59–66.

Sorokin, Pitirim A. 1927. *Social Mobility*. New York: Harper & Brothers.

Treiman, Donald. 1970. "Industrialization and Social Stratification." Pp. 207–34 in *Social Stratification: Research and Theory for the 1970s*, edited by E. O. Laumann. Indianapolis: Bobbs-Merrill.

Treiman, Donald J., and Kam-Bor Yip. 1989. "Educational and Occupational Attainment in 21 Countries." Pp. 373–94 in *Cross-National Research in Sociology*, edited by M. L. Kohn. Newbury Park, CA: Sage.

U.S. Department of Commerce, Bureau of the Census. 2001. *Survey of Income and Program Participation (SIPP), 1986 Panel (Wave 1-4 Core Microdata File, Wave 4 Topical Module Microdata File), 1996 Panel (Wave 1-3 Core Microdata File, Wave 3 Topical Module Microdata File)* [computer file]. Washington, DC: U.S. Dept. of Commerce.

Winship, Christopher, and Stephen L. Morgan. 1999. "The Estimation of Causal Effects from Observational Data." *Annual Review of Sociology* 25:659–706.

Wolff, Edward N. 1998. "Recent Trends in the Size Distribution of Household Wealth." *Journal of Economic Perspectives* 12:131–50.

CHAPTER EIGHT

Family Attainment Norms and Educational Stratification in the United States and Taiwan: The Effects of Parents' School Transitions

Robert D. Mare and Huey-Chi Chang

The most commonplace observation in the study of educational stratification and mobility is that how far an individual goes in school is strongly associated with how far his or her parents have gone in school. Although the reasons for this association are the subject of a rich field of investigation and the strength of the association varies across time and place, the positive correlation of parents' and offsprings' educational attainments is nearly universal. Whereas early studies of educational inequality focused on educational attainment as a *status*, typically measured by total years of schooling attained (Duncan 1965, 1967; Blau and Duncan 1967; Hauser and Featherman 1976), more recent studies have assumed that schooling is a dynamic *process*. The process is conceived of and measured as a sequence of school transitions between levels of schooling, whether measured as years of school completed or enrollment in major organizational divisions of school systems (e.g., Duncan 1968; Mare 1980, 1981a; Shavit and Blossfeld 1993; Breen and Jonsson 2000). Viewing educational stratification in this way shows where in the schooling process social inequalities are greatest, allows comparisons of stratification across dissimilar school systems, allows more precise linkage of market and institutional changes to individual level probabilities of making

Earlier versions of this chapter were prepared for presentation at the meetings of the Research Committee on Social Stratification of the International Sociological Association in Taipei, Taiwan, in January 1998 and the World Congress of Sociology in Montreal, Canada, in July 1998. This research was supported by the John D. and Catherine T. MacArthur Foundation, the Institute for Research on Poverty, the Graduate School of the University of Wisconsin-Madison, and the National Science Foundation. The authors are grateful to Stephen Morgan for helpful comments on an earlier draft.

school transitions, and provides estimates of the effects of family background characteristics on school continuation decisions that do not depend on the shape of the distribution of educational attainment (Mare 1980, 1981a, 1981b; Shavit and Blossfeld 1993; Breen and Jonsson 2000).

THE EFFECTS OF PARENTS' SCHOOL
CONTINUATION DECISIONS

Given the usefulness of viewing the schooling of children as a series of discrete transitions in models of the intergenerational transmission of educational attainment, it is surprising that researchers have devoted little attention to the conceptualization and measurement of parents' educational attainments. Typically, we measure mother's and father's schooling in the same way as offspring's schooling was measured in the earliest educational stratification studies, namely as highest grade of school completed, and estimate their linear effects on the log odds of school continuation. Although parsimonious, this specification does not incorporate other potentially important effects of parents' schooling, some of which correspond rather closely to scholarly and popular notions of the reasons behind the positive association of parents' and offsprings' schooling.

It is widely recognized that parents' aspirations for their offsprings' socioeconomic achievements are heavily conditioned by their own accomplishments. In many countries parents desire and expect that their children will grow up to achieve at least as high a standard of living as they themselves enjoy and that educational attainment is the primary avenue to socioeconomic success. In an era of secularly rising average levels of educational attainment, one criterion of successful parenthood is for children go at least as far in school as their parents. Moreover, theorists of educational inequality suggest that parents' educational attainments set a floor for the attainments of their offspring because individuals face psychic costs to downward intergenerational mobility (Boudon 1974; Breen and Goldthorpe 1997; Breen and Yaish [this volume]). Yet studies of educational stratification seldom explicitly incorporate this idea into the analysis of school transitions. One specification of this idea, straightforward to implement with the typical data used to study educational mobility, is that parents affect whether their offspring make a particular school transition not only through their own completed levels of educational attainment but also through whether they themselves have made the school transition in question. This formulation recognizes a norm or, at the least, a statistical regularity that offspring go at least as far as their parents in school and that, for the great majority of families, the educational attainments of parents is a floor under the attainments of offspring. This chapter develops the rationale for and presents empirical demonstration of this type of effect.[1]

PARENTAL SOCIALIZATION AND ATTAINMENT NORMS

A tendency for individuals to go at least as far in school as their parents raises the question of how this regularity develops. Individuals appear to behave *as if* one of their main goals is not to experience downward educational mobility and, given this assumption, it may be possible to derive predictions about trend and variation in educational stratification (Breen and Goldthorpe 1997). However, one may ask why they are driven by this particular function of their parents' attainments, rather than some other. A large literature on the social psychology of socioeconomic attainment points to the socializing influences of significant others, including parents, teachers, and peers on the aspirations and expectations of young persons regarding educational and occupational attainment (e.g., Kahl 1957; Sewell, Haller, and Portes 1969; Sewell and Hauser 1975). For the most part, studies of socialization influences focus on just the positive associations between the social environments provided by significant others and the aspirations of youths. These positive correlations, however, are necessary but not sufficient conditions for parents' attainments to set a floor on those of their offspring. For the latter nonlinear effects of parents' educational attainment to appear, additional mechanisms must be at work. One possibility is simply that parents (and possibly other influencers) can best shape the aspirations and aptitudes of young people for the part of the educational attainment process with which they have direct experience. Once young persons supercede their parents' attainment, parents have little direct experience to draw on and thus their influence subsides. Another possibility is that parents are motivated by their failures as well as successes. Sheridan (2001) suggests that parents who aspire to a particular education level but do not attain it make an extra effort to see that their children accomplish their unmet goals (relative to parents who obtain the same amount of education but do not aspire to go further). These are possible mechanisms that may underpin family attainment norms that give rise to nonlinear effects of parental educational attainment on the school continuation decisions of young persons. It is, however, beyond the scope of this chapter to adjudicate among alternative mechanisms.

PARENT TRANSITION EFFECTS AND OCCUPATIONAL "INHERITANCE"

That parents' own school transitions may affect the school attainment of their offspring and thus be an important feature of intergenerational educational mobility is in keeping with standard approaches to the study of mobility on other dimensions of stratification, especially occupational mobility. Almost all studies of occupational mobility that treat occupations as a set of discrete locations recognize a strong tendency for offspring to "inherit" the occupational categories of their parents (e.g., Erikson and Goldthorpe 1992; Hout 1988; Hout and Hauser 1992) that goes beyond what would be expected on the basis of a strong positive association between scalar measures of parents' and offsprings' occupational characteristics. This tendency is subject to a variety of interpretations, including direct inheritance of a job or the physical capital associated with a business; socialization and education in the norms, values, and knowledge of a field of work; or simply the aggregation of detailed occupations into broad categories, combined with the preponderance of short over long distance intergenerational mobility. Whatever the interpretation, however, the statistical analysis of intergenerational mobility almost always requires special attention to the strong resemblance of parents' and offsprings' occupations. In addition to high intergenerational persistence within occupation categories, occupational mobility data also show a tendency for parents' occupational attainments to set a floor on the attainments of offspring. Societies that have undergone sectoral transformations of the labor force from farm to nonfarm, primary to secondary and tertiary, nonmanual to manual, and manufacturing to service, typically have substantial intergenerational structural mobility. In such transformations the lines between broad segments of the occupational structure, such as white collar versus blue collar or nonagricultural versus farm workers have often served as differentially permeable barriers to mobility. For example, in the mid-twentieth-century United States, sons of blue collar workers were much more likely to move into white collar occupations than were the sons of white collar workers to move into blue collar occupations. The less successful sons of white collar workers tended to move into relatively low status and poorly paid white collar occupations rather than into relatively high status and better paying blue collar positions (Blau and Duncan 1967). The approach to the study of educational stratification proposed in this chapter, then, echoes well-established themes in the analysis of occupational stratification and mobility.

If the members of families follow the rule that offspring must go at least as far in school as their parents, this premise suggests a number further questions about how they implement this rule. How this rule is applied to families of varying size and gender composition, how it varies by the birth order and sex of children, and how the sometimes varying educational attainments of mother and father combine to set the expectations for offspring are all important empirical issues. The main goal of this chapter is to document the effects of whether parents achieve selected educational milestones on whether their offspring make those same school transitions; to estimate the size of these effects; and to explore how these effects depend on characteristics of individual offspring and their families. Our empirical investigations focus on two societies—the United States and Taiwan—that have broadly similar educational systems, but also important cultural differences that may illuminate the ways that family effects on educational stratification come about.

ATTAINMENT NORMS AND THE EFFECTS OF PARENTS' EDUCATION

We explore the idea that parents affect their offspring's schooling through resources that are tied to whether they have completed specific levels of schooling as well as to their highest grade of school completed. That is, we conjecture that whether parents complete specific milestones in the schooling process affect whether their offspring achieve those same milestones. Although this hypothesis is simple, it leads to a set of subsidiary issues and hypotheses about the way that the effect of parental school transitions works. The issues that we consider in our empirical analyses include:

1. Is the specific nonlinear effect of parental schooling that we propose, in conjunction with the well-established linear effect sufficient to account for the full association between parents' and offsprings' schooling? That is, are there other important nonlinearities in the effects of parental schooling? We address this question through statistical tests of alternative models of association.

2. A commonly observed pattern of the effects of mother's or father's years of school completed is that these effects decline systematically from the early to the later stages of the schooling process (Mare 1980; Shavit and Blossfeld 1993). This variation may be due to the effects of unmeasured heterogeneity or other specific mechanisms of social selection and exclusion that are most tightly tied to parental socioeconomic circumstances at the earliest stages of the schooling process. If in fact the effects of parents' school transitions on offspring's schooling are large, we ask whether these parental effects also decline over the schooling process or exhibit some other nonproportionality (interaction) with the discrete hazard of school attrition. Although the transition-specific pattern of these effects may also reflect unmeasured heterogeneity, it may well be that parental transition effects are more stable across school transitions to the extent that a common norm governing the link between parent and offspring schooling persists at all levels of schooling. We investigate this question empirically through comparisons among models for proportional (transition-invariant) and nonproportional (transition-dependent) effects of the measures of parental schooling.

3. If the school transitions that parents make establish a floor for the attainments of their children, does just one parent or do both parents have this effect and if the school transitions of both parents affect offsprings' schooling, which parent has a stronger effect? Despite the high correlation of mother's and father's schooling, the educational attainments of both parents typically influence the attainment of their offspring (e.g., Mare 1980). It is an open question whether the same holds for parental school transitions.[2]

4. A further issue in characterizing the effects of parental educational attainment on the schooling of offspring is whether parental effects are similar for male and female children. If parents wish to establish a floor on the school attainment of their children, they may do so differentially between boys and girls if their ultimate socioeconomic and lifestyle aspirations for their daughters differ from those of their sons. Levels of educational attainment and regimes of educational stratification in the contemporary United States are very similar for men and women (e.g., Mare 1995) and for this society sex differences in the effects of parents' school transitions may be small. In other societies and eras in which gender inequalities in educational attainment are large, the effects of parents' transitions may differ between boys and girls. These effects, moreover, may interact with whether it is mother's or father's school transitions that exert a larger effect. Mother's

educational attainment may set a floor under the attainments of a daughter whereas father's attainment may set a floor under the attainment of a son. Thomas (1994), for example, demonstrates same sex effects of parents' educational attainments on the health and nutritional status of their offspring.

5. Although families may try to follow a norm that children go at least as far in school as their parents, these efforts may be constrained by parental resources. Insofar as families have limited cultural as well as economic resources that facilitate success in school, some families may not be able to achieve their goals for the attainments of their offspring. One way that resources may constrain educational attainment is through the number of children in the family. As is well known, educational attainment and school continuation probabilities are inversely associated with the size of an individual's sibship, presumably reflecting the resource scarcities experienced by larger families (e.g., Hauser and Featherman 1976; Mare 1980; Blake 1989). Although the effects of years of parents' schooling on offsprings' schooling do *not* vary with sibship size in the United States (Mare and Chen 1986), to the extent that the effects of parent school transitions indicate the results of a family strategy to set a floor on children's attainments, these effects may in fact be weaker in the resource-limited context of large families than in small families where these constraints are minimal.[3]

In addition to the effects discussed thus far, several other issues are related to the effects of whether parents make school transitions on their offsprings schooling. These issues include whether the effects of parents' school transitions depend on the sex composition of a sibship or by birth order,[4] whether parents are more likely to require all of their children or only selected children to achieve their own schooling levels, and whether the tendency for parents to set a floor under their children's schooling has strengthened or weakened over time. Although these issues are amenable to empirical investigation using variants of the models presented here, they are beyond the scope of this chapter. We return to these and other issues for future research at the conclusion of the chapter.

EDUCATIONAL STRATIFICATION IN TAIWAN AND THE UNITED STATES

We investigate these issues through a analysis of the effects of family background on educational attainment for two populations, Taiwan in 1989 and the United States in 1994, which may differ substantially in the ways in which families affect educational inequality, especially in their treatment of male and female children. Despite pervasive gender stratification in the United States, historical and contemporary differences in educational attainment between men and women are relatively small (Mare 1995). School enrollment rates, average levels of educational attainment, and the effects of parents' socioeconomic characteristics are similar for males and females. It remains an open question, however, whether the specific effects of family background emphasized in this chapter, the effects of whether a mother or father has made a specific school transition, may interact with the sexes of their children.

In contrast to the United States, Taiwan exhibits both a contemporary and historical regime of substantial gender inequality in educational attainment (Tsai 1998). In traditional Taiwanese families, parental aspirations for daughters' educational attainments are less ambitious than for sons and are much more likely to be oriented toward the marriage market than the market economy. When family resources are scarce, daughters are more likely than sons to be constrained in their educational attainment (Parish and Willis 1993). Although this regime of gender stratification is expected to weaken with the emergence of "love" marriages, the secular trend toward affluence, and the urbanization of the population, its vestiges remain very apparent in the contemporary population (Tsai 1998). In view of these gender inequalities, we seek to learn whether the tendency of parents to set a floor on the educational attainments of their children is interdependent with the different roles and statuses of men and women in Taiwanese families.

STATISTICAL MODELS

We analyze the effects of personal and family background characteristics, including mother's and father's educational attainment, size of sibship, and sex on the probability of making selected school transitions. Although we consider four transitions for both Taiwan and the United States, we examine somewhat different transitions for the two countries, in recognition of their different distributions of educational attainment. For the United States we consider the following transitions:

1. Completes at least 9th grade;
2. Completes at least high school (12th grade) given 9th grade completion;

3. Completes at least some college (13th grade) given high school completion;

4. Completes at least a college degree (16th grade) given some college completion.

For Taiwan the transitions are:

1. Completes elementary school (6th grade);

2. Completes junior high school (9th grade) given elementary school completion;

3. Completes senior high school (12th grade) given junior high school completion;

4. Completes at least some college (13th grade) given senior high school completion.

For both societies, these outcomes represent transitions between major institutional divisions of schooling.[5]

Our basic analyses of the effects of parental characteristics use a time survival model that employs a logit transformation of the probabilies of making transitions between successive levels of schooling and, for some regressors, allows for nonproportional effects. That is, we allow the effects of the independent variables to vary across school transitions. In such models the unit of analysis is the "person-decision," that is, the binary outcome of whether or not an individual makes a given transition given that he or she has made all transitions up to the one in question. This procedure is a general one for the analysis of event histories (e.g., Allison 1982; Kalbfleisch and Prentice 1980; Vermunt 1997) and has been extensively used to study educational attainment (e.g., Mare 1980, 1981a; Shavit and Blossfeld 1993). In keeping with the prior literature on the analysis of school transitions, most of the regressors that we include in our schooling models are fixed across transitions for a given individual. An exception to this are the variables that denote whether an individual's mother and father have made the school transition in question, which are the variables of central interest to this study. Although parents' educational attainments are fixed covariates, the measures for whether they have made a given school transition are, by definition transition dependent.

Let p_{it} be the probability that the ith individual makes the tth school transition ($i = 1, \ldots, I; t = 1, \ldots, T$); X_{ik} be the individual's value on the kth (fixed regressor) ($k = 1, \ldots, K$); M_{it} and F_{it} be dichotomous variables that denote whether or not the individual's mother and father have made the *t*th transition; and α_t, β_k, γ^m, and γ^f be parameters to be estimated. Then the logit model for school transitions is:

$$\text{logit}\,(p_{it}\,|\,X_i,\,M_{it},\,F_{it}) = \alpha_t + \Sigma_k\,\beta_k\,X_{ik} + \gamma^m M_{it} + \gamma^f F_{it} \tag{1}$$

This model can be estimated by maximum likelihood using standard statistical software. Because some of our individual-level observations belong to the same families, our sample is clustered. We obtain maximum likelihood estimates of the individual-level models with Huber-White adjustments for clustering using Stata (StataCorp 2003).

DATA

We use two data sources in the present investigation, the 1989 Taiwan Women and Family Survey (TWAF)[6] and the 1994 General Social Survey (GSS). Both of these samples have national coverage, include information on the educational attainments of siblings, and contain enough information on individual educational attainment and sociodemographic and family background characteristics to permit the analysis of educational stratification.

The TWAF is a sample of 3,803 women, aged 20–66 and includes reports about the educational attainments of these women, their full sibships, their husbands, and their husbands' sibships. From these data we construct a sample consisting of respondents, their siblings, their husbands and their husbands' siblings. We included all TWAF respondents who were aged 20–66 in 1989, the siblings of these respondents, the older siblings of respondents who were aged less than 20 in 1989, the respondents' husbands who were aged 20–79, the siblings of these husbands, the older siblings of husbands aged less than 20, and the younger siblings of husbands aged more than 79.[7] This provides a sample of 39,294 individuals. Although the TWAF is not a representative sample of the male population, the husbands, brothers, and brothers-in-law of the respondents provide a large number of males for analysis. We believe that this sample is adequate for estimating the effects of family characteristics on the probability of progression through school in the adult male Taiwanese population and for drawing inferences about sex differences in these effects.

The GSS is a nationally representative sample of the 2,992 persons in the United States aged 18 and over in 1994. In addition to the sociodemographic and attitudinal data that the GSS obtains annually, the 1994 survey obtained information on a randomly selected sibling of the GSS respondent.[8] First, for the individual-level analysis of the effects of parental educational attainment and parents' school transitions on offsprings' schooling, we selected all GSS respondents and their randomly selected siblings who were aged 20 to 80 in 1994. Respondents or siblings who have invalid or missing data on sex or educational attainment are excluded. The resulting sample included 4,949 individuals and 16,497 transition records.

GRADE PROGRESSION IN THE UNITED STATES AND TAIWAN

Table 8.1 shows patterns and intercohort trends in levels of educational attainment and school continuation rates from the TWAF and GSS data. Average levels of attainment and continuation rates have grown dramatically during the twentieth century in both nations, although the United States is much further along in the spread of secondary and postsecondary education. In the United States, the increase in average levels of school completed has slowed in recent cohorts (Mare 1995), whereas Taiwan is still in a phase of rapid growth. In both societies, school attrition is substantial in the transition from high school completion to college attendance, but in Taiwan substantial attrition remains at the secondary level as well.

The most striking difference between the two societies lies in the educational inequalities between men and women. Average levels of attainment in the United States have been similar for men and women born throughout the twentieth century. Among cohorts born early in the century the distributions of schooling differ between men and women in their dispersion but not their mean. In those cohorts women have higher transition rates early in the schooling process and lower rates at the college level, resulting in a more compressed distribution among women compared to men. Thus in these cohorts a larger fraction of women than men achieved at least some education but a smaller fraction achieved the highest levels of education. In the more recent cohorts, this pattern largely disappears. Among the most recent cohorts, gender stratification in educational attainment is largely invisible in these data and is only revealed when one examines attainment patterns in specific postsecondary and graduate fields of study (Mare 1995).

In Taiwan, in contrast, gender inequality in educational attainment has declined, but still remains far greater than can be observed in the United States at any time in the twentieth century. Women born in the first half of

TABLE 8.1
Indicators of Educational Trends for Taiwan and the United States

	TAIWAN YEAR OF BIRTH				UNITED STATES YEAR OF BIRTH			
	1923–67	1923–45	1946–55	1956–67	1915–74	1915–34	1935–54	1955–74
Males								
Mean Years Attended	9.20	7.74	10.24	11.40	13.26	11.97	13.55	13.51
SD (Years Attended)	4.26	4.45	3.78	2.84	3.00	3.41	3.17	2.44
Transition 1*	0.938	0.875	0.993	1.000	0.944	0.847	0.942	0.986
Transition 2	0.599	0.451	0.657	0.901	0.882	0.806	0.899	0.892
Transition 3	0.756	0.726	0.793	0.722	0.588	0.430	0.616	0.612
Transition 4	0.457	0.476	0.474	0.385	0.561	0.634	0.616	0.490
Total Observations	3,502	1,668	1,378	456	2,408	419	1,003	986
Females								
Mean Years Attended	7.53	4.45	7.99	10.05	13.22	12.05	13.47	13.55
SD (Years Attended)	4.41	4.04	3.99	3.28	2.69	2.93	2.69	2.40
Transition 1	0.844	0.610	0.922	0.983	0.959	0.874	0.972	0.988
Transition 2	0.511	0.252	0.437	0.758	0.882	0.830	0.903	0.885
Transition 3	0.697	0.593	0.757	0.679	0.579	0.403	0.582	0.646
Transition 4	0.306	0.241	0.385	0.259	0.505	0.503	0.525	0.488
Total Observations	3,801	1,188	1,434	1,179	2,655	517	1,061	1,077

*Transitions for Taiwan are (1) completes 6+, (2) completes 9+ given completes 6+, (3) completes 12+ given completes 9+, (4) completes 13+ given completes 12+. Transitions for United States are: (1) completes 9+, (2) completes 12+ given completes 9+, (3) completes 13+ given completes 12+, (4) completes 16+ given completes 13+. For further discussion see text.

SOURCES: 1989 Taiwan Women and Family Survey and 1994 General Social Survey.

the century average almost three years of schooling less than their male counterparts, a gap that has been cut by about half in the most recent cohorts represented in the TWAF data. In the most recent cohorts, school continuation rates for women are similar to those of men at the elementary level, but still lag substantially at the secondary and postsecondary levels. These patterns imply that for the parents of TWAF respondents the differences in educational attainments of mothers and fathers are very large. Overall, the much greater inequality between men and women in educational attainment in Taiwan compared to the United States suggests that more general patterns of educational stratification, including the effects of parents' socioeconomic characteristics and other aspects of family life may vary between male and female children in Taiwan in ways that we do not see in the United States.

THE EFFECT OF PARENTS' SCHOOLING ON THE SCHOOL TRANSITIONS OF SONS AND DAUGHTERS

The Effects of Parents' School Transitions

Before examining the effects of sex and family size on schooling, we consider first a set of models that include only the effects of mother's and father's schooling on offspring's schooling. These models show the basic form of the relationships between parents' and offsprings' schooling and the effects of parental school transitions net of the well-known linear effects of parents' schooling on their sons' and daughters' odds of school progression. Table 8.2 summarizes the fit of these models, which vary in whether they incorporate unrestricted discrete effects of mother's and father's schooling, linear effects, and effects of whether mother and father make the transition that is faced by their son or daughter.[9] The models also vary by whether these effects are proportional—that is, invariant across offsprings' school transitions—or nonproportional—that is, they depend on the school transition of interest.

Model 1.1 allows for nonproportional, unrestricted discrete effects of mother's and father's schooling. Inasmuch as all of the other models of mother's and father's schooling effects that we consider are nested within this unrestricted model, it is a useful baseline for comparison. It also shows whether the data are broadly consistent with the hypothesis that parents' schooling levels set floors under the attainments of their offspring. Figures 8.1a through 8.1d plot these unrestricted effects separately for mother's and

TABLE 8.2

Fit of Models of Mother's and Father's Schooling Effects

	PARAMETERIZATION OF PARENTS' SCHOOLING EFFECTS					TAIWAN			UNITED STATES		
Model	Discrete Effects	Linear Effects	Parent Transition Effects	Missing Data Effects	df	Log Likelihood	G^2 vs. 1.1	BIC	Log Likelihood	G^2 vs. 1.1	BIC
1.1	Varying	No	No	Varying	0	−52,286	0	0	−6,274	0	0
1.2	No	No	No	No	40	−58,737	12,902	12,451	−6,951	1,355	966
1.3	Constant	No	No	Constant	30	−53,411	2,250	1,914	−6,385	223	−68
1.4	Constant	No	Constant	Constant	28	−52,834	1,096	784	−6,321	95	−177
1.5	Constant	No	Varying	Varying	16	−52,598	623	450	−6,285	23	−132
1.6	No	Varying	No	Varying	24	−52,393	213	−53	−6,339	131	−103
1.7	No	Constant	No	Constant	36	−53,448	2,324	1,919	−6,404	261	−89
1.8	No	Varying	Varying	Varying	16	−52,323	73	−100	−6,286	25	−130
1.9	No	Constant	Constant	Constant	34	−52,984	1,396	1,014	−6,327	106	−224
1.10	No	Varying	Constant	Varying	22	−52,338	103	−139	−6,295	43	−171
1.11	No	Constant	Varying	Varying	22	−52,668	763	521	−6,296	44	−170

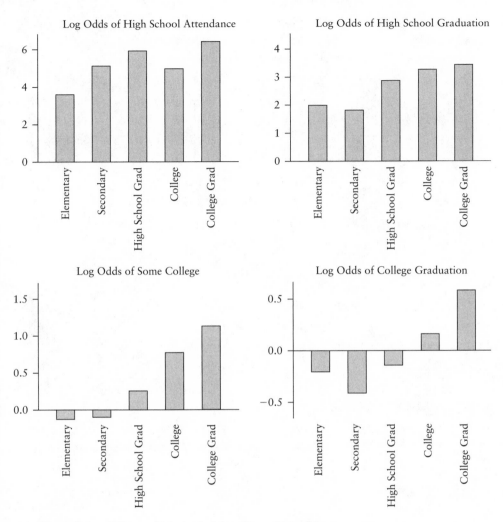

Figure 8.1a   Effects of Mother's Schooling—United States

father's schooling. These discrete effects show the general monotonic relationship between parents' and offsprings' schooling that is typically captured
in the linear effects of parents' schooling. In addition, in many of these figures,
the largest discrete contrast in the log odds of making a given school transition by a son or daughter is between those whose parents who have and have
not made that transition themselves. For example, in the United States, the
effects of mother's schooling are both monotonically positive and also show

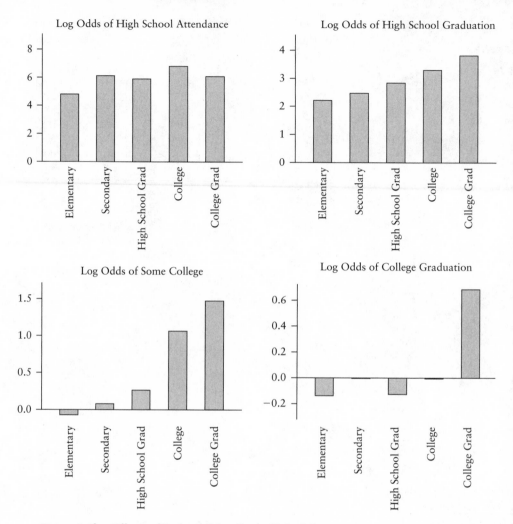

Figure 8.1b   Effects of Father's Schooling—United States

distinct upward steps between the adjacent levels of mother's schooling that correspond to the offspring's school transition in question. For fathers, there is one exception to this pattern—at high school graduation where the effect of father's schooling is purely linear—but there is an unmistakable father's transition effect at the other three transitions. For Taiwan, the evidence for a parent's transition effect is weaker, although whether the mother or the father has attended college has an unusually large impact on the transition to college

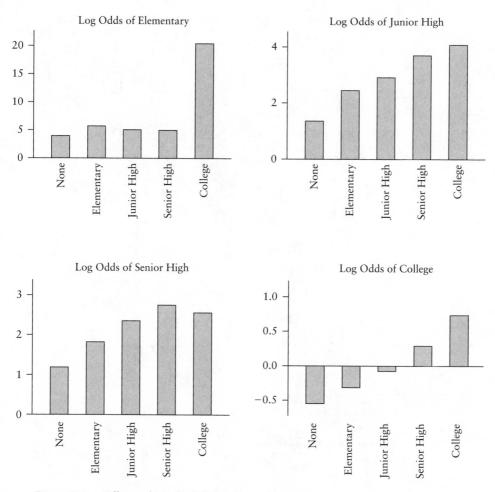

Figure 8.1c Effects of Mother's Schooling—Taiwan

for offspring. Whether the Taiwan data are consistent with the general hypothesis of parental transition effects requires more specific analyses. On balance, however, for both the United States and Taiwan, we see enough evidence of transition effects in the data to motivate a more systematic investigation.

The statistics of relative fit in Table 8.2 suggest that both a linear and a parental transition component are necessary and sufficient to summarize the unrestricted effects of mother's and father's schooling.[10] By the Bayesian Information Criterion (BIC), the only models that fit better that the unrestricted model for Taiwan are the three that allow for nonproportional

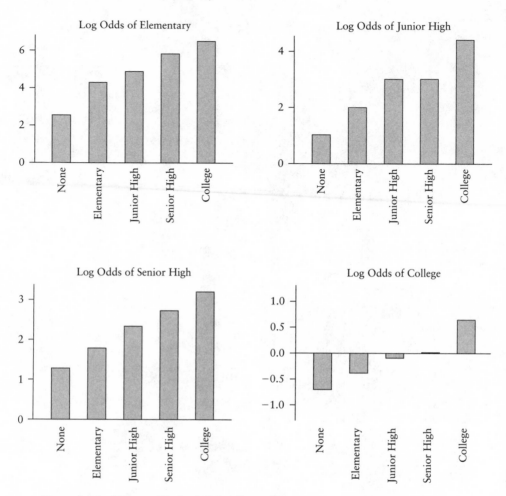

Figure 8.1d   Effects of Father's Schooling—Taiwan

linear effects of mother's and father's schooling on offspring's school transitions (1.6, 1.8, and 1.10). Among these three, the two that incorporate the effects of parents' transitions (1.8 and 1.10) fit better that the model that omits the transition effects (1.6), and the model that allows for proportional (transition invariant) effects of parents' school transitions fits the best of all (1.10). This conclusion is broadly supported by the log likelihood comparisons as well, although the very large sample for Taiwan, as well as the clustered nature of the data makes the likelihood statistics difficult to interpret.

For the United States, many more models fit better than the unrestricted model than for Taiwan, but models that incorporate the effects of parents' school transitions on offsprings' transitions (1.4, 1.5, and 1.8–1.11) fit better by the BIC than those that do not incorporate these effects (1.3, 1.6, and 1.7). Among the models that incorporate parental transition effects, those that specify those effects as proportional (1.4, 1.9, and 1.10) fit better than those that allow the transition effects to vary across offsprings' transitions (1.5, 1.8, and 1.11). These better fitting models vary in the specification of the linear effects of parental schooling. Although the evidence for nonproportional (varying over transitions) linear effects of parents' schooling is weak in these data, the model of nonproportional linear effects is consistent with both the Taiwan data and other studies for the United States (e.g., Mare 1980; Hout, Raftery, and Bell 1993).[11]

All of the parameters for model 1.10 are reported in Table 8.3 and those for the effects of fathers' school transitions are plotted in Figures 8.2a and 8.2b. For the United States and, to a lesser extent, for Taiwan as well, the effects of parental school transitions are substantial, even after the linear effects are taken into account. In the United States, averaged over all school transitions, if one's mother has made a given transition, the odds that one also makes that transition are about 65 percent higher than if one's mother did not make the transition. For fathers, the transition effect is about 85 percent. For Taiwan we also observe a substantial effect for fathers' transitions, but the estimated effect of mothers is statistically insignificant, a result consistent with the patterns shown in Figure 8.1c and possibly with the relatively lower status of women in Taiwanese families (Tsai 1998).

One can see the size of the parental transition effects by comparing them to the linear effects of parental educational attainment. In the United States, each year of mother's schooling multiplies the odds of attending high school by about 38 percent, indicating that the effect of whether the mother has made a given transition is equivalent to somewhat less than the linear effect of two years of mother's schooling. For the odds of graduating from high school, each year of a mother's schooling multiplies the odds by about 13 percent (1.378×0.817), indicating that the effect of whether the mother has made a given transition equals approximately four years of mother's schooling. These order of magnitude calculations—which yield even larger effects for fathers—suggest that whether parents complete specific school transitions are major influences on the educational attainments of their sons and daughters.

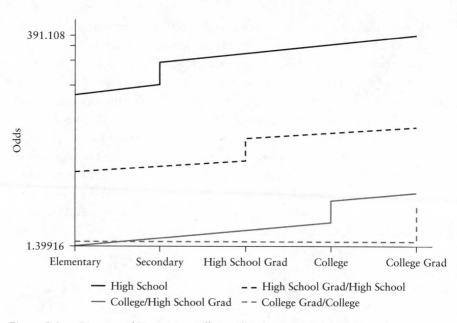

Figure 8.2a   Linear and Transition Effects of Father's Schooling—United States

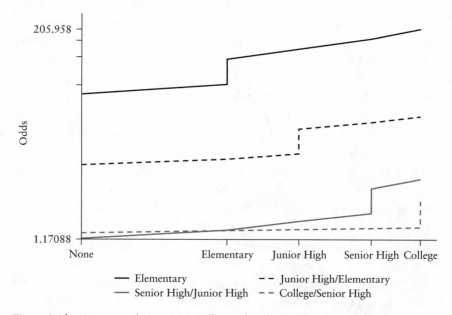

Figure 8.2b   Linear and Transition Effects of Father's Schooling—Taiwan

TABLE 8.3
Effects of Mother's and Father's Schooling
on Odds of Making School Transitions

Variable	TAIWAN		UNITED STATES	
	exp(β)	|z(β)|	exp(β)	|z(β)|
(Tr1)				
Tr2	0.143	41.5	1.956	0.9
Tr3	0.281	22.7	0.334	1.5
Tr4	0.077	38.7	1.241	0.9
Mother's Schooling (Linear)	1.250	5.7	1.378	3.8
MS × Tr2	0.961	1.1	0.817	2.4
MS × Tr3	0.892	2.9	0.793	2.8
MS × Tr4	0.845	4.2	0.758	3.3
Father's Schooling (Linear)	1.250	12.0	1.132	1.5
FS × Tr2	0.941	−3.4	0.951	0.6
FS × Tr3	0.878	−7.0	0.982	0.2
FS × Tr4	0.850	−8.4	0.899	1.3
Mother Made Transition	1.235	1.3	1.648	5.1
Father Made Transition	1.508	6.1	1.859	5.9
Log Likelihood	−52,338		−6,295	
N	104,540		16,497	

NOTE: Effects are based on Model 1.10 in Table 8.2. Models also include indicators for missing data on mother's and father's schooling and for interactions between missing data indicators and categorical variables for transition.

Parents' Transitions and Gender Stratification

To see whether parents' educational attainment and specifically parents' school transitions affect sons and daughters differently, we incorporate sex and its interactions with parents schooling into model 1.10 of Table 8.2. Table 8.4 reports fit statistics for a variety of specifications of the sex effects relative to a model that allows unrestricted interactions of gender with each of the effects contained in model 1.10. The overall pattern of model fit differs dramatically between Taiwan and the United States. For the United States, by the BIC, the best fitting model contains no sex effects at all (2.2). Using the informal likelihood ratio test criterion, the only significant sex

TABLE 8.4

Fit of Models of Sex Interactions with Mother's and Father's Schooling Effects

| | PARAMETERIZATION OF SEX EFFECTS | | | | | | TAIWAN | | | UNITED STATES | | |
	Main Effect of Sex	Interaction with Transition Effects	Interaction with Linear Effects	Interaction with Parent Transitions	Interaction with Missing Data Effects	df	Log Likelihood	G² vs. 2.1	BIC	Log Likelihood	G² vs. 2.1	BIC
Model												
2.1	Yes	Yes	Yes	Yes	Yes	0	−51,328	0	0	−6,281	0	0
2.2 (1.10)	No	No	No	No	No	22	−52,338	2,020	1,765	−6,295	28	−186
2.3	Yes	No	No	No	No	21	−51,453	249	6	−6,295	27	−177
2.4	Yes	Yes	No	No	No	18	−51,364	70	−138	−6,289	16	−159
2.5	Yes	Yes	No	Yes	Yes	14	−51,351	44	−117	−6,287	13	−123
2.6	Yes	Yes	Yes	Yes	Yes	12	−51,347	37	−102	−6,286	11	−106
2.7	Yes	Yes	Yes	No	Yes	14	−51,351	46	−116	−6,287	11	−125
2.8	Yes	Yes	No	No	Yes	16	−51,361	66	−119	−6,288	13	−142

effect is for the interaction with transition; that is, the difference in the log odds of making school transitions between men and women may vary across school transitions. As suggested by Table 8.1, transition rates do vary between the sexes in cohorts born in the early part of the century, although not in more recent cohorts.

For Taiwan, in contrast to the United States, all models that incorporate sex effects improve fit over the model that does not (2.2). By the BIC, model 2.4, which includes only a nonproportional effect of gender is the best fitting model, although the differences in fit among models 2.4–2.8 are small. By the informal likelihood ratio criterion, in contrast, virtually all of the sex effects are significant. Although the BIC statistic suggests that a simple model of transition-specific main effects of sex is appropriate for Taiwan, we nonetheless focus on the parameters of model 2.6, which also allows for proportional effects of the interactions of gender with parents' highest year of school completed and with whether parents' have completed the given school transition.[12] Table 8.5 reports the parameters of this model for Taiwan and the United States and Figures 8.3a–8.3d plot the predicted log odds from this model for Taiwan.

As implied by the fit statistics, the process of educational stratification is largely independent of sex in the United States, except for variation in the effects of gender across school transitions. In particular, compared to men, women are more likely to make the early school transitions and less likely to make the later transitions. There is, however, no evidence of sex differences in the effects of parents' schooling on offsprings' schooling.

In Taiwan, in contrast, women are disadvantaged at every school transition, although the effect is especially large at the transition into elementary school. Moreover, the effects of parents' schooling vary substantially with not only the sex of offspring but also the sex of parent. As shown above, whether a Taiwanese father has made a given school transition affects his children's transitions much more strongly than whether the mother has made the transition. The estimates in Table 8.5 show that this effect is much larger for sons than for daughters. For a son, the odds of making a transition increase by about 80 percent if his father has made that transition but only by about 40 percent ($\approx 1.835 \times 0.779 - 1.0$) for a daughter. Whether or not a mother has made a transition does not significantly affect either her son's or her daughter's odds of school continuation. Unlike for the United States, the linear effects of parents' schooling on their children's school

TABLE 8.5
Effects of Mother's and Father's Schooling and Sex
on Odds of Making School Transitions

Variable	TAIWAN		UNITED STATES	
	exp(β)	|z(β)|	exp(β)	|z(β)|
(Tr1)				
Tr2	0.108	38.6	3.289	2.5
Tr3	0.181	25.8	0.687	3.0
Tr4	0.053	39.5	21.206	2.9
Mother's Schooling (Linear)	1.249	5.4	1.351	3.5
MS × Tr2	0.960	1.0	0.814	2.5
MS × Tr3	0.890	2.9	0.789	2.9
MS × Tr4	0.847	4.0	0.754	3.3
Father's Schooling (Linear)	1.273	12.3	1.138	1.5
FS × Tr2	0.937	3.5	0.952	0.6
FS × Tr3	0.871	7.2	0.983	0.2
FS × Tr4	0.845	8.5	0.901	1.3
Mother Made Transition	1.146	0.7	1.896	2.3
Father Made Transition	1.835	6.4	2.048	2.3
Female (vs. Male)	0.388	22.4	1.093	0.2
Fem. × Tr2	1.405	6.8	0.719	1.6
Fem. × Tr3	1.910	10.7	0.636	2.1
Fem. × Tr4	1.402	4.9	0.501	2.9
Fem. × Mother's Schooling (Linear)	1.017	2.1	1.045	1.3
Fem. × Father's Schooling (Linear)	0.986	2.1	0.988	0.4
Fem. × Mother Made Transition	1.068	0.4	0.914	0.5
Fem. × Father Made Transition	0.779	2.7	0.937	0.3
Log Likelihood	−51,347		−6,286	
N	104,540		16,497	

NOTE: Estimates are for Model 2.6 in Table 8.4. Models also include indicators for missing data on mother's and father's schooling and for interactions between missing data indicators and transition and sex.

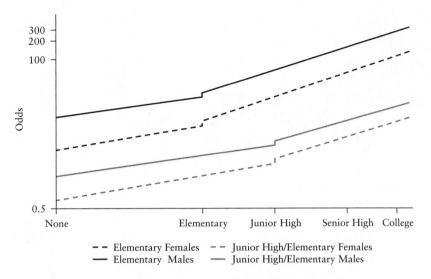

Figure 8.3a   Linear and Step Effects of Mother's Schooling by Sex—Taiwan

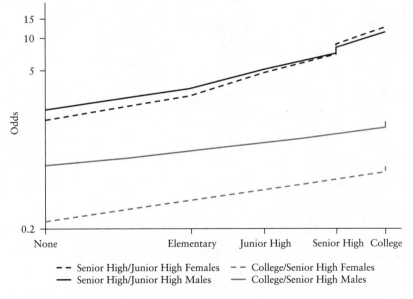

Figure 8.3b   Linear and Step Effects of Mother's Schooling by Sex—Taiwan

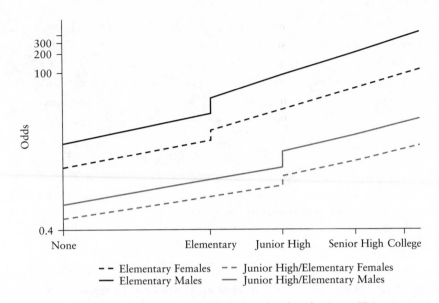

Figure 8.3c   Linear and Step Effects of Father's Schooling by Sex—Taiwan

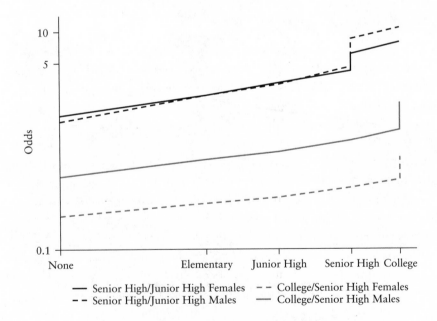

Figure 8.3d   Linear and Step Effects of Father's Schooling by Sex—Taiwan

progression also vary between men and women, but these differences are small. A year of mother's schooling raises a daughter's school continuation odds by about 2 percent more than a son's odds, whereas a year of father's schooling raises a daughter's odds by about 2 percent less than a son's odds. The much more important way that the intergenerational transmission of educational attainment differs between men and women is through the sex difference in how the floor effect of parental schooling occurs. Unlike the relatively gender neutral regime of educational stratification in the United States, in Taiwan it is fathers and not mothers who ensure that their offspring go at least as far as they do in school and they enforce this norm more rigidly for their sons than for their daughters.

Parents' Transitions and the Effects of Sibship Size

To see whether variations in sibship size constrain the effect of parents' school transitions on their children's schooling, we enhance model 2.6 with measures of number of siblings and their interactions with gender and parents' educational attainment. Table 8.6 presents fit statistics for these models. In the United States sibship size negatively effects school progression and, by the BIC, a model that includes a simple linear effect fits the best. In Taiwan, the data suggest a more complex pattern of sibling effects. First, a discrete rather than linear pattern of parameters improves the fit of the model, suggesting nonlinearity in the effect of sibship size (model 3.4 versus 3.3). Second, although the effect of sibship size does not vary significantly between men and women (3.6 and 3.7 versus 3.4), it does vary across school transitions (3.5) and with parents' educational attainment (3.8–3.10). Among the latter three models, the smallest BIC value for Taiwan is for model 3.9 in which the effects of parents' school transitions vary linearly with sibship size.[13] Table 8.7 shows the parameters of this model for Taiwan and the United States and Figures 8.4a and 8.4b show the key effects for Taiwan.

For the United States, the odds of school continuation decrease monotonically with sibship size, but no other sibship size effects are statistically significant. For Taiwan, in contrast, the odds of school continuation increase with sibship size to a maximum for sibships of size four and then subside. Of greater interest is the interaction between the effects of sibship size and whether or not parents have made given school transitions. As shown above, in Taiwan fathers' transitions but not those of mothers affect the school continuation of their children. Table 8.7 shows, however, that *for only children,*

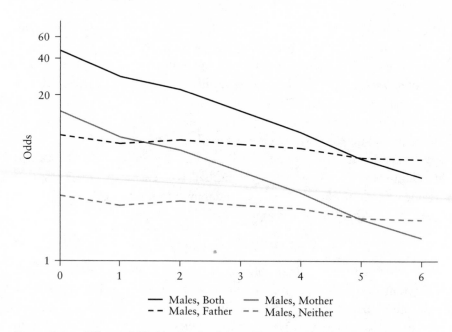

Figure 8.4a Effects of Sibship Size by Parent Transitions—Taiwan Males

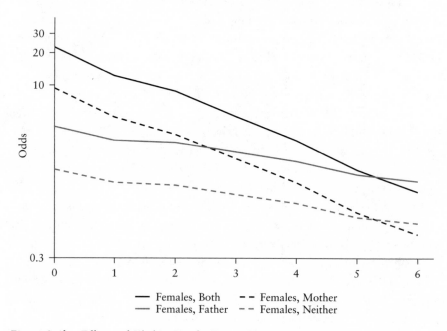

Figure 8.4b Effects of Sibship Size by Parent Transitions—Taiwan Females

TABLE 8.6
Fit of Models of Sibship Size Interactions with Mother's and Father's Schooling and Sex Effects

	PARAMETERIZATION OF SIBLING EFFECTS							TAIWAN			UNITED STATES		
Model	Main Effect	Interaction with Transition	Interaction with Sex	Interaction with Linear Effects	Interaction with Parent Transitions	Interaction with Missing Data	df	Log Likelihood	G^2 vs. 3.1	BIC	Log Likelihood vs. 3.1	G^2 vs. 3.1	BIC
3.1	Discrete	Discrete	Discrete	Discrete	Discrete	Discrete	0	−51,057	0	0	−6,091	0	0
3.2 (2.6)	No	No	No	No	No	No	218	−51,347	580	−1,939	−6,286	391	−1,726
3.3	Linear	No	No	No	No	No	217	−51,248	382	−2,126	−6,250	319	−1,788
3.4	Discrete	No	No	No	No	No	211	−51,210	287	−2,152	−6,240	299	−1,750
3.5	Discrete	Linear	No	No	No	No	208	−51,171	228	−2,176	−6,233	285	−1,735
3.6	Discrete	Linear	Yes	No	No	No	207	−51,170	228	−2,165	−6,233	285	−1,726
3.7	Discrete	Linear	Yes	No	No	Linear	206	−51,168	222	−2,159	−6,232	282	−1,718
3.8	Discrete	Linear	No	Linear	No	Linear	204	−51,140	167	−2,191	−6,224	267	−1,714
3.9	Discrete	Linear	No	No	Linear	Linear	204	−51,135	157	−2,201	−6,231	280	−1,701
3.10	Discrete	Linear	No	Linear	Linear	Linear	202	−51,126	139	−2,195	−6,221	261	−1,701

TABLE 8.7
Effects of Mother's and Father's Schooling, Sex, and Number of Siblings
on Odds of Making School Transitions

Variable	TAIWAN		UNITED STATES	
	exp(β)	|z(β)|	exp(β)	|z(β)|
(Tr1)				
Tr2	0.188	13.6	2.100	0.9
Tr3	0.198	11.8	0.864	1.8
Tr4	0.051	20.0	0.876	0.2
Mother's Schooling (Linear)	1.262	5.7	1.322	3.2
MS × Tr2	0.944	1.5	0.816	2.4
MS × Tr3	0.877	3.3	0.800	2.6
MS × Tr4	0.834	4.3	0.765	3.1
Father's Schooling (Linear)	1.281	12.5	1.116	1.3
FS × Tr2	0.930	4.0	0.955	0.5
FS × Tr3	0.863	7.6	0.995	0.1
FS × Tr4	0.837	8.8	0.914	1.1
Mother Made Transition	4.948	3.2	1.888	3.7
Father Made Transition	3.152	6.2	2.120	4.1
Female (vs. Male)	0.387	22.4	1.045	0.1
Fem. × Tr2	1.419	6.9	0.715	1.6
Fem. × Tr3	1.912	10.7	0.627	2.1
Fem. × Tr4	1.397	4.9	0.492	3.0
Fem. × Mother's Schooling (Linear)	1.017	2.0	1.048	1.4
Fem. × Father's Schooling (Linear)	0.986	2.0	0.989	0.3
Fem. × Mother Made Transition	1.125	0.6	0.926	0.4
Fem. × Father Made Transition	0.783	2.6	0.918	0.5
(0 Sibs)				
1 Sib	0.930	0.5	0.719	2.2
2 Sibs	1.131	0.9	0.504	5.4
3 Sibs	1.170	1.1	0.411	6.2
4 Sibs	1.218	1.3	0.376	4.6
5 Sibs	1.145	0.8	0.389	0.2
6+ Sibs	1.022	0.1	0.285	2.5

(continued)

TABLE 8.7
(*continued*)

Variable	TAIWAN		UNITED STATES	
	exp(β)	|z(β)|	exp(β)	|z(β)|
Sibs × Tr2	0.894	4.9	1.011	0.2
Sibs × Tr3	0.979	0.8	1.094	1.7
Sibs × Tr4	1.007	0.3	1.109	1.8
Sibs × Mother Made Transition	0.723	3.2	0.973	0.8
Sibs × Father Made Transition	0.889	3.1	0.974	0.7
Log Likelihood	−51,135		−6,231	
N	104,540		16,497	

NOTE: Estimates are for Model 3.9 in Table 8.6. Models also include indicators for missing data on mother's and father's schooling and for interactions between missing data indicators and transition, sex, and number of siblings.

both parents' transitions have substantial positive effects on the odds that their children will make the corresponding school transitions. (For a male only child, if his mother made a transition, their odds of making that transition are nearly five times greater than if she did not; if his father made a transition their odds of making that transition are more than three times greater than if he did not.) The coefficients for the interaction between parents' transitions and the linear effect of sibship size indicate that this large effect changes as sibships grow, albeit at different rates for the mother's and father's effects and for sons and daughters. As illustrated in Figures 8.4a and 8.4b, whereas the effect of mother's school transitions declines dramatically as the number children increases, the decline in the effect of father's transitions is much more modest. What decline does occur for fathers, moreover, is confined to their daughters. In short, sibship size is not an obstacle to sons achieving at least as much schooling as their fathers. Daughters, however, find it much harder to make the same transitions as their mothers and only have a large chance of doing so when they come from small families.

Our analyses show that whether or not parents make a given school transition has a large positive effect on the probabilities that their sons or daughters make that transition themselves. In this sense families do much to ensure that parents' educational attainment sets a floor on the attainments of offspring. The comparison between Taiwan and the United States illustrates the diverse ways that this floor effect can work. For the United States the effect of parents' transitions is pervasive and largely independent of the sex of the parent, the sex of the offspring, or family size. For Taiwan, the effect of parents' school transitions is interdependent with the regime of gender inequality in family life and educational attainment. The parent transition effect is a key mechanism through which fathers facilitate the educational attainments of their sons. Whether mothers can benefit their offspring or daughters can benefit from their parents' school transitions is much more contingent on family resources.

CONCLUSION

Although we have learned much about educational stratification from statistical models of the linear effect of parents' schooling on offsprings' school transitions, such models leave out an important part of the process. Parents do indeed try to have their children go at least as far in school as they do, which results in a clear nonlinear effect. This effect of parental schooling greatly improves the fit of our models to standard data on the association between parents' and offsprings' schooling. More important, this effect appears to be sensitive to cultural differences in educational stratification in a particularly revealing way. Gender inequalities in levels of educational attainment are small in the United States and overall differences in the education distributions of men and women have disappeared. In other societies, such as Taiwan, inequalities in how girls and women are treated in the family and in ultimate educational attainment remain large. Whereas these societal differences do not affect the linear effects of parents' schooling on the school progression of their offspring, they do show up in how the two societies implement the norm that children match or surpass their parents' attainment. In the United States, this is a large, pervasive effect that is independent of the sex of parent, sex of offspring, and family resource constraints. But in Taiwan this effect is mainly confined to the school attainments of fathers and its benefit goes mainly to sons. These results suggest that the presence or absence of the effects of whether parents make school transitions can provide concrete clues about important variations in how educational stratification works.

This nonlinear effect of parents' school transitions is straightforward to estimate with the typical data that we use to study educational stratification and, in the future, should be estimated in a wide variety of nations. More work is also needed on how this effect comes about and its implications. It remains to investigate whether parents set a floor under the attainments of all of their children or are more concerned that selected children achieve this goal. Our results suggest that in Taiwan, this goal is more important for sons than daughters, but there are other bases of intrafamily educational stratification than sex, such as birth order, academic ability, and other characteristics of children. Additionally, several other issues are related to the effects of whether parents make school transitions on their offsprings' schooling. These issues include whether the effects of parents' school transitions depend on the sex composition of a sibship, whether the effects vary by birth order, whether in multiple child families parents are more likely to require every child to achieve the parents' schooling level or to require that *at least one* child achieve the parents' schooling level, and whether the tendency for parents to set a floor under their children's schooling has strengthened or weakened over successive cohorts of children and parents. A further issue is whether parents' educational attainment is a "hard" floor for offspring's schooling—that is, the probability that offspring fall below their parents' level of schooling is not significantly different from zero—or simply has the sort of stochastic effect investigated in the present analysis. Finally, future research should also examine the role that the parent transition effect has played in secular educational growth. Incorporating parental transition effects into models of intercohort trends in educational growth may provide a more complete demographic explanation of changes in levels of educational attainment and grade progression and provide a better basis for forecasting the direction and momentum of educational change.

Notes

1. Earlier evidence for parent transition effects on offspring's school transitions is reported by Mare (1995) and, in an earlier, unpublished version of this paper by Mare and Chang (1998). More recent empirical investigations of this idea are provided by Need and De Jong (2001); Davies, Heinesen, and Holm (2002); and Breen and Yaish (this volume).

2. An interesting family of hypotheses not considered here is whether it is the maximum, the minimum, or some other function of the schooling of the two parents that exerts the biggest effect on offsprings' schooling.

3. These arguments assume that the number of siblings is predetermined with respect to parents' decisions to invest in children. Although this assumption is

common in most sociological investigations of these relationships, it is not maintained in many economic analyses of the family, which assume that parental investments in children are made jointly with decisions about how many children to have (Becker 1991).

4. Our preliminary analyses suggest that for both Taiwan and the United States, the effects of the sex composition on school continuation probabilities are negligible. Beyond the number of siblings, neither the main effect of sex composition, nor the interaction of sex composition and sex of individual child, nor the interaction of sex composition and whether or not mother or father has made a school transition has a significant effect on school continuation.

5. The transitions for Taiwan are the same as those used by Tsai and Chiu (1993) in their analysis of educational stratification in Taiwan.

6. The Taiwan Women and Family Survey was collected by William L. Parish, Ching-Hsi Chang, Ying-chuan Liu, and Ching-lung Tsay with the support of the National Institute of Child Health and Development (Grant Number: RO1 HD23322-01); the National Science Council, Republic of China; and the Ministry of the Interior, Republic of China. We are grateful to William Parish and staff of NORC for making the data available to us.

7. The TWAF survey ascertained whether respondents' siblings are older or younger than the respondents, but not their exact ages. Likewise, the survey ascertained whether husbands' siblings are older or younger than the husbands, but not their exact ages.

8. In a supplementary telephone interview with the randomly selected sibling, the Survey of American Families, obtained much more extensive information from the sibling. This information, however, is not used in the analyses reported in this chapter.

9. Models also include dummy variables for whether or not data are missing on mother's and father's schooling and, when interactions involving parents schooling are included in the model, analogous interactions with these missing data indicators.

10. The log likelihood and BIC comparisons in Table 8.3 and elsewhere in this chapter are informal. Whereas likelihood ratio tests assume simple random samples, these samples are clustered by sibship. Although we have adjusted the standard errors of coefficient estimates for clustering, we have not adjusted the likelihood and BIC statistics.

11. The superior fit of model 1.9 for the United States by the BIC is misleading because the relative fits of the models are influenced by the presence or absence of parameters for missing data on parents' schooling. Because some parental schooling effects are nonproportional in models 1.10 and 1.11 it is necessary to include nonproportional effects of these missing data indicators, which are largely insignificant. Because model 1.9 includes only proportional effects of parents' schooling, the missing data effects are specified as proportional. The contrasts among these models are almost entirely due to the absence of nonproportional missing data effects in model 1.9.

12. The superior fit of model 2.4 compared to models 2.5–2.7 is an artifact of restrictions on the insignificant effects of missing data indicators in 2.4, which must be included in the other models. When those indicators are included in 2.4, the BIC statistic is no longer clearly favorable relative to 2.5–2.7 (see model 2.8). The BIC statistics for 2.5–2.7 suggest that a gender interaction with either one but not both parental schooling indicators yields the best fitting model. However, because there may be important differences between interactions with mother's and father's schooling in Taiwan, we focus on model 2.6, which includes all of the parameters of potential interest.

13. Variants of models 3.5–3.10 that include nonlinear terms for sibship size interactions with sex, transition, and parents' schooling do not improve the fit over these linear specifications.

References

Allison, Paul D. 1982. "Discrete-Time Methods for the Analysis of Event Histories." *Sociological Methodology 1982* (12):61–98.

Becker, Gary S. 1991. *A Treatise on the Family*, 2nd ed. Cambridge, MA: Harvard University Press.

Blake, Judith. 1989. *Family Size and Achievement*. Berkeley: University of California Press.

Blau, Peter M., and Otis Dudley Duncan. 1967. *The American Occupational Structure*. New York: Wiley.

Boudon, Raymond. 1974. *Education, Opportunity, and Social Inequality*. New York: Wiley.

Breen, Richard, and John H. Goldthorpe. 1997. "Explaining Educational Differentials: Towards a Formal Rational Action Theory." *Rationality and Society* 9:275–305.

Breen, Richard, and Jan O. Jonsson. 2000. "Analyzing Educational Careers: A Multinomial Transition Model." *American Sociological Review* 65: 754–72.

Davies, Richard, Eskil Heinesen, and Anders Holm. 2002. "The Relative Risk Aversion Hypothesis." *Journal of Population Economics* 15:683–713.

Duncan, Beverly. 1965. *Family Factors and School Dropout: 1920–1960*. Ann Arbor, University of Michigan Cooperative Research Project No. 2258, U.S. Office of Education.

———. 1967. "Education and Social Background." *American Journal of Sociology* 72:363–72.

———. 1968. "Trends in the Output and Distribution of Schooling." In *Indicators of Social Change*, edited by E. B. Sheldon and W. E. Moore. New York: Russell Sage Foundation.

Easterlin, Richard A. 1968. *Population, Labor Force, and Long Swings in Economic Growth: The American Experience*. New York: Columbia University Press.

Erikson, Robert, and John H. Goldthorpe. 1992. *The Constant Flux: A Study of Class Mobility in Industrial Societies*. Oxford: Clarendon.

Hauser, Robert M., and David L. Featherman. 1976. "Equality of Schooling: Trends and Prospects." *Sociology of Education* 49:99–120.

Hout, Michael. 1988. "More Universalism, Less Structural Mobility: The American Occupational Structure in the 1980s." *American Journal of Sociology* 93: 1358–1400.

Hout, Michael, and Robert M. Hauser. 1992. "Symmetry and Hierarchy in Social Mobility: A Methodological Analysis of the CASMIN Model of Class Mobility." *European Sociological Review* 8:239–66.

Hout, Michael, Adrian Raftery, and Eleanor O. Bell. 1993. "Making the Grade: Educational Stratification in the United States." Pp. 25–50 in *Persistent Inequality: Changing Educational Stratification in Thirteen Countries*, edited by Y. Shavit and H.-P. Blossfeld. Boulder, CO: Westview.

Kalbfleisch, John, and Ross Prentice. 1980. *The Statistical Analysis of Failure Time Data*. New York: John Wiley.

Kahl, Joseph A. 1957. "Educational and Occupational Aspirations of 'Common Man' Boys." *Harvard Educational Review* 23:186–203.

Mare, Robert D. 1980. "Social Background and School Continuation Decisions." *Journal of the American Statistical Association* 75:295–305.

———. 1981a. "Change and Stability in Educational Stratification." *American Sociological Review* 46:72–87.

———. 1981b. "Market and Institutional Sources of Educational Growth." Pp. 205–45 in *Research in Social Stratification and Mobility* 1, edited by Donald J. Treiman and Robert V. Robinson. Greenwich, CT: JAI.

———. 1995. "Changes in Educational Attainment and School Enrollment." Pp. 155–213 in *State of the Union: America in the 1990s*, edited by R. Farley. Vol. I: Economic Trends. New York: Russell Sage Foundation.

Mare, Robert D., and Meichu D. Chen. 1986. "Further Evidence on Number of Siblings and Educational Stratification." *American Sociological Review* 51: 403–12.

Mare, Robert D., and Huey-Chi Chang. 1998. "Family Strategies and Educational Attainment Norms in Taiwan and the United States: Some New Models for Educational Stratification." Presented to Research Committee on Social Stratification and Mobility of the International Sociological Association, Taipei.

Need, Ariana, and Uulkje De Jong. 2001. "Educational Differentials in the Netherlands: Testing Rational Action Theory." *Rationality and Society* 13:71–83.

Parish, William L., and Robert J. Willis. 1993. "Daughters, Education, and Family Budgets: Taiwan Experiences." *Journal of Human Resources* 28:763–98.

Shavit, Yossi, and Hans-Peter Blossfeld. 1993. *Persistent Inequality: A Comparative Analysis of Educational Stratification in Thirteen Countries*. Boulder, CO: Westview.

Sheridan, Jennifer. 2001. "Getting the College Education That I Didn't Get: The Effects of Parent's Unrealized Educational Aspirations on Children's Educational Outcomes." Unpublished Paper. Center for Demography and Ecology. University of Wisconsin-Madison.

Sewell, William H., Archibald O. Haller, and Alejandro Portes. 1969. "The Educational and Early Occupational Attainment Process." *American Sociological Review* 34:82–92.

Sewell, William H., and Robert M. Hauser. 1975. *Education, Occupation, and Earnings: Achievement in the Early Career.* New York: Academic Press.

StataCorp. 2003. *Stata Statistical Software Release 8.0.* College Station, TX: Stata Corporation.

Thomas, Duncan. 1994. "Like Father, Like Son; Like Mother, Like Daughter: Parental Resources and Child Height." *Journal of Human Resources* 19:950–88.

Tsai, Shu-Ling. 1998. "Families and Social Stratification in Taiwan: Three Hypotheses Proposed for a Survey Module." Pp. 350–93 in Proceedings of the Conference on Social Stratification and Mobility: Newly Industrializing Economies Compared, Vol. II. Taipei: Institute of Sociology, Academia Sinica.

Tsai, Shu-Ling, and Hei-Yuan Chiu. 1993. "Changes in Educational Stratification in Taiwan." Pp. 193–227 in *Persistent Inequality: Changing Educational Stratification in Thirteen Countries*, edited by Y. Shavit and H.-P. Blossfeld. Boulder, CO: Westview.

Vermunt, Jeroen K. 1997. *Log-Linear Models for Event Histories.* Thousand Oaks, CA: Sage.

CHAPTER NINE

Testing the Breen-Goldthorpe Model of Educational Decision Making

Richard Breen and Meir Yaish

In 1997, Richard Breen and John Goldthorpe (henceforth B&G) published a model of educational decision making that sought to explain why differentials in educational attainment between young people from different social classes changed rather little, if at all, over the greater part of the twentieth century. The central mechanism that B&G used to account for this is "relative risk aversion": that is, young people (and their families) have, as their major educational goal, the acquisition of a level of education that will allow them to attain a class position at least as good as that of their family of origin. Some subsequent studies have found support for this argument (Need and deJong 2001; Davies, Heinesen, and Holm 2002). Another (Schizzerotto 1997) has applied the model to explain cross-national differences in average levels of educational attainment. In this chapter we first reformulate the B&G model as a more general model of decision making when students are faced with a sequence of risky choices. One result of this reformulation is that some of the assumptions made by B&G prove to be unnecessary and so their model has wider applicability than might have appeared. The reformulated model is then tested using the case for which it seems most likely to apply: namely men (cf. B&G 1997:296) in England and Wales.

WHAT NEEDS TO BE EXPLAINED?

The starting point for the B&G model is the volume edited by Shavit and Blossfeld (1993). This volume comprised studies of thirteen countries: the

Thanks to John Goldthorpe, to participants at the RC28 meeting at New York University, August 2003, and to the editors and their referees, for comments on an earlier version.

United States, Germany, the Netherlands, Sweden, Britain, Italy, Switzerland, Taiwan, Japan, Czechoslovakia, Hungary, Poland, and Israel. In all cases, retrospective data, collected mainly in the 1980s, were used to measure the extent of class and gender inequality in educational attainment in successive age cohorts born during the first two-thirds of the twentieth century.[1] The major findings were that, notwithstanding substantial expansion of educational systems during the century, particularly at the lower secondary level, in only Sweden and the Netherlands (and, possibly, West Germany) was any clear reduction found in the strength of the association between social class origins and educational attainment. Blossfeld and Shavit (1993:19) conclude that "there has been *little change in socioeconomic inequality of educational opportunity*" (1993:21, italics in original). This conclusion echoed, to a large extent, earlier findings from the United States (Featherman and Hauser 1978), France (Garnier and Raffalovich 1984), the Netherlands (Dronkers 1983), Britain (Halsey, Heath, and Ridge 1980), and elsewhere.[2] It contrasted with the position with respect to gender: ten of the countries had data on both men and women and in all of them there was "a substantial reduction" in male/female differences in attainment.

CONSTANCY OF CLASS DIFFERENTIALS VIA RELATIVE RISK AVERSION[3]

The B&G model was developed in order to explain the constancy of class inequalities over time as these derive from what Boudon (1974) calls "secondary effects." Primary effects are those that give rise to an association between social origins and children's academic ability: their explanation lies outside the B&G model. Secondary effects then come into play to account for educational choices conditional on differences in demonstrated ability or performance. The model is therefore concerned with why children of similar abilities but different class backgrounds are observed to make different educational choices (B&G 1997:277). It has three main elements. First is the structure of the decision problem. B&G argue that within all educational systems there exist points at which young people face the choice of pursuing a more risky or a less risky option. The examples they give are the choice of an academic (risky) *versus* a vocational (less risky) track; and the choice of continuing to a further educational level rather than leaving the educational system. Risk arises because of the pattern of expected utilities of the different choices and because there exists the possibility that students who choose the more risky course may in fact fail to complete it.[4] Second, the ith student has a threshold, T_i that determines his or her minimum acceptable level of educational attainment. B&G define T_i to be a social class position at least as good as that from which the student originated. Third, each student has a belief about the probability of succeeding in each of the risky options. B&G call their subjective belief parameter π_i.

The B&G model can in fact be given a simpler and more parsimonious expression as follows. The educational system consists of a set of levels, $k = 1, \ldots K$, the first M of which are compulsory. At each level of postcompulsory education there are two terminal educational outcomes (henceforth *outcomes*). These outcomes are failing (F_k where k indicates the level of education); and leaving having succeeded and chosen not to continue to the next level, L_k. Failing, in this context, means not completing (or not completing satisfactorily) the kth level of education and so being unable to continue to the $k + 1$th level. These terminal educational outcomes can be ranked in terms of (expected) utility and this ranking is agreed on by all students: $U(L_k) > U(L_{k-1})$ and $U(F_k) > U(F_{k-1})$ for all k.

Students who fail at a given educational level must leave the educational system. Students who complete a given educational level have the choice of leaving the system at that point or continuing to the next level of education. Thus, the utility of succeeding at level k can be written:

$$U(S_k) = \max(U(L_k), V(k + 1))$$
(1)

where $U(S_k)$ is the expected utility of succeeding at level k and $V(k + 1)$ is the expected utility of continuing to level $k + 1$. V can be written:

$$V(k) = \pi_k U(S_k) + (1 - \pi_k)U(F_k)$$
(2)

where π_k is the student's subjective probability of succeeding at level k.[5]

The student's decision rule is that she continues to level k of the educational system if

$$V(k) > U(L_{k-1})$$
(3)

If this inequality is not met[6] the student leaves the educational system. $V(k)$ then depends on the returns to leaving the educational system at all higher levels and the subjective probabilities of succeeding at these higher levels.

Let $(r_1, \ldots, r_M)$ be a set of outcomes that are a (probabilistic) function of educational outcomes, L_k and F_k, $k = 1, \ldots, K$; and T_i be the outcome that acts as the threshold point for the ith student. For all outcomes with $U(r_m) \leq U(T)$, the change in utility, as a student moves to more preferred outcomes, is non-declining. For all outcomes having $U(r_m) > U(T)$ the marginal utility as a student moves to higher ranked outcomes, is declining.[7]

On what basis do students determine T? B&G assume that T is the securing of a class position equal to that of the student's family of origin and so T is defined in terms of labor market outcomes, which are themselves probabilistic functions of educational outcomes. In other cases T might simply be the highest level of education attained by one or other parent (as in Mare and Chang 1998; Need and deJong 2001; Davies, Heinesen, and Holm 2002). The central point is that, given a definition of T, the fact that students differ in where T is located implies that they will differ in their educational choices.

As an example of the application of the B&G model, we focus on the particular educational choice of staying in the system or leaving it as this is depicted in Figure 9.1 (reproduced from B&G 1997:280). Here there are three possible educational outcomes—P (stay and succeed), F (stay and fail), and L (leave immediately)—and each is associated with probabilities of gaining access to positions in three particular classes: Professionals, Managers, and Administrators (denoted S^* for service class), the working class (W^*) and the underclass (U^*).[8] These probabilities are denoted by α, β, and γ. Parameters subscripted 1 refer to the conditional probability of entering the service class; 2 to the conditional probability of entering the working class; and the conditional probability of entering the underclass is equal to one minus the sum of the other two parameter values. The α parameters relate to transitions to class positions among those who continue and succeed at a given educational level; β among those who fail; and γ those who choose not to continue to that level. B&G assume that continuing and succeeding is a sure way of avoiding the underclass (i.e., $\alpha_1 + \alpha_2 = 1$) though this is not a necessary feature of the model. B&G (1997:282) also impose four assumptions about the relative sizes of these conditional probabilities.[9]

1. $\alpha > \beta_1$ and $\alpha > \gamma_1$. It is generally believed that remaining at school and succeeding affords a better chance of access to the service class than does remaining at school and failing or leaving school.

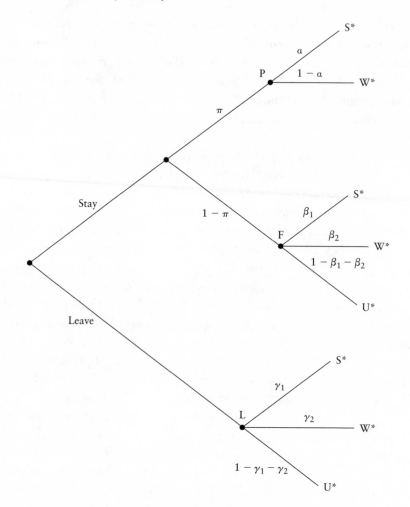

Figure 9.1. A Multiple Decision Tree

2. $\gamma_1 + \gamma_2 > \beta_1 + \beta_2$. Remaining at school and failing increases the chances of entering the underclass. This means that there is a risk involved in choosing to continue to the next level of education.

3. $\gamma_2 > \gamma_1$; $(\gamma_2/\gamma_1) \geq (\beta_2/\beta_1)$. Students who leave immediately have a better chance of access to the working than to the service class. The odds of entering the service rather than the working class are at least as good for those who leave immediately as for those who fail.

4. $\alpha > 0.5$. Staying in education and succeeding makes entry to the service class more likely than entry to the working class.

We now show that the definition of T, given above, together with the assumptions about the probabilistic relationship between educational outcomes and class positions, yields differences in the probabilities of continuing to further levels of education between students from service class (S) and working class (W) backgrounds.

Define, for S students,

$$U(S^*) = U(W^*) + \lambda_1$$
$$U(W^*) = U(U^*) + \lambda_2$$

and for W students

$$U(S^*) = U(W^*) + \varphi_1$$
$$U(W^*) = U(U^*) + \varphi_2$$

The λ and φ parameters capture the differences in utility between different class positions. Following B&G, the thresholds are set at $T_S = S^*$ and $T_W = W^*$.

Let π_S^* be the subjective probability below which an S student will prefer the L option to continuing in education; and similarly for π_W^* in the case of a W student. The class difference that emerges from B&G's analysis is that $\pi_S^* < \pi_W^*$: that is, working class students will require a higher subjective probability of success than will service class students in order to choose to continue.

Write

$$\pi_S^* = \frac{(\gamma_1 - \beta_1)(U(U^*) + \lambda_1 + \lambda_2) + (\gamma_2 - \beta_2)(U(U^*) + \lambda_2) + (\beta_1 + \beta_2 - \gamma_1 - \gamma_2)U(U^*)}{(\alpha_1 - \beta_1)(U(U^*) + \lambda_1 + \lambda_2) + (\alpha_2 - \beta_2)(U(U^*) + \lambda_2) + (\beta_1 + \beta_2 - \alpha_1 - \alpha_2)U(U^*)}$$

In the case shown in Figure 9.1, α_1 is equal to α and α_2 is equal to B&G's $1 - \alpha$. A similar expression applies for π_W^*. Some algebra gives

$$\pi_S^* < \pi_W^* \Rightarrow \frac{\lambda_1(\gamma_1 - \beta_1) + \lambda_2(\gamma_1 + \gamma_2 - \beta_1 - \beta_2)}{\lambda_1(\alpha_1 - \beta_1) + \lambda_2(\alpha_1 + \alpha_2 - \beta_1 - \beta_2)}$$
$$< \frac{\varphi_1(\gamma_1 - \beta_1) + \varphi_2(\gamma_1 + \gamma_2 - \beta_1 - \beta_2)}{\varphi_1(\alpha_1 - \beta_1) + \varphi_2(\alpha_1 + \alpha_2 - \beta_1 - \beta_2)}$$

and this reduces to

$$\lambda_1\varphi_2[(\gamma_1 - \beta_1)(\alpha_1 + \alpha_2 - \beta_1 - \beta_2) - (\alpha_1 - \beta_1)(\gamma_1 + \gamma_2 - \beta_1 - \beta_2)]$$
$$< \lambda_2\varphi_1[(\gamma_1 - \beta_1)(\alpha_1 + \alpha_2 - \beta_1 - \beta_2) - (\alpha_1 - \beta_1)(\gamma_1 + \gamma_2 - \beta_1 - \beta_2)] \quad (4)$$

The assumption about the shape of the utility functions implies that

$$\lambda_1/\lambda_2 > \varphi_1/\varphi_2 \tag{5}$$

In words: the change in utility between a W^* and S^* destination relative to the change in utility between U^* and W^* is larger for S students (for whom these changes occur beneath their threshold) than for W students. This means that the term in square brackets in (4) must be negative:[10] that is

$$(\gamma_1 - \beta_1)(\alpha_1 + \alpha_2 - \beta_1 - \beta_2) < (\alpha_1 - \beta_1)(\gamma_1 + \gamma_2 - \beta_1 - \beta_2)$$

This reduces to

$$\gamma_1(\alpha_2 - \beta_2) - \beta_1\alpha_2 < \gamma_2(\alpha_1 - \beta_1) - \alpha_1\beta_2$$

or

$$\gamma_1 < \beta_1 + \frac{(\alpha_1 - \beta_1)(\gamma_2 - \beta_2)}{(\alpha_2 - \beta_2)} \tag{6}$$

But, if there are to be class differences in π^*, it must also be the case that at least $\pi_W^* > 0$ and this requires that

$$\frac{\varphi_1(\gamma_1 - \beta_1) + \varphi_2(\gamma_1 + \gamma_2 - \beta_1 - \beta_2)}{\varphi_1(\alpha_1 - \beta_1) + \varphi_2(\alpha_1 + \alpha_2 - \beta_1 - \beta_2)} > 0$$

By assumption (i), $\alpha > \beta_1$, so the denominator of this expression is positive and $\pi_W^* > 0$ requires

$$\frac{\beta_1 + \beta_2 - \gamma_1 - \gamma_2}{\beta_1 - \gamma_1} < \frac{-\varphi_1}{\varphi_2} \tag{7}$$

This condition can be met if either $\beta_1 > \gamma_1$ and $\gamma_1 + \gamma_2 > \beta_1 + \beta_2$ or $\beta_1 < \gamma_1$ and $\gamma_1 + \gamma_2 < \beta_1 + \beta_2$. The fact that γ_1 can be smaller or larger than β_1 means that it could, for example, be the case that a young person's chances of access to the service class are improved simply by acquiring more years of education, even if this does not lead to examination success. Alternatively—and, in many European educational systems, more plausibly—such time spent in education may be wasted in the sense that leaving school and embarking earlier on a career will yield a better chance of access to the service class. Of the assumptions invoked by B&G, it is perhaps the second, $\gamma_1 + \gamma_2 > \beta_1 + \beta_2$ (staying and failing yields a higher probability of underclass entry than leaving immediately), which might be thought most controversial.

We now see that such an assumption is not necessary for the model to produce their results. What is necessary is that the returns to staying and failing do not strictly dominate those to leaving immediately—it cannot be that case that both $\beta_1 > \gamma_1$ and $\beta_2 > \gamma_2$ hold. But this does not prohibit the expected return to staying and failing from being higher than that to leaving immediately—which is analogous to the result, reported in many American studies, of a marginal increase in lifetime earnings even for an uncompleted additional year of education.

The definition of a threshold, together with the assumptions that $T_S = S^*$ and $T_W = W^*$ and that (6) and (7) hold, are sufficient to show that W and S students have different probabilities of choosing the stay rather than leave option. Class differences in the distribution of π (the subjective probability of succeeding if a student continues in education) and in the distribution of resources with which to meet the costs of education will then act to accentuate the class differences to which relative risk aversion gives rise. Such differences in π will exist because "the mean level of ability is higher in the service class than in the working class" (B&G 1997:285) and this difference is reflected in differences in educational performance that students then use to form their expectations of success and failure in the future. "If pupils' expectations about how well they will perform at the next level of education are upwardly bounded by how well they have performed in their most recent examination . . . then ability differences will be wholly captured in differences in the subjective parameter π" (B&G 1997:286).

TESTING THE MODEL

The data we use to test the model come from the National Child Development Study (NCDS). The NCDS is a longitudinal study of an entire cohort born in Britain in the week of 3–9 March 1958. The initial sample size was 17,414 (Shepherd 1995). To date, data have been collected at seven points: 1958 (shortly after birth), 1965 (when the studied children were age 7), 1969 (age 11), 1974 (age 16), 1991 (age 33), and 2000 (age 42).

The NCDS provides rich information. Parents were interviewed at the first three sweeps, providing detailed information on the children's social background. Data were also collected directly from the children through tests and questionnaires administered at school at ages 7, 11, and 16. Extensive information on examination results was also collected from the respondents' schools in 1978. From the age of 16 onward, the respondents themselves were interviewed. We restrict the analysis to boys who were born in England and Wales (henceforth E&W, for short) or had emigrated there by age 5. Because of sample attrition (the achieved sample size in the 1974 survey was 14,761), the geographical and gender restriction of the sample we use and missing data our sample size is 2,804.

Since 1974 the minimum school leaving age in E&W has been 16. This limit applied to members of the NCDS cohort (who became 16 in March 1974). At this age respondents would normally take their first public examination (in 1974 these were either Ordinary Level General Certificate of Education—known as O-level—or the Certificate of Secondary Education, CSE). Reaching the minimum leaving age introduces pupils to their first decision concerning their career, and at this point they are faced with three main alternatives: leaving school and entering the labor market, leaving school and entering apprenticeship, or continuing in school. The next main decision point in the English educational system comes at the end of secondary school, usually at age 18. At this age respondents are expected to take their second public examination (Advanced Level), and to make their second decision concerning their career. At this point pupils are faced with three main alternatives: leaving school and entering the labor market, leaving school and entering non-university postsecondary education or training, or entering university.

We focus on the former decision because access to university or other tertiary course is determined by exam performance (as we show below). Thus, all choices at O-level are solved by backward induction. The decision tree is shown in Figure 9.2 and this also reports the proportion of our sample members who followed the different paths. Perhaps most striking is that only a minority—roughly one in five—of male pupils continued to A-level, but that just over half of them then entered university.

VARIABLES

The B&G model argues that, even when controlling for ability and financial resources, there will still be class differences in educational decisions, and thus we need to measure three factors that should affect pupil's educational choices: financial resources, class background, and ability.

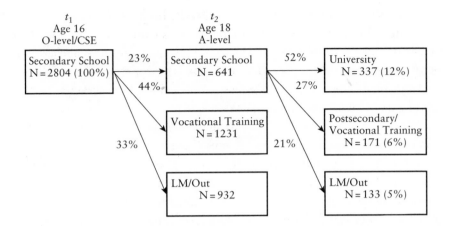

Figure 9.2. Pathways in the English and Welsh Educational Systems

To tap the available financial resources of the respondent's family we use a dummy variable for type of accommodation (council, rented, private) when the respondent was 16 (N2471). We also control for the number of rooms in that accommodation (N2476). Ideally we would have used a more direct variable, such as household income, but it is not possible to compute a valid household income variable because, at the time of the 1974 wave, industrial action led to an unspecified share of the sample working a three-day week.

To control for ability and performance we have three measures. First, we use the results, on an 80-point scale, of a General Ability Test at age 11 (N920). As Breen and Goldthorpe (1999) point out, performance on this test would appear to give the best proxy available in the NCDS data set to IQ scores. Second, we control for demonstrated ability measures at age 16 as these stem from performances in public examinations in England and Wales. The NCDS data set includes equivalent scales of 21 CSE and O-level exams (1 = O-level, grade A or B; 2 = O-level, grade C and CSE grade 1; 3 = O-level, grade D or E and CSE grade 2 or 3; 4 = CSE grade 4 or 5; 5 = other result; 6 = no entry), which we inverted and summarized.[11] We further identify all those with no entry score across all the twenty-one subjects (i.e., with 0 score) with a dummy variable. Third, we control for performance in the Advanced level (A-level) at age 18 (i.e., in 1976 irrespective of where these exams were taken). The NCDS data set includes A-level grades in the form of a 15-point scale formed by summing the three best A-level grades (A = 5). Again, we identify those with zero score with a dummy variable.[12]

We use the Goldthorpe class schema (see Erikson and Goldthorpe 1992, chapter 2 for a complete description) initially to identify seven classes: (I) upper service class, (II) lower service class, (III) routine non-manual class, (IV) petty bourgeoisie, (V) supervisors etc., (VI) skilled manual class, (VII) unskilled manual class. In the NCDS data set the respondent's class at age 33 is coded to the Goldthorpe class schema, and other class variables, such as class origins and respondent's class prior to age 33, are coded to the Office of National Statistics' Socio-Economic Groups (SEGs). However, a fair approximation to the Goldthorpe schema in its seven class version can be derived from the latter (Heath and McDonald 1987). For class origins, then, we derived the Goldthorpe class schema from information on the respondent's father's SEG at respondent's age 16 (N2385), or, if that information was missing, at age 11 (N1175). If the information was missing at both sweeps we derived class from the information on the respondent's mother's SEG at respondent's age 16 (N2394), or if necessary birth (N490). We also use three measures of class destination: first class position after completion of highest qualification, current or last class position by age 23, and current or last class position by age 33. For the first two of these we derived the Goldthorpe class schema from the respondent's SEG (N6130 and N6147, respectively), while the latter is already coded to the Goldthorpe class schema (N540080).

In the analysis we also omit the self-employed and petty bourgeoisie (class IV). We do this for two main reasons: first, an important aspect of the B&G theory is that educational attainment is governed by the desire for intergenerational class maintenance: but among the self-employed and petty bourgeoisie, education is much less important in maintaining class position than is the direct inheritance of capital (Ishida et al. 1995; Marshall et al. 1997). Secondly, the model requires that the class categories should have a clear rank order and this can be easily achieved only among employees. A key criterion for the way in which one can hierarchically order the employees' class categories is that of employment relations (Goldthorpe 2000). Thus, after omitting class IV we rearranged the Goldthorpe class schema into four hierarchical categories: Class I (higher service relationship), II (lower service relationship), III + V + VI (classes with mixed employment relations), and VII (labor contract).

The distinctive feature of the B&G model is the predictions that it makes about the propensities of children from different classes to make different educational choices, even when they differ neither in their subjective beliefs about the probability of succeeding in the educational system nor in their capacities to meet the relevant costs. We therefore devise a test for such differences that is based on the idea that the threshold expected probability of success required to make a student choose a more over a less risky alternative should show significant differences according to class origins.

For the educational setup that we have just described and that is shown in Figure 9.2, the expected utility of leaving the educational system after completing a particular level is

$$EU(k) = \sum_{j=1}^{VII} U_j p_j^k \tag{8}$$

Here k denotes the educational outcomes V^O (enter vocational training after O-level or CSE—henceforth, for brevity, we refer only to O-level), L^O (enter the labor market after O-level), V^A (enter vocational training after A-level), L^A (enter the labor market after A-level), and T (enter university or "tertiary" education). We use p to denote the probability of entering destination class j (j = I, II, III + V + VI, and VII) conditional on the kth educational outcome.[13]

If we let π denote the subjective probability of doing well enough at A-level to enter university and δ the subjective probability of doing well enough at A-level to enter vocational training, we can write the choice of whether to stay in the educational system after O-level rather than enter vocational training immediately after O-level as

$$\pi EU(T) + \delta EU(V^A) + (1 - \delta)EU(L^A) > EU(V^O) \tag{9}$$

and a similar expression can be written for the choice of whether to stay rather than leave the educational and training system. Because it is easier to enter post-A-level vocational training than to enter university we specify δ as a function of π thus:

$$\delta = \pi + (1 - \pi)m \tag{10}$$

where m is a constant. Using (10) and rearranging (9) we get an expression for the threshold value of π required to continue to A-level:

$$\tilde{\pi} > \frac{EU(V^O) - EU(L^A) - m[EU(V^A) - EU(L^A)]}{EU(T) - EU(L^A) + (1 - m)[EU(V^A) - EU(L^A)]} \tag{11}$$

If we now write the origin class specific marginal utilities between one class and another as

$$U(j = VII) = 0 \forall i$$
$$U(j = III) - U(j = VII) = \Delta_3^i$$
$$U(j = II) - U(j = III) = \Delta_2^i$$
$$U(j = I) - U(j = II) = \Delta_1^i$$

where i indexes origin classes. Using these marginal utilities (and omitting the i superscript for convenience) we can write

$$\tilde{\pi} > \frac{\Delta_1 a_1 + \Delta_2 a_2 + \Delta_3 a_3}{\Delta_1 b_1 + \Delta_2 b_2 + \Delta_3 b_3} \tag{12}$$

where

$$a_1 = p_I^{V^O} - p_I^{L^A} - m(p_I^{V^A} - p_I^{L^A}),$$
$$a_2 = a_1 + p_{II}^{V^O} - p_{II}^{L^A} - m(p_{II}^{V^A} - p_{II}^{L^A}),$$
$$a_3 = a_1 + a_2 + p_{III}^{V^O} - p_{III}^{L^A} - m(p_{III}^{V^A} - p_{III}^{L^A}),$$
$$b_1 = p_I^{T} - p_I^{L^A} + (1 - m)(p_I^{V^A} - p_I^{L^A}),$$
$$b_2 = b_1 + p_{II}^{T} - p_{II}^{L^A} + (1 - m)(p_{II}^{V^A} - p_{II}^{L^A}),$$
$$b_3 = b_1 + b_2 + p_{III}^{T} - p_{III}^{L^A} + (1 - m)(p_{III}^{V^A} - p_{III}^{L^A})$$

A similar expression to (12), and coefficients corresponding to a_1 to a_3 and b_1 to b_3, can also be derived for the choice of whether to continue in education rather than leave and enter the labor market. In terms of B&G's theory, the a and b coefficients capture the beliefs that individuals hold about the class returns to different levels and types of education (what we earlier labeled, following B&G, the αs, βs and γs) while the Ds capture the marginal utility attached to different class destinations.

DERIVING TESTABLE HYPOTHESES

Testable hypotheses can be derived from (12) provided, of course, that we can replace the coefficients in that expression with actual values. We have no independent measures of the Δs but we assume that, for all classes, all the marginal utilities are positive, and, following our earlier reformulation of the model, that

$$\Delta_1^I \geq \Delta_2^I \geq \Delta_3^I,$$
$$\Delta_2^{II} \geq \Delta_3^{II} > \Delta_1^{II}, \tag{13}$$

$$\Delta_3^{III} > \Delta_2^{III} > \Delta_1^{III},$$
$$\Delta_3^{VII} > \Delta_2^{VII} > \Delta_1^{VII}$$

As far as beliefs about the returns to different levels of educational attainment (the a and b coefficients in [12]), B&G say nothing about how they might be formed and the NCDS data contain no questions from which we might empirically establish these beliefs. We therefore investigated a number of different proxies. Our first, and most preferred among the methods available to us, uses the Oxford Mobility Survey (OMS). This was a survey of adult men, fielded in 1972, shortly before the NCDS cohort had to make the educational decisions with which we are concerned, and it provides data on the Goldthorpe class position of respondents and on their education: furthermore, the latter can be coded to approximately the same five categories as we have used for the NCDS respondents. We therefore assume that the educational attainment and class position of adult men who have reached "occupational maturity" (which we take to mean between ages 35 and 60) are a good proxy for the information that young people in our data used to form their beliefs about the social class returns to educational attainment. To operationalize this we cross-tabulated current class position by educational attainment, and the probabilities of being found in each of our four destination classes, conditional on having reached one of our five terminal educational states, V^O, L^O, V^A, L^A, and T, are reported in Table 9.1.[14] As we might have anticipated, the probability of being found in classes I and II increases the higher the educational attainment, while the risk of being found in class VII is greatest among those who enter the labor market directly after one or other public examination.

Using the figures shown in Table 9.1 we derive the following expression for the threshold subjective probability of success at A-level that makes a pupil indifferent between continuing in school and entering vocational training:

$$\tilde{\pi}_V > \frac{-\Delta_1 0.007 - \Delta_2 0.075 + \Delta_3 0.022}{\Delta_1 0.259 + \Delta_2 0.240 - \Delta_3 0.150} \tag{14a}$$

and the same in respect of the choice of staying in school versus leaving and entering the labor market:[15]

$$\tilde{\pi}_L > \frac{-\Delta_1 0.032 - \Delta_2 0.160 + \Delta_3 0.021}{\Delta_1 0.259 + \Delta_2 0.240 - \Delta_3 0.150} \tag{14b}$$

TABLE 9.1
Probability of Class Position, Conditional on Educational
Attainment, All Men Ages 35–60 in England and Wales

Educational level	DESTINATION CLASS AT AGE 33				
	I	*II*	*III + V + VI*	*VII*	*N*
L^O	.388	.220	.328	.064	250
V^O	.413	.280	.244	.063	332
L^A	.418	.345	.145	.091	55
V^A	.433	.383	.167	.017	60
T	.663	.292	.035	.009	202

SOURCE: Oxford Mobility Study 1972.

As far as the choice of staying rather than entering training is concerned, it is clear from (14a) that any pupil for whom $\Delta_2 \geqslant \Delta_3$ will always prefer to continue in education, regardless of their value of π. As we saw in (13), this is true of pupils from origin classes I and II. But pupils from classes III + V + VI and VII attach greater weight to Δ_3 than to Δ_2 and this is particularly true of those from class III + V + VI for whom Δ_3 is the difference in utility between downward mobility and maintaining their class position. For pupils from both these class origins, we can expect that not all will choose to continue in education (note that more weight attached to Δ_3 increases the numerator and decreases the denominator), and that those from class III + V + VI will be particularly likely to leave at this point and take up some vocational training.[16] Thus our first hypothesis is:

> Controlling for the subjective probability of success at A-level and for family resources, there will be class differences in the choice of continuing in school or entering vocational training. Pupils from class origins I and II will be most likely to continue, followed by those from class VII, with those from class III + V + VI the least likely to do so.

As for the choice of staying rather than entering the labor market directly, the same considerations apply, though in this case, only pupils who attached very considerable weight to Δ_3 would choose to leave rather than continue to A-level.[17] Thus our second hypothesis is:

> Controlling for the subjective probability of success at A-level and for family resources, only those pupils who attached a great deal of utility to entering classes

III + V + VI relative to VII, and very little additional utility to gaining access to classes II and I will choose to leave school and enter the labor market.

In cases where both leaving and entering a vocational course are preferred to staying, we expect the latter to be preferred to the former if

$$c_1\Delta_1 + c_2\Delta_2 + c_3\Delta_3 > 0 \tag{15}$$

where

$$c_1 = p_I^{Vo} - p_I^{Lo},$$
$$c_2 = c_1 + p_{II}^{Vo} - p_{II}^{Lo},$$
$$c_3 = c_2 + p_{III}^{Vo} - p_{III}^{Lo}$$

Given the OMS data, all the c coefficients in (15) are positive, leading to our final hypothesis:

pupils from all class backgrounds should prefer a vocational course to direct labor market entry after O-level.

Testing the Hypotheses

These hypotheses can then be tested quite straightforwardly. Table 9.2 shows the estimated coefficients from a multinomial logit model in which the dependent categories are the choices at A-level. As we can see by comparing the columns labeled 1 with those labeled 2, once we control for educational performance at A-level there are no class differences in choices whatsoever. This confirms our earlier argument that access to university or other tertiary course is determined by exam performance and that the decision after O-level is the only one of any consequence.

Table 9.3 then reports the coefficients from a multinomial logit model of decisions after O-level. Columns (1a) and (1b) show the gross class differences in the odds of choosing to enter vocational training rather than continue to A-level and in the odds of entering the labor market rather than continuing to A-level, but these are greatly reduced when we control for ability, performance, and family resources.[18] Nevertheless, in support of H1, pupils from origins in classes III + V + VI and VII are significantly more likely to enter vocational training in preference to staying to A-level than are pupils from classes I and II, though there is no significant difference between the propensities of class III + V + VI and class VII students. To assess hypothesis H2 would require information on the detailed shape of students' utility

TABLE 9.2

Multinomial Logit Regression Models on T3

(Standard Errors in Parentheses)

Model	(1a)	(1b)	(2a)	(2b)
Contrasts	LM vis-à-vis University	Voc vis-à-vis University	LM vis-à-vis University	Voc vis-à-vis University
Class Origins I (reference)				
II	0.481+	0.209	0.193	−0.081
	(0.277)	(0.241)	(0.313)	(0.270)
III + V + VI	0.724*	0.329	0.416	0.033
	(0.269)	(0.238)	(0.305)	(0.267)
VII	0.736+	0.414	0.250	−0.018
	(0.443)	(0.172)	(0.500)	(0.452)
Performance				
A-level			−0.275*	−0.272*
			(0.052)	(0.040)
A-level control			0.654+	0.002
			(0.335)	(0.249)
Intercept	−1.378*	−0.874*	−0.371	0.470
	(0.208)	(0.172)	(0.357)	(0.293)
N	641		641	

* $p < 0.05$

+ $p < 0.1$

functions, but it would seem to follow from B&G's arguments that the largest value of Δ_3 should be held by pupils from class III + V + VI, and therefore they should be the most likely to prefer to leave and enter the labor market. In fact, it is pupils from class VII origins who are significantly more likely than all others to go directly into the labor market after O-level. The class difference that persists here is due neither to poorer resources nor to lower expectations of success, and it can be attributed to the mechanism of relative risk aversion that B&G propose only if we assume that pupils from class VII origins attach zero marginal utility to attaining any position higher than class VII (i.e. $\Delta_1 = \Delta_2 = \Delta_3 = 0$). This seems implausible (though not impossible), and there must therefore be something (else) about coming

TABLE 9.3
Multinomial Logit Regression Models on T2
(Standard Errors in Parentheses)

Model	(1a)	(1b)	(2a)	(2b)
Contrasts	LM vis-à-vis Acad	Voc vis-à-vis Acad	LM vis-à-vis Acad	Voc vis-à-vis Acad
Class Origins				
I (reference)				
II	0.650*	0.776*	−0.002	0.105
	(0.169)	(0.164)	(0.214)	(0.211)
III + V + VI	1.617*	2.014*	0.277	0.682*
	(0.156)	(0.151)	(0.210)	(0.204)
VII	2.601*	2.542*	0.745*	0.770*
	(0.215)	(0.213)	(0.279)	(0.276)
Ability				
Ability			−0.041*	−0.029*
			(0.006)	(0.006)
Ability control			0.236	−0.134
			(0.216)	(0.220)
Performance				
O-level			−0.149*	−0.167*
			(0.009)	(0.009)
O-level control			−2.161*	−3.110*
			(0.308)	(0.308)
Resources				
Owned accommodation (reference)				
Council accommodation			0.725*	0.536*
			(0.179)	(0.175)
Rented accommodation			0.455	0.090
			(0.244)	(0.245)
Number of rooms			−0.066+	−0.200+
			(0.051)	(0.053)
Intercept	−0.851	−0.791	5.489*	6.251*
	(0.132)	(0.129)	(0.503)	(0.499)
N	2804		2804	

*p < 0.05
+p < 0.1

from class VII that depresses the likelihood of continuing to A-level. Lastly, hypothesis H3 is confirmed by our data: given the choice of leaving and entering the labor market or leaving and entering vocational training, pupils of all classes would prefer the latter (as we see from the larger coefficients in column 2b compared with those in 2a).

Although these results are favorable to the B&G hypothesis, it should be noted that the OMS data are far from ideal for the purpose to which we have put them. As well as the problem of the small sample it is also the case that these men experienced an educational system that was in some respects quite different from that experienced by the NCDS cohort (for example, O-levels and A-levels were not introduced until 1950). Thus, although it is certainly plausible that these data provide a reasonable proxy to whatever sources of information young people in the early 1970s might have used as the basis for their educational decisions, there are also good grounds for skepticism.

Thus far it appears that the B&G model has not fared too badly. But the major difficulty of testing the model is to find estimates of the beliefs that young people hold about the class returns to various educational options and so we examined three other sets of estimates using empirical probabilities derived from the sample members' own experiences after leaving the educational system. In other words, we took the jobs that respondents later occupied and used the observed relationship between educational attainment and the class of those jobs as a proxy for the beliefs they held when they made the choice of education. Recall that we have three measures of post-education class position, based on first job, most recent job held at age 23, and most recent job held at age 33. Assuming that respondents' expectations are accurate but somewhat myopic, we begin with first job. This yields the cross-tabulation shown in Table 9.4a and from that we derive threshold values as follows:

$$\tilde{\pi}_V > \frac{-\Delta_1 0.048 - \Delta_2 0.152 + \Delta_3 0.104}{\Delta_1 0.269 + \Delta_2 0.458 + \Delta_3 0.151} \tag{16a}$$

$$\tilde{\pi}_L > \frac{-\Delta_1 0.034 - \Delta_2 0.133 - \Delta_3 0.119}{\Delta_1 0.269 + \Delta_2 0.458 + \Delta_3 0.151} \tag{16b}$$

These results are similar to equations 14a and 14b but more straightforward because the denominator is now always positive. In this case, men for whom Δ_3 is sufficiently large compared to Δ_2 and Δ_1 will certainly prefer to leave after O-level to enter vocational training: given our assumptions about the relative sizes of the Δs this is most likely to be true of men of class III + V + VI, followed by men of class VII. On this basis, then, we should expect young men from these two classes to be more likely than those from classes I and II to leave school and enter training after O-level, and as we have already seen in Table 9.3, this is true of both classes III + V + VI and VII. But the numerator of equation (16b) is negative suggesting that no pupils would choose to leave school and enter the labor market directly in preference to continuing to A-level,[19] and, as we have already seen, the survey does not support this.

The distribution of classes by educational attainment at age 23 shown in Table 9.4b yields threshold equations as follows:

$$\tilde{\pi}_V > \frac{-\Delta_1 0.064 - \Delta_2 0.337 - \Delta_3 0.127}{\Delta_1 0.285 + \Delta_2 0.215 - \Delta_3 0.404} \tag{17a}$$

$$\tilde{\pi}_L > \frac{-\Delta_1 0.075 - \Delta_2 0.304 - \Delta_3 0.272}{\Delta_1 0.285 + \Delta_2 0.215 - \Delta_3 0.404} \tag{17b}$$

and using the data at age 33 (shown in Table 9.4c) yields equations as follows:

$$\tilde{\pi}_V > \frac{-\Delta_1 0.261 - \Delta_2 0.390 - \Delta_3 0.140}{\Delta_1 0.196 + \Delta_2 0.179 - \Delta_3 0.102} \tag{18a}$$

$$\tilde{\pi}_L > \frac{-\Delta_1 0.230 - \Delta_2 0.345 - \Delta_3 0.252}{\Delta_1 0.196 + \Delta_2 0.179 - \Delta_3 0.102} \tag{18b}$$

In all four equations,[20] the numerator will always be negative, showing that the relative risk aversion mechanism will lead to no class differences in choice of educational option. The reason is evident in Tables 9.4b and 9.4c, where the class returns to entering the labor market directly after A-level (i.e., the worst outcome for someone who chose to remain in school after O-level) dominate those to entering vocational training after O-level (i.e., the best outcome for those who chose to leave school after O-level). There is therefore no risk involved in continuing in education and so no incentive to leave at this point. The reason for the difference in the expectations we would hold when using these measures of class position, rather than the class of first job, arises from the massive upward mobility that this cohort experienced between their first job and the job they held at age 33. This appears part of a more general upward shift in the British class structure over the period from the late 1970s to 1991. The NCDS respondents could not have been expected to know that this would happen and so their actual class positions at a point near "occupational maturity" cannot really be taken as a

TABLE 9.4A
Probability of Entering First Class Positions, Conditional on
Educational Attainment, All Men Ages 35–60 in England and Wales

Educational level	DESTINATION CLASS IN FIRST JOB				
	I	II	III + V + VI	VII	N
L^O	0.027	0.055	0.556	0.362	1593
V^O	0.014	0.048	0.799	0.139	1263
L^A	0.055	0.147	0.546	0.252	203
V^A	0.123	0.207	0.507	0.163	163
T	0.263	0.282	0.274	0.182	358

TABLE 9.4B
Probability of Class Position at Age 23, Conditional on
Educational Attainment, Men in England and Wales

Educational level	DESTINATION CLASS AT AGE 23				
	I	II	III + V + VI	VII	N
L^O	0.030	0.181	0.468	0.321	1245
V^O	0.041	0.137	0.646	0.176	1070
L^A	0.096	0.416	0.440	0.048	147
V^A	0.184	0.361	0.401	0.054	125
T	0.302	0.395	0.220	0.083	205

TABLE 9.4C
Probability of Entering First Class Position at Age 33, Conditional on
Educational Attainment, Men in England and Wales

Educational level	DESTINATION CLASS AT AGE 33				
	I	II	III + V + VI	VII	N
L^O	0.217	0.148	0.326	0.309	1175
V^O	0.186	0.134	0.483	0.197	884
L^A	0.437	0.268	0.232	0.063	171
V^A	0.532	0.222	0.240	0.006	142
T	0.547	0.293	0.148	0.004	331

guide to their beliefs. On the other hand, to take their class position derived from their first job as their beliefs about the class that their educational choices will finally lead them to attain is to attribute to them an unreasonable degree of myopia.[21]

CONCLUSION

We have reformulated the B&G model of educational decision making and derived hypotheses, which we then tested using data on young men in England and Wales in the early 1970s who were making the transition from compulsory to post-compulsory secondary education. Our tests follow from the idea that, because young people from different class origins have different threshold levels of education that they seek to reach as a minimum, they will differ in the marginal utility they attach to higher educational levels, giving rise to different propensities to choose alternative educational and non-educational options. These class differences in the incentives to continue in education can be derived from the reformulated model, but the tests also depend on our ability to operationalize the assumed common (among students of all class origins) beliefs about the returns to educational attainment. These were not measured in the NCDS data set we used, and it turns out that our results depend on which particular source of information about the class returns to different levels and types of educational attainment we use. But, we suggest, the most plausible of these is the first source, the OMS survey, and the results from this survey give some measure of support to the B&G model. Hypothesis 1 predicted that, as far as the choice of whether to continue to A-level studies or enter vocational training is concerned, students from classes I and II would be most likely, those from VII less likely, and those from III + V + VI least likely, to prefer A-level. Our results suggested that, while I and II were indeed the most likely, there was no difference between students from the other two classes. Hypothesis 2 predicted that students from class III + V + VI would be most likely to prefer direct entry into the labor market over continuing to A-level: this was not borne out by our analysis in which students from class VII were most likely to do this, with the other classes showing no significant differences. Lastly, hypothesis 3, that all students would prefer vocational training to direct labor market entry, was supported by our results.

However, perhaps the clearest conclusion that comes from our analysis is, indeed, the important role played by students' beliefs and the difficulty of adequately proxying them. Our results are sensitive to our choice of proxy: when we used beliefs based on the students' own first job the results were somewhat less supportive of the B&G model, and when we used proxies based on their later jobs the predictions of the model were not borne out at all. The difficulty of adequately proxying beliefs is an old refrain: Manski's (1993) paper is perhaps the best known plea for attempts to measure pupil beliefs, and it is one that we can only echo. Our analysis clearly shows the dependence of the success or failure of the B&G model on whether or not pupils hold the "right" set of beliefs.

It is noticeable that the earlier attempts to test the B&G model, to which we referred at the start of this chapter, have circumvented this problem by assuming that pupils define the threshold value, T, not in terms of their future class position, but in terms of a particular level of educational attainment (typically the level attained by one or other parent). One way of reconciling this with the original formulation of the model would be to suppose that, in the absence of adequate information about the likely future returns to education, students simply use parents' educational level as a heuristic: that is, they assume that attaining the same educational level as their parents is likely to lead them to attain much the same class position. But whether or not this is so is better dealt with as an empirical matter than as an assumption.

Notes

1. Partial exceptions to this are Britain, where the data come from cohorts born between 1913 and 1952; Japan, where they come from cohorts born between 1905 and 1955; and Switzerland, where the data come from two cohorts one born in 1950, the other in 1960.

2. Subsequent research has confirmed Sweden (Jonsson and Erikson 2000) and Germany (Jonsson, Mills, and Muller 1996) as exceptions to this pattern of stability, and research using more recent French (Thelot and Vallet 2000) and Dutch (Ganzeboom and Luijkx, 2004) data suggests declining class inequalities there too.

3. This reformulation of the model is taken from Breen (2001).

4. This may also be true of the less risky choice but for simplicity of exposition B&G assume that there is no chance of educational failure in this case.

5. For convenience we drop the student-specific subscript except where this would cause confusion.

6. B&G (1997:286) add a second condition. Students will continue in education at level k only if both condition (3) and the condition $r_i > c_k$ are met, where r is the student's family's resources and c is the cost of education at that level. Because the latter condition is rather straightforward we do not discuss it any further.

7. The model is thus a special case of Kahneman and Tversky's (1979) prospect theory.

8. We are here following B&G's original choice of classes, which are chosen for illustrative purposes and are not meant to be exhaustive. So, for example, S^* does not include clerical workers. U^* would include unskilled workers, the chronically unemployed and similar.

9. Although, as noted in the introduction, there have been a number of recent tests of the model that have been largely supportive of it, the assumptions of the model might themselves be subjected to further empirical scrutiny. The model assumes that students hold beliefs about the relationship between educational attainment and the attainment of class position that do not vary by class background, and that they have a threshold level of attainment, which does. In principle these assumptions could be tested. Additionally, some consideration might be given to the degree of sensitivity of the results of the model to these assumptions. Certainly if the model were to be extended to explain, say, ethnic group differences in educational decision making, it would be unrealistic to assume common beliefs about the returns to education given that minority groups often believe themselves to be discriminated against. As Macleod's (1995) work illustrates very well, this diversity of beliefs about educational returns can be an important explanation for variation in educational decisions.

10. B&G examine two sets of values for the λ and φ parameters. Initially they set the utility of outcomes S^* and W^* to one for working class students while $U(U^*)$ is zero, and to $U(S^*) = 1$ for service class students and both $U(W^*)$ and $U(U^*)$ are set to zero. This implies $\lambda_1 = 1$; $\lambda_2 = 0$; $\varphi_1 = 0$; $\varphi_2 = 1$. Later B&G allow S students to attach different utility to W^* and U^* and W students to attach more utility to S^* than to W^*. So we have: $U(S^*) = 1$; $U(W^*) = 0$; and $U(U^*) = -x$, for S students; and $U(S^*) = x^*$; $U(W^*) = 1$; and $U(U^*) = 0$ for W students. These give

$$\lambda_1 = 1; \lambda_2 = x$$
$$\varphi_1 = (x^* - 1); \varphi_2 = 1$$

The earlier formulation is consistent with the requirement that $\lambda_1/\lambda_2 > \varphi_1/\varphi_2$ and, if one sets $1 \leqslant x^* < 2$ and $x \leqslant 1$, so is the latter. Setting $x^* = 1$ and $x = 0$ in the latter reduces to the earlier formulation.

11. The twenty-one subjects include E443-modern languages, E446-French, E449-English, E452-Art, E455-Arts, E458-History, E461-Biology, E464-Chemistry, E467-General Science, E470-Geology, E473-General Studies, E476-Law and Economics, E479-Social Sciences, E482-Domestic Sciences, E485-Commercial Subjects, E488-Technical Subjects, E491-Mathematics, E494-Other Math, E497-Statistics, E500-Other Sciences, and E503-Physics.

12. The reason for this is that some of those with a zero score may in fact be cases whose examination results were not reported.

13. Our p_j^k are thus equivalent to the α, β, and γ parameters in the original formulation of the B&G model.

14. It should be noted that, although the OMS sample is large (just over 10,000 men), we have rather small numbers at each educational level, and this is mainly because a very high proportion of men in the survey had not taken O-level or an equivalent examination: thus the estimates shown in Table 9.1 will, in some cases, have rather large standard errors.

15. Both (14a) and (14b) are derived setting m = 0.1. Other values of m do not change the signs of any coefficients in either equation but a larger value of m (which corresponds to easier access to post-A-level vocational training) makes it less likely that pupils of classes III + V + VI and VII will choose to enter post-O-level vocational training (as one would have expected since this reduces the risk associated with remaining in school).

16. For example, given $\Delta_1 = 1$ and $\Delta_2 = 2$, (13a) implies that for $5.21 < \Delta_3 < 7.14$ the threshold value of π required in order to continue in school declines as Δ_3 increases. For $\Delta_3 > 7.14$ all pupils prefer to stay.

17. Continuing the example from the previous note, given Δ_3 in the range 6.38 to 16.76 the threshold value of π needed to remain at school declines as Δ_3 increases and for $\Delta_3 > 16.76$ all prefer to remain.

18. We also experimented with other specifications and measures of resources, including the number of siblings, persons per room, and whether the respondent received free school lunches but our results remained unchanged.

19. The exception, as earlier noted, would be any student who held $\Delta_1 = \Delta_2 = \Delta_3 = 0$.

20. Again, the figures in the text are based on $m = 0.1$.

21. Using the respondents' fathers' education and class position to proxy beliefs is not possible in the NCDS because father's education cannot be coded to the five educational categories we are using.

References

Blossfeld, H.-P., and Yossi Shavit. 1993. "Persisting Barriers: Changes in Educational Opportunities in Thirteen Countries." Pp. 1–24 in *Persistent Inequality: Changing Educational Attainment in Thirteen Countries*, edited by Yossi Shavit and Hans-Peter Blossfeld. Boulder, CO: Westview.

Boudon, Raymond. 1974. *Education, Opportunity and Social Inequality*. New York: Wiley.

Breen, Richard. 2001. *A Rational Choice Model of Educational Inequality*. Working Paper 166, Centro de Estudios Avanzados in Ciencias Sociales, Instituto Juan March de Estudios e Investigaciones, Madrid.

Breen, Richard, and John H. Goldthorpe. 1997. "Explaining Educational Differentials: Towards a Formal Rational Action Theory." *Rationality and Society* 9(3):275–305; reprinted in pp. 459–70 in David B. Grusky ed. 2001. *Social Stratification: Class, Race and Gender*. Boulder, CO: Westview.

Breen, Richard, and John H. Goldthorpe. 1999. "Class Inequality and Meritocracy: A Critique of Saunders and an Alternative Analysis." *The British Journal of Sociology* 50(1):1–27.

Dronkers, J. 1983. "Have Inequalities in Educational Opportunities Changed in the Netherlands? A Review of Empirical Evidence." *Netherlands Journal of Sociology* 19:133–50.

Davies, Richard, Eskil Heinesen, and Anders Holm. 2002. "The Relative Risk Aversion Hypothesis." *Journal of Population Economics* 15:683–713.

Erikson, Robert, and John H. Goldthorpe. 1992. *The Constant Flux: A Study of Class Mobility in Industrial Societies.* Oxford: Clarendon.

Featherman, D. L., and R. M. Hauser. 1978. *Opportunity and Change.* New York: Academic Press.

Ganzeboom, Harry B. G., and Ruud Luijkx. 2004. "Recent Trends in Intergenerational Occupational Class Reproduction in the Netherlands 1970–1999." Pp. 345–82 in *Social Mobility in Europe*, edited by Richard Breen. Oxford: Oxford University Press.

Garnier, M. A., and L. Raffalovich. 1984. "The Evolution of Equality of Educational Opportunity in France." *Sociology of Education.* 57:1–11.

Goldthorpe, John H. 2000. *On Sociology: Numbers, Narratives and the Integration of Research and Theory.* Oxford: Oxford University Press.

Grusky, David B., ed. 2001. *Social Stratification: Class, Race and Gender.* Boulder, CO: Westview.

Halsey, A. H., A. F. Heath, and J. M. Ridge. 1980. *Origins and Destinations: Family, Class and Education in Modern Britain.* Oxford: Clarendon.

Heath, A. F., and S. K. MacDonald. 1987. "Social Change and the Future of the Left." *Political Quarterly* 53:364–77.

Ishida, H., J. M. Ridge, and W. Müller. 1995. "Class Origin, Class Destination and Education: A Cross National Study of Ten Industrial Nations." *American Journal of Sociology* 101(1):145–93.

Jonsson, J., and Robert Erikson. 2000. "Understanding Educational Inequality: The Swedish Experience." *L'Annee Sociologique* 50:345–82.

Jonsson, J., Colin Mills, and Walter Müller. 1996. "Half a Century of Increasing Educational Openness? Social Class, Gender and Educational Attainment in Sweden, Germany and Britain." Pp. 183-206 in *Can Education Be Equalized?*, edited by R. Erikson and J. Jonsson. Boulder, CO: Westview.

Kahneman, Daniel, and Amos Tversky. 1979. "Prospect Theory: An Analysis of Decision Under Risk." *Econometrica* 47(2):263–91.

Macleod, J. 1995. *Ain't No Makin' It: Aspirations and Attainment in a Low Income Neighbourhood.* Boulder, CO: Westview.

Manski, Charles. 1993. "Adolescent Econometricians: How Do Youth Infer the Returns to Schooling?" Pp. 57–60 in *Studies of Supply and Demand in Higher Education*, edited by Charles T. Clotfelter and Michael Rothschild. Chicago: University of Chicago Press.

Mare, Robert D., and Huey-Chi Chang. 1998. "Family Attainment Norms and Educational Attainment: New Models for School Transitions." Paper presented at RC28 meeting Taipei, Taiwan.

Marshall, G. Swift, A., and Stephen Roberts. 1997. *Against the Odds: Social Class and Social Justice in Industrial Societies*. Oxford: Oxford University Press.

Need, Ariana, and Uulkje De Jong. 2001. "Educational Differentials in the Netherlands: Testing Rational Action Theory." *Rationality and Society* 13(1):71–98

Schizzerotto, Antonio. 1997. "Perche' in Italia ci sono pochi diplomati e pochi laureati? Vincoli strutturali e decisioni razionali degli attori come cause delle contenuta espansione della scolarite' superiore." *Polis* 11(3):345–65.

Shavit, Yossi, and Hans-Peter Blossfeld, eds. 1993. *Persistent Inequality: Changing Educational Attainment in Thirteen Countries*. Boulder, CO: Westview.

Shepherd, P. 1995, "The National Child Development Study: An Introduction to the Origin of the Study and the Method of Data Collection." NCDS User Support Group, Working Paper 1.

Thelot, C., and L.-A. Vallet. 2000. "La réduction des inégalities socials devant l'ecole depuis le début du siécle." *Economie et Statistique* 334:3–32.

CHAPTER TEN

Mental Ability—Uni or Multidimensional? An Analysis of Effects

David Epstein and Christopher Winship

For the better part of the past century, psychologists have argued about whether mental ability is unidimensional or multidimensional. This debate has focused almost exclusively on the appropriate interpretation of results from various factor analyses of test score data. Although these analyses typically indicate that much of the variance in test items can be explained by a single factor, there has been sharp disagreement as to whether this outcome supports the claim that mental ability is unidimensional or rather whether this is simply evidence that different abilities are highly correlated with each other.

Research by psychologists has focused solely on the internal structure of various test batteries. That is, the issue of unidimensionality versus multidimensionality has only been examined in terms of the appropriateness of different models for observed covariance structures of test items. Totally unexamined by psychologists has been the question of whether the *effects* of mental ability on different outcomes can be adequately modeled by assuming that mental ability is unidimensional or whether it is necessary to posit multiple dimensions. In fact, John Carroll, one of the most prominent psychologists currently working on the dimensionality of mental ability, has asserted that it makes no sense to examine the possible effects of mental ability until research has resolved the question about its internal structure (Carroll 1993).

What Carroll and other psychologists have overlooked is that the relationship between performance on a test battery and various outcomes

We are grateful to Steve Morgan for various comments and suggestions. Of course the usual disclaimer applies.

provides potential evidence as to whether mental ability is uni- or multidimensional. This is true in two important respects. First, in terms of the pure technical question of model fit, the inclusion of outcomes in the analysis can considerably expand the size of the covariance matrix to be modeled. As such, a model containing effects with a single dimension of mental ability implies many more additional restrictions that can be tested against the data. Second, to the degree that it is found that there are different dimensions to mental ability and these different dimensions differentially affect various outcomes, this is evidence that mental ability needs to be conceptualized as being multidimensional.

In this chapter, we analyze the Armed Service Vocational Aptitude Battery (ASVAB), a mental ability test given to all applicants to the Armed Forces. The ASVAB consists of ten different subcomponents. Four of the components make up what is know as the Armed Forces Qualifying Test or AFQT. In 1980, the ASVAB was given to nearly the entire National Longitudinal Survey of Youth (NLSY) sample (Center for Human Resources 1995). This sample consists of a nationally representative sample of youth ages 14 to 21 in 1979, the first year of the sample, and over-samples of blacks, Hispanics, and poor whites. We restrict our analysis to the white men from the national sample.

Using the NLSY, we examine the effects of mental ability on different measures of social and economic success. We consider three different models for mental ability—a unidimensional model similar to that favored by many psychometricians, a model with four dimensions proposed by Bock and Moore (1986), and a model containing three of the dimensions in the Bock and Moore model that treats four of the test subcomponents as achievement tests. We find that the unidimensional model fits the data poorly. Bock and Moore's four dimension model fits the data considerably better, though the data provides somewhat stronger support for the model with three dimensions plus a set of achievement tests. The three dimensions of mental ability consist of mathematical aptitude, verbal aptitude, and fluency. Bock and Moore's fourth dimension, technical knowledge, depends on four separate subtests measuring different types of technical knowledge. In the three dimension model, these dimensions are treated as separate achievement items.

Our analysis suggests that Quantitative and Verbal Ability are the primary predictors of educational attainment. However, Fluent Production (basically a measure of how fast an individual can carry out a set of different mental tasks) has little or no effect on educational attainment. Fluent Production, though, is the most important predictor of economic success as measured by wages and family income, where neither Quantitative nor Verbal Ability appears to be important. The lack of fit of the unidimensional model of ability discussed above, and the differential effect of these three measures of ability strongly suggests that intelligence needs to be conceptualized as having a multidimensional structure.

In the next section of the chapter we review previous literature on the dimensionality of mental ability and the separate literature on the effects of mental ability on social and economic success. The following section describes the data and methods we use in detail. The subsequent section then provides the various analyses that we have carried out. Finally, in the discussion and conclusion section we examine the implications of our findings for the debate as to whether mental ability is uni- or multidimensional.

PREVIOUS RESEARCH

Two different literatures are relevant to our analysis. We begin by looking briefly at psychological literature on intelligence. Here, we discuss the several different ways intelligence or mental ability has been conceptualized. In the second section, we examine research on the effects of intelligence on different measures of social and economic success.

Psychological Research

Research on mental ability can be thought of as following two general traditions: the classical and the revisionist. Brody (1992) provides an extended discussion of the classical tradition.

The Classical Tradition Charles Spearman, who made many important contributions to modern statistical methods, is generally acknowledged as the father of the classical perspective. In his research, he identifies mental intelligence, or what he called "*g*," as being a unidimensional quality that determines an individual's performance on a battery of tests. In his seminal work, *The Abilities of Man* (1927) Spearman describes his many investigations that purportedly show the pervasiveness of *g*.

Following Spearman, Thurstone (1931) developed multiple factor analysis as a method for modeling the correlations between a set of test items in terms of a set of latent factors (Brody 1992). In his initial research, Thurstone obtained thirteen factors, nine of which he assigned a psychological label.[1] Thurstone, however, conducted further research (Thurstone and Thurstone 1941) that failed to provide strong support of multidimensional models of mental ability and, as such, left him "without a convincing refutation of Spearman's" theory (Brody 1992). Subsequently, intelligence, or more precisely *g*, became identified with the first principle component in a factor analysis of a set of test items and was assumed to be determined by individuals' intelligence.

A key issue for classicists has been what *g* really represents. Cyril Burt, another early psychometrician, argued that *g* or intelligence is an "innate (inherited), general (applicable to a wide variety of circumstances), cognitive (as opposed to motivational or emotional) capacity" (Snyderman and Rothman 1988:51). Arthur Jensen, the most prominent modern day classicist states:

> The *g* factor is manifested in tests to the degree that they involve *mental manipulation* of the input elements . . . , *choice, decision, invention* in contrast to reproduction, *reproduction* in contrast to selection, *meaningful memory* in contrast to rote memory, *long-term memory* in contrast to short-term memory, and *distinguishing relevant information* from irrelevant information in solving complex problems. (Jensen 1980:250)

The Revisionist Tradition   Revisionists argue that intelligence is multidimensional, though a variety of different theories concerning the multidimensionality of intelligence have been offered. Perhaps the most influential perspective has been that of Cattell (1971), who has argued that there are three different types of intelligence: fluid, crystallized, and visual-spatial. Fluid intelligence is the ability to learn new things and solve problems that have not been seen before. Crystallized intelligence is what one currently knows. Fluid intelligence is assumed to decline with age and crystallized to increase. Cattell posits that in general individuals with high initial fluid intelligence will later in life have high crystallized intelligence because of their greater ability to learn. Visual-spatial intelligence is assumed quite separate and involves the ability to solve spatial reasoning problems. Sternberg (1985) offers a similar theory. He, however, argues that there is such a thing as general intelligence, but that this is a meta-factor involving the ability to use specific components of one's ability.

Revisionists have different positions with respect to the concept of "*g*." Ceci (1990) argues that *g* is essentially a statistical concept that appears to apply across individuals. He, however, suggests that we have little understanding of either the physiological or psychological mechanisms underlying it. He further contends that *g* may be the result of an interlocking set of cognitive abilities that are not easily identified through factor analysis. Hunt (1995:357) admits that there is a *g*, but qualifies this statement by saying that "there are alternate explanations for the data . . . even when one restricts oneself to the notion that intelligence is what the tests measure." Specifically, he argues that it is possible to reject the unidimensional model of intelligence *and* remain within the psychometric tradition of factor analysis. In particular, he argues that Cattell's framework of crystallized, fluid, and spatial intelligence could be specified as a multifactor model. He goes on to argue that the interdependency between different factors overlaps among individuals with low levels of intelligence; that is, individuals that are low on one dimension of intelligence are highly likely to be low on others. He argues that, in contrast, at the high end there is very little overlap.

Carroll (1993) has proposed the most sophisticated multidimensional theory of intelligence. He argues the intelligence should be conceptualized in terms of three strata. His theory comes about as a result of his extensive survey of 477 data sets that he selected for analysis. Carroll summarizes his theory using six points:

> 1. "The interpretation of individual factors, at each stratum, is a process of theory construction that specifies testable hypotheses regarding the characteristics of variables that measure (load significantly on) each factor at a higher stratum. . . .
> 2. The three strata . . . are not intended to be rigidly defined. . . . Further, it is not assumed that the three strata exhibit strict subsumption relations. . . .
> 3. The three-stratum theory assumes a hierarchical rather than a taxonomic model. . . .
> 4. Factors, at whatever stratum, may be assumed to correspond to real phenomena, in individuals, that govern cognitive performance. . . .
> 5. The three-stratum theory is an *explicit* theory of cognitive abilities in the sense that it seeks to account for observed covariation in the total range of cognitive performances. . . .
> 6. The three-stratum theory provides a framework within which correlations between psychometric variables and information-processing variables are to be interpreted." (Carroll 1993:654)

Mental Ability and Socioeconomic Success

Work on the effects of mental ability on socioeconomic success falls into two subtypes. One line of work goes back to at least Jencks' 1972 book *Inequality* and has examined whether intelligence conceptualized as a single factor affects social economic success. Other work in this tradition includes *Who Gets Ahead?* (Jencks 1979), Duncan et al. (1972), and more recently Herrnstein and Murray's controversial 1994 book, *The Bell Curve*, along with the flood of work that has responded to it, for example, Fienberg et al. (1997) and Arrow et al. (2000). All of this work has found that intelligence affects success, though there is disagreement as to how important intelligence and its importance relative to other factors such as family background (Korenman and Winship 2000). This work is of limited importance to the present study in that it simply assumes that intelligence is unidimensional and fails to investigate whether intelligence has different components that differentially affect different components of social and economic success.

A much more limited literature has examined whether different possible dimensions of mental ability affect success. Janet Currie and Duncan Thomas' 1995 paper "Nature vs. Nurture? *The Bell Curve* and Children's Cognitive Achievement" looks at the relationships between different components of the ASVAB for mothers in the NLSY and the test scores of their children. As such, their analysis parallels that carried out here. As in our analysis, they find that different components of the ASVAB have different effects on different children's outcome. They also show that even after controlling for the AFQT component of the ASVAB, individual components of the ASVAB have a significant effect, with the results varying by race, age, and outcome. As a result, they conclude that "the AFQT does not summarize all the information contained in the ASVABs" (Currie and Thomas 1995:21).

Cawley et al. (1997) also analyze the importance of different components of the ASVAB. They show that the Numerical Operations item has a more important effect on log wages than the AFQT or the first component taken from a factor analysis of the four AFQT items. In an earlier paper, Heckman (1995) notes that the Numerical Operations and Coding Speed subtests are represented by the second component of a factor analysis, which by construction is orthogonal to the first component that is assumed to measure *g*. He hypothesizes that this factor is a measure of "fluid intelligence" or "problem solving."

Corcoran (1996), like Currie and Duncan, examines whether additional components of the ASVAB have predictive power for various outcomes net of the effect of the AFQT. Using regression analysis, Corcoran finds that for the vast majority of outcomes that F-tests reject the null hypothesis that the AFQT is the only component of the ASVAB that is predictive of the outcome. The exceptions are poverty, being out of the labor force, being unemployed, divorced, or jailed.

Corcoran also posits a five dimensional mental ability model consisting of quantitative and verbal ability, fluent production, general science knowledge, and technical knowledge. She then examines the importance of these factors for different outcomes. Although she fails to find a set of results that are consistent across outcomes, she does find that fluent production and mathematical ability have large and independent effects on different measures of success, providing evidence against the position that mental ability is unidimensional.

DATA AND METHODOLOGY

This study uses NLSY. The NLSY consists of a nationally representative sample of Americans aged 14–22 when first surveyed in 1979, and three over-samples. The respondents were then surveyed in each subsequent year. The original NLSY sample contained 12,686 people, with a low rate of sample attrition in future years: in 1990, the last year for which data is used in this study, 10,436 respondents, or 89.9 percent of the original sample, were interviewed. We restrict our analysis to white males found in the national subsample (NLS Handbook 11) leading to a sample 2,297 respondents.

Our analysis employs a number of different variables taken from the NLSY. The first set is the ten subject tests that comprise the Armed Services Vocational Aptitude Battery (ASVAB). The ten tests, in the order in which they were given, are General Science (GS), Arithmetic Reasoning (AR), Word Knowledge (WK), Paragraph Comprehension (PC), Numerical Operations (NO), Coding Speed (CS), Auto and Shop Information (AS), Mathematics Knowledge (MK), Mechanical Comprehension (MC), and Electronics Information (EI). These variables were used in standardized form. Bock and Moore (1986) provide a detailed description of the ASVAB.

The second set of variables contains exogenous control variables. The two variables in this category are the respondent's level of education in 1980 and a socioeconomic status (SES) variable initially constructed by Herrn-stein and Murray (1994). The SES variable is a combination of mother's and father's level of education, average family income for 1978 and 1979, mea-sured in 1990 dollars, and a variable coded for the higher of the two parents' occupational status. We use both variables in standardized form in order to facilitate comparisons between estimates.

The third set of variables consists of outcomes. There are three main types of outcomes: educational attainment, economic/labor outcomes, and social outcomes. The educational outcome is level of attainment in 1990 variable. The economic/labor outcomes are the natural log of the respon-dent's income and wages and his or her poverty status. In addition, there are dummy variables indicating whether or not the respondent was out of the labor force for one or more months or was unemployed for one or more months. All of the economic/labor outcome variables are taken from the 1989 survey. Although many of these variables may seem to be measuring similar characteristics, they do, in fact, measure different aspects of eco-nomic well-being and may be affected by different types of ability in differ-ent ways.

The last four outcomes are social outcomes. The first is a dummy vari-able coded yes if the respondent had been interviewed while incarcerated. The three remaining social outcomes all deal with marriage. The next vari-able is coded yes if the respondent was married by age 30 and is exclusive to those respondents thirty years or older as of the 1990 interview. The second marriage variable is another dummy variable and is coded yes if the respon-dent divorced within five years of marriage. This variable excludes unmar-ried respondents as well as those married after 1985. Spouse's income is the fourth and final social outcome. As with the previous income measure, this variable is used in its log form. The mean and standard deviation for each of the variables can be found in Supplementary Appendix Table S1. The corre-lation matrix for these variables can be found in Supplementary Appendix Table S2.

Our analysis uses structural equation modeling methods (Bollen 1989). The structural equation modeling program AMOS (Arbuckle and Wotke 1995) was used in this analysis to obtain maximum likelihood estimates. AMOS allows for the imputation of missing values using a full information maximum likelihood procedure under the assumption that the data are missing at random. This is particularly important given that large number of cases that have missing data on at least one variable. An important limitation of AMOS is that it does not allow either logit or probit specifications for equations with dichotomous dependent variables. As a result, in cases where we have dichotomous dependent variables we estimate linear probability models. AMOS produces a wide variety of measures of fit. We use three: the Tucker-Lewis Index (TLI), the Incremental Fit Index (IFI), and the Root Mean Square of Approximation (RMSEA).

ANALYSIS

We start by considering the general model that forms the basis for all of our analyses. Our analysis was done in three steps. First, we examined different models for the structure of mental ability. We then analyze the effects of parental background and education on mental ability. Finally, we examine the effects of mental ability, modeled as a unitary and as a multidimensional entity on different measures of social and economic success.

Basic Model

Figure 10.1 presents the basic model underlying our analysis. The model is hierarchical with variables causally ordered from left to right. As such, we do not allow for any simultaneity between variables. On the left side of Figure 10.1 are variables that we treat as exogenous—Parent's SES and Educational Attainment in 1980, the year respondents took the ASVAB. Although other exogenous variables could certainly have been used, it was determined that education in 1980 and socioeconomic status were the most vital. Because we have restricted the sample to white males, neither race/ethnicity or gender are included as controls. To the right of these variables are the (mental) ability factors that, depending on the model being analyzed, may consist of a single or multiple dimensions. Mental ability, however modeled, is assumed to depend on both Parental SES and Education in 1980. Mental Ability is measured by the ten separate tests that constitute the ASVAB. These variables are shown at the top of Figure 10.1. Next in the causal sequence is 1990 Educational Attainment. This is assumed to be affected by all prior variables. Finally, at the right side of the diagram are the outcome variables that are assumed to be affected by all other variables.

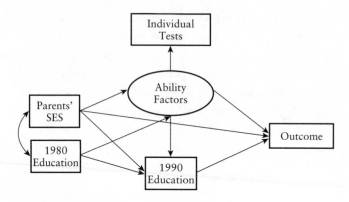

Figure 10.1.   The Basic Model

Alternative Models of Mental Ability

We have chosen to look intensively at three particular factor models of the ability component of our overall model. The first is a single-factor model of the AFQT. The second is the four-factor model discussed by Bock and Moore (1986) in their extensive work with the ASVAB. The last is our original model. This model is based on the Bock and Moore model, though it constructs the factors slightly differently in addition to decomposing the technical ability factor. We label this "The New Model."

The AFQT Model We began by looking at the model used by Herrnstein and Murray (1994), the AFQT. This model assumes there is one ability factor based on four of the ASVAB subtests: arithmetic reasoning, mathematics knowledge, paragraph comprehension, and word knowledge. Herrnstein and Murray argue that the AFQT is a very high quality measure of the psychometricans' concept of *g* (Herrnstein and Murray 1994). Figure 10.2 displays the model. The first three rows of Table 10.1 provide the factor loadings for this model and our different measures of fit.

As can be seen in Table 10.1, the factor loadings for the two quantitative items, Mathematics Knowledge (ZMK) and Arithmetic Skill (ZAR) have the largest factor loadings on the single factor, 0.908 and 0.892 respectively. The loading for the verbal subtests, Work Knowledge (AWK) and Paragraph Comprehension, are considerably lower at 0.686 and 0.734, respectively.

The fit of the one dimensional model is generally poor. As will be the case with all our models, chi square is highly significant at 463.012 with two

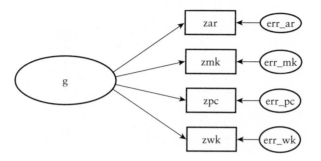

Figure 10.2. AFQT Model

degrees of freedom. The IFI for the AFQT model is in the acceptable range at 0.941, but the values for the TLI and RMSEA fall well into the poor range, at 0.706 and 0.317, respectively.

The Bock and Moore Model Another possible model is the one proposed by Bock and Moore in their extensive work with the ASVAB (Bock and Moore 1986). This model is shown in Figure 10.3.

As described in a previous section, their model involves all ten ASVAB subtests and four ability factors. The four factors are defined as follows:

> Quantitative Ability: Arithmetic Reasoning, Mathematics Knowledge, and Mechanical Comprehension;
> Verbal Attainment: Word Knowledge, Paragraph Comprehension, General Science, and Electronics Information
> Fluent Production: Numerical Operations and Coding Speed.
> Technical Knowledge: General Science, Mechanical Comprehension, Electronics Information, and Auto and Shop Information Tests.

The factor loadings and measures of fit for this model are also shown rows four through twelve in Table 10.1. Numerical Operations (ZNO) and Coding Speed (ZCS) have moderately high loadings on Fluent Production factor at 0.78 and 0.703 respectively. As in the AFQT model, Mathematical Knowledge and Arithmetic Reasoning correlate highly with their underlying factor, here Quantitative Ability, with loadings, respectively, of 0.908 and 0.892. In the Bock and Moore model, Quantitative Ability is also assumed to be measured by the Mechanism Comprehension subtest, which has a factor loading of 0.268. In general, if a variable is to be a good measure of an underlying construct, it should have a factor loading of at least 0.7 and preferably above 0.85. The extremely low factor loading for Mechanical

TABLE 10.1
Factor Loadings

	g	zno	zcs	zmk	zar	zwk	zpc	zgs	zei	zas	zmc
AFQT — g				0.908 (0.019)	0.892 (0.017)	0.686 (0.015)	0.734 (0.016)				
		n = 2297	DF = 2	Chi2 = 463.012	IFI = 0.941	TLI = 0.706	RMSEA = 0.317				
Bock & Moore											
Fluent Production		0.78 (0.017)	0.703 (0.017)								
Quantitative				0.933 (0.018)	0.924 (0.017)						
Verbal						0.762 (0.014)	0.76 (0.016)	0.65 (0.02)	0.386 (0.021)		0.298 (0.02)
Technical Knowledge								0.185 (0.019)	0.463 (0.021)	0.742 (0.017)	0.593 (0.02)
		n = 2297	DF = 26	Chi2 = 327.658	IFI = 0.987	TLI = 0.973	RMSEA = 0.071				
New Model											
Fluent Production		0.781 (0.017)	0.703 (0.017)								
Quantitative				0.938 (0.018)	0.917 (0.017)						
Verbal						0.768 (0.014)	0.763 (0.016)				
GS Factor								0.9 (0.014)			
EI Factor									0.896 (0.014)		
AS Factor										0.876 (0.013)	
MC Factor											0.939 (0.014)
		n = 2297	DF = 18	Chi2 = 235.173	IFI = 0.991	TLI = 0.972	RMSEA = 0.072				

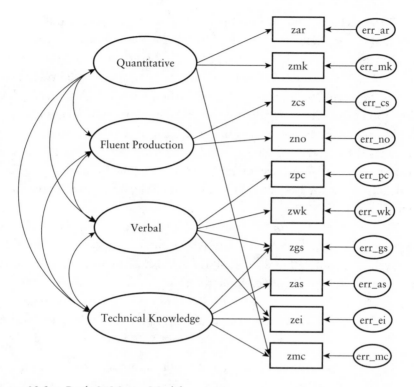

Figure 10.3.   Bock & Moore Model

Comprehension casts considerable doubt on whether it is a measure of Quantitative Ability.

Also similar to the AFQT model, Word Knowledge and Paragraph Comprehension correlate moderately highly with their underlying factor, here Verbal Ability, with loadings, respectively, of 0.762 and 0.76. In the Bock and Moore model General Science and Electronic Information are also assumed to be related to the Verbal Ability factor. Their factor loadings are, respectively, 0.65 and 0.386. These factor loadings are sufficiently low to raise doubts about whether they should be considered measures of Verbal Ability.

The Technical Knowledge factor is a function of General Science, Electronics Information, Auto and Shop Knowledge, and Mechanical Comprehension. The factor loadings here are, respectively, 0.185, 0.463, 0.742, and 0.593. The fact that three of the four factor loadings are as low as they are raises considerable doubt about whether these four variables are measuring the same underlying factor.

The correlations among the latent dimensions of mental ability in the Bock and Moore model and in what we call the New Model are reported in Supplementary Appendix Table S3. Fluent Production has a 0.75 correlation with Verbal Ability and 0.808 correlation with Quantitative Ability. The correlation between Quantitative and Verbal Ability is 0.859. All three of these correlations are relatively high, but low enough to make unclear whether we should think of there being three different dimensions to ability as opposed to only one. The correlations of Technical Knowledge with Fluent Production, Quantitative, and Verbal are lower, 0.443, 0.565, 686, indicating that Technical Knowledge may be something distinctly different from the other three dimensions.

The measures of fit for the Bock and Moore model are substantially better than the measures those for the AFQT model. In this case, the IFI is 0.987, the TLI is 0.973 and the RMSEA is 0.071. The first of these two fall in to the very good fit range, while the third is near the middle of the acceptable range. Based on these results, it seems that the Bock and Moore approach does a much better job of explaining performance on the ASVAB than does that taken by Herrnstein and Murray and the other classicists.

A New Model While the Bock and Moore approach contains four ability factors with some backing in the literature, it does raise questions. The most important is "Does the placement of the ten subtests into these four factors make theoretical sense?" The four factors seem logical, but there are some curious groupings. Although it might be argued that mechanical comprehension could be related to quantitative ability, it is much more difficult to discern why verbal ability should have any effect on general science or electronics information. Furthermore, the technical knowledge factor, while certainly not an absurd grouping, might not be as logical as it seems. While these four tests certainly represent different aspects of technical knowledge, they appear to be measures of quite distinct domains of knowledge. Though one might expect an individual with a strong understanding of general science to have strong earning power, the same might not be true for an individual who scores highly on the auto and shop information test.

With this in mind, we looked for a third model that both fit the ASVAB tests and was backed by solid theory. We explored the fit of a large number of models. In the end, we settled on a model that is similar to the Bock and Moore model, but which removes some of its more troubling aspects. This model is shown in Figure 10.4.

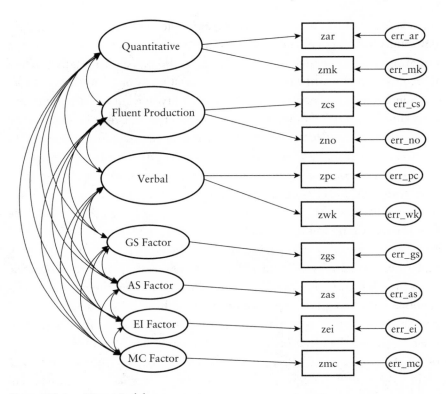

Figure 10.4. New Model

This model, like the Bock and Moore model, includes all ten subtests. It, too, has ability factors called quantitative ability, verbal attainment, and fluent production, though the measures of these factors are slightly different. In our model, the quantitative factor is measured by arithmetic reasoning and mathematical knowledge, but not mechanical comprehension; the verbal attainment factor is measured by word knowledge and paragraph comprehension, but not general science or electronics information; and the fluent production factor, which is the same as in the Bock and Moore model, is measured by numerical operations and coding speed. Because the remaining four tests do not logically fit into one ability factor, we have allowed each of these tests—general science, mechanical comprehension, electronics information, and auto and shop information—to be its own factor.

The factor loadings for the New Model are very similar to those in the Bock and Moore model, generally only differing in the third decimal place. Because there is one factor associated with each of the four Technical

Knowledge items, the factor loadings here are solely a function of the standard deviations of each item. If we had used the whole sample and not restricted our analysis to white males, these loadings would all be one because each of these variables is scaled to have standard deviation of one in the population.

The correlations between the different dimensions of mental ability can be found in Supplementary Appendix Table S3. The correlations among fluent production, verbal ability, and quantitative ability are very close to those in the Bock and Moore model. The correlation of the four technical dimensions with both each other and the three other dimensions are surprisingly high. The correlations range from 0.397 (Fluent Production and Auto-Shop Information) to 0.852 (Verbal and General Science). Most of the correlations are between 0.5 and 0.8.

The fit statistics for the new model are very similar to that of the Bock and Moore model. The IFI and TLI are 0.991 and 0.972, respectively, while the RMSEA is 0.072. Like the Bock and Moore model, the first two measures lie in the very good range, while the third falls in the acceptable part of the spectrum. The chi square for the new model, 235.173 with 18 DF is considerably lower than that for the Bock and Moore model with a chi square of 327.658 and 26 DF. This represents a difference in chi squares of 92.485 with a difference in degrees of freedom of 6. A formal difference in chi squares, however, is not appropriate here as the Bock and Moore model is not strictly nested within the New Model.

Before moving on to the full model, a couple of things should be noted. After adding the two exogenous variables, level of education in 1980 and socioeconomic status, to each of the three models for mental ability, the factor loadings remain remarkably constant. This remains true as we add the different outcomes to the model. These results are available in the Supplementary Appendix.

Effects of Parental SES and 1980 Education on Mental Ability

Table 10.2 presents the effect of Parental SES and 1980 Education for our three different models of mental ability. In our analysis, the exogenous variables parental socioeconomic status and level of education in 1980 have positive and substantial effects on ability, independent of how ability is conceived. These results are largely as would be expected. In the single-factor, AFQT model, the effects of parental SES and education are very similar, with that of SES playing a slightly larger role.

TABLE 10.2
Effects of PSES and 1980 Education on Ability

| | AFQT | BOCK AND MOORE | | | | NEW MODEL | | | | | | |
	AFQT or g	Quant.	Fl. Prod.	Verbal	Tech.	Quant.	Fl. Prod.	Verbal	GS Factor	AS Factor	EI Factor	MC Factor
PSES	0.591	0.544	0.445	0.554	0.188	0.548	0.445	0.546	0.43	0.146	0.297	0.302
	(0.03)	(0.029)	(0.031)	(0.03)	(0.03)	(0.03)	(0.031)	(0.03)	(0.027)	(0.026)	(0.026)	(0.026)
ed80	0.527	0.469	0.479	0.512	0.426	0.475	0.479	0.505	0.427	0.382	0.441	0.345
	(0.03)	(0.03)	(0.032)	(0.03)	(0.031)	(0.03)	(0.032)	(0.031)	(0.027)	(0.027)	(0.027)	(0.027)
n	2297	2297				2297						
DF	8	38				24						
Chi2	535.159	413.925				296.062						
IFI	0.942	0.985				0.989						
TLI	0.847	0.969				0.965						
RMSEA	0.169	0.066				0.07						

The two multifactor models tell a similar story, though there are a few points worth emphasizing. In the Bock and Moore model, the effect of education on the four factors ranges from 0.426 on technical ability to 0.512 on verbal ability. The values of the effect of SES on ability are quite similar, with the exception of Technical Ability. Here, the effect falls to 0.188. These numbers make a good deal of intuitive sense, as one would expect Parental SES and Education to have the largest effects on the more traditional academic ability factors.

The results for the New Model are very similar to that of the Bock and Moore model, but they add insight into the effects of Parental SES and Education on Bock and Moore's Technical Ability factor. We see that the effect of parental SES on the general science factor is much more in line with that of the effects on Quantitative and Verbal Ability, and Fluent Production, while for the more career competency-oriented variables the effect of Parental SES is quite a bit smaller, as was the case with Technical Knowledge in the Bock and Moore model.

The model fit statistics shown in Table 10.2 suggest that the AFQT model does not fit the data satisfactorily. Although the IFI is acceptable, the TLI is below 0.9 (0.847), and RMSEA is greater than 0.1 (0.169). The fit statistics for the Bock and Moore model and the New Model all indicate adequate levels of fit and are quite comparable to each other.

1990 Education as an Outcome

In our model, Education in 1990 is both an outcome of and a mediator variable for Parental SES and Education 1980 and for Mental Ability, however measured. The results for our three different models, each of which treat mental ability differently, are found in Table 10.3.

If we look at direct effects, the AFQT model shows that intelligence has a stronger effect on education than does SES. This is consistent with Herrnstein and Murray's (1994) findings. However, Korenman and Winship (2000) show that when more extensive measures of family background are used, Family Background and the AFTQ seem to have roughly similar size effects. In the Bock and Moore model and the New Model, the effects of family background are similar in size to those in the AFQT model. Somewhat surprisingly, the effects of 1980 education are actually larger in the Bock and Moore and New Model than in the AFQT model. This is unexpected, since in the Bock and Moore and New Model, mental ability is multidimensional,

TABLE 10.3
Outcome: ed90

	AFQT	Bock & Moore	New Model
zed1980	0.151	0.205	0.193
	(0.022)	(0.022)	(0.022)
zses	0.277	0.247	0.263
	(0.022)	(0.022)	(0.021)
g	0.387		
	(0.019)		
Quantitative		0.393	0.425
		(0.041)	(0.042)
Fluent Production		−0.053	−0.021
		(0.032)	(0.034)
Verbal		0.225	0.087
		(0.042)	(0.046)
Technical Knowledge		−0.316	
		(0.027)	
GS Factor			0.078
			(0.03)
AS Factor			−0.204
			(0.024)
EI Factor			−0.053
			(0.027)
MC Factor			−0.048
			(0.025)
n	2297	2297	2297
DF	11	44	27
R2	0.533	0.602	0.585
Chi2	643.225	493.985	345.31
IFI	0.940	0.983	0.988
TLI	0.848	0.965	0.96
RMSEA	.158	0.067	0.072

which allows it to have a greater effect on 1990 Education, which presumably would lead to a decrease in the effect of 1980 Education.

The Bock and Moore and the New Model posits a multidimensional structure for mental ability. In both cases this provides important new insights. In both models Quantitative Ability has a large effect on 1990 Education. Fluent Production's effect, however, is quite small, actually negative, and statistically insignificant. Verbal Ability has a large effect in the Bock and Moore model and a much smaller and not quite statistically significant effect in the New Model. It is unclear to us why this would be the case.

Surprisingly, the Technical Knowledge factor in the Bock and Moore model has a large negative effect (−0.316). Decomposing this factor into its four constituent parts, as done in the New Model, provides insight as to why this might be the case. The General Science (GS) factor has a positive effect on education, as would be expected. The Auto and Shop knowledge (AS) factor, however, has a large negative effect (−0.204), which is highly statistically significant. The Electrical Information (EI) and Mechanical Comprehension (MC) factors have much smaller negative effects, −0.053 and −0.046, respectively, that are on the margin of significance at the 2 σ level. What these results suggest is these last three factors that are part of Bock and Moore Technical Knowledge factor are capturing the decision by some individuals to pursue a blue collar career. The most obvious example would be Auto and Shop Information, which may be, at least partially, a measure of whether individuals intend to pursue a career as an auto mechanic. This makes particular sense if we think of these as attainment measures as opposed to measures of specific components of mental ability. We would expect that individuals who intended to become auto mechanics would know a lot about automobiles. More generally, these results demonstrate the conceptual superiority of our New Model over the Bock and Moore model. By using a single Technical Knowledge factor the Bock and Moore model are combining "apples with oranges." General Science knowledge appears to behave in a way that is broadly similar to the other components of mental ability. The other three technical factors, however, appear to be attainment measures, capturing the amount of knowledge individuals have attained in very specific and narrow areas.

The fit statistics for the three models are similar to what has been found previously. Only the IFI indicates that the AFQT model fits adequately, while the fit statistics for the Bock and Moore model and the New Model are again satisfactory and quite similar.

DETERMINANTS OF SOCIAL AND ECONOMIC SUCCESS

Ideally, we would have preferred to include all of the outcomes in a single model. Due to the limitations of AMOS, however, it was necessary to run a separate analysis for each outcome. With a model as complex as ours, it is not entirely surprising that we ran up against the limits of AMOS' capabilities. In trying to fit the model in a very high-dimensional space, such as would be found in a model including eight or more outcomes, AMOS sometimes produced results that were simply nonsensical. In addition, missing data can also cause these types of problems in complex models.

In all we estimate twenty-seven separate models, nine models for the nine different outcomes for each of the three different specifications of the structure of mental ability. Estimates are found in Tables 10.4, 10.5, and 10.6 with one table for each specification of mental ability. Each column represents the estimates from a different model. In each table we only report the estimates of the effects for those variables that affect the nine different outcomes.[2] Rather than discussing all the outcomes together, we break them into four groups—economic outcomes, labor market outcomes, jail, and marital outcomes.

Economic Outcomes

We start by looking at the three economic outcomes in the study: log wage, log income, poverty. For all three economic outcomes in the AFQT model, Ed90 and Parent SES have similar effects. The effect of the AFQT (g), however, is considerably larger than for these other two variables. As already noted above this is consistent with Herrnstein and Murray's (1994) findings, though as Korenman and Winship (2000) have shown, the effects Family Background and the AFQT are similar if a more extensive set of family background measures are used.

In the Bock and Moore model, Fluent Production is by far the strongest predictor of the three economic outcomes. Quantitative Ability and Technical Knowledge have only very small effects. The effect of Verbal Ability is negative for log wage and log income, though neither effect is statistically significant. What is most important to note is that these findings are the complete opposite of those found in Table 10.3 for 1990 Education. There in the Bock and Moore model, Quantitative and Verbal Ability were the strongest predictors of 1990 Education. Technical Knowledge actually had a large negative effect, and the effect of Fluent Production was small, negative, and

TABLE 10.4
AFQT Model

	OUTCOMES								
	logwage	loginc	pov	unemp	olf	jail	wedby30	div5	lgspin90
ed90	0.046	0.07	-0.007	-0.002	0.008	-0.007	-0.103	-0.046	0.122
	(0.023)	(0.024)	(0.008)	(0.01)	(0.01)	(0.005)	(0.022)	(0.019)	(0.05)
zses	0.048	0.057	-0.008	0.001	0.021	0	-0.003	0.004	0.117
	(0.022)	(0.023)	(0.007)	(0.009)	(0.01)	(0.005)	(0.022)	(0.018)	(0.048)
g	0.125	0.13	-0.032	-0.027	-0.034	-0.018	0.058	-0.007	-0.001
	(0.019)	(0.02)	(0.006)	(0.008)	(0.009)	(0.004)	(0.019)	(0.016)	(0.042)
n	2297	2297	2297	2297	2297	2297	2297	2297	2297
DF	15	15	15	15	15	15	15	15	15
R2	0.139	0.13	0.053	0.019	0.013	0.032	0.031	0.018	0.04
Chi2	664.7	661.475	650.984	646.896	647.208	648.368	656.993	644.907	648.834
IFI	0.964	0.967	0.941	0.941	0.941	0.941	0.945	0.941	0.956
TLI	0.914	0.922	0.858	0.858	0.859	0.858	0.868	0.859	0.893
RMSEA	0.137	0.137	0.136	0.135	0.135	0.136	0.137	0.135	0.136

TABLE 10.5
Bock & Moore Model

	OUTCOMES								
	loguage	loginc	pov	unemp	olf	jail	wedby30	div5	lgspin90
ed90	0.074	0.094	-0.012	0.002	0	-0.01	-0.048	-0.045	0.081
	(0.025)	(0.026)	(0.009)	(0.011)	(0.012)	(0.006)	(0.024)	(0.021)	(0.055)
zses	0.052	0.059	-0.007	0	0.019	0	-0.003	0.006	0.119
	(0.022)	(0.023)	(0.007)	(0.009)	(0.01)	(0.005)	(0.021)	(0.018)	(0.048)
Quantitative	0.033	0.02	0.025	-0.013	-0.025	0.001	-0.059	-0.006	0.015
	(0.041)	(0.043)	(0.014)	(0.018)	(0.019)	(0.01)	(0.04)	(0.035)	(0.091)
Fluent Production	0.155	0.171	-0.036	-0.01	-0.025	-0.014	0.143	-0.022	0.077
	(0.03)	(0.032)	(0.01)	(0.013)	(0.014)	(0.007)	(0.029)	(0.026)	(0.067)
Verbal	-0.095	-0.08	-0.024	-0.014	0.031	-0.006	-0.118	0.023	-0.01
	(0.042)	(0.043)	(0.014)	(0.018)	(0.019)	(0.01)	(0.04)	(0.035)	(0.091)
Technical Knowledge	0.078	0.065	-0.005	0.009	-0.025	-0.003	0.151	-0.016	-0.08
	(0.027)	(0.028)	(0.009)	(0.012)	(0.012)	(0.006)	(0.026)	(0.023)	(0.06)
n	2297	2297	2297	2297	2297	2297	2297	2297	2297
DF	51	51	51	51	51	51	51	51	51
R2	0.173	0.158	0.068	0.021	0.02	0.034	0.137	0.02	0.049
Chi2	506.734	502.801	503.599	502.01	498.436	502.142	518.017	502.688	503.698
IFI	0.987	0.988	0.983	0.983	0.984	0.983	0.983	0.983	0.985
TLI	0.973	0.974	0.966	0.966	0.966	0.966	0.966	0.966	0.97
RMSEA	0.062	0.062	0.062	0.062	0.062	0.062	0.063	0.062	0.062

TABLE 10.6
New Model

	OUTCOMES								
	loguage	loginc	pov	unemp	olf	jail	wedby30	div5	lgspin90
ed90	0.059	0.082	−0.013	0.001	0.003	−0.01	−0.061	−0.037	0.087
	(0.024)	(0.025)	(0.008)	(0.01)	(0.011)	(0.006)	(0.023)	(0.02)	(0.053)
zses	0.053	0.06	−0.006	−0.001	0.019	−0.005	0.002	0.002	0.113
	(0.022)	(0.023)	(0.007)	(.009)	(0.01)	(0.005)	(0.021)	(0.018)	(0.048)
Quantitative	0.048	0.02	0.025	−0.012	−0.024	0.001	−0.048	0.002	−0.011
	(0.043)	(0.045)	(0.015)	(0.019)	(0.02)	(0.01)	(0.042)	(0.037)	(0.096)
Fluent Production	0.15	0.17	−0.034	−0.014	−0.022	−0.011	0.136	−0.042	0.083
	(0.033)	(0.034)	(0.011)	(0.014)	(0.015)	(0.008)	(0.032)	(0.028)	(0.072)
Verbal	−0.094	−0.073	−0.032	0.002	0.017	−0.015	−0.127	0.087	0.026
	(0.046)	(0.048)	(0.016)	(0.02)	(0.021)	(0.011)	(0.045)	(0.039)	(0.102)
GS Factor	0.009	0.007	0.003	−0.002	−0.003	0.002	0.031	−0.067	−0.001
	(0.03)	(0.031)	(0.01)	(0.013)	(0.014)	(0.007)	(0.029)	(0.026)	(0.067)

AS Factor	0.059	0.034	−0.006	0.019	−0.025	−0.005	0.116	0.01	−0.059
	(0.023)	(0.024)	(0.008)	(0.01)	(0.011)	(0.005)	(0.023)	(0.02)	(0.052)
EI Factor	0.028	0.021	0.008	−0.021	0.014	0.011	0.034	−0.02	−0.079
	(0.027)	(0.028)	(0.009)	(0.012)	(0.012)	(0.006)	(0.026)	(0.022)	(0.059)
MC Factor	−0.024	0	−0.006	0.001	−0.003	−0.003	−0.018	−0.005	0.04
	(0.025)	(0.026)	(0.009)	(0.011)	(0.012)	(0.006)	(0.024)	(0.021)	(0.056)
n	2297	2297	2297	2297	2297	2297	2297	2297	2297
DF	31	31	31	31	31	31	31	31	31
R2	0.173	0.156	0.071	0.024	0.02	0.037	0.124	0.037	0.051
Chi2	355.628	354.631	352.061	348.571	346.51	349.572	360.405	346.295	353.126
IFI	0.991	0.991	0.988	0.988	0.988	0.988	0.988	0.988	0.989
TLI	0.968	0.97	0.96	0.96	0.961	0.96	0.96	0.961	0.964
RMSEA	0.068	0.067	0.067	0.067	0.067	0.067	0.068	0.067	0.067

statistically insignificant. Another way of understanding this result is that whereas Fluent Production primarily has a direct effect on the three economic outcomes, the effects of Quantitative and Verbal Ability are primarily indirect, going through 1990 Education. (The Supplementary Appendix provides a more detailed discussion and analysis of the decomposition of effects into total, direct, and indirect effects.)

The results for Quantitative Ability, Fluent Production, and Verbal Ability are similar in our New Model to those in the Bock and Moore model. With the exception of Mechanical Comprehension, which has essentially zero effect, the effects of the technical knowledge factors on economic success are generally in the expected direction—positive with respect to log wage and log income, and negative with respect to poverty. Interestingly, the effect of General Science is extremely small with the effects of Auto and Shop Information and Electronics Information being positive and larger. Here also, the results differ considerably from those found for 1990 Education where General Science had a large and positive effect and the effects of the other three technical factors were negative.

The results of the fit statistics are somewhat different than those found in the previous analyses. Both the IFI and TLI show an adequate fit for the AFQT model. As before, the RMSEA does not. The fit statistics for the Bock and Moore and New Model, however, are considerably stronger and as before are quite similar.

Labor Market Outcomes

Unemployment status and labor force participation comprise the second set of outcomes. The squared multiple correlations for these outcomes are some of the smallest in our study, ranging from 0.013 to 0.024. Therefore, only 1 or 2 percent of the variance in these outcomes is explained by any of the models. Clearly, factors other than those included in the model affect unemployment and labor force participation.

In the AFQT model, intelligence is a better predictor for each of these outcomes than is SES. In the Bock and Moore model, none of the ability measures has a significant effect. Looking at our more complex model does add more information about the technical factors, but no clear pattern emerges. For the outside, the labor force outcome, Auto and Shop Information, Mechanical Comprehension, and General Science have negative weights, while the weight on Electronics Information is positive. For unemployment,

Auto and Shop and Mechanical Information are negative while Electronics Information and General Science are positive.[3]

In summary, in the context of labor market outcomes differentiating between different components of ability is not particularly useful. Although AFQT (g) substantially affects these outcomes, Fluent Production, Quantitative Ability, Verbal Ability, and Technical Knowledge do not. Allowing the separate components of Technical Knowledge to have different effects in the New Model does suggest that some of these components may affect our two labor market outcomes. However, from the inconsistent pattern of these effects it is difficult to understand what the nature of these effects might be.

The pattern of fit statistics is similar to what we have found before. Only the IFI indicates an adequate fit for the AFQT model. The fit statistics for the Bock and Moore model and the New Model are similar, appreciably better, and all indicate an adequate fit.

Social Outcomes

Like the employment and labor force outcomes, the R-squares for the social outcomes are quite low. The only R-squares that are higher than 0.05 for any of the social outcomes are those for the Wed By 30 variable. For the Bock and Moore model, the result is 0.137, while for the New Model where the squared multiple correlation is only 0.031.

For the AFQT model, for all social outcomes but spouse's income, the direct effect of intelligence is greater than that of SES. The four ability factor model of Bock and Moore adds more detail to this picture. For each of the four social outcomes, Fluent Production is one of the two most important ability factors. The other important factor for each outcome varies and does not seem to follow any pattern.

Expanding Bock and Moore's technical ability factor by using the New Model provides substantial new information only for the spouse's income outcome. In the Bock and Moore model, the effect of technical ability on spouse's income is negative and the largest of the four ability factors. The New Model suggests that this comes mostly from the Electronics Information ability and the Auto and Shop factors. The effects of the other two technical ability factors, Mechanical Comprehension and General Science, are quite small and statistically insignificant.

The pattern of fit statistics here is similar to what we have found before. Only the IFI indicates an adequate fit for the AFQT model. The fit statistics for the Bock and Moore model and the New Model are similar, appreciably better, and all indicate an adequate fit.

DISCUSSION AND CONCLUSION

Our goal in this chapter has been to examine whether a uni- or multidimensional model of intelligence provides a better understanding of the ways in which intelligence affects different dimensions of economic and social success. Our analyses have focused on three models: a model that assumes that intelligence is unidimensional, what we term the AFQT model; Bock and Moore's model which assumes that intelligence, at least as measured by the ASVAB, consists of four dimensions: Quantitative and Verbal Ability, Fluent Production, and Technical Knowledge; and what we term our New Model, which assumes that the ASVAB captures the same first three measures of intelligence as in the Bock and Moore model, but that technical knowledge consists of four separate factors that are more appropriately thought of as achievement measures.

Two broad conclusions are possible. First, we find throughout that a model that assumes that intelligence is unidimensional provides a poor fit to the data. This is true whether the model simply treats intelligence as a function of Parental SES and Education in 1980 or in the various models that estimate the effect of intelligence on different measures of economic and social success. Both the Bock and Moore and our New Model fit the data considerably better and by standard criteria provide adequate fits.

In terms of fit, the Bock and Moore and our New Model do about equally well. We, however, believe that the New Model should be preferred because it is theoretically more defensible and in a number of cases provides more sensible results. Specifically, results from our analysis suggest that General Science behaves more like an intelligence measure, whereas the other three components of Technical Knowledge (Auto and Shop Information, Mechanical Comprehension, and Electronics Information) act more like indicators of interest in a vocational education and career. In particular, General Science Knowledge positively predicts educational attainment and economic success, whereas the other three components of technical knowledge have negative effects on educational attainment, but positive or insignificant effects on economic success. We also see little theoretical justification of the linkages in the Bock and Moore model between the latent Quantitative Ability factor and Mechanical Comprehension, but not the other Technical Knowledge items or between the latent Verbal Ability factor and General Science.

The second conclusion is that in both the Bock and Moore Model and the New Model different dimensions of mental ability differentially effect different measures of economic and social success. Specifically, in both the Bock and Moore Model and the New Model, Quantitative Ability is the most important predictor of educational attainment in 1990. In both models, Fluent Production has no effect on educational attainment. Verbal Ability has a statistically significant effect on 1990 educational attainment in the Bock and Moore Model, but not in the New Model.

With respect to other outcomes, the results are quite different. The findings are clearest with respect to economic outcomes. Here, in both the Bock and Moore model and the New Model, Fluent Production is the most important predictor, whereas the effects of Quantitative and Verbal Ability are either close to zero or negative, but statistically insignificant. With respect to other outcomes, the effects of different dimensions vary and it is difficult to find any overall consistent pattern.

In conclusion, we would argue that the evidence from our analysis argues strongly against a unidimensional model of mental ability. Our analysis suggests that a unidimensional model both fits the data poorly, and that different dimensions of mental ability differentially affect different measures of social and economic success. Specifically, Quantitative Ability and possibly Verbal Ability are the most important predictors of educational attainment, but appear to have no direct effect on economic success. Rather they affect economic success indirectly through 1990 educational attainment. Fluent Production is the most important predictor of economic success, but appears to have no effect on educational attainment. A question of considerable interest is why Fluent Production should directly affect economic success, but Quantitative Ability and Verbal Ability should only affect economic success through educational attainment. One possibility is that education serves as a relatively accurate signal to employers as to individual's actual Quantitative and Verbal Ability. If this is correct, then education may affect economic success both because of the human capital it represents and because it is an indicator for individuals' Quantitative and Verbal Ability.

Notes

1. However, Eysenck (1939) and Carroll (1988) reanalyzed Thurstone's data and found that a common factor accounted for more of the variance than Thurstone had reported.

2. Each model also provides estimates of the effects of Parental SES and 1980 Education on Mental Ability and the effects of these variables on 1990 Education. In addition, each model provides estimates for the factor loading associated with the different test items in each mental ability structure. In general, results vary only modestly across models.

3. There is one source of concern when looking at the results of the economic/labor outcomes using the Bock and Moore model and our model. It revolves around the direction of the effect of verbal ability on several of these variables. In the Bock and Moore model, the sign of the effect on wages, income, and labor force participation is the opposite of what one would expect. When examining our model, this is true of the effects on wages, income, labor force participation, and unemployment status. It should be noted, however, that the effect of verbal ability differs significantly from zero only on wages for each model. Nonetheless, we decided that it was worthwhile to look at these outcomes in a slightly different manner in order to see whether we could alleviate some of this concern. Our solution was to restrain the effect of verbal ability on the outcomes in question to zero and then to check that this operation did not dramatically affect our previous results. Results are reported in the Supplementary Appendix Tables S7 and S8.

References

Arbuckle, James L. and Werner Wothke. 1995. *Amos 4.0 User's Guide*. Chicago: SmallWaters Corporation.

Arrow, Kenneth, Samuel Bowles, and Steve Durlauf, eds. 2000. *Meritocracy and Society*. Princeton, NJ: Princeton University Press.

Bock, R. Darrell and Elsie G.J. Moore. 1986. *Advantage and Disadvantage: A Profile of American Youth*. Hillsdale, NJ: Lawrence Erlbaum Associates.

Bollen, Kenneth A. 1989. *Structural Equations with Latent Variables*. Wiley Series in Probability and Mathematical Statistics. New York: Wiley.

Brody, Nathan. 1992. *Intelligence*. San Diego: Academic Press.

Carroll, J. B. 1988. *Yes, There's* g, *and What Else*. Unpublished manuscript based on a colloquium presented at the University of Delaware, November 17, 1988.

Carroll, J. B. 1993. *Human Cognitive Abilities: A Survey of Factor-Analytic Studies*. New York: Cambridge.

Cattell, R. B. 1971. *Abilities: Their Structure, Growth, and Action*. Boston: Houghton Mifflin.

Cawley, John, Karen Coneely, James Heckman, and Edward Vytlacil. 1997. "Cognitive Ability, Wages, and Meritocracy." In *Intelligence, Genes, and Success:*

Scientists Respond to The Bell Curve, edited by Bernie Devlin, Stephen Fienberg, Daniel P. Resnick, and Kathryn Roeder. New York: Springer-Verlag.

Ceci, Stephen J. 1990. *On Intelligence . . . More or Less*. Englewood Cliffs, NJ: Prentice Hall.

Center for Human Resource Research, The Ohio State University. 1995. *NLS Handbook*.

Corcoran, Jill. 1996. "Beyond *The Bell Curve* and G: Rethinking Ability and its Correlates." Senior Thesis. Department of Sociology. Harvard University.

Currie, Janet, and Duncan Thomas. 1995. "Nature vs. Nurture? Race, Children's Cognitive Achievement and *The Bell Curve*." NBER Working Paper no. 5240, August.

Devlin, Bernie, Stephen Fienberg, Daniel P. Resnick, and Kathryn Roeder. 1997. *Intelligence, Genes, and Success: Scientists Respond to The Bell Curve*. New York: Springer-Verlag.

Duncan, O. D., D. L. Featherman, and B. Duncan. 1972. *Socioeconomic Background and Achievement*. New York: Seminar Press.

Eysenck, H. J. 1939. "Primary Mental Abilities." *British Journal of Educational Psychology* 9:81–98.

Fienberg, Stephen, Daniel Resnick, Bernie Devlin, and Kathryn Roeder, eds. 1997. *Intelligence and Success: Is It All in the Genes: Scientists Respond to The Bell Curve*. New York: Springer-Verlag.

Heckman, James J. 1995. "Lessons from the Bell Curve." *Journal of Political Economy* 103(5):1091–1120.

Herrnstein, Richard J., and Charles Murray. 1994. *The Bell Curve: Intelligence and Class Structure in American Life*. New York: Free Press.

Hunt, Earl. 1995. "The Role of Intelligence in Modern Society." *American Scientist* 83 (July–August): 356–68.

Jencks, Christopher. 1979. *Who Gets Ahead? The Determinants of Economic Success in America*. New York: Basic Books.

Jensen, Arthur R. 1980. *Bias in Mental Testing*. New York: Free Press.

Korenman, Sanders, and Christopher Winship. 2000. "A Reanalysis of *The Bell Curve*: Intelligence, Family Background, and Schooling." Pp. 137–78 in *Meritocracy and Society*, edited by Kenneth Arrow, Samuel Bowles, and Steve Durlauf. Princeton, NJ: Princeton University Press.

Snyderman, Mark, and Stanley Rothman. 1988. *The IQ Controversy, the Media and Public Policy*. New Brunswick: Transaction.

Spearman, Charles. 1927. *The Abilities of Man: Their Nature and Measurement*. New York: Macmillan.

Sternberg, Robert J. 1985. *Beyond IQ: A Triarchic Theory of Human Intelligence*. Cambridge: Cambridge University Press.

Thurstone, L. L. 1931. Multiple Factor Analysis. *Psychological Review* 38:406–27.

Thurstone, L. L., and T. G. Thurstone. 1941. *Factorial Studies of Intelligence*. Chicago: University of Chicago Press.

CHAPTER ELEVEN

Counterfactual Analysis of Inequality and Social Mobility

Flavio Cunha, James Heckman, and Salvador Navarro

I. INTRODUCTION

Most studies of income inequality and social mobility are descriptive in nature. Studies of inequality compare differences in the location in the overall distribution of income among groups at a point in time and over time and the evolution of income distributions over time. Studies of mobility measure movements of income within lifetimes or across generations.[1] These exercises present factual summaries of income inequality and income mobility.

For the purposes of policy analysis, and for interpreting facts within a scientific model, it is necessary to move beyond factual description to construct counterfactuals. They can be used to determine what would happen to mobility or inequality if different policies or interventions were tried than the policies historically observed. They can also be used to decompose observed inequality and mobility into components due to genuine uncertainty ("luck" as described by Jencks et al. 1972) and components of heterogeneity and individual differences that are predictable, at least by a certain age or stage of the life cycle.

This chapter describes recent methodological advances that enable analysts to construct counterfactual distributions and separate heterogeneity (predictable variability across persons) from uncertainty.[2] In general, the welfare consequences of predictable heterogeneity and unpredictable uncertainty are not the same. Using the tools reviewed here, analysts can determine how much inequality and mobility is forecastable at a given age and how much is unforecastable luck.

These methods allow analysts to move beyond aggregate summary measures of inequality that are based on the anonymity postulate to determine which groups in an initial distribution are affected by a policy change and how they are affected. The anonymity postulate treats two aggregate distributions as equally good if, after income is redistributed among persons, the overall distribution is the same. With our methods we can determine, for reforms that are contemplated but have never been implemented, which groups in an initial position benefit or lose, how much they lose, how they would vote in advance of a reform, and how they would vote after it is implemented, once the *ex ante* uncertainty surrounding the outcomes of the reform is resolved.

The methods we develop are more powerful than randomization. Evidence from randomized trials yields marginal distributions of outcomes separately for treatments and controls (Heckman 1992; Heckman, Smith, and Clements 1997). Our methods identify joint distributions of treatment and no-treatment outcomes. Thus we can identify how persons in one quantile of an initial no-treatment distribution will be shifted to quantiles of the treatment distribution, something an experiment cannot do unless additional assumptions are invoked (see Heckman, Smith, and Clements 1997; or Heckman and Smith 1998). Our methods can also be used to construct the joint distributions of outcomes across policy states, whether or not the policies have been implemented. Panel data can sometimes be used to construct these outcomes when policies are observed. Our analysis allows us to construct these joint distributions even if none of the policies has been observed.

We can move beyond aggregate summary measures of policy outcomes to gauge the effects of a policy on subgroups defined by *unobserved* potential outcomes within the overall population distribution. Thus, we can move beyond traditional inequality and social mobility analysis to consider how a policy shifts persons from a position in one potential outcome distribution to another even though joint potential outcome distributions cannot be directly measured, but must be derived from marginal outcome distributions for program participants and nonparticipants. Conventional studies of inequality consider movements of persons among observed (measured) states (see, e.g., Ravallion 2003).

The plan of the rest of the chapter is as follows. In section 2, we discuss the conventional criteria used to evaluate social outcomes as a way of placing our work in context. In section 3, we present a choice-theoretic framework for constructing counterfactuals and we consider limitations of our approach.

Section 4 presents our method for constructing distributions of counterfactuals based on factor models, extending methods developed by Goldberger and Jöreskog (1975) and Jöreskog (1977) to consider the construction of counterfactuals. We summarize results on identification derived in a number of previous papers. Section 5 shows how we can use information about choices and subsequent realizations to infer how much agents know about future earnings when making their choices about college. This section reviews a method for estimating "luck" and separating it from predictable heterogeneity that is developed in Carneiro, Hansen, and Heckman (2003) and Cunha, Heckman, and Navarro (2005). Section 6 reports the empirical results that demonstrate the power of the method. Among other things, we find in our data that roughly 80 percent of the variance in the returns to college are forecastable at the time students make their college decisions. We present an analysis of counterfactuals that shows the effects of a tuition policy on inequality and mobility. With our methodology it is possible to present a much richer analysis of the inequality and mobility consequences of policies. Section 7 concludes.

2. WELFARE ECONOMICS AND SOCIAL CHOICE

In order to place our work in context, we briefly review the welfare measures used in the policy evaluation literature. The literature on welfare economics and social choice presents different criteria to assess the desirability of alternative policies. The standard model of welfare economics postulates a social welfare function V defined over the utilities u_i under policy j of the N members of society,

$$V_j = V[u^j_1, u^j_2, \ldots, u^j_N],$$

where V_j is the society's welfare under policy j and u^j_i is the utility of person i under policy j. One example is the Benthamite social welfare function $V_j = \sum_{i=1}^{N} u^j_i$. Another possibility is the Rawlsian social welfare function $V_j = \min\{u^j_1, u^j_2, \ldots, u^j_N\}$.

Standard criteria used to evaluate policies and compare income distributions including those based on the preceding welfare criteria, as well as conventional cost-benefit analysis, invoke the anonymity axiom (Cowell 2000). To define this concept, let $(Y^A_1, Y^A_2, \ldots, Y^A_N)$ and $(Y^B_1, Y^B_2, \ldots, Y^B_N)$ denote the observed income in a society with N agents under policy A and policy B, respectively. The subscripts denote individuals. Assume that under policy B everything else is the same as under policy A, except that the outcomes for agents 1 and 2 under policy B are exchanged:

$$(Y_1^B, Y_2^B, \ldots, Y_N^B) = (Y_2^A, Y_1^A, \ldots, Y_N^A).$$

According to the anonymity axiom, any social welfare ordering over these two policies or states of affairs should be indifferent between policies A and B, because overall inequality is the same.

Adopting the anonymity axiom is empirically convenient because its implementation only requires information on the marginal distributions of outcomes under different policies, and not the joint distributions of outcomes across policy states. However, as noted by Cowell (2000), the anonymity axiom makes strong assumptions. The main problem is that individual outcomes under alternative policies are either assumed to be independent or any such dependence of outcomes across policy states is assumed to be irrelevant in assessing the merits of alternative policies. The initial position of persons is assumed not to affect judgments about final outcomes of a policy. However, if the joint distributions of policy outcomes can be recovered, we can assess how the median voter would evaluate a proposed reform, both *ex post* and *ex ante*, and see what percentage of a population would favor the reform given their initial position—the desiderata of modern positive political economy (see Persson and Tabellini 2000). If only the two marginal distributions (pre- and post-policy) are available, we cannot assess how the median voter, who is interested in how a policy affects his or her movements from the baseline to the final state, would evaluate that policy unless one assumes something about the dependence of outcomes for persons across policies.

In any actual policy setting, it is likely that persons, or groups of persons, have at least partial knowledge about how they will fare under different policy regimes. Thus, even if outcomes in alternative policy regimes are not completely known, outcomes under the policy in place are known. The outcomes in different regimes are likely to be dependent so that persons who benefit under one policy are also likely to benefit under another. However, due to uncertainty, these outcomes are unlikely to be perfectly dependent. Consequently, for a variety of actual social choice mechanisms, both the initial and final positions of each agent are relevant for evaluation of social policy, but the exact dependence is unknown to the analyst. Below we show how the methodology presented here can be applied to identify who gains or loses from each policy at various deciles of initial or final distributions, relaxing the anonymity axiom. We can do such analyses for factual or counterfactual distributions. We also allow for uncertainty in the evaluation of outcome states not yet experienced. Thus, we can distinguish between *ex ante* and *ex post* evaluations of a reform.

3. THE EVALUATION OF SOCIAL PROGRAMS: CHOICES WITHIN POLICY STATES AND COMPARISONS ACROSS POLICY STATES

Social programs such as job training and college tuition subsidies are central features of the modern welfare state. Because different parties may gain or lose from such programs, there is a demand for knowledge about the redistributive effects of government policies. The central problem in the literature on the evaluation of social policies is the construction of counterfactuals. In the tradition of the literature on income distribution, Bourguignon and Ferreira (2003) call this construction *ex ante* analysis, although we prefer the term counterfactual analysis, reserving "*ex ante*" and "*ex post*" to describe resolution of the uncertainty about a proposed policy before and after it is implemented. Counterfactuals can be constructed for both *ex ante* and *ex post* evaluations.

In the simplest form of the evaluation problem, there are two possible outcomes within each policy regime. Let $S = 0$, and $S = 1$ denote nonreceipt and receipt of education, respectively, within a policy regime. In our empirical analysis, $S = 0$ denotes a worker who is a high school graduate, and $S = 1$ denotes a worker who is a college graduate. In an analysis of unions, workers who are not members of a union are designated by $S = 0$ while those who are members are denoted $S = 1$. S can denote many possible treatments, and our methodology applies to all of them.

Associated with each level of education is a potential outcome. Let (Y_0, Y_1) denote potential outcomes in state $S = 0$ and $S = 1$, respectively within a given policy regime. Each person has a (Y_0, Y_1) pair. We assume that (Y_0, Y_1) have finite means and can be expressed in terms of conditioning variables X in the following manner:

$$Y_0 = \mu_0(X) + U_0 \tag{1a}$$

$$Y_1 = \mu_1(X) + U_1, \tag{1b}$$

where $E(Y_0 \mid X) = \mu_0(X)$, $E(Y_1 \mid X) = \mu_1(X)$ and $E(U_0 \mid X) = E(U_1 \mid X) = 0$. The gain for an individual who moves from the $S = 0$ to $S = 1$ within a policy regime is Δ, where $\Delta \equiv Y_1 - Y_0$.

If Y_1 and Y_0 could be observed for each individual at the same time, the gain of going to school designated by $S = 1$ would be known for each person. An evaluation problem within a policy regime arises because we do not observe the pair (Y_0, Y_1) for anybody. This is a missing data problem: in calculating the gains to attending college for a particular individual who chooses to be a college graduate, we observe her college earnings (Y_1), but not her high school earnings (Y_0). The solution to this missing data problem is to construct counterfactuals: how much a college graduate would earn if she had chosen to be a high school graduate. To identify these counterfactuals, different approaches in the literature of program evaluation make different assumptions about how the missing data are related to the available data, and what data are available. The econometric approach features the use of choice data in constructing counterfactuals.

For simplicity, and in accordance with a well-established tradition in econometrics, we write index I as a net utility

$$I = Y_1 - Y_0 - C \tag{2}$$

where C is the cost of participation in sector 1. We write $C = \mu_C(Z) + U_C$ where the Z are observed (by the analyst) determinants of cost and U_C denotes unobserved determinants of C from the point of view of the analyst. In reduced form (substituting out for Y_1, Y_0 and C), we may write

$$I = \mu_I(X, Z) + U_I$$

where

$$\mu_I(X, Z) = \mu_1(X) - \mu_0(X) - \mu_C(Z)$$

and

$$U_I = U_1 - U_0 - U_C.$$

We write

$$S = 1 \text{ if } I \geq 0; \, S = 0 \text{ otherwise.} \tag{3}$$

Thus, if the net utility of state 1 is positive, $S = 1$ is chosen. Other decision rules may be used, but the model of (Y_1, Y_0, S) is sufficiently rich to serve our purposes.[3]

Overall income within the policy regime is $Y = SY_1 + (1 - S)Y_0$. Traditional analyses of inequality compare the distribution of Y across policy regimes that are observed. Analyses of social mobility document the dynamics of life cycle or intergenerational movements. Our approach delves more deeply. We consider the consequences of choices ($S = 0$ or $S = 1$) within policy regimes and how alternative policies cause people to change their S decisions and relocate into different portions of the overall distribution. Under our approach, we can estimate the proportion who switch from $S = 0$ to $S = 1$, where they come from in both the distribution of Y_0 and of Y (in one policy regime), and where they go to in the distribution of Y_1 and of Y (in the other policy regime). We can do a parallel analysis for those who switch from $S = 1$ to $S = 0$, reversing the roles of Y_0 and Y_1. We can do this for counterfactuals as well as for factuals. We can also do counterfactual social mobility analysis. Another major advantage of our approach is that we control for the econometric consequences of endogeneity in the choice of S and thereby avoid self-selection biases. In our empirical work, we control for the endogeneity of schooling.

Traditionally, the literature on program evaluation has focused on estimating mean impacts of S and not distributions. The most commonly studied parameter in the literature is the average treatment effect:

$$ATE = E(\Delta \mid X) = E(Y_1 - Y_0 \mid X).$$

Another popular parameter is the effect of treatment on the treated,

$$TT = E(\Delta \mid X, S = 1) = E(Y_1 - Y_0 \mid X, S = 1).$$

The modern literature allows for the possibility that the gains to switching from $S = 0$ to $S = 1$, $Y_1 - Y_0$, are heterogenous across agents even conditioning on X. Further, the agents act on this difference when choosing S. In the analysis of this model, two problems emerge.

The first is an interpretive problem. If the gains (Δ) vary across agents, there is no single number that summarizes the distribution of gains for all purposes of policy evaluation. For each specific policy question we want to address, we must carefully define the parameter of interest (see Heckman and Vytlacil 2005, 2006a). In general, the average gain of those who are in the program is not the relevant parameter of interest. Consider an example from the economics of education: if we want to determine the gains of a policy that reduces tuition, we need to know (1) how many entrants into education will be induced by the tuition policy, and (2) from where in the distribution of gains to schooling $(Y_1 - Y_0)$ the new entrants are coming. Given (1) and (2), we can compute aggregate gains from the tuition policy. We can then check whether the return of the marginal entrant is above or below that of the typical person enrolled in the program. For other problems of distributional analysis, it is of interest to determine where in an initial distribution beneficiaries come from and where they end up in the treatment outcome distribution.

The second problem is an econometric one. Once we have defined the parameter of interest, say the gain to the median voter, how can we estimate it? If we wish to avoid special assumptions like statistical independence between Y_0 and Y_1 or perfect dependence, the solution is to recover the joint distribution of (Y_0, Y_1). Once we know this distribution, it is possible to calculate the distribution of $(Y_1 - Y_0)$ for any group of people we are interested in and obtain its median or any other quantile. We may compute several measures of interest from this distribution.

The proportion of people taking schooling that benefit from it in terms of gross returns $\Delta(= Y_1 - Y_0)$ is $\Pr(\Delta > 0 \mid S = 1)$. This parameter is one way to measure how widely program gains are distributed among participants. The proportion of the total population benefiting from participating in schooling is $\Pr(\Delta > 0 \mid S = 1) \cdot \Pr(S = 1)$. It is of interest to determine how many people in society at large benefit (in the sense of $Y_1 - Y_0$ gains) from participating in schooling.

The distribution of gains from schooling for agents who are at selected base state values is $\Pr(\Delta \leq a \mid S = 1, Y_0 = y_0)$. This measure interests Rawlsian evaluators who seek to determine the impact of schooling on recipients in the lower tail of the base state distribution.

The increase in the level of outcomes above a certain threshold, say the poverty line $\bar{y}$, due to schooling is $\Pr(Y_1 > \bar{y} \mid S = 1) - \Pr(Y_0 > \bar{y} \mid S = 1)$. This is a parameter that describes how the distribution of the outcomes for the participants compares to the distribution of the outcomes for the same agents if they had not participated in schooling.

We can also form measures for people affected by a specific policy. Let A and B denote two policy states, say a high tuition and a low tuition policy, respectively. The proportion of people who benefit from a policy that induces them into schooling (e.g., a reduction in tuition) is $\Pr(\Delta > 0 \mid S_A = 0, S_B = 1)$, where the measure of benefit is a gross gain measure and S^A and S^B are choice indicators under policy A and B, respectively. We can also measure the proportion of the total population that benefits from the policy-induced movement: $\Pr(\Delta > 0 \mid S_A = 0, S_B = 1) \cdot \Pr(S_A = 0, S_B = 1)$. Our empirical analysis reports these and other measures of impact that we can define and estimate both within a policy and across policy regimes.

In this chapter, we report on recent research that solves the problem of constructing counterfactuals by identifying the joint distribution of (Y_1^A, Y_0^A) and the potential outcomes under policy A, conditional on S (or I), using a factor structure model. These models generalize the LISREL models of Jöreskog (1977) and the MIMIC model of Goldberger and Jöreskog (1975) to produce counterfactual distributions. Before we proceed to explain the methodology, we discuss the types of policies we evaluate.

It is fruitful to distinguish between two kinds of policies: (1) those that affect potential outcomes (Y_0^A, Y_1^A) for outcomes and costs (C^A) under policy regime A through price and quality effects and (2) those that affect sectorial choices (through C^A), but do not affect potential outcomes. Tuition and educational access policies that do not produce general equilibrium effects fall into the second category of policy. It is the second kind of policy that receives the most attention in empirical work on the economics of education, either when estimating gains to schooling under a policy regime $(Y_1^A - Y_0^A)$ (see e.g., Card 1999) or evaluating schooling policies (e.g., Kane 1994).[4]

Consider two general policy environments denoted A and B. These policies might affect the costs of schooling including access to it. In the general case, we could have (Y_0^A, Y_1^A, C^A) and (Y_0^B, Y_1^B, C^B) for each person. There might be general equilibrium policies or policies that operate in the presence of social interactions that affect both costs and outcomes.[5]

A special case of this policy produces two social states for outcomes that we wish to compare. However, in this special case, interventions have no effect on potential outcomes and can be described as producing two choice sets (Y_0, Y_1, C^A) and (Y_0, Y_1, C^B) for each person. They affect costs and the choice of outcomes, but not the potential outcomes as a full-fledged general equilibrium or social interaction analysis would do. We focus most of our attention on policies that keep potential schooling outcomes unchanged but that vary C in selecting who takes schooling.

This chapter analyzes two sets of counterfactuals: (1) (Y_0^A, Y_1^A) within policy regime A and (Y_0^B, Y_1^B) within policy regime B, and (2) aggregate income across policy regimes (Y^A, Y^B) where $Y^A = Y_1^A S^A + Y_0^A (1 - S^A)$ is the observed income under regime A and $Y^B = Y_1^B S^B + Y_0^B (1 - S^B)$ is the income under regime B, where $S^A = 1$ if a person chose $S = 1$ under regime A and S^B is defined in an analogous fashion. The tradition in the analysis of income inequality is to make comparisons across regimes, that is, to compare the distribution of $Y^A = Y_1^A S^A + Y_0^A(1 - S^A)$ with the distribution of $Y^B = Y_1^B S^B + Y_0^B(1 - S^B)$. When both A and B are observed, such comparisons are straightforward if there are panel data on incomes of the same persons in both states.

With our methods, we can construct counterfactual distributions of (Y_1^A, Y_0^A) and (Y_1^B, Y_0^B) within each policy regime and can also construct comparisons across policy states based on $Y_1^A S^A + Y_0^A(1 - S^A)$ and $Y_1^B S^B + Y_0^B(1 - S^B)$. We can also compare movements from Y_0^A to Y_1^B as well as other comparisons whether or not A and B are observed. This method allows us to obtain a much richer understanding of the inequality and social mobility consequences of policy change than are available from inequality measures based on the anonymity axiom, and allows us to go more deeply than panel data analyses that compare movements from the distribution of Y_A to the distribution of Y_B. We can use our analysis to generate counterfactual states never measured.

4. IDENTIFYING COUNTERFACTUAL DISTRIBUTIONS USING FACTOR MODELS

Identifying the joint distribution of potential outcomes is a difficult problem because we do not observe both components of (Y_0, Y_1) for anyone except in special panel data situations (see Heckman and Smith 1998). Thus, one cannot in general directly form the joint distribution of potential outcomes (Y_0, Y_1). Heckman and Honoré (1990) show that, if we know that $C = 0$ for every person, decision rule (2)–(3) applies, there are distinct variables in $\mu_1(X)$ and $\mu_0(X)$, X is independent of (U_1, U_0), and other mild regularity restrictions are satisfied, then one can identify the joint distribution of (Y_0, Y_1) given X.[6] In this case, the agents choose S solely in terms of the differences in outcomes. This information buys identification. However, if C varies across people and contains some variables unobserved by the analyst, this method breaks down.

As shown by Heckman (1990) and Heckman and Smith (1998), under the assumptions that (Z, X) are statistically independent from (U_0, U_1, U_I), $\mu_I(X, Z)$ is a nontrivial function of Z given X, and full support on $\mu_0(X)$, $\mu_1(X)$ and $\mu_I(X, Z)$, and an assumption that the elements of the pairs $(\mu_0(X), \mu_I(X, Z))$ and $(\mu_1(X), \mu_I(X, Z))$ can be varied independently of each other, then one can identify the joint distributions of $(U_0, \frac{U_I}{\sigma_I})$ and $(U_1, \frac{U_I}{\sigma_I})$

and also $\mu_0(X)$, $\mu_1(X)$, and $\frac{\mu_I(X, Z)}{\sigma_I}$.[7] Thus, one can identify the joint distributions of (Y_0, I^*) and (Y_1, I^*) given X and Z where $I^* = I/\sigma_I$. One cannot recover the conditional (on X, Z) joint distribution of (Y_0, Y_1) or (Y_0, Y_1, I^*) without further assumptions.

We provide an intuitive motivation for why $F(Y_0, I^*)$ and $F(Y_1, I^*)$ are identified in Appendix A, drawing on standard results in the semiparametric discrete choice literature. The thrust of this literature is that under the stated conditions, we can identify the distribution of I up to a factor of proportionality, σ_I. We can also identify

$$F(Y_0, I \mid I < 0, X, Z) = F(Y_0 \mid D = 0, X, Z) \Pr(D = 0 \mid X, Z)$$

and

$$F(Y_1, I \mid I \geq 0, X, Z) = \Pr(Y_1 \mid D = 1, X, Z) \Pr(D = 1 \mid X, Z).$$

By varying X, Z we can trace out the full distributions of $F(Y_0, I)$ and $F(Y_1, I)$ respectively. Once we estimate the distributions, we perform conventional factor analysis on (Y_0, I^*) and (Y_1, I^*) because, effectively, we observe these two distributions.

4.1 Factor Models

The factor structure approach developed by Aakvik, Heckman, and Vytlacil (1999, 2005) presents a solution to the problem of constructing counterfactual distributions. Our presentation follows that of Carneiro, Hansen, and Heckman (2001, 2003) and we show the essential idea. Suppose that the unobservables follow a one factor structure. Our methods generalize to the multifactor case, but for the sake of simplicity we focus on the one factor case in our exposition although we estimate models with multiple factors in our empirical work reported below.[8]

We assume that all of the dependence across (U_0, U_1, U_{I^*}) is generated by a scalar factor θ as in Aakvik, Heckman, and Vytlacil (1999, 2005),

$$U_0 = \alpha_0\theta + \varepsilon_0$$
$$U_1 = \alpha_1\theta + \varepsilon_1$$
$$U_{I^*} = \alpha_{I^*}\theta + \varepsilon_{I^*}.$$

We assume that θ is statistically independent of $(\varepsilon_0, \varepsilon_1, \varepsilon_{I^*})$ and satisfies $E(\theta) = 0$, and $E(\theta^2) = \sigma_\theta^2$. All the ε's are mutually independent with $E(\varepsilon_0) = E(\varepsilon_1) = E(\varepsilon_{I^*}) = 0$, and $\text{Var}(\varepsilon_0) = \sigma_{\varepsilon_0}^2$, $\text{Var}(\varepsilon_1) = \sigma_{\varepsilon_1}^2$, and

$\mathrm{Var}(\varepsilon_{I^*}) = \sigma^2_{\varepsilon_{I^*}}$ (the ε terms are called uniquenesses). Because the factor loadings may have different signs and magnitudes, the factor may affect outcomes and choices in very different ways.

To show how one can recover the joint distribution of (Y_0, Y_1) using factor models, we break the argument in two parts. First, we show how to recover the factor loadings, factor variance, and the variances of the uniquenesses. This part is like traditional factor analysis except that a latent variable (e.g., I^*) is only observed up to scale so its scale must be normalized. Then, we show how to construct joint distributions of counterfactuals.

4.2 Recovering the Factor Loadings

4.2.1 The Case When There Is Information Only on Y_0 for $I < 0$ and Y_1 for $I > 0$ but the Decision Rule Is (2)–(3) Under conditions stated in Heckman and Smith (1998) and Carneiro, Hansen, and Heckman (2003), one can identify $F(U_0, U_{I^*})$ and $F(U_1, U_{I^*})$. These conditions were discussed in section 4.1. From these distributions one can identify the left-hand sides of the following two equations:

$$\mathrm{Cov}(U_0, U_{I^*}) = \alpha_0 \alpha_{I^*} \sigma^2_\theta$$
$$\mathrm{Cov}(U_1, U_{I^*}) = \alpha_1 \alpha_{I^*} \sigma^2_\theta.$$

As previously noted, the scale of the unobserved I is normalized, a standard condition for discrete choice models. A second normalization that we need to impose is that $\sigma^2_\theta = 1$. This is required because the factor is not observed and we must set its scale. That is, because $\alpha\theta = k\alpha^\theta_k$ for any constant $k \neq 0$, we need to set the scale by, say, normalizing the variance of θ. We could alternatively normalize some α_0 or α_1 to one. Finally, if we set $\alpha_{I^*} = 1$ (something we can relax, as noted below and in the next section), then we identify α_1 and α_0 from the known covariances above. Because

$$\mathrm{Cov}(U_1, U_0) = \alpha_1 \alpha_0 \sigma^2_\theta$$

we can identify the covariance between Y_1 and Y_0 even though we do not observe both Y_0 and Y_1 for anyone. We then use the variances $\mathrm{Var}(U_1)$, $\mathrm{Var}(U_0)$ and the normalization $\mathrm{Var}(U_{I^*}) = 1$ to recover the variances of the uniquenesses $\sigma^2_{\varepsilon_0}, \sigma^2_{\varepsilon_1}, \sigma^2_{\varepsilon_{I^*}}$.

The fact that we needed to normalize both $\sigma^2_\theta = 1$ and $\alpha_{I^*} = 1$ is a consequence of our assumption that we have only one observation for Y_1 or Y_0 for each person. If we have access to more observations (say from panel data), we can relax the normalizations, say $\sigma_\theta^2 = 1$. In this case we can form, for a panel of length T, the left-hand sides of the following equations:

$$\frac{\text{Cov}(Y_{1,t'}, I^*)}{\text{Cov}(Y_{1,t'}, Y_{1,t})} = \alpha_{1,t}, t = 1, \ldots, T$$

$$\frac{\text{Cov}(Y_{0,t'}, I^*)}{\text{Cov}(Y_{0,t'}, Y_{0,t})} = \alpha_{0,t}, t = 1, \ldots, T$$

and recover σ_θ^2 from, say, $\text{Cov}(Y_{1,t}, I^*) = \alpha_{1,t}\sigma_\theta^2$, given the normalization $\sigma_{I^*}^2 = 1$. The variances of the uniquenesses follow as before.

The crucial idea motivating this identification strategy is that even though we never observe (Y_0, Y_1) as a pair, both Y_0 and Y_1 are linked to S through the choice equation. From information on choice S we can recover I^* from a standard identification argument in econometrics. Thus, we essentially observe (Y_0, I^*) and (Y_1, I^*). The common low dimensional dependence of Y_0 and Y_1 on I^* secures identification of the joint distribution of Y_0, Y_1, I^*. We next develop an alternative strategy based on the same idea where in addition to a choice equation, we have a measurement equation observed for all observations whether or not Y_1 or Y_0 is observed. This plays the role of I^* and in certain respects identification with a measurement is more transparent and more traditional.

4.2.2 Adding a Measurement Equation One interesting extension arises when we have a measurement for θ that is observed irrespective of whether $S = 1$ or $S = 0$. This information is in addition to the outcomes Y_0 or Y_1 and S. In educational statistics, a test score is often used to proxy ability. Suppose that the analyst has access to one ability test M for each person. Measured ability M is

$$M = \mu_M(X) + U_M.$$

We can estimate $\mu_M(X)$ by standard methods and we can form the residual from this equation. Assume that the residual has a factor structure

$$U_M = \alpha_M\theta + \varepsilon_M,$$

where ε_M is mutually independent from $(\varepsilon_0, \varepsilon_1, \varepsilon_I)$ and θ.[9] We assume $\alpha_M \neq 0$. We can, in addition to the covariances presented in Section 4.2.1, determine the left-hand sides of

$$\text{Cov}(U_M, U_0) = \alpha_M \alpha_0 \sigma_\theta^2$$
$$\text{Cov}(U_M, U_1) = \alpha_M \alpha_1 \sigma_\theta^2$$
$$\text{Cov}(U_M, U_{I^*}) = \alpha_M \alpha_{I^*} \sigma_\theta^2.$$

These are obtained, respectively, from correlations of the residuals of U_M with the residuals from (selection corrected) Y_0:

$$Y_0 - \mu_0(X) = U_0,$$

from correlations of U_M with the residuals from (selection corrected) Y_1:

$$Y_1 - \mu_1(X) = U_1,$$

as well as the residuals of U_M with the residuals of I^* using discrete choice analysis. Details are provided in Carneiro, Hansen, and Heckman (2003). Intuitively, we can construct the residuals needed to construct each covariance from the bivariate distributions (conditional on X) of (M, Y_0), (M, Y_1), and (M, I), correcting for selection into $S = 0$ and $S = 1$, respectively, the first two joint distributions. If we impose the normalization $\alpha_M = 1$, which can be interpreted as requiring that higher ability signals a higher level of factor θ, we can form the ratio

$$\frac{\text{Cov}(U_0, U_{I^*})}{\text{Cov}(U_M, U_{I^*})} = \alpha_0$$

and identify α_0. In a similar fashion,

$$\frac{\text{Cov}(U_1, U_{I^*})}{\text{Cov}(U_M, U_{I^*})} = \alpha_1$$

we recover α_1. Now, from

$$\text{Cov}(U_M, U_0) = \alpha_0 \sigma_\theta^2,$$

we can obtain σ_θ^2. Finally, we can identify α_{I^*} based on information from

$$\text{Cov}(U_M, U_{I^*}) = \alpha_{I^*} \sigma_\theta^2,$$

so we can obtain α_{I^*} up to scale. Thus, with one measurement, one choice equation and two outcomes we can identify σ_θ^2 and α_{I^*} up to scale. We can use the identified variances $\text{Var}(U_0)$, $\text{Var}(U_1)$, $\text{Var}(U_{I^*}) = 1$, and $\text{Var}(U_M)$ to recover the variance of the uniquenesses $\sigma_{\varepsilon_0}^2$, $\sigma_{\varepsilon_1}^2$, $\sigma_{\varepsilon_{I^*}}^2$, and $\sigma_{\varepsilon_M}^2$. Thus, having access to a measurement (M) and choice data generated by decision rule

(2)–(3), allows us to estimate the covariances among the outcomes across the two counterfactual states. The measurements can replace the choice equation provided that the analyst surmounts the selection problem that Y_0 is observed only if $S = 0$ and Y_1 is observed only if $S = 1$.[10]

Remaining is the problem of identifying the distributions of the unobservables. Traditional factor analysis assumes normality. We present a more general nonparametric analysis.

4.3 Recovering the Distributions Nonparametrically

Given the identification of factor loadings, factor variances, and uniquenesses, we show how to identify the distribution of θ and $\sigma_{\varepsilon_0}^2, \sigma_{\varepsilon_1}^2, \sigma_{\varepsilon_{I^*}}^2$ nonparametrically (the last variance is obtained up to a normalization). The method is based on a theorem by Kotlarski (1967). We state his theorem.

Theorem 1 *Suppose that we have two random variables T_1 and T_2 that satisfy:*

$$T_1 = \theta + v_1$$
$$T_2 = \theta + v_2$$

with θ, v_1, v_2 mutually statistically independent, $E(\theta) < \infty, E(v_1) = E(v_2) = 0$, that the conditions for Fubini's theorem are satisfied for each random variable, and the random variables possess nonvanishing characteristic functions, then the densities $f_\Theta(\theta), f_{Y_1}(v_1),$ and $f_{Y_2}(v_2)$ are identified.
Proof. See Kotlarski (1967).∎

Applied to the current problem, we have a choice equation, two outcome equations, and a measurement equation. Assume that we normalize $\alpha_M = 1$. As a consequence of this assumption and the analysis of the preceding subsection, all factor loadings, factor variance, and the variances of the uniquenesses are known. The system is

$$I^* = \mu_{I^*}(X, Z) + \alpha_{I^*}\theta + \varepsilon_{I^*}$$
$$Y_0 = \mu_0(X) + \alpha_0\theta + \varepsilon_0$$
$$Y_1 = \mu_1(X) + \alpha_1\theta + \varepsilon_1$$
$$M = \mu_M(X) + \theta + \varepsilon_M.$$

This system can be rewritten as

$$\frac{I^* - \mu_{I^*}(X, Z)}{\alpha_{I^*}} = \theta + \frac{\varepsilon_{I^*}}{\alpha_{I^*}}$$

$$\frac{Y_0 - \mu_0(X)}{\alpha_0} = \theta + \frac{\varepsilon_0}{\alpha_0}$$

$$\frac{Y_1 - \mu_1(X)}{\alpha_1} = \theta + \frac{\varepsilon_1}{\alpha_1}$$

$$M - \mu_M(X) = \theta + \varepsilon_M.^{11}$$

Applying Kotlarski's theorem to any pair of equations, we conclude that we can identify the densities of θ, $\frac{\varepsilon_{I^*}}{\alpha_{I^*}}$, $\frac{\varepsilon_0}{\alpha_0}$, $\frac{\varepsilon_1}{\alpha_1}$, ε_M. Because we know α_{I^*}, α_0, and α_1 we can identify the densities of θ, ε_{I^*}, ε_0, ε_1, ε_M.[12] Thus, we can identify the distributions of all of the error terms. Finally, to recover the joint distribution of (Y_1, Y_0) given X, denoted $F(Y_1, Y_0 \mid X)$, note that

$$F(Y_1, Y_0 \mid X) = \int F(Y_1, Y_0 \mid \theta, X) dF(\theta),$$

where $F(\theta)$ is the distribution of θ. From Kotlarski's theorem, $F(\theta)$ is known. Because of the factor structure, Y_1, Y_0 and S are independent once we condition on θ. So

$$F(Y_1, Y_0 \mid \theta, X) = F(Y_1 \mid \theta, X) F(Y_0 \mid \theta, X).$$

But $F(Y_1 \mid \theta, X)$ and $F(Y_0 \mid \theta, X)$ are identified once we condition on the factors because

$$F(Y_1 \mid \theta, X, S = 1) = F(Y_1 \mid \theta, X)$$
$$F(Y_0 \mid \theta, X, S = 0) = F(Y_0 \mid \theta, X).$$

Note further that if θ were known to the analyst, this procedure would be matching on θ and X (which is equivalent, for identification, to matching on the propensity score $\Pr(S = 1 \mid X, Z, \theta)$).[13] Our method generalizes matching by allowing the variables that would produce the conditional independence assumed in matching to be unobserved by the analyst.

Over the support of $\mu_I(X, Z)$, $\mu_1(X)$ and $\mu_0(X)$, we can evaluate policies that change Z for each X. We can evaluate new policies that can be expressed as some value of (X, Z) in the historical support. We can extrapolate to new supports by making functional form assumptions, for example,

$\mu_1(X) = X\beta_1, \mu_0(X) = X\beta_0$ and $\mu_I(X, Z) = (X, Z)\beta_I$. See Heckman and Vytlacil (2005, 2006b) for further discussion of the extrapolation issue.

Observe that without making additional assumptions our method is more powerful than randomization. Randomized assignments would only produce identification of $F(Y_0)$ and $F(Y_1)$ and not $F(Y_0, Y_1)$ (Heckman 1992).

5. DISTINGUISHING BETWEEN HETEROGENEITY AND UNCERTAINTY

In the literature on earnings dynamics (e.g., Lillard and Willis 1978), it is common to estimate an earnings equation of the sort

$$y_{i,t} = X_{i,t}\beta + \delta S_i + v_{i,t}, \tag{4}$$

where $y_{i,t}$, $X_{i,t}$, S_i, $v_{i,t}$ denote, respectively, earnings, observable characteristics, educational attainment and unobservable characteristics of person i at time t. Often the error term $v_{i,t}$ is decomposed into two or more components. For example,

$$v_{i,t} = \phi_i + \varepsilon_{i,t}. \tag{5}$$

The term ϕ_i is a person-specific fixed effect. The error term $\varepsilon_{i,t}$ is generally assumed to be serially correlated, say $\varepsilon_{i,t} = \rho\varepsilon_{i,t-1} + \eta_{i,t}$ where $\eta_{i,t}$ is an independently and identically distributed innovation with mean zero. It is widely accepted that components of $X_{i,t}$, ϕ_i, and $\varepsilon_{i,t}$ all contribute to measured inequality. However, the literature is silent about the difference between heterogeneity and uncertainty, the unforecastable part of earnings— what Jencks et al. (1972) call "luck." On intuitive grounds, the predictable components of $v_{i,t}$ have a different effect on welfare than the unpredictable components, especially if people are risk averse and cannot fully insure against the uncertainty. Is uncertainty ϕ_i? Is it $\varepsilon_{i,t}$? Is it $\phi_i + \varepsilon_{i,t}$? Or $\eta_{i,t}$? Statistical decompositions such as (4) and (5) tell us nothing about which components of (4) are unforecastable by agents.

The methodology summarized in this chapter, and developed more fully in Cunha, Heckman, and Navarro (2005), provides a framework within which it is possible to identify and separate components that are forecastable from ones that are not. The essential idea of the method can be illustrated in the case of educational choice. In order to choose between high school and college, say at age 17, agents forecast future earnings (and other returns) at each schooling level. Using this information from educational choice at age 17, together with the realization of earnings that are observed at later ages, it is possible to estimate and test which part of future earnings are forecast by the agent at age 17.

In this method, we use choice information to extract *ex ante* or forecast earnings to distinguish them from *ex post* or realized earnings. The difference between forecast and realized earnings allows us to identify the components of uncertainty facing agents at the time they make their schooling decisions. With this method, we can distinguish predictable heterogeneity from uncertainty.

In order to make this point clearly, we formalize the argument by considering a version of the Roy (1951) economy with two sectors. As before, let S_i denote different sectors: $S_i = 0$ denotes choice of the high school sector, and $S_i = 1$ denotes choice of the college sector. Each person can choose to be in either sector. Let the two potential outcomes be represented by the pair $(Y_{0,i}, Y_{1,i})$, only one of which is observed by the analyst, because it is assumed that only one option can be chosen. As before, we denote by C_i the cost of choosing sector 1. The cost C_i reflects the costs associated with choosing the college sector (e.g., tuition, and non-pecuniary costs of attending college expressed in monetary values), $Y_{1,i}$ is the present value of earnings in the college sector discounted over horizon T for person i choosing at a fixed age set to zero:

$$Y_{1,i} = \sum_{t=0}^{T} \frac{y_{1,i,t}}{(1 + r)^t},$$

and $Y_{0,i}$ is the present value of earnings in the high school sector for person i at a fixed age set to zero:

$$Y_{0,i} = \sum_{t=0}^{T} \frac{y_{0,i,t}}{(1 + r)^t},$$

where r is the one-period risk-free interest rate. Underlying $Y_{1,i}$ and $Y_{0,i}$ are time series of potential earnings in the two states: $(y_{0,i,0}, \ldots, y_{0,i,T})$ for high school and $(y_{1,i,0}, \ldots, y_{1,i,T})$ for college.

Let $\mathcal{I}_i$ denote the information set of agent i at the time the schooling choice must be made. The decision rule governing sectorial choice is, in the population,

$$S_i = \begin{cases} 1, \text{ if } E(Y_{1,i} - Y_{0,i} - C_i | \mathcal{I}_i) \geq 0 \\ 0, \text{ otherwise.} \end{cases}$$

In this economy, the decision rule is quite simple: one attends school if the expected gains from schooling are greater than or equal to the expected costs. To fix ideas, write

$$y_{0,i,t} = X_{i,t}\beta_{0,t} + v_{0,i,t}$$
$$y_{1,i,t} = X_{i,t}\beta_{1,t} + v_{1,i,t}$$
$$C_i = Z_i\gamma + v_{i,C}.$$

Suppose there exists a vector of factors $\vec{\theta} = (\theta_1, \theta_2, \ldots, \theta_L)$ such that θ_j and θ_k are mutually independent random variables for $j, k = 1, \ldots, L, j \neq k$. Assume we can decompose the error term in earnings at age t in the following manner:

$$v_{0,i,t} = \vec{\theta}_i\alpha_{0,t} + \varepsilon_{0,i,t}$$
$$v_{1,i,t} = \vec{\theta}_i\alpha_{1,t} + \varepsilon_{1,i,t},$$

where now, $\alpha_{0,t}$ and $\alpha_{1,t}$ are vectors. We can also decompose the cost function C in similar fashion:

$$C_i = Z_i\gamma + \vec{\theta}_i\alpha_C + \varepsilon_{i,C}.$$

The parameters α_C, and $\alpha_{s,t}$ for $s = 0, 1$, and $t = 0, \ldots, T$ are called the factor loadings. The choice equation can then be written as:

$$I_i = E\left(\sum_{t=0}^{T} \frac{(X_{i,t}\beta_{1,t} + \vec{\theta}_i\alpha_{1,t} + \varepsilon_{1,i,t}) - (X_{i,t}\beta_{0,t} + \vec{\theta}_i\alpha_{0,t} + \varepsilon_{0,i,t})}{(1 + r)^t} \right.$$
$$\left. - (Z_i\gamma + \vec{\theta}_i\alpha_C + \varepsilon_{i,C}) | \mathcal{I}_i \right).$$

$S_i = 1$ if $I_i \geq 0$; $S_i = 0$ otherwise.

If there is an element of the vector $\vec{\theta}_i$, say $\theta_{i,2}$ (factor 2), that has nonzero loadings on future earnings, say at age 40, in either counterfactual state, $\alpha_{2,s,40} \neq 0$, for $s = 0$ or 1 and factor $\theta_{i,2}$ is a determinant of schooling choices, then one can say that at the time of the schooling choice, the agent knew the unobservable captured by the factor 2 that affects future earnings. If $\theta_{i,2}$ does not enter the choice equation but explains future earnings, then $\theta_{i,2}$ is uncertain (not predictable) at the age the decisions are made. By assumption $\varepsilon_{i,C}$ is predictable but the future $\varepsilon_{1,i,t}$ and $\varepsilon_{0,i,t}$ are not predictable.

The idea of our test is thus very simple: the components of future earnings that are forecastable are captured by the factors that are known by the agents when they make their educational choices.[14] The predictable factors are estimated with a nonzero loading in the choice equation. The uncertainty in the decision regarding college is captured by the factors that the agent does not act on when making the decision of whether to attend college or not. In this case, the loadings (coefficients on these factors) in the choice equation would be zero. Carneiro, Hansen, and Heckman (2003) provide exact conditions for identifying the factor loadings.[15] Cunha, Heckman, and Navarro (2005) develop this analysis further.

In the next section, we estimate a model of schooling choice; show how one can recover the distribution of $\vec{\theta}$, α_C and $\alpha_{s,t}$, $s = 0, 1, t = 0, \ldots, T$; and we put our analysis to use to estimate counterfactual distributions for different policies, to compute their consequences for mobility and inequality, and to measure the contributions of "luck" to post-schooling earnings. We answer how much of the post-schooling earnings is predictable at the age schooling decisions are made.

6. EMPIRICAL RESULTS

6.1 The Data, Equations, and Estimation

In our empirical analysis, we use a sample of white males from the NLSY data. Following the preceding theoretical analysis, we consider only two schooling choices: high school and college graduation. From now on we use c to denote college and h to denote high school. We assume perfect credit markets for simplicity and familiarity. By this we mean that restrictions on borrowing against future earnings are assumed not to be important. See Cameron and Taber (2004) and Carneiro and Heckman (2002) for evidence supporting this assumption. Carneiro, Hansen, and Heckman (2003) assume the absence of credit markets and obtain empirical results on the extent of uncertainty similar to the ones presented here, so the issue of whether credit markets function or not does not affect the main conclusions of our analysis.

Appendix Table 11.1 (posted at the website for this book) presents the descriptive statistics of the variables used in our empirical analysis. They show that college graduates have higher present value of earnings than high school graduates. College graduates also have higher test scores and come from better family backgrounds. They are more likely to live in a location where a college is present, and where college tuition is lower.

TABLE 11.1
List of Covariates

Variable Name	Cost Function (Z)	Test System (X_T)	PV Earnings* (X)
South at Age 14	Yes	Yes	Yes
Urban at Age 14	Yes	Yes	Yes
Parents Divorced	Yes	Yes	No
Number of Siblings	Yes	Yes	No
Mother's Education	Yes	Yes	No
Father's Education	Yes	Yes	No
Family Income Age 17	Yes	Yes	No
Dummy 1957	Yes	No	Yes
Dummy 1958	Yes	No	Yes
Dummy 1959	Yes	No	Yes
Dummy 1960	Yes	No	Yes
Dummy 1961	Yes	No	Yes
Dummy 1962	Yes	No	Yes
Dummy 1963	Yes	No	Yes
Dummy 1964	No	No	No
Age in 1980	No	Yes	No
Grade Completed 1980	No	Yes	No
Enrolled in 1980	No	Yes	No
Distance to College	Yes	No	No
Tuition at age 17	Yes	No	No

* Present Value of Earnings in thousands of dollars.

To simplify the empirical analysis, we divide the lifetimes of individuals into two periods. The first period covers ages 17 through 28 and the second goes from 29 through 65. We impute missing wages and project earnings for the ages not observed in the NLSY data using the procedure described in Appendix B of Carneiro, Hansen, and Heckman (2003). In Cunha, Heckman, and Navarro (2005), we consider alternative ways to create full life cycle histories. Some type of combination of data sets is required because the NLSY does not contain information on the full life cycle of earnings. We augment the NLSY data with data from the PSID to estimate the lifetime earnings of the NLSY sample members. For each schooling level $s \in \{c, h\}$, for each period $t \in \{1, 2\}$ we calculate the present value of earnings at age 17, $Y_{s,t}$. We assume that the error term for $Y_{s,t}$ is generated by a two factor model,

$$Y_{s,t} = X\beta_{s,t} + \theta_1\alpha_{s,t,1} + \theta_2\alpha_{s,t,2} + \varepsilon_{s,t}. \tag{6}$$

We omit the "i" subscripts to eliminate notational burden. This model is all that is required to fit the data. Additional factors, when entered, do not contribute to the fit of the model. In Table 11.1 we list the elements of X used in our empirical analysis. They are listed in the column "PV Earnings." We normalize $\alpha_{h,1,2} = 1$.

For the measurement system of cognitive ability we use five components of the ASVAB test battery: arithmetic reasoning, word knowledge, paragraph composition, math knowledge, and coding speed. We link the first factor to this system of ability tests and exclude the other factor from it. Thus, we adopt two normalizations. First, the loading on the first factor on the arithmetic reasoning test is set to one. Second, the loading on the second factor is set to zero in all test equations. Thus, the test scores are devoted to measuring ability. We include family background variables among the covariates X_T in the ASVAB test equations. Table 11.1 lists the variables used in X_T. They are listed in the column "Test System." Formally, let T_j denote the test score j:

$$T_j = X_T\omega_j + \theta_1\alpha_{test_j,1} + \varepsilon_{test_j}. \tag{7}$$

The cost function C is given by:

$$C = Z\gamma + \theta_1\alpha_{C,1} + \theta_2\alpha_{C,2} + \varepsilon_C \tag{8}$$

where the Z are variables that affect the costs of going to college and include variables that do not affect outcomes $Y_{s,t}$ (such as local tuition and distance to college). Table 11.1 shows the full set of covariates used in Z under the column "Cost Function."

For the educational choice equation, we assume that agents know X, Z, ε_C, and some, but not necessarily all, components of θ. Let the components known to the agent be $\bar{\theta}$. The decision rule for attending college is based on:

$$V = E\left(Y_{c,1} + \frac{Y_{c,2}}{1 + r} - Y_{h,1} - \frac{Y_{h,2}}{1 + r} \,\middle|\, X, \bar{\theta} \right) - E(C \,|\, Z, X, \bar{\theta}, \varepsilon_C) \tag{9}$$

where future earnings are discounted at interest rate $r = .03$. Individuals go to college if $V > 0$. We test and do not reject the hypothesis that individuals, at the time they make their college decisions, know their cost functions, the factors $\bar{\theta}$, and unobservables in cost ε_C. However, they do not know $\varepsilon_{s,t}, s \in \{c, h\}, t \in \{1, 2\}$ at the time they make their educational choices, and they may not know other components of $\vec{\theta}$. The factor loadings on the θ not in $\bar{\theta}$ are estimated to be zero. See Cunha, Heckman, and Navarro (2005) for further discussion of this test and for extensions of the method.

We assume that each factor $k \in \{1, 2\}$ is generated by a mixture of J_k normal distributions:

$$\theta_k \sim \sum_{j=1}^{J_k} p_{k,j}\phi(f_k | \mu_{k,j}, \tau_{k,j})$$

where $\phi(\eta | \mu_j, \tau_j)$ is a normal density for η with mean μ_j and variance τ_j. As shown in Ferguson (1983), mixtures of normals with a large number of components approximate any distribution of θ_k arbitrarily well.[16] Even though the $\varepsilon_{s,t}$ are nonparametrically identified, we assume in the empirical work reported here that they are normally distributed.[17] We estimate the model using Markov Chain Monte Carlo methods. In Appendix Tables 2a–2c, available at our website, we present estimated coefficients and factor loadings for the model.

6.2 Results

6.2.1 *How the Model Fits the Data* To assess the validity of our estimates, we perform a variety of checks of fit of predictions against the data. We first compare the proportions of people who choose each schooling level. In the NLSY data, 55 percent choose high school and 45 percent choose college. The model predicts 56 percent and 44 percent, respectively. The model replicates the observed proportions, and formal tests of equality of predicted and actual proportions cannot be rejected.

In Figure 11.1 we show the densities of the predicted and actual present value of earnings for the overall sample of high school and college graduates. The fit is good. Figures 11.2 and 11.3 show the same densities restricted to the sample of those who choose high school (2) and college (3). The fit is good. When we also perform formal tests of equality of predicted and actual distributions, we cannot reject the hypothesis of equality of the distributions for each schooling choice using a chi-squared goodness of fit test at a 5 percent significance level for all three cases (Table 11.2). We conclude that a two factor model is enough to fit the data. From this analysis, we conclude that

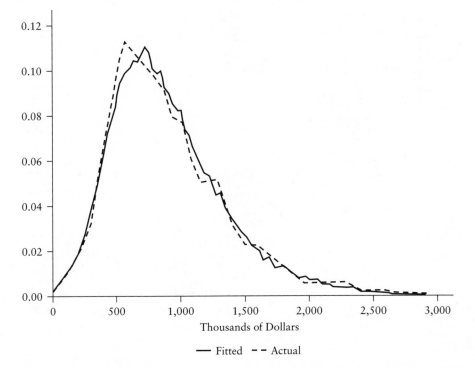

Figure 11.1.   Densities of Fitted and Actual Present Value of Earnings for Overall Sample.

NOTE: Present value of earnings from age 17 to 65 discounted using an interest rate of 3%. Let (Y_0, Y_1) denote potential outcomes in high school and college sectors, respectively. Let $S = 0$ denote high school sector and $S = 1$ denote college sector. Define observed earnings as $Y = SY_1 + (1 - S)Y_0$. Let $f(y)$ denote the density function of observed earnings. Here we plot the density functions f generated from the data (the dashed line) against that fitted by the model (the solid line). We use kernel density estimation to produce these functions.

earnings innovations $\varepsilon_{s,t}$ relative to a two factor model are not in the agents' information sets at the time they are making schooling decisions. If they were, additional factors would be required to capture the full covariance between educational choices and future earnings, but when we enter additional factors, they do not improve the fit of the model to data and have zero estimated factor loadings in the choice equation.

6.2.2 The Factors: Non-normality and Evidence on Selection In order to fit the data, one must allow for non-normal factors, as one can see from the evidence summarized in Figure 11.4. To generate Figure 11.4, we compute

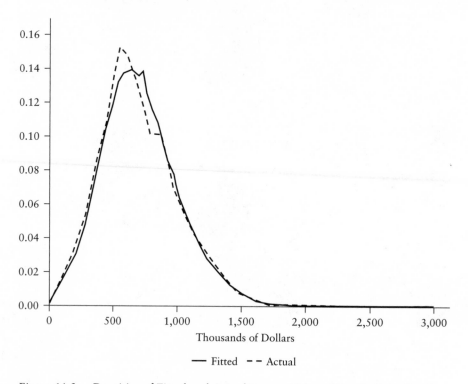

Figure 11.2.   Densities of Fitted and Actual Present Value of Earnings for People Who Choose to Graduate from High School

NOTE: Present value of earnings from age 17 to 65 discounted using an interest rate of 3%. Let Y_0 denote potential outcome in the high school sector. Let $S = 0$ denote choice of the high school sector. Let $f(y \mid S = 0)$ denote the density function of observed earnings conditioned on agents who are high school graduates. Here we plot the density functions $f(y \mid S = 0)$ generated from the data (the dashed line) against that predicted by the model (the solid line) We use kernel density estimation to produce these functions.

the variance of the distribution of factor 1, say σ_{θ_1}. Because the factors have mean zero, we can plot the estimated density of factor 1 against that of a normal random variable with mean zero and variance σ_{θ_1}. We proceed in a similar fashion for factor 2. Neither factor is normally distributed. A traditional assumption used in factor analysis (see, e.g., Jöreskog 1977) is violated. Our approach is more general and does not require normality.

Figure 11.5 plots the density of factor 1 conditional on educational choices. The solid line is the density of factor 1 for agents who are high school graduates, while the dashed line is the density for agents who are college graduates. Because factor 1 is associated with cognitive tests, we can interpret it

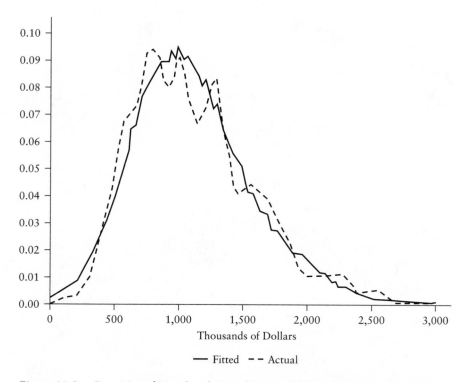

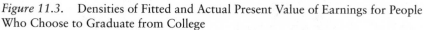

— Fitted − − Actual

Figure 11.3. Densities of Fitted and Actual Present Value of Earnings for People Who Choose to Graduate from College

N O T E : Present value of earnings from age 17 to 65 discounted using an interest rate of 3%. Let Y_1 denote potential outcome in the college sector. Let $S = 1$ denote choice of the college sector. Let $f(y \mid S = 1)$ denote the density function of observed earnings conditioned on agents who are college graduates. Here we plot the density functions $f(y \mid S = 1)$ generated from the data (the dashed line) against that predicted by the model (the solid line) We use kernel density estimation to produce these functions.

TABLE 11.2
Goodness of Fit Test for Lifetime Earnings

	χ^2 *Statistic*	*Critical Value**
Overall	48.9251	53.1419
High School	25.4820	26.0566
College	32.2506	33.2562

* 95 percent confidence, equiprobable bins with approximately 23 people per bin.

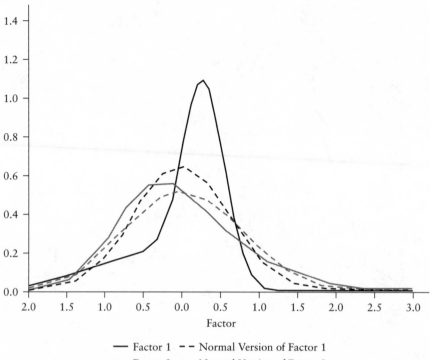

Figure 11.4.   Densities of Factors and Their Normal Equivalents

N O T E : Let $f(\theta_1)$ denote the density probability function of factor θ_1. We assume that $f(\theta_1)$ is a mixture of normals. Assume $\mu_1 = E(\theta_1)$, $\sigma_1 = \text{Var}(\theta_1)$. Let $\phi(\mu_1, \sigma_1)$ denote the density of a normal random variable with mean μ_1 and variance σ_1. The solid curve is the actual density of factor θ_1, $f(\theta_1)$, while the dashed curve is the density of a normal random variable with mean and variance of factor θ_1, $\phi(\mu_1, \sigma_1)$. We proceed similarly for factor 2, where the fitted density is plotted in light grey and the normal version is plotted in light grey dashes.

as an index of "ability." The agents who choose college have, on average, higher ability. Factor 1 is purged of the effect of parental background and level of education at the date of the ASVAB test. Figure 11.5 shows that selection on ability is an important factor in explaining college attendance. A similar analysis of factor 2 reveals that schooling decisions are not very much affected by it. However, factor 2 is important for predicting future earnings, as we show below.

6.2.3 Estimating Joint Distributions of Counterfactuals: Returns, Costs, and Ability as Determinants of Schooling In estimating the distribution of

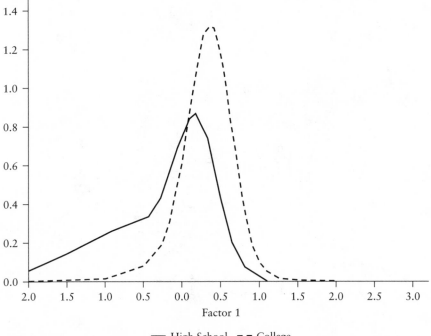

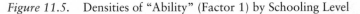

─── High School   ‑ ‑ College

Figure 11.5.   Densities of "Ability" (Factor 1) by Schooling Level

NOTE: Let $f(\theta_1)$ denote the density function of factor θ_1. We assume that $f(\theta_1)$ is a mixture of normals. The solid line is the estimated density of factor 1 conditional on choosing the high school sector, that is, $f(\theta_1 \mid \text{Choice} = \text{High School})$. The dashed line plots the density of factor 1 conditional on choosing the college sector, that is, $f(\theta_1 \mid \text{Choice} = \text{College})$.

earnings in counterfactual schooling states within a policy regime (e.g., the distributions of college earnings for people who actually choose to be high school graduates), the usual approach is to assume that both distributions are the same except for an additive constant—the coefficient of a schooling dummy in an earnings regression. More recently developed methods partially relax this assumption by assuming preservation of ranks across potential outcome distributions, but do not freely specify the two outcome distributions (see Heckman, Smith, and Clements 1997; Vytlacil 2002; Chernozhukov and Hansen 2005). Our approach relaxes this assumption by allowing for arbitrary dependence across potential outcome distributions. Table 11.3 presents the conditional distribution of *ex post* potential college earnings given *ex post* potential high school earnings decile by decile. The table displays a

TABLE 11.3

Ex Post Conditional Distribution (College Earnings Conditional on High School Earnings)

$$\Pr(d_i < Y_c < d_i + 1 \mid d_j < Y_b < d_j + 1)^*$$

High School	COLLEGE									
	1	2	3	4	5	6	7	8	9	10
1	0.6980	0.2534	0.0444	0.0032	0.0011	0.0000	0.0000	0.0000	0.0000	0.0000
2	0.2270	0.4150	0.2470	0.0890	0.0180	0.0040	0.0000	0.0000	0.0000	0.0000
3	0.0450	0.2160	0.3420	0.2610	0.1070	0.0260	0.0030	0.0000	0.0000	0.0000
4	0.0140	0.0950	0.2120	0.2930	0.2390	0.1090	0.0370	0.0010	0.0000	0.0000
5	0.0000	0.0300	0.1130	0.2190	0.2940	0.2170	0.1100	0.0170	0.0000	0.0000
6	0.0000	0.0040	0.0340	0.0980	0.2030	0.3080	0.2470	0.0990	0.0070	0.0000
7	0.0000	0.0000	0.0100	0.0340	0.1130	0.2390	0.3190	0.2350	0.0500	0.0000
8	0.0000	0.0000	0.0000	0.0030	0.0240	0.0910	0.2360	0.4010	0.2320	0.0130
9	0.0000	0.0000	0.0000	0.0000	0.0010	0.0060	0.0470	0.2360	0.5400	0.1700
10	0.0000	0.0000	0.0000	0.0000	0.0000	0.0000	0.0010	0.0110	0.1710	0.8170

* d_i is the ith decile of the College Lifetime Earnings Distribution and d_j is the jth decile of the High School Lifetime Earnings Distribution.

strong positive dependence between the relative positions of individuals in the two distributions. In particular, for all high school deciles, more than 50 percent of the individuals located at any decile in the high school earnings distribution will be within one decile of their original position in the college earnings distribution. However, the dependence is far from perfect. For example, almost 10 percent of those who are at the sixth decile of the high school distribution would be in the eighth decile of the college distribution. Observe that this comparison is not being made in terms of positions in the overall distribution of earnings. We can determine where individuals are located in the distribution of population potential high school earnings and the distribution of potential college earnings although in the data we only observe them in either one or the other state. The assumption of perfect dependence across counterfactual distributions that is maintained in much of the recent literature (e.g., Juhn, Murphy, and Pierce 1993) is, however, too strong, at least in this application.

Figures 11.6 and 11.7 present the marginal densities of predicted and counterfactual earnings for college (Figure 11.6) and high school (Figure 11.7). When we compare the densities of present value of earnings in the college sector for persons who choose college against the counterfactual densities of college earnings for high school graduates, the density of the present value of earnings for college graduates is to the right of the counterfactual density of the present value of earnings of high school graduates if they were college graduates. Figure 11.7 reveals that college graduates are more likely to be successful in the high school sector than actual high school graduates. The surprising feature of both figures is that the overlap of the distributions is substantial. Many high school graduates have earnings as large as those of college graduates.

Tables 11.4 and 11.5 provide further evidence against the hypothesis of perfect dependence across counterfactual distributions. In Table 11.4, we report the fitted and counterfactual present value of earnings for agents who choose high school. The typical high school student would earn $703,780 over the life cycle. She would earn $1,021,970 if she had chosen to be a college graduate.[18] This implies a return of 46 percent to a college education over the whole life cycle (i.e., a monetary gain of $318,190). In Table 11.5, we note that the typical college graduate earns $1,122,690 (above the counterfactual earnings of what a typical high school student would earn in college), and would make only $756,130 over her lifetime if she chose to be a

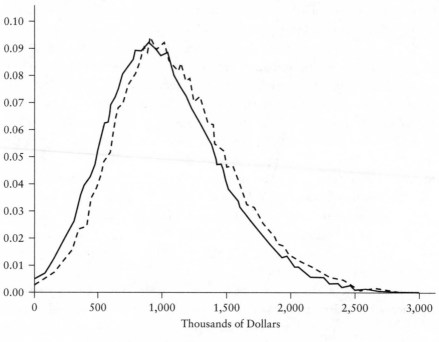

Figure 11.6.   Densities of Present Value of Earnings in the College Sector

N O T E : Let Y_1 denote present value of earnings (discounted at a 3% interest rate) in the college sector. Let $f(y_1)$ denote its density function. The dashed line plots the fitted Y_1 density conditioned on choosing college, that is $f(y_1 \mid S = 1)$, while the solid line shows the estimated counterfactual density function of Y_1 for those agents that are actually high school graduates, that is, $f(y_1 \mid S = 0)$.

high school graduate instead. The returns to college education for the typical college graduate (which in the literature on program evaluation is referred to as the effect of Treatment on the Treated) is 50 percent above that of the return for a high school graduate. In monetary terms we would say that a college graduate has a gain of going to college almost $500,000 higher over her lifetime than does the typical high school graduate.

Figure 11.8 plots the density of returns to education for agents who are high school graduates (the solid curve), and the density of returns to education for agents who are college graduates (the dashed curve). College graduates have returns distributed somewhat "to the right" of high school graduates, so the difference is not only a difference for the mean individual

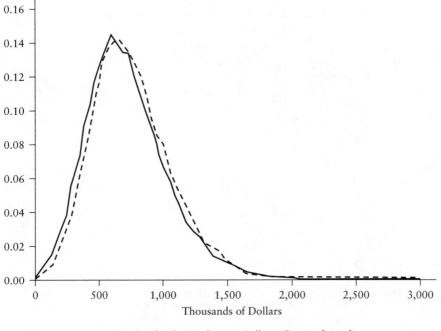

Thousands of Dollars

— High School (Fitted)   – – College (Counterfactual)

Figure 11.7.   Densities of Present Value of Earnings in the High School Sector

NOTE: Let Y_0 denote present value of earnings (discounted at a 3% interest rate) in the high school sector. Let $f(y_0)$ denote its density function. The solid line plots the fitted Y_0 density conditioned on choosing college, that is $f(y_0 \mid S = 0)$, while the dashed line shows the counterfactual density function of Y_0 for those agents that are actually college graduates, that is, $f(y_0 \mid S = 1)$.

but is actually present over the entire distribution. An economic interpretation of Figure 11.8 is that agents who choose a college education are the ones who tend to gain more from it.

With the methodology proposed here, we can also determine returns to the marginal student. Table 11.6 reveals that the average individual who is just indifferent between a college education and a high school diploma earns $743,400 as a high school graduate or $1,089,970 as a college graduate. This implies a return of 48 percent. The returns to people at the margin are above those of the typical high school graduate, but below those for the typical college graduate. Because persons at the margin are more likely to be affected by a policy that encourages college attendance, their returns are the

TABLE 11.4

Average Present Value of Earnings* for High
School Graduates
Fitted and Counterfactual,
White Males from NLSY79

	High School (fitted)	College (counterfactual)
High School	703.780	1021.970
SE	14.626	78.214
Random**	726.590	1065.900
SE	20.513	43.054

AVERAGE RETURNS*** FOR HIGH SCHOOL GRADUATES	
	High School vs. Some College
High School	0.4600
SE	0.1401

* Thousands of dollars. Discounted using a 3 percent interest rate.
** It defines the result of taking a person at random from the population regardless of his schooling choice.
*** As a fraction of the base state, that is (PV Earnings (Col) − PV Earnings (HS))/PV Earnings (HS).

ones that should be used in order to compute the marginal benefit of policies that induce people into schooling.

A major question that emerges from our analysis is why, if high school graduates have positive returns to attending college, don't all attend? People do not pick schooling levels based only on monetary returns. Recall that their choice criterion [equation (9)] includes also the pecuniary and non-pecuniary costs of actually attending college. Figure 11.9 shows the estimated density of the monetary value of this cost both overall and by schooling level. While almost no high school graduate perceives a negative cost (i.e., a benefit) of attending college; around one-third of college graduates actually perceive it as a benefit. Table 11.7 explores this point in more detail by presenting the mean total cost of attending college (first rows) and the mean cost that is due to ability (i.e., factor 1), given in the second rows. While in both cases the cost of attending college is positive for both the average college graduate and the average high school graduate, costs on average are smaller for college

TABLE 11.5
Average Present Value of Earnings*
for College Graduates
Fitted and Counterfactual,
White Males from NLSY79

	High School (counterfactual)	College (fitted)
College	756.13	1,122.69
SE	40.57	25.89
Random**	726.59	1,065.90
SE	20.51	43.05

AVERAGE RETURNS*** FOR COLLEGE GRADUATES	
High School vs. Some College	
College	0.50
SE	0.08

* Thousands of dollars. Discounted using a 3 percent interest rate.
** It defines the result of taking a person at random from the population regardless of his schooling choice.
*** As a fraction of the base state, that is (PV Earnings (Col) − PV Earnings (HS))/PV Earnings (HS).

graduates. From Figure 11.5 we know that college graduates have higher ability. The average contribution of ability to costs is positive for high school graduates (a true cost). It is negative for college graduates, so it is perceived as a benefit. This is the answer to our puzzle: people do not only (or even mainly) make their schooling decisions by looking at their monetary returns in terms of earnings. Psychic costs play a very important role. Differences in ability are one force behind this result.[19,20]

6.2.4 Mobility and Heterogeneity versus Uncertainty In Figures 11.10 through 11.12, we separate the effect of heterogeneity from uncertainty in earnings. The information set of the agent is $\mathcal{I} = \{X, Z, X_T, \varepsilon_C, \Theta\}$ where Θ contains some or all of the factors. Focusing on Figure 11.10 we start by assuming that the agents do not know their factors; consequently, $\Theta = \emptyset$. If we let the agent learn about factor 1,[21] so that, $\Theta = \{\theta_1\}$, then the reduction in the forecast variance is basically nil. This exercise shows that while factor 1 is important for forecasting educational choices, it does not do a very good

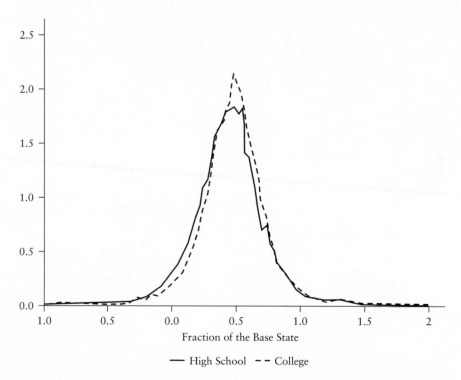

Figure 11.8.   Densities of *Ex Post* Returns to College by Schooling Level Chosen

NOTE: Let Y_0, Y_1 denote the present value of earnings in the high school and college sectors, respectively. Define *ex post* returns to college as the ratio $R = \frac{(Y_1 - Y_0)}{Y_0}$. Let $f(r)$ denote the density function of the random variable R. The solid line is the density of *ex post* returns to college for high school graduates, that is, $f(r \mid S = 0)$. The dashed line is the density of *ex post* returns to college for college graduates, that is, $f(r \mid S = 1)$.

job in forecasting earnings. Now, assume that the agent is given knowledge of factor 2, but not factor 1, so that $\Theta = \{\theta_2\}$. Then the agent is able to substantially reduce the forecast variance of earnings in high school. Thus, while factor 2 does not greatly affect college choices, it greatly informs the agent about his or her future earnings. When the agent is given knowledge of both factors 1 and 2, that is, $\Theta = \{\theta_1, \theta_2\}$, he can forecast earnings marginally better. Factor 1 provides information on ability, but almost none on future earnings. Figure 11.11 reveals much the same story about college earnings. These results suggest that selection into college is not based primarily on expected economic returns to education. Cost factors play an important role.

TABLE 11.6

Average Present Value of Earnings* for
People Indifferent Between High School and College
Conditional on Education Level,
White Males from NLSY79

	High School	College
Average	743.400	1089.970
SE	24.152	33.255

AVERAGE RETURNS** FOR PEOPLE INDIFFERENT BETWEEN HIGH SCHOOL AND COLLEGE	
	High School vs. Some College
Average	0.4800
SE	0.0853

* Thousands of dollars. Discounted using a 3 percent interest rate.
** As a fraction of the base state, that is (PV Earnings (Col) −
PV Earnings (HS))/PV Earnings (HS).

Table 11.8 presents the variance of potential earnings in each state and re-turns under different information sets available to the agent. We conduct this exercise for the forecast of period 1, period 2, and lifetime earnings. We report baseline variances and covariances without conditioning and the remaining uncertainty state as a fraction of the baseline no information state when different components are given to the agents. Note that knowledge of factor 2 is fundamentally important in reducing forecast variance for period 2 earnings.

This discussion sheds light on the issue of distinguishing predictable heterogeneity from uncertainty. We have demonstrated that there is a large dispersion in the distribution of the present value of earnings. This dispersion is largely due to heterogeneity, which is forecastable by the agents at the time they are making their schooling choices. Recall that by our tests agents know θ_1 and θ_2. The remaining dispersion is due to luck, or uncertainty or unforecastable factors as of age 17. Its contribution is smaller.

It is interesting to note that knowledge of the factors enables agents to make better forecasts. Figure 11.12 presents an exercise for returns to college $(Y_1 - Y_0)$ similar to that presented in Figures 11.10 and 11.11 regarding information sets available to the agent. Knowledge of factor 2 also greatly improves the forecastability of returns, 80 percent of the variability

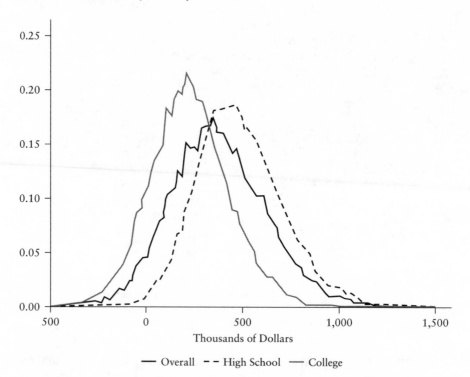

Figure 11.9.   Density of Monetary Value of Psychic Cost Both Overall and by Schooling Level

NOTE: In this figure we plot the monetary value of psychic costs. Let C denote the monetary value of psychic costs. The monetary value of psychic costs is given by: $C = Z\gamma + \theta_1\alpha_{C1} + \theta_2\alpha_{C2} + \varepsilon_C$. The contribution of ability to the costs of attending college, in monetary value, is $\theta_1\alpha_{C1}$.

in returns is forecastable at age 17. The levels are even more predictable (94 percent for high school; 97 percent for college). Most variability across people is due to heterogeneity and not uncertainty.

6.2.5 *Ex Ante* versus *Ex Post*   Once the distinction between heterogeneity and uncertainty is made, we can talk about the distinction between *ex ante* and *ex post* decision making. From our analysis, we conclude that, at the time agents pick their schooling, the ε's in their earnings equations are unknown to them. These are the components that correspond to "luck" as defined by Jencks et al. (1972). It is clear that decision making would be different, at least for some individuals, if the agent knew these chance components when choosing schooling levels because decision rule (2)–(3) would now be

TABLE 11.7
Mean Monetary Value of Total Cost
of Attending College

High School	College	Overall
488.24	232.56	375.27

MEAN MONETARY VALUE OF COST OF ATTENDING COLLEGE DUE TO ABILITY		
High School	*College*	*Overall*
40.97	-51.27	0.0

Let C denote the monetary value of psychic costs. Then C is given by:

$$C = Z\gamma + \theta_1 a_{C1} + \theta_2 a_{C2} + \varepsilon_C$$

The contribution of ability to the costs of attending college in monetary value is $\theta_1 a_{C1}$. Recall that, on average, the ability is different between those who attend college and those who attend high school.

$$V = Y_{c,1} + \frac{Y_{c,2}}{1+r} - Y_{h,1} - \frac{Y_{h,2}}{1+r} - C > 0$$

$$S = 1 \text{ if } V > 0; \ S = 0 \text{ otherwise,}$$

where no expectation is taken to calculate V because all terms on the right-hand side of the top equation are known with certainty by the agent.

In our empirical model, if individuals could pick their schooling level using their *ex post* information (i.e., after learning their luck components in earnings), 13.81 percent of high school graduates would rather be college graduates and 17.15 percent of college graduates would have stopped their schooling at the high school level.

6.2.6 Analyzing a Cohort Specific Cross-Subsidized Tuition Policy: Constructing Joint Distributions of Counterfactuals Across Policy Regimes As an example of the power of our method to evaluate the consequences of policy on income inequality, we analyze a cross-subsidized tuition policy indexed by family income level. We construct joint distributions of outcomes within policy regimes (treatment and no treatment or schooling and no schooling) and joint distributions of choices ($Y = SY_1 + (1 - S)Y_0$) across

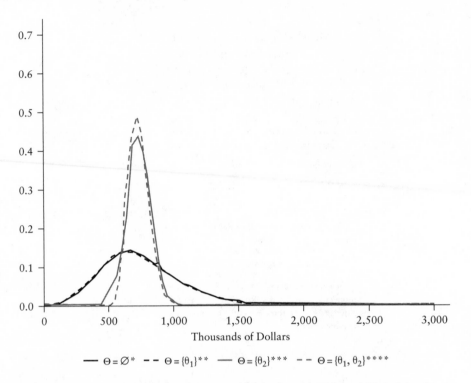

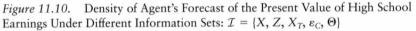

Figure 11.10. Density of Agent's Forecast of the Present Value of High School Earnings Under Different Information Sets: $\mathcal{I} = \{X, Z, X_T, \varepsilon_C, \Theta\}$

NOTE: Let Y_0 denote the agent's forecast of present earnings in the high school sector. These are formed over the whole population, not just the subpopulation who go to high school. We assume that agents know all coefficients. Let $\mathcal{I} = \{X, Z, X_T, \varepsilon_C, \Theta\}$ denote the agent's information set. Let $f(y_0 \mid \mathcal{I})$ denote the density of the agent's forecast of present value of earnings in high school, conditioned on the information set $\mathcal{I}$. Then:
* Plot of $f(y_0 \mid \mathcal{I})$ under no information, *i.e.*, $\Theta = \varnothing$.
** Plot of $f(y_0 \mid \mathcal{I})$ when only factor 1 is in the information set, *i.e.*, $\Theta = \{\theta_1\}$.
*** Plot of $f(y_0 \mid \mathcal{I})$ when only factor 2 is in the information set, *i.e.*, $\Theta = \{\theta_2\}$.
**** Plot of $f(y_0 \mid \mathcal{I})$ when both factors are in the information set, *i.e.*, $\Theta = \{\theta_1, \theta_2\}$.

policy regimes. The policy analyzed is as follows. A prospective student whose family income at age 17 is below the mean is allowed to attend college free of charge. The policy is self-financing within each schooling cohort. To pay for this policy, persons attending college with family income above the mean pay a tuition charge equal to the amount required to cover the costs of the students from lower income families as well as their own.

Total tuition raised covers the cost K of educating each student. Thus, if there are N_P poor students and N_R rich students, total costs are $(N_P + N_R)K$.

Agent's Forecast Variance of Present Value of Earnings
Under Different Information Sets: $\mathcal{I} = \{X, Z, X_T, \varepsilon_C, \Theta\}$
(as a fraction of the variance when no information is available)

	Var(Y_c)	Var(Y_h)	Var($Y_c - Y_h$)	Cov(Y_c, Y_h)
For time period 1:*				
Variance when $\Theta = \varnothing$	7,167.20	5,090.46	3,073.94	4,591.86
Percentage of variance remaining after controlling for the indicated factor:				
$\Theta = \{\theta_1\}$	97.50%	98.34%	99.43%	97.33%
$\Theta = \{\theta_2\}$	18.50%	32.83%	89.52%	2.67%
$\Theta = \{\theta_1, \theta_2\}$	16.01%	31.17%	88.94%	0.00%
For time period 2:**				
Variance when $\Theta = \varnothing$	49,690.64	167,786.87	41,137.80	88,169.85
Percentage of variance remaining after controlling for the indicated factor:				
$\Theta = \{\theta_1\}$	97.18%	97.54%	98.25%	97.28%
$\Theta = \{\theta_2\}$	7.39%	4.73%	16.55%	2.72%
$\Theta = \{\theta_1, \theta_2\}$	4.57%	2.27%	14.80%	0.00%
For lifetime:***				
Variance when $\Theta = \varnothing$	56,857.84	172,877.33	44,211.74	92,761.72
Percentage of variance remaining after controlling for the indicated factor:				
$\Theta = \{\theta_1\}$	97.22%	97.57%	98.33%	97.28%
$\Theta = \{\theta_2\}$	8.79%	5.56%	21.62%	2.72%
$\Theta = \{\theta_1, \theta_2\}$	6.01%	3.13%	19.95%	0.00%

We use an interest rate of 3 percent to calculate the present value of earnings. In all cases, the information set of the agent is $\mathcal{I} = \{X, Z, X_T, \varepsilon_C, \Theta\}$ and we change the contents of Θ.

* Variance of the unpredictable component of earnings between ages 17 and 28 as predicted at age 17.
** Variance of the unpredictable component of earnings between ages 29 and 65 as predicted at age 17.
*** Variance of the unpredictable component of earnings between ages 17 and 65 as predicted at age 17.

So we would say that the variance of the unpredictable component of period 1 college earnings when using factor 1 in the prediction is 97.5 percent of the variance when no information is available (i.e., 0.975*7167.2).

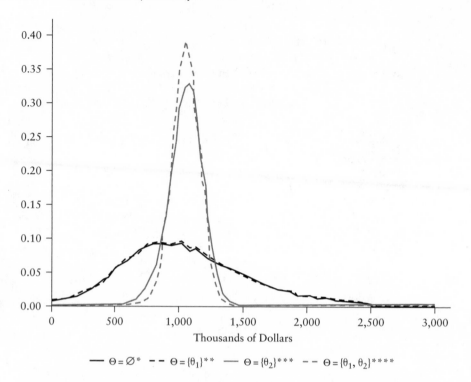

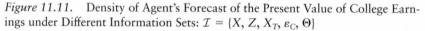

Figure 11.11.   Density of Agent's Forecast of the Present Value of College Earnings under Different Information Sets: $\mathcal{I} = \{X, Z, X_T, \varepsilon_C, \Theta\}$

N O T E : Let Y_1 denote the agent's forecast of present earnings in the college sector. These are formed over the whole population, not just the subpopulation who go to college. We assume that agents know all coefficients. Let $\mathcal{I} = \{X, Z, X_T, \varepsilon_C, \Theta\}$ denote the agent's information set. Let $f(y_1 \mid \mathcal{I})$ denote the density of the agent's forecast of present value of earnings in college, conditioned on the information set $\mathcal{I}$. Then:
* Plot of $f(y_1 \mid \mathcal{I})$ under no information, *i.e.*, $\Theta = \varnothing$.
** Plot of $f(y_1 \mid \mathcal{I})$ when only factor 1 is in the information set, *i.e.*, $\Theta = \{\theta_1\}$.
*** Plot of $f(y_1 \mid \mathcal{I})$ when only factor 2 is in the information set, *i.e.*, $\Theta = \{\theta_2\}$.
**** Plot of $f(y_1 \mid \mathcal{I})$ when both factors are in the information set, *i.e.*, $\Theta = \{\theta_1, \theta_2\}$.

In the proposed policy, the poor pay nothing. So each rich person is charged a tuition $T = K(1 + \frac{N_P}{N_R})$. To determine T, notice that $N_P = N_P(T)$; $N_R = N_R(T)$. We iterate to find the unique self-financing T. Notice that $N_P(0)$, the number of poor people who attend college when tuition is zero, is the same for all values of T ($N_P(T) = N_P(0)$ for all T). N_R is sensitive to the tuition level charged.

Figure 11.13 shows that the marginal distributions of income in both the pre-policy state and the post-policy state are essentially identical. Under

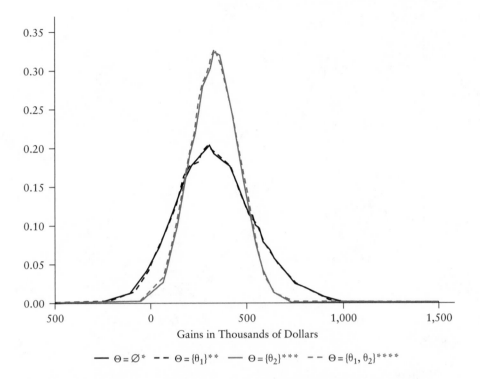

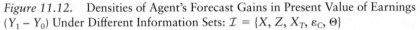

Figure 11.12.   Densities of Agent's Forecast Gains in Present Value of Earnings
$(Y_1 - Y_0)$ Under Different Information Sets: $\mathcal{I} = \{X, Z, X_T, \varepsilon_C, \Theta\}$

NOTE: Let Y_1, Y_0 denote the agent's forecast of present value of earnings in the high school and college sectors, respectively. We define the difference in present value of earnings as $\Delta = Y_1 - Y_0$. We assume that agents know all coefficients. Let $\mathcal{I} = \{X, Z, X_T, \varepsilon_C, \Theta\}$, $f(\Delta \mid \mathcal{I})$ denote the agent's information set and the density of the agent's forecast of gains in present value of earnings in choosing college, conditioned on the information set $\mathcal{I}$, respectively. These are defined over the whole population. Then:
*Plot of $f(\Delta \mid \mathcal{I})$ under no information, *i.e.*, $\Theta = \varnothing$.
**Plot of $f(\Delta \mid \mathcal{I})$ when only factor 1 is in the information set, *i.e.*, $\Theta = \{\theta_1\}$.
***Plot of $f(\Delta \mid \mathcal{I})$ when only factor 2 is in the information set, *i.e.*, $\Theta = \{\theta_2\}$.
****Plot of $f(\Delta \mid \mathcal{I})$ when both factors are in the information set, *i.e.*, $\Theta = \{\theta_1, \theta_2\}$.

anonymity we would judge these two situations as equally good using Lorenz measures or second order stochastic dominance. We move beyond anonymity and analyze the effect that the policy has on what Fields (2003) calls "positional" mobility.

Panel 1 of Table 11.9 presents this analysis by describing how the 9.2 percent of the people who are affected by the policy move between deciles of the distribution of income. These statistics describe movements from one

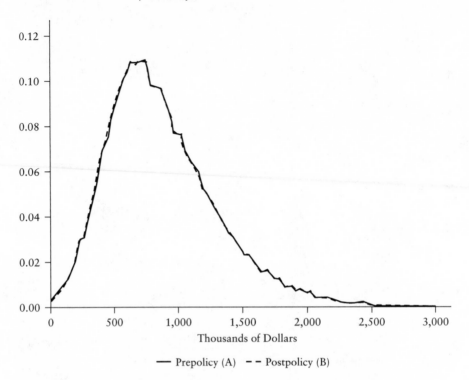

Figure 11.13. Densities of Present Value of Lifetime Earnings Before and After Implementing Cross Subsidy Policy

NOTE: Let Y^A, Y^B denote the observed present value of earnings pre- and post-policy, respectively. Define $f(y^A)$, $g(y^B)$ as the marginal densities of present value of earnings pre- and post-policy. In this figure we plot $f(y^A)$, $g(y^B)$.

income distribution in the initial regime to another income distribution associated with the new regime. The policy affects more people at the top deciles than at the lower deciles. Around half of the people affected who start at the first decile remain at the first decile. People in the middle deciles are spread both up and down, and a large proportion of people in the upper deciles is moved into a lower position (only 16 percent of those starting on the top decile remain there after the policy is implemented). Moving beyond the anonymity postulate (which instructs us to examine only marginal distributions), we learn much more about the effects of the policy on different groups.

Thus far, we have focused on constructing and interpreting the joint distribution of outcomes across the two policy regimes. If outcomes under both regimes are observed, these comparisons can be made using panel data. No

TABLE 11.9

Mobility of People Affected by Cross-subsidizing Tuition

OVERALL: FRACTION OF TOTAL POPULATION WHO SWITCH SCHOOLING LEVELS: 0.0932

PROBABILITY OF MOVING TO A DIFFERENT DECILE OF THE LIFETIME EARNINGS DISTRIBUTION

Fraction by Decile of Origin	Deciles of Origin	1	2	3	4	5	6	7	8	9	10
0.0728	1	0.5565	0.2011	0.1220	0.0634	0.0283	0.0074	0.0012	0.0000	0.0000	0.0000
0.0867	2	0.2079	0.1712	0.1715	0.1690	0.1585	0.0870	0.0322	0.0025	0.0002	0.0000
0.0955	3	0.1148	0.1489	0.0935	0.1137	0.1573	0.1888	0.1387	0.0409	0.0034	0.0000
0.0998	4	0.0619	0.1557	0.0910	0.0534	0.0764	0.1615	0.2084	0.1557	0.0360	0.0000
0.1032	5	0.0296	0.1495	0.1387	0.0630	0.0304	0.0571	0.1411	0.2456	0.1396	0.0055
0.1050	6	0.0066	0.0959	0.1726	0.1471	0.0520	0.0142	0.0415	0.1671	0.2605	0.0425
0.1084	7	0.0006	0.0336	0.1411	0.1956	0.1269	0.0420	0.0082	0.0348	0.2346	0.1827
0.1089	8	0.0000	0.0046	0.0519	0.1765	0.2211	0.1495	0.0388	0.0034	0.0513	0.3029
0.1101	9	0.0000	0.0000	0.0055	0.0421	0.1570	0.2733	0.2302	0.0447	0.0014	0.2459
0.1069	10	0.0000	0.0000	0.0000	0.0002	0.0041	0.0517	0.2082	0.3242	0.2490	0.1626

HIGH SCHOOL: FRACTION OF TOTAL POPULATION WHO SWITCH FROM HIGH SCHOOL TO COLLEGE DUE TO THE POLICY: 0.0450

Fraction by Decile of Origin	Deciles of Origin	1	2	3	4	5	6	7	8	9	10
0.1012	1	0.3954	0.2557	0.1775	0.0936	0.0417	0.0110	0.0018	0.0000	0.0000	0.0000
0.1279	2	0.0382	0.1220	0.2176	0.2325	0.2200	0.1210	0.0448	0.0035	0.0003	0.0000
0.1369	3	0.0023	0.0188	0.0692	0.1536	0.2244	0.2701	0.1984	0.0584	0.0049	0.0000
0.1367	4	0.0000	0.0016	0.0088	0.0368	0.1116	0.2417	0.3123	0.2332	0.0540	0.0000
0.1285	5	0.0000	0.0000	0.0007	0.0052	0.0277	0.0903	0.2324	0.4047	0.2300	0.0090
0.1122	6	0.0000	0.0000	0.0000	0.0004	0.0024	0.0151	0.0792	0.3209	0.5004	0.0816
0.1017	7	0.0000	0.0000	0.0000	0.0000	0.0000	0.0009	0.0101	0.0761	0.5133	0.3997

TABLE 11.9
(continued)

Fraction by Decile of Origin	Deciles of Origin										
		OVERALL: FRACTION OF TOTAL POPULATION WHO SWITCH SCHOOLING LEVELS: 0.0932									
		PROBABILITY OF MOVING TO A DIFFERENT DECILE OF THE LIFETIME EARNINGS DISTRIBUTION									
		1	2	3	4	5	6	7	8	9	10
0.0797	8	0.0000	0.0000	0.0000	0.0000	0.0000	0.0000	0.0000	0.0067	0.1440	0.8493
0.0557	9	0.0000	0.0000	0.0000	0.0000	0.0000	0.0000	0.0000	0.0000	0.0032	0.9968
0.0173	10	0.0000	0.0000	0.0000	0.0000	0.0000	0.0000	0.0000	0.0000	0.0000	1.0000
		COLLEGE: FRACTION OF TOTAL POPULATION WHO SWITCH FROM COLLEGE TO HIGH SCHOOL DUE TO THE POLICY: 0.0473									
0.0459	1	0.8941	0.0866	0.0055	0.0000	0.0000	0.0000	0.0000	0.0000	0.0000	0.0000
0.0475	2	0.6423	0.2972	0.0534	0.0062	0.0009	0.0000	0.0000	0.0000	0.0000	0.0000
0.0560	3	0.3763	0.4510	0.1501	0.0211	0.0015	0.0000	0.0000	0.0000	0.0000	0.0000
0.0647	4	0.1860	0.4648	0.2559	0.0868	0.0059	0.0007	0.0000	0.0000	0.0000	0.0000
0.0791	5	0.0753	0.3801	0.3518	0.1522	0.0347	0.0059	0.0000	0.0000	0.0000	0.0000
0.0982	6	0.0138	0.2001	0.3602	0.3064	0.1059	0.0133	0.0004	0.0000	0.0000	0.0000
0.1148	7	0.0011	0.0618	0.2598	0.3603	0.2337	0.0766	0.0066	0.0000	0.0000	0.0000
0.1366	8	0.0000	0.0071	0.0807	0.2744	0.3436	0.2323	0.0603	0.0015	0.0000	0.0000
0.1618	9	0.0000	0.0000	0.0073	0.0559	0.2084	0.3628	0.3056	0.0593	0.0008	0.0000
0.1920	10	0.0000	0.0000	0.0000	0.0002	0.0044	0.0561	0.2260	0.3519	0.2702	0.0911

NOTE: Cross-subsidy consists in making tuition 0 for people with family income below average and making the budget balance by raising tuition for college students with family income above the average. For example, we read from the first panel row 1, column 1 that 7.28 percent of the people who switch schooling levels come from the lowest decile. Out of those, 55 percent are still in the first decile after the policy while 2.83 percent jump to the fifth decile. Panel 2 has the same interpretation but it only looks at people who switch from high school to college while panel 3 looks at individuals who switch from college to high school.

TABLE 11.10
Mobility of People Affected
by Cross-subsidizing Tuition,
Fraction of the Total Population
Who Switch Schooling Levels: 0.0932

	FRACTION OF HIGH SCHOOL GRADUATES:	
PREPOLICY CHOICE:	*Do Not Switch*	*Become College Graduates*
High School	0.9197	0.0803

	FRACTION OF COLLEGE GRADUATES:	
	Do Not Switch	*Become High School Graduates*
College	0.8923	0.1077

NOTE: Cross-subsidy consists in making tuition zero for people with family income below average and making the budget balance by raising tuition for college students with family income above the average.

use of counterfactuals is necessary. However, our methods will apply if either or both policy regimes are unobserved but are proposed. Taking advantage of the fact that we can identify not only joint distributions of earnings over policy regimes but also over counterfactual states within regimes we can learn a great deal more about the effects of this policy, whether or not policy regimes are observed.[22]

Table 11.10 and panels 2 and 3 of Table 11.9 reveal that not only is 9.2 percent of the population affected by the policy, but that actually about half of them moved from high school into college (4.5 percent of the population) and half moved from college into high school (4.7 percent of the population). This translates into saying that, of those affected by the policy, 92 percent of the high school graduates stay in high school in the post-policy regime while only 89 percent of college graduates stay put. Thus, the policy is slightly biased against college attendance. We can form the joint distributions of lifetime earnings by initial schooling level. Figure 11.14 summarizes some of the evidence presented in Table 11.10. Figure 11.14 and

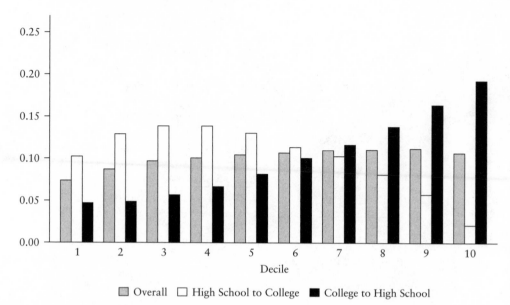

Figure 11.14.   Fraction of People Who Switch Schooling Levels When Tuition Is Cross-subsidized, By Decile of Origin from the Lifetime Earnings Distribution

N O T E : Cross subsidy consists in making tuition zero for people with family income below the average and making the budget balance by raising tuition for college students with family income above the average.

the evidence in panels 2 and 3 of Table 11.9 show that the policy affects very few high school graduates at the top end of the income distribution (only 1.7 percent of those affected come from the tenth percentile) and a lot of college graduates in the same situation (19 percent of college graduates affected come from the top decile). We can also see that the policy tends to move high school graduates up in the income distribution and moves college graduates down. As another example of the generality of our method and the new insight into income mobility induced by policy that it provides, we can determine where people come from and where they end up at in the counterfactual distributions of earnings. Table 11.11 shows where in the pre-policy distribution of high school earnings persons induced to go to college come from and where in the post-policy distribution of college earnings they go to. Most people stay in their decile or move to closely adjacent ones. Given that some people benefit from the policy while others lose, it is not clear whether society as a whole values this policy positively. An advantage of our method is that it allows us to calculate the effect that the policy has

TABLE 11.11

Mobility of People Affected by Cross-subsidizing Tuition Across Counterfactual Distributions,
High School: Fraction of Total Population who from High School to College After the Policy: 0.0450

Fraction by Decile of Origin in the Prepolicy High School Distribution	Deciles of Origin	PROBABILITY OF MOVING TO A DIFFERENT DECILE OF THE POSTPOLICY COLLEGE LIFETIME EARNINGS DISTRIBUTION									
		1	2	3	4	5	6	7	8	9	10
0.0667	1	0.8266	0.1227	0.0140	0.0020	0.0000	0.0000	0.0000	0.0000	0.0000	0.0000
0.0811	2	0.4044	0.4110	0.1490	0.0296	0.0055	0.0000	0.0000	0.0000	0.0000	0.0000
0.0908	3	0.1488	0.3544	0.3059	0.1419	0.0445	0.0039	0.0005	0.0000	0.0000	0.0000
0.0998	4	0.0401	0.2343	0.3096	0.2490	0.1234	0.0379	0.0053	0.0004	0.0000	0.0000
0.1047	5	0.0089	0.0713	0.2081	0.3053	0.2348	0.1282	0.0365	0.0068	0.0000	0.0000
0.1058	6	0.0004	0.0202	0.0950	0.2155	0.2761	0.2416	0.1273	0.0239	0.0000	0.0000
0.1062	7	0.0000	0.0033	0.0243	0.0896	0.1888	0.3026	0.2662	0.1155	0.0096	0.0000
0.1116	8	0.0000	0.0004	0.0016	0.0159	0.0630	0.1690	0.3220	0.3228	0.1024	0.0028
0.1138	9	0.0000	0.0000	0.0000	0.0016	0.0043	0.0293	0.1227	0.3271	0.4568	0.0582
0.1173	10	0.0000	0.0000	0.0000	0.0000	0.0000	0.0000	0.0027	0.0333	0.2626	0.7014

TABLE 11.11
(continued)

PROBABILITY OF MOVING TO A DIFFERENT DECILE
OF THE POSTPOLICY COLLEGE LIFETIME EARNINGS DISTRIBUTION

COLLEGE: FRACTION OF TOTAL POPULATION WHO SWITCH FROM COLLEGE TO HIGH SCHOOL DUE TO THE POLICY: 0.0473

Fraction by Decile of Origin in the Prepolicy High School Distribution	Deciles of Origin	1	2	3	4	5	6	7	8	9	10
0.1095	1	0.5473	0.2945	0.1135	0.0316	0.0062	0.0012	0.0000	0.0000	0.0000	0.0000
0.1056	2	0.1076	0.3257	0.2937	0.1789	0.0716	0.0204	0.0016	0.0004	0.0000	0.0000
0.1035	3	0.0180	0.1473	0.2776	0.2657	0.1833	0.0857	0.0200	0.0024	0.0000	0.0000
0.1013	4	0.0004	0.0355	0.1535	0.2349	0.2866	0.1890	0.0847	0.0150	0.0004	0.0000
0.1012	5	0.0000	0.0050	0.0467	0.1503	0.2654	0.2705	0.1903	0.0668	0.0050	0.0000
0.0979	6	0.0000	0.0000	0.0091	0.0513	0.1678	0.2683	0.2972	0.1786	0.0276	0.0000
0.0977	7	0.0000	0.0000	0.0000	0.0087	0.0463	0.1609	0.3071	0.3387	0.1362	0.0022
0.0953	8	0.0000	0.0000	0.0000	0.0004	0.0044	0.0430	0.1560	0.4020	0.3617	0.0324
0.0964	9	0.0000	0.0000	0.0000	0.0000	0.0000	0.0009	0.0127	0.1337	0.5355	0.3173
0.0882	10	0.0000	0.0000	0.0000	0.0000	0.0000	0.0000	0.0000	0.0034	0.0915	0.9051

NOTE: Cross-subsidy consists in making tuition 0 for people with family income below average and making the budget balance by raising tuition for college students with family income above the average. For example, we read from the first panel row 1, column 1 that 6.67 percent of the people who switch from high school to college come from the lowest decile of the prepolicy high school distribution. Out of those, 82.66 percent are still in the first decile of the postpolicy college earnings distribution after the policy is implemented while 1.40 percent "jump" to the third decile. Panel 2 has the same interpretation but it only looks at people who switch from college to high school.

TABLE 11.12
Voting Outcome of Proposing Cross-subsidizing* Tuition,
Fraction of the Total Population
Who Switch Schooling Levels: 0.0932

Average prepolicy lifetime earnings**	920.55
Average postpolicy lifetime earnings**	905.96
Fraction of the population who votes	
Yes	0.0716
No	0.6152
Indifferent	0.3132

* Cross-subsidy consists in making tuition zero for people with family income below average and making the budget balance by raising tuition for college students with family income above the average.
** In thousands of dollars.

on welfare. An individual's relative utility is not only given by earnings but also by the monetary value of psychic costs. We can predict how people would vote if the policy analyzed in this section were proposed. Table 11.12 shows the result of such an exercise. The policy lowers the mean earnings for people affected by it. Most people not indifferent to the policy would vote against it.

Finally, because we are able to distinguish heterogeneity from uncertainty, we can also simulate the effects of the policy in the case in which people decide using their *ex post* information (i.e., after their luck components are realized). The outcomes for this case are very similar to the ones we just presented (although fewer people are affected by the policy). For the sake of brevity we do not report them in this chapter.[23] This finding reinforces our earlier conclusion. Uncertainty is not a major factor in explaining college choices. This suggests that the large estimated role for psychic costs cannot be due to expectational errors about uncertain components of future income. The role of luck, long emphasized in the literature on education and earnings, appears to be small.

7. SUMMARY AND CONCLUSION

This chapter summarizes and applies a new body of research on counterfactual analyses of income inequality and mobility. We construct counterfactuals within policy regimes and counterfactuals across policy regimes. Using the methods presented here, it is possible to understand the sources of inequality, and the inequality and mobility consequences of social policies, much more deeply than is possible using traditional measures based on the anonymity axiom.

We show how to construct distributions of counterfactuals within policy regimes using factor models. With these same tools, we show how to separate variability into two components: (1) those that are predictable by a certain age (heterogeneity) and (2) those that are not (luck).

We apply these methods to analyze the returns to college education. We find that by age 17, when college decisions are made, prospective students can forecast roughly 80 percent of the lifetime variance in their returns to schooling. Heterogeneity and not uncertainty drives the variance in earnings both cross-sectionally and over time. Given the relatively small role for uncertainty, it is unlikely that expectational errors about future earnings play a major role in explaining college choices.

We also find that counterfactual outcomes both within and across policy regimes are highly correlated. However there is a lot of slippage in ranks across potential outcomes within one policy regime and the outcomes chosen across policy regimes. Ranks are by no means identical across these counterfactual distributions. One justification for the use of the anonymity postulate in the analysis of data on income distributions is that outcomes are independent across policies. That justification is strongly rejected in our data, as is the polar assumption that ranks are perfectly dependent across policies.

We show how our methods can reveal where in initial and final distributions persons induced to change their education by a tuition subsidy policy will come from and where they end up. Such analyses can be made both in terms of initial and final outcome distributions and in distributions of potential outcomes associated with each educational choice. We present a much richer analysis of the inequality and mobility consequences of policies than are available from analyses based on panel data or data from social experiments.

This chapter has ignored the analysis of general equilibrium effects operating through factor markets even though such effects are empirically important for large scale programs. Substantial changes in educational enrollments will affect the wages of college and high school students. The next step in our research program is to graft the methods in this paper to the general equilibrium framework of Heckman, Lochner, and Taber (1998a, 1998b,

1998c, 1999) to provide a more comprehensive analysis of the effects of policies on inequality.

APPENDIX A. A MOTIVATION FOR THE NONPARAMETRIC IDENTIFICATION OF THE JOINT DISTRIBUTION OF OUTCOMES AND THE BINARY CHOICE EQUATION

The following intuition motivates the conditions under which $F(Y_0, I^* \mid X, Z)$ is identified. A formal proof is given in Carneiro, Hansen, and Heckman (2003). A parallel argument holds for $F(Y_1, I^* \mid X, Z)$. First, under the conditions given in Cosslett (1983), Manski (1988), and Matzkin (1992), we can identify $\frac{\mu_I(X, Z)}{\sigma_I}$ from the choice probability $\Pr(S = 1 \mid X, Z) = \Pr(\mu_I(X, Z) + U_I \geq 0 \mid X, Z)$. We can also identify the distribution of $\frac{U_I}{\sigma_I}$. Second, from this information and the distribution of outcomes for those for whom $F(Y_0 \mid S = 0, X, Z) = \Pr(Y_0 \leq y_0 \mid \mu_I(X, Z) + U_I \leq 0, X, Z)$, we can form

$$F(Y_0 \mid S = 0, X, Z)\Pr(S = 0 \mid X, Z) = \Pr(Y_0 \leq y_0, I^* \leq 0 \mid X, Z).$$

The left-hand side of this equation is known (we observe Y_0 when $S = 0$ and we know the probability that $S = 0$ given X, Z). The right-hand side can be written as

$$\Pr\left(Y_0 \leq y_0, \frac{U_I}{\sigma_I} < -\frac{\mu_I(X, Z)}{\sigma_I} \,\middle|\, X, Z \right).$$

We know $\frac{\mu_I(X, Z)}{\sigma_I}$ and can vary it for each fixed X. In particular, if $\mu_I(X, Z)$ gets small ($\mu_I(X, Z) \to -\infty$), we can recover the marginal distribution Y from which we can recover $\mu_0(X)$.

Using equation (1a), we can express this probability as

$$\Pr\left(U_0 \leq y_0 - \mu_0(X), \frac{U_I}{\sigma_I} \leq \frac{-\mu_I(X, Z)}{\sigma_I} \,\middle|\, X, Z \right).$$

Note that the X and Z can be varied and y_0 is a number. Thus, we can trace out the joint distribution of $(U_0, \frac{U_I}{\sigma_I})$. We can thus recover the joint distribution of

$$(Y_0, I^*) = \left(\mu_0(X) + U_0, \frac{\mu_I(X, Z) + U_I}{\sigma_I} \right).$$

Notice the three key ingredients: (1) the independence of (U_0, U_I) and (X, Z), (2) the assumption that we can set $\frac{\mu_I(X, Z)}{\sigma_I}$ to be very small (so we get the marginal distribution of Y_0 and hence $\mu_0(X)$), and (3) the assumption that $\frac{\mu_I(X, Z)}{\sigma_I}$ can be varied independently of $\mu_0(X)$. This enables us to trace out the joint distribution of $\left(U_0, \frac{U_I}{\sigma_I}\right)$.

Another way to see how identification works is to note that from Cosslett (1983), Manski (1988), Matzkin (1992), and ingredients (1) and (2) we can express

$$F(Y_0 \mid S = 0, X, Z) \, \Pr(S = 0 \mid X, Z)$$

as a function of $\mu_0(X)$ and $\frac{\mu_I(X, Z)}{\sigma_I}$. This is called index sufficiency in the discrete choice literature. Varying the $\mu_0(X)$ and $\frac{\mu_I(X, Z)}{\sigma_I}$ traces out the distribution of $\left(U_0, \frac{U_I}{\sigma_I}\right)$.

Notes

This research was supported by NIH R01-HD043411. Cunha acknowledges support from CAPES grant 1430/99-8. We thank Gary Fields for helpful comments on the first draft of this paper. Cunha is affiliated with the Department of Economics, University of Chicago. Heckman is affiliated with that department as well as with the American Bar Foundation and University College London. Navarro is affiliated with the University of Wisconsin-Madison.

1. See Fields (2003) for a comparison of inequality and mobility measures.

2. We draw on results reported in Heckman (1992); Heckman, Smith, and Clements (1997); Aakvik, Heckman, and Vytlacil (1999, 2005); Carneiro, Hansen, and Heckman (2003); and Cunha, Heckman, and Navarro (2005).

3. See Heckman (2001) for a survey of this literature. These models for counterfactuals and potential outcomes are called Roy (1951) or generalized Roy models and have an ancient lineage in econometrics. The decision maker may be a parent, and the outcomes may be for a child.

4. Heckman, Lochner, and Taber (1998a, 1998b, 1999) develop general equilibrium policy analysis computing distributional consequences of alternative policies. See also Bourguignon and Silva (2003).

5. Thus a large scale expansion of the educational system may depress the returns to schooling.

6. Exclusion restrictions in $\mu_1(X)$ and $\mu_0(X)$ are not strictly required if the gradients of $\mu_1(X)$ and $\mu_0(X)$ differ. Exclusions give simple sufficient conditions.

7. Full support means that the support of $\mu_1(X)$ matches (or contains) the support of U_1; the support of $\mu_0(X)$ matches (or contains) the support of U_0 and the support of $\mu_I(X, Z)$ matches (or contains) the support of U_I. (See Heckman and Honoré 1990, for details.) The support of a random variable is the set of values where it has a positive probability density.

8. See Carneiro, Hansen, and Heckman (2003) for a discussion of the model with multiple factors.

9. For simplicity, we assume that this is a continuous measurement. Discrete measurements can also be used. See Carneiro, Hansen, and Heckman (2003).

10. We cannot dispense with the information from the choice equation in securing identification unless we have data on measurements to form $F(Y_0, M)$ and $F(Y_1, M)$. This information might be obtained if we have limit sets $\mathcal{Z}_u$ and $\mathcal{Z}_l$ such that $\Pr(S = 1 \mid X, Z) = 1$ for $z \in \mathcal{Z}_u$ and $\Pr(S = 0 \mid X, Z) = 0$ for $z \in \mathcal{Z}_l$. Then M can take the place of I, and we can do factor analysis if we have two or more measurement variables. See Carneiro, Hansen, and Heckman (2001).

11. Again, for the sake of simplicity, we assume that M is continuous but our methods work for discrete measurements. See Carneiro, Hansen, and Heckman (2003).

12. Recall that U_I is only known up to scale σ_I.

13. Carneiro, Hansen, and Heckman (2003) discuss the relationship between factor and matching models. For a discussion of factor models and control functions, see Heckman and Navarro (2004).

14. This is related to Flavin's (1981) test of the permanent income hypothesis and her measurement of unforecastable income innovations. See Cunha, Heckman, and Navarro (2005).

15. Identification depends on the length of the panel, the number of measurement equations and the variation in Z and X.

16. In the ℓ^1 norm.

17. Models where the $\varepsilon_{s,t}$ are allowed to be mixtures do not change the conclusions of this chapter. However, they increase the complexity of the simulation analysis. For this reason, we use the simple normal framework to estimate the uniquenesses. We stress, however, that it is not a requirement, just a matter of convenience.

18. These numbers may appear to be large but are a consequence of using a 3 percent discount rate.

19. Furthermore, we know that this result is not sensitive to the specification of the credit market. Carneiro, Hansen, and Heckman (2003) obtain a similar conclusion in a model where people are not allowed to borrow or lend. In our model, on the other hand, there are no constraints to borrowing or lending. Cuhna, Heckman, and Navarro (2005) present additional evidence on this issue.

20. "Psychic costs" can stand in for expectational errors and attitudes towards risk. We do not distinguish among these explanations in this chapter. The estimated costs are too large to be due to tuition alone. As noted below, given that returns are strongly forecastable, an important role for expectational errors seems unlikely. See the discussion in Cunha, Heckman, and Navarro (2005).

21. As opposed to the econometrician who never gets to observe either θ_1 or θ_2.

22. It is implausible that we would have panel data on policy regimes where under one regime a person goes to school and under another he does not.

23. They are available on request from the authors.

References

Aakvik, Arild, James J. Heckman, and Edward J. Vytlacil. 1999. "Training Effects on Employment when the Training Effects Are Heterogenous: An Application to Norwegian Vocational Rehabilitation Programs." Department of Economics, University of Bergen 0599.

Aakvik, Arild, James J. Heckman, and Edward J. Vytlacil. 2005. "Estimating Treatment Effects for Discrete Outcomes When Responses to Treatment Vary: An Application to Norwegian Vocational Rehabilitation Programs." *Journal of Econometrics* 125:15–51.

Bourguignon, François, and Francisco H. G. Ferreira. 2003. "Ex Ante Evaluation of Policy Reforms Using Behavioral Models." Pp. 123–41 in *The Impact of Economic Policies on Poverty and Income Distribution*, edited by F. Bourguignon and L. A. P. Silva. Washington, DC: The World Bank.

Bourguignon, François, and Luiz A. Pereira da Silva, eds. 2003. *The Impact of Economic Policies on Poverty and Income Distribution*. Washington, DC: The World Bank.

Cameron, Stephen V., and Christopher Taber. 2004. "Estimation of Educational Borrowing Constraints Using Returns to Schooling." *Journal of Political Economy* 112:132–82.

Card, David. 1999. "The Causal Effect of Education on Earnings." Pp. 1801–63 in *Handbook of Labor Economics*, vol. 3A, edited by O. Ashenfelter and D. Card. New York: North-Holland.

Carneiro, Pedro, Karsten T. Hansen, and James J. Heckman. 2001. "Removing the Veil of Ignorance in Assessing the Distributional Impacts of Social Policies." *Swedish Economic Policy Review* 8:273–301.

Carneiro, Pedro, Karsten T. Hansen, and James J. Heckman. 2003. "Estimating Distributions of Treatment Effects with an Application to the Returns to Schooling and Measurement of the Effects of Uncertainty on College Choice." *International Economic Review* 44:361–422.

Carneiro, Pedro, and James J. Heckman. 2002. "The Evidence on Credit Constraints in Post-Secondary Schooling." *Economic Journal* 112:705–34.

Chernozhukov, Victor, and Christian Hansen. 2005. "An IV Model of Quantile Treatment Effects." *Econometrica* 73:245–261.

Cosslett, Stephen R. 1983. "Distribution-Free Maximum Likelihood Estimator of the Binary Choice Model." *Econometrica* 51:765–82.

Cowell, Frank A. 2000. "Measurement of Inequality," Pp. 87–166 in *Handbook of Income Distribution*, vol. 1, edited by A. B. Atkinson and F. Bourguignon. New York: North-Holland.

Cunha, Flavio, James J. Heckman, and Salvador Navarro. 2005. "Separating Heterogeneity from Uncertainty in Life Cycle Earnings." Hicks Lecture, Oxford University, April 2004, *Oxford Economics Papers* 57:191–261.

Ferguson, Thomas S. 1983. "Bayesian Density Estimation by Mixtures of Normal

Distributions." Pp. 287–302 in *Recent Advances in Statistics*, edited by
M. Rizvi, J. Rustagi, and D. Siegmund. New York: Academic Press.

Fields, Gary S. 2003. "Economic and Social Mobility Really Are Multifaceted."
Paper presented at the Conference on Frontiers in Social and Economic Mobility, Cornell University, Ithaca, New York, March.

Flavin, Marjorie A. 1981. "The Adjustment of Consumption to Changing Expectations about Future Income." *Journal of Political Economy* 89:974–1009.

Goldberger, Arthur S., and Karl G. Jöreskog. 1975. "Estimation of a Model with
Multiple Indicators and Multiple Causes of a Single Latent Variable." *Journal
of the American Statistical Association* 70:631–39.

Heckman, James J. 1990. "Varieties of Selection Bias." *American Economic Review* 80:313–18.

Heckman, James J. 1992. "Randomization and Social Policy Evaluation." Pp.
201–30 in *Evaluating Welfare and Training Programs*, edited by C. F. Manski
and Irwin Garfinkel, Cambridge, MA: Harvard University Press.

Heckman, James J. 2001. "Micro Data, Heterogeneity, and the Evaluation of Public Policy: Nobel Lecture." *Journal of Political Economy* 109:673–748.

Heckman, James J., and Bo Honoré. 1990. "The Empirical Content of the Roy
Model." *Econometrica* 58:1121–49.

Heckman, James J., Lance Lochner, and Christopher Taber. 1998a. "Tax Policy
and Human-Capital Formation." *American Economic Review* 88:293–97.

Heckman, James J., Lance Lochner, and Christopher Taber. 1998b. "General-
Equilibrium Treatment Effects: A Study of Tuition Policy." *American
Economic Review* 88:381–86.

Heckman, James J., Lance Lochner, and Christopher Taber. 1998c. "Explaining
Rising Wage Inequality: Explorations with a Dynamic General Equilibrium
Model of Labor Earnings with Heterogeneous Agents." *Review of Economic
Dynamics* 1:1–58.

Heckman, James J., Lance Lochner, and Christopher Taber. 1999. "General-
Equilibrium Cost-Benefit Analysis of Education and Tax Policies." Pp.
291–349 in *Trade, Growth and Development: Essays in Honor of Professor
T. N. Srinivasan, Contributions to Economic Analysis*, vol. 242, edited by
G. Ranis and L. Raut. New York: North-Holland.

Heckman, James J., and Salvador Navarro. 2004. "Using Matching Instrumental
Variables and Control Functions to Estimate Economic Choice Models." *Review of Economics and Statistics* 86:30–57.

Heckman, James J., and Jeffrey A. Smith. 1998. "Evaluating the Welfare State."
Pp. 241–318 in *Econometrics and Economic Theory in the 20th Century: The
Ragnar Frisch Centennial*. Econometric Society Monograph Series, edited by
S. Strom. Cambridge: Cambridge University Press.

Heckman, James J., Jeffrey A. Smith, and Nancy Clements. 1997. "Making the Most
Out of Programme Evaluations and Social Experiments: Accounting for Heterogeneity in Programme Impacts." *Review of Economic Studies* 64:487–535.

Heckman, James J., and Edward J. Vytlacil. 2005. "Structural Equations, Treatment Effects and Econometric Policy Evaluation." *Econometrica* 73:669–738.

Heckman, James J., and Edward J. Vytlacil. 2006a. "Econometric Evaluation of Social Programs. Part I: Causal Models, Structural Models and Econometric Policy Evaluation." In *Handbook of Econometrics,* vol. 6, edited by J. Heckman and E. Leamer. Amsterdam: Elsevier Science.

Heckman, James J., and Edward J. Vytlacil. 2006b. "Econometric Evaluation of Social Programs. Part II: Using Economic Choice Theory and the Marginal Treatment Effect to Organize Alternative Econometric Estimators." In *Handbook of Econometrics,* vol. 6, edited by J. Heckman and E. Leamer. Amsterdam: Elsevier Science.

Jencks, Christopher, Marshall Smith, Henry Acland, Mary Jo Bane, David K. Cohen, Herbert Gintis, Barbara Heyns, and Stephen Michelson. 1972. *Inequality: A Reassessment of the Effect of Family and Schooling in America.* New York: Basic Books.

Jöreskog, Karl G. 1977. "Structural Equations Models in the Social Sciences: Specification, Estimation and Testing." Pp. 265–87 in *Applications of Statistics,* edited by P. R. Krishnaih. Amsterdam: North-Holland.

Juhn, Chinhui, Kevin M. Murphy, and Brooks Pierce. 1993. "Wage Inequality and the Rise in Returns to Skill." *Journal of Political Economy* 101:410–42.

Kane, Thomas J. 1994. "College Entry by Blacks Since 1970: The Role of College Costs, Family Background, and the Returns to Education." *Journal of Political Economy* 102:878–911.

Kotlarski, Ignacy I. 1967. "On Characterizing the Gamma and Normal Distribution." *Pacific Journal of Mathematics* 20:729–38.

Lillard, Lee A., and Robert J. Willis. 1978. "Dynamic Aspects of Earning Mobility." *Econometrica* 46:985–1012.

Manski, Charles F. 1988. "Identification of Binary Response Models." *Journal of the American Statistical Association* 83:729–38.

Matzkin, Rosa. 1992. "Nonparametric and Distribution-Free Estimation of the Binary Threshold Crossing and the Binary Choice Models." *Econometrica* 60:239–70.

Persson, Torsten, and Guido E. Tabellini. 2000. *Political Economics: Explaining Economic Policy.* Cambridge, MA: MIT Press.

Ravallion, Martin. 2003. "Assessing the Poverty Impact of an Assigned Program." Pp. 103–22 in *The Impact of Economic Policies on Poverty and Income Distribution,* edited by F. Bourguignon and L. A. P. Silva. Washington, DC: The World Bank.

Roy, A. D. 1951. "Some Thoughts on the Distribution of Earnings." *Oxford Economic Papers* 3:135–46.

Vytlacil, Edward J. 2002. "Independence, Monotonicity, and Latent Index Models: An Equivalence Result." *Econometrica* 70:331–34.

PART FIVE   CONTEXTS OF
MOBILITY: INCOME
DYNAMICS AND
VULNERABILITY TO
POVERTY

CHAPTER TWELVE

Estimating Individual Vulnerability to Poverty with Pseudo-Panel Data

François Bourguignon, Chor-ching Goh, and Dae Il Kim

Studying individual earning dynamics requires panel data of individuals that are seldom available in developing countries. Hence, it is difficult to study such issues as the propensity of earners to fall into poverty or vulnerability to poverty due to earning changes. Because of the absence of suitable panel data in most developing countries, there is no direct way to examine individual earning dynamics nor vulnerability to poverty. It may seem a priori that repeated cross-sectional data are of no use to identify individual earning dynamics, because by definition, such data do not refer to the same individuals at various points of time. However, this chapter explores a methodology that permits recovering some parameters of individual earnings dynamics from cross-sectional data under a set of simplifying assumptions. The methodology is based on pseudo-panel techniques focusing on second order moments, as pioneered by (Deaton and Paxson 1994). Based on these parameters, it is then possible to derive estimates on the vulnerability to poverty making use of all the cross-sectional information available at a point of time.

Our motivation for studying vulnerability to poverty, defined as the probability of earning below a poverty threshold conditional on initial earnings, stems from concerns expressed by opponents of globalization that integration exposes individuals to the vagaries of international markets, and such shocks may be transmitted to greater volatility and uncertainty in earnings of individual workers. The East Asian financial crisis rekindled this anxiety. There

We wish to thank Gary Fields for his helpful comments on an earlier draft and suggestion that we make a comparison of results between panel and cross-sectional data that forms the gist of this chapter.

has been little empirical work to investigate the linkage between shocks at the macro level and vulnerability at the level of individual workers. Within the large literature on wage inequality and wage differentials in relation to globalization, only a handful of studies—mostly on Latin American economies (perhaps because macroeconomic volatility appears to be structurally higher there)—examine this relationship, taking changes in employment as the indicator of vulnerability.[1] De Ferranti et al. (2000) summarizes issues of worker insecurity and economic openness in Latin America: they find that wage volatility is affected more by inflation than by openness, and that many countries experienced more stable wages during the more open 1990s. Bourguignon and Goh (2004) made a first attempt to investigate this topic in an East Asian context. They find that there was no correlation between trade liberalization and vulnerability to poverty in that region.

The objectives of this chapter are to present an original method to study individual earning dynamics using repeated cross-sectional or pseudo-panel data, and to compare the accuracy of these estimates with those produced from a true panel data. In our case, a pseudo panel is formed by following cohorts of randomly selected individuals born in a five-birth-year interval over time in successive cross-sectional surveys; that is, we are tracking over time male workers born in 1946–50 as one homogeneous group or cohort; male workers born in 1951–55 as another group or cohort and so on. We discuss in Section 1 the method that recovers features of individual earning dynamics from pseudo-panel data. The idea is as follows: if it may be assumed that all individuals within a cohort face a stochastic earning process that has common characteristics, these characteristics may be recovered at the aggregate level, without observing actual earning paths. Observing the evolution of the mean and the variance of earnings within a cohort is sufficient to estimate the common characteristics of individual earning processes. On this basis, simple estimates of the probability of a worker observed in year t to fall into poverty in year $t + 1$ can be worked out. In Section 2, we apply this method to repeated cross-sectional data in Korea, using them as a pseudo panel. We also check the relevance of this approach by applying it to a pseudo panel constructed from a true panel data in Korea. Korea was selected because few other developing countries have reasonably long and representative panel data on earnings. The panel data sets that are suitably long enough for us to check the quality of earning dynamics estimates based on pseudo panel are the Korea Labor Institute Panel Study data and the Korean's Urban Worker Household Income and Expenditure Surveys. In Section 3, we evaluate the quality of the approximation of pseudo-panel estimates vis-à-vis direct individual panel estimates.

Our results show that the basic earning dynamics parameter—that is, the persistence of earnings shocks from a period to the next—recovered from repeated cross-sectional data, or a pseudo panel, are not significantly different from those estimated from a true panel. Another parameter of the model, the variance of the earning "innovations," recovered from a pseudo panel also approximate those estimated from a true panel. With regards to our variable of interest, the vulnerability to poverty, estimates simulated from a pseudo panel track very closely those from a panel.

I. A MODEL FOR RECOVERING EARNING DYNAMICS FEATURES FROM REPEATED CROSS-SECTIONAL DATA

Assume that the earnings, w_{it}^j, of individual i belonging to cohort group j at time t may be represented by the following equation:

$$\ln w_{it}^j = X_{it}^j \beta_t^j + \xi_{it}^j \tag{1}$$

where X_{it} is a set of individual characteristics like age or educational attainment and ξ_{it}^j stands for unobserved permanent earning determinants as well as the transitory component of earnings. Accordingly, assume that this residual term ξ_{it}^j follows an autoregressive process $AR(1)$:

$$\xi_{it}^j = \rho^j \xi_{it-1}^j + \varepsilon_{it}^j \tag{2}$$

where ε_{it}^j is the "innovation" in earnings and is supposed to have a variance $\sigma_{\varepsilon jt}^2$.

Suppose now that repeated cross-sectional data are available for periods $t = 1, 2, \ldots T$. If the sample is representative of the whole population at each period, a sample of individuals belonging to each cohort j is observed in each period. It is thus possible to follow cohort j over time. But, because individuals in two successive cross-sections are not identical, it is not possible to observe ξ_{it}^j and ξ_{it-1}^j for the same person i. Thus, model (1)–(2) cannot be readily estimated. Nevertheless, it is possible to extract from these cross-sections some information on the basic dynamic parameters ρ^j and $\sigma_{\varepsilon jt}^2$. Under the assumption that individuals enter and exit randomly the labor force between two successive periods, it is the case from (2) that the variance $\sigma^2_{\xi jt}$ of the residual ξ^j_{it} behaves according to the following process:

$$\sigma^2_{\xi jt} = \rho^{j2}\sigma^2_{\xi jt-1} + \sigma^2_{\varepsilon jt} \tag{3}$$

The preceding equation may be used to recover the dynamic parameters ρ^j and $\sigma^2_{\varepsilon jt}$. After having estimated equation (1) on each cohort j separately for each period t, it is a simple matter to get estimates of the residual variance $\sigma^2_{\xi jt}$. We will need at least three periods to be able to estimate ρ^j by OLS[2] from equation (3); then, the residuals provide estimates of the variance of the innovation term $\sigma^2_{\varepsilon jt}$.

Although technically three cross-sections will allow us to estimate equation (3), very likely that ρ^j will be very imprecisely estimated with such few time observations. This might be remedied by imposing some restrictions on the parameter ρ^j across cohorts j. For instance, one could impose this coefficient to be the same across a number of cohorts, or among members of the same cohort belonging to various sociodemographic groups.

If the model is well specified and enough time observations are available, then the estimated $\hat{\rho}^j$ and $\hat{\sigma}^2_{\varepsilon jt}$ will have the expected signs and magnitude, that is, $0 < \hat{\rho}^j < 1$ and $\hat{\sigma}^2_{\varepsilon jt} > 0$ for all t. If estimates are not well behaved, the hypotheses behind equation (3)—that is, the first order autoregressive process on earnings or the randomness of entries/exits—have to be rejected. The preceding method has been applied to cross-sectional data from Indonesia, Korea, and Thailand (Bourguignon and Goh 2004). Reasonable estimates of the parameters of the model were obtained for all countries.

Before discussing the results, two remarks are in order. The first remark concerns how the preceding assumption about individual earning dynamics leads to the mean vulnerability of individuals, observed in cross-section t, to poverty in period $t + 1$, conditional on their initial earnings and characteristics. Some additional assumptions are necessary for this last step. The first assumption is that the innovation term is distributed as a normal with mean 0 and variance $\hat{\sigma}^2_{\varepsilon jt}$, so that earnings are distributed as a log-normal variable, conditional on individual characteristics, X. The second assumption is that some prediction of future individual characteristics $\hat{X}^j_{it+1}$ is available— this is easy for variables like age or educational attainment, other variables might have to be assumed stationary. The same applies to future earning coefficients $\hat{\beta}^j_{it+1}$ and the variance of the innovation, $\hat{\sigma}^2_{\varepsilon jt+1}$. In both cases, the simplest assumption is that the parameters are stationary. Yet, the intercept coefficient in $\hat{\beta}^j_{it+1}$ may be modified so as to capture the expected growth rate in earnings, whereas $\hat{\sigma}^2_{\varepsilon jt+1}$ may in some cases reflect the effect of macroeconomic shock or, on the contrary, a stabilization.

Under the preceding assumptions, and denoting $\hat{\xi}^j_{it}$ the estimated residual of the earning equation (1) in period t, it can be figured out that the probability of earning less than a poverty threshold, $\overline{w}$, at time $t + 1$, conditional on characteristics of period t is given by:

$$v^j_{it} = pr(Ln \, w^j_{it+1} < Ln \, w \, | \, X^j_{it}, \hat{X}^j_{it+1}, \hat{\beta}^j_{t+1}, \hat{\sigma}^2_{\varepsilon jt+1}) = \Phi\left(\frac{Ln \, \overline{w} - \hat{X}^j_{it+1}\hat{\beta}^j_{t+1} - \hat{\rho}^j\hat{\xi}^j_{it}}{\hat{\sigma}^2_{\varepsilon jt+1}}\right)$$

(4)

where $\Phi(.)$ denotes the cumulative density of the standard normal. Thus, $\hat{v}^j_{it}$ is the vulnerability of individual j, belonging to cohort j and observed at time t, to falling into poverty at time $t + 1$.

The second remark is about the possibility of checking the relevance of the approximation of earning dynamics by the preceding method. Doing so requires true individual panel data. If such data are available, one can compare the indirect estimates of the dynamic parameters $\hat{\rho}^j$ and $\hat{\sigma}^2_{\varepsilon jt}$ obtained through equation (3) using the cross-sectional nature of the data to the direct estimates of model (1)–(2) obtained using the full panel dimension of the data. It can be seen that the latter is equivalent to estimating the model:

$$\ln w^j_{it} = \rho^j \ln w^j_{it-1} + X^j_{it}\beta^j_t + \gamma^j_{it-1}X^j_{it-1} + \varepsilon^j_{it} \, with \, E(\varepsilon^j_{it}) = 0 \, and \, V(\varepsilon^{j2}_{it}) = \sigma^2_{\varepsilon jt} \quad (5)$$

In this expression, γ^j_{it-1} actually stands for $-\rho^j\beta^j_{t-1}$ but this is not a restriction as long as the coefficients β^j_t are allowed to change with time. It may also be noted that estimating the preceding model through OLS may be done even when the individual characteristics X^j_{it} do not change over time.

Of course, checking whether the pseudo-panel estimates of earning dynamics are satisfactory can also be done by looking at the implications of the model rather than the estimated parameters. In the present case, this means comparing the estimates of vulnerability to poverty obtained through expression (4) with the actual frequency of falling into (or remaining in) poverty in the panel data.

2. APPLICATION TO KOREA

Repeated cross-sectional data on individual earnings are available in a large number of developing countries whereas panel data are not easily available. Korea is among the few countries where suitable, albeit very short, panel data are available for evaluating the relevance of the preceding methodology.

The largest cross-sectional data set on individual earnings in Korea is the Wage Structure Survey (WSS), formerly the Occupational Wage Survey, 1991–2000. This is an establishment survey and only wage earners in non-agricultural private firms with ten or more workers are in the sample.[3] Sectors with larger firms tend to be over-sampled.

Panel data sets on individual earnings in Korea are much smaller in size and much shorter in the time dimension. Two data sets are available: the Korea Labor Institute Panel Study Data (KLIP), 1998–2001, and the Urban Worker Household Income and Expenditure Survey (UWH), 1994–2000. The KLIP first sampled 5,000 households in the urban areas in 1998, approximately 70 percent of which has remained in the sample by 2001.[4]

The UWH is a household panel survey covering the urban areas. It provides earnings information only for those households headed by a wage/salary worker.[5] Although data are available for 1994–2000, the entire sample is replaced every five years. Actually, only two short panels are thus available: 1994–97, and 1998–2000, respectively.

The pseudo-panel methodology discussed above requires the maximum number of time observations to yield more precise estimates of earning dynamic parameters. In their true panel dimension, the two panel data sets available in Korea actually permit no more than three observation periods, because the use of lagged values in the equations to be estimated eliminates the first period. Yet, because two data sets are available in the UWH data source, it is possible to use slightly more observation periods in that case. This is the reason our results discussed in this section are based only on the cross-sections of data available in the WSS and the UWH; the KLIP has too short a series to construct a pseudo panel. For brevity, results are presented and discussed only for male earners—and male household heads in the case of UWH.

Table 12.1 presents the estimated persistence in the residuals of earning equation (1), $\hat{\rho}^j$, for the two pseudo panels. Explanatory variables in that regression include years of age, age squared, educational attainment, marital status, and a dummy variable denoting self-employment (for UWH). Because

TABLE 12.1
Estimates of $\hat{\rho}^j$'s Based on Pseudo Panels
Constructed from the Cross-sectional
Wage Structure Survey (WSS),
1990–2000, and the Urban Worker
Household Income and Expenditure
Survey (UWH), 1994–2000.

	$\hat{\rho}^j$ (SE)	
Cohort, by Birth Year:	WSS	UWH
1941–45	0.686	0.769
	(.189)	(.199)
1946–50	0.617	0.935
	(.182)	(.179)
1951–55	0.478	0.947
	(.153)	(.221)
1956–60	0.421	0.866
	(.138)	(.186)
1961–65	0.688	0.957
	(.201)	(.181)
1966–70	0.874	0.444
	(.150)	(.146)
1971–75	0.762	0.756
	(.198)	(.221)
All Cohorts Combined	0.625	0.850
	(.189)	(.202)

the persistence parameter in equation (3) comes as the square of $\hat{\rho}^j$, a simple transformation was used to obtain an estimate of the standard error of $\hat{\rho}^j$. It can be seen that the estimates of $\hat{\rho}^j$ for both pseudo panels are reasonably between zero and one, with $\hat{\rho}^j$'s significantly different from zero. The $\hat{\rho}^j$'s are not very precisely measured due to very few observation periods. As a F-test indicates that the $\hat{\rho}^{2j}$'s are not statistically different among cohorts, one can hope to increase precision by pooling the cohorts together and assuming a common $\hat{\rho}$. The last row of Table 12.1 presents the cohort-combined $\hat{\rho}$'s for the two pseudo panels, which are 0.63 and 0.85, respectively. Contrary to what we hoped, the precision of these estimates is not better than that of cohort-specific estimates because of too much cohort heterogeneity.

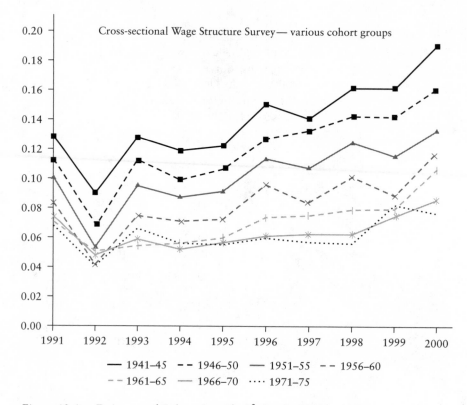

Figure 12.1.   Estimates of Cohort-Specific $\hat{\sigma}^2_{\varepsilon jt}$ for the WSS and UWH Pseudo-panels

That the estimate of persistence is higher with UWH than with WSS is not surprising given that UWH data cover household heads whose earnings are less volatile and more predictable from a year to the next. In addition, there is likely to be fewer entries and exits from the labor force among household heads, which may reinforce the stability of earnings in UWH.

Based on the estimated persistence in shocks, $\hat{\rho}$, we plot the cohort-specific variance of innovation terms, $\hat{\sigma}^2_{\varepsilon jt}$, for both pseudo panels in Figure 12.1. The repeated cross-sections drawn from the UWH (right graph) shows a sharp spike of variance in 1998, reflecting the shock of the financial crisis. Interestingly enough, the WSS data (left graph) shows a gradual rise in the variance of the earning innovation that started with the crisis in 1998 and continued an upward trend into 2000. It is tempting to relate these differences

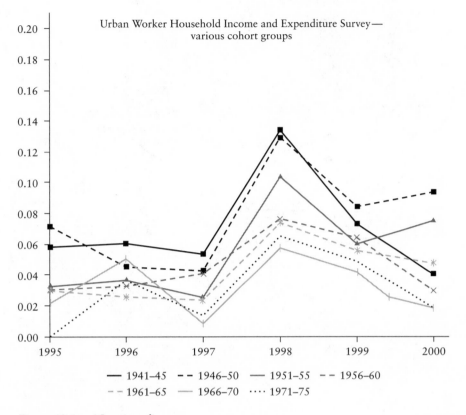

Figure 12.1. (*Continued*)

again to the definition of the two samples. The story suggested by the two charts in Figure 12.1 is that the destabilization of the labor market due to the 1998 crisis was limited to the crisis year for household heads, people who generally have steadier career paths and earning profiles. It went beyond the crisis years for secondary, or "marginal" workers, traditionally more mobile across jobs than household heads. This interpretation is reinforced by the fact that, except for the oldest cohort, the variance of earning innovation for household heads fell back after the crisis to a level higher than that observed before the crisis.

Figure 12.2 presents the vulnerability measures based on the pseudo panels and computed according to equation (4). Unsurprisingly, the time evolution of vulnerability to poverty reflects closely the trend of the $\hat{\sigma}^2_{\varepsilon jt}$. Both

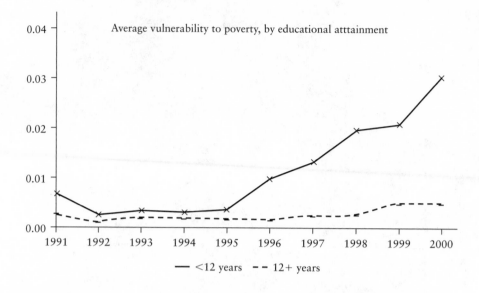

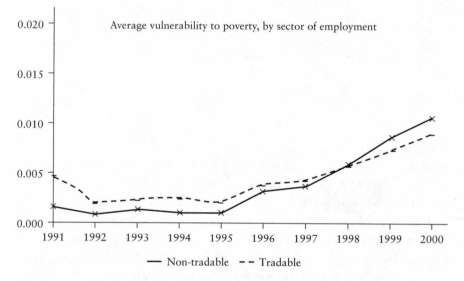

Figure 12.2. Measures of Vulnerability to Poverty, by Educational Attainment and by Sectors of Employment, for the WSS and UWH Pseudo-panels

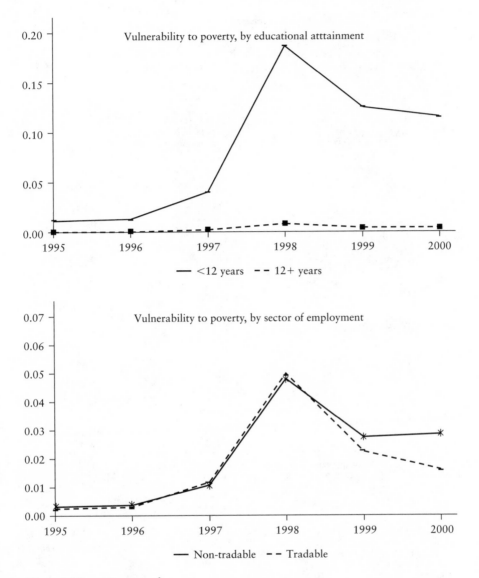

Figure 12.2.   (*Continued*)

data sets show that workers with less education experience greater vulnerability to falling into poverty. They also confirm that labor market in Korea is fluid, and workers are mobile between sectors.[6] Whether a worker is in the tradable manufacturing sector or the non-tradable sector, there is no difference in vulnerability to poverty between sectors.

TABLE 12.2
Estimates of Persistence Parameter, $\hat{\rho}^j$, for Two Panel Data
Sets, the Korea Labor Institute Panel Study data (KLIP),
and the Korea's Urban Worker Household Income
and Expenditure Survey (UWH)

Cohort, by Birth Year:	PERSISTENCE PARAMETER (SE)	
	KLIP	UWH
1941–45	0.722	0.828
	(.035)	(.018)
1946–50	0.670	0.888
	(.025)	(.015)
1951–55	0.675	0.754
	(.026)	(.014)
1956–60	0.548	0.763
	(.023)	(.013)
1961–65	0.588	0.776
	(.022)	(.012)
1966–70	0.570	0.816
	(.023)	(.017)
1971–75	0.439	0.640
	(.032)	(.041)

	$\hat{\rho} = \hat{R} + \hat{\gamma}*$ COHORT			
	$\hat{R}$ (SE)	$\hat{\gamma}$ (SE)	$\hat{R}$ (SE)	$\hat{\gamma}$ (SE)
Cohorts Combined:	0.748	−0.036	0.868	−0.019
	(.022)	(.006)	(.014)	(.004)

3. RESULTS FROM TRUE PANEL DATA

In this section, we estimate individual earning dynamics based on true panel data and compare the true panel estimates with the cross-sectional (pseudo-panel) estimates to check the precision of the latter. Two sets of panel data are used: the KLIP (1998–2001) and the UWH (1994–2000).

Table 12.2 presents the persistence in earnings shocks, $\hat{\rho}^j$, for the two panels. As it was the case when comparing pseudo-panel estimates obtained with WSS and UWH, true panel estimates of persistence parameters differ between

TABLE 12.3
Estimates of Persistence Parameter:
Comparison Between the Cross-sectional
WSS and Panel KLIP

PSEUDO PANEL WSS	PANEL KLIP		
		$\hat{\rho} = \hat{R} + \hat{\gamma}*$ COHORT	
$\hat{\rho}$ (SE)	$\hat{\rho}$ (SE)	$\hat{R}$ (SE)	$\hat{\gamma}$ (SE)
0.625	0.614	0.748	−0.036
(.189)	(.010)	(.022)	(.006)

the two panel data sets, KLIP and UWH. They are higher for the sample of male household heads in UWH than for the sample of all male wage/salary workers in KLIP. In both cases, one also observes that the persistence parameter declines when moving from an older cohort to a younger cohort, a fact well documented in the literature on earnings mobility.[7] In effect, pooling together all cohorts and allowing the persistence parameter to depend linearly on the middle birth year of each cohort (i.e., $\hat{\rho} = \hat{R} + \hat{\gamma}*cohort$) does not reduce significantly the information compared to cohort-specific parameters. In contrast with what was observed with pseudo panels, however, imposing a constant persistence parameter across cohorts is restrictive.

We now compare the estimates obtained with the pseudo panel made up of the WSS cross-sections in the previous section with estimates obtained from true panel estimates. The best comparison is with KLIP, which does not restrict the sample to household heads. The respective estimates of persistence parameters are shown in Table 12.3 under alternative restrictions for KLIP. It turns out that the $\hat{\rho}$ based on the repeated WSS cross-section is not significantly different from the $\hat{\rho}$ based on the true panel KLIP when the latter is restricted to be identical across cohorts. The former is 0.625 whereas the latter is 0.614. This seems extremely satisfactory. But, it should not hide the fact that going back to cohort-specific estimates in Tables 12.1 and 12.2, WSS cross-sectional estimates do not pick up at all the age or cohort profile of persistence parameters apparent in true panel estimates. This is possibly because of a lack of precision of the cross-sectional estimates. Indeed, comparing the first column of Tables 12.1 and 12.2 shows no significant difference.

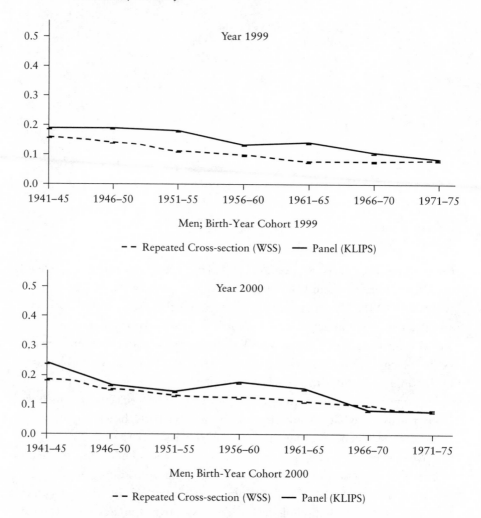

Figure 12.3.   Estimates of the Variance of Earning Innovation $\hat{\sigma}^2_{\varepsilon jt}$ from Cross-sectional WSS and Panel KLIPS, 1999 and 2000

Figure 12.3 presents the cohort-specific $\hat{\sigma}^2_{\varepsilon jt}$'s obtained from cross-sectional WSS estimates and those estimated on the basis of the true panel KLIP for years 1999 and 2000. The cohort specificity of $\hat{\sigma}^2_{\varepsilon jt}$ based on the re-peated cross-sections approximate very closely those of $\hat{\sigma}^2_{\varepsilon jt}$ estimated from the panel. Overall, however, KLIP estimates are slightly higher than WSS es-timates. From 1999 to 2000, there is slight increase in the variance of inno-vation with both estimation techniques. While the change is uniform with

TABLE 12.4
Estimates of the Persistence Parameter
Based on UWH: Comparison Between
Pseudo and True Panel Estimates

PSEUDO PANEL	TRUE PANEL		
	$\hat{\rho} = \hat{R} + \hat{\gamma} *$ COHORT		
$\hat{\rho}$ (SE)	$\hat{\rho}$ (SE)	$\hat{R}$ (SE)	$\hat{\gamma}$ (SE)
0.850	0.801	0.868	−0.019
(.202)	(.006)	(.014)	(.004)

WSS, it is more cohort specific with the true panel estimates obtained with KLIP.

Instead of comparing pseudo-panel and true panel estimates obtained from different data sources, it is also informative to compare the two estimates using the same panel data set. In one case, the panel dimension of the data is ignored and only the repeated cross-sections are used to estimate equation (3). In the second case, the panel dimension is being used to estimate model (5). The KLIP panel is not very interesting from that point of view because the time dimension of the data is simply too short. This is the reason we now switch to the UWH data set.

Table 12.4 presents the $\hat{\rho}$ based on the pseudo and true panels obtained from UWH. When the persistence parameter is constrained to be constant across cohorts, the pseudo-panel estimate, at 0.85, is close to, and certainly not significantly different from the panel estimate, at 0.80. As in the preceding comparison, however, the pseudo-panel estimate misses the cohort specificity of the persistence parameters apparent in the true panel estimates.

Figure 12.4 presents the trend of variance of earning innovation, $\hat{\sigma}^2_{\varepsilon jt}$, for all cohort groups combined, based on pseudo and true panels. Note that there are only four overlapping years (i.e., 1995–97, and 1999) for the pseudo and true panel because the UWH survey renewed its sample in 1998, and we have a first-order autoregressive model. The comparison of pseudo- and true panel estimates for each cohort during the overlapping years (not presented here) shows very close approximation, similar to that in Figure 12.3.

Note that the variance estimated on the basis of the true panel is on average larger than that estimated on the basis of pseudo panel. These

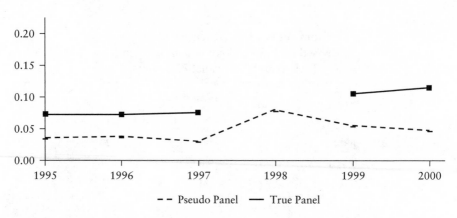

Figure 12.4.   Estimates of the Variance of Earning Innovation $\hat{\sigma}^2_{\varepsilon jt}$ Based on UWH: Pseudo- Versus True Panel Estimates

discrepancies can easily be explained. One will first note that the estimated persistence parameter from the pseudo panel is above the corresponding estimate from the true panel—0.85 versus 0.80 on average. It follows from equation (3) that the variance of earning innovation, $\sigma^2_{\varepsilon jt}$, is smaller with the pseudo panel. The gap between the two estimates depends on the variance of earnings residuals of the previous period, $\sigma^2_{\xi jt-1}$. The variance of earnings is higher during the financial crisis years 1998–99. Accordingly, the gap between pseudo- and true panel estimates of the $\sigma^2_{\varepsilon jt}$ is larger on average in 1999 and 2000. Also, the levels of $\sigma^2_{\varepsilon jt}$ for both pseudo and true panel in 1999 and 2000 are higher than levels in pre-crisis years.

According to the preceding argument, the time evolution of the innovation variance with the pseudo- and true panel estimates should be approximately parallel for all cohorts. That this is not the case is due to the fact that the pseudo-panel estimates are not defined on a balanced panel whereas the true panel estimates are. That this makes a difference suggests that exits from the panel cannot always be considered as randomly distributed in the population.

Table 12.5 presents our variable of interest, vulnerability to poverty, for the first of the two preceding comparisons—that is, the cross-sectional WSS and the KLIP panel—for 1999 and 2000. The poverty threshold is defined as 50 percent of the median. Although the point estimates are not identical, cross-sectional and panel vulnerability measures are very close to each other.

TABLE 12.5
Vulnerability to Poverty Based on the Cross-sectional WSS
and the Panel KLIP, 1999 and 2000

		VULNERABILITY TO POVERTY: $\Phi\left(\dfrac{Ln\overline{w} - \hat{X}^i_{it+1}\hat{\beta}^i_{t+1} - \hat{\rho}^i\hat{\xi}^i_{it}}{\sigma^2_{ejt+1}}\right)$	
YEAR		Pseudo Panel from Repeated Cross-section	True Panel
1999	All	.043	.057
	Tradable Sector	.045	.056
	Non-tradable Sector	.041	.057
2000	All	.045	.078
	Tradable Sector	.046	.074
	Non-tradable Sector	.044	.080
1999	With Less than 12 years of Schooling	.090	.14
	With 12 or More years of Schooling	.036	.031
2000	With Less than 12 years of Schooling	.11	.19
	With 12 or More Years of Schooling	.035	.043

In both cases, we find that vulnerability does not differ by sectors, but depends on educational attainment.

Figure 12.5 presents the evolution of vulnerability to poverty for our second set of comparisons (that is, the pseudo- and true panel of the UWH) between 1995 and 2000. We present the comparison between pseudo- and true panel estimates for the tradable and non-tradable sectors. Both graphs are close images of each other, reflecting the similar trends of vulnerability in tradable and non-tradable sectors. The trends of pseudo-panel estimates of vulnerability approximate closely the trends of true panel estimates within each sector of employment.

It may be tempting to make a comparison of point estimates of vulnerability measures between pseudo and true panel data and make a statement about the precision of the pseudo-panel estimates. However, it's not very meaningful to make an assessment of the point estimates especially in our first set of comparison between cross-sectional WSS and panel KLIP (Table 12.5). In this case, we are looking at two different samples. Besides the $\hat{\sigma}^2_{ejt}$ and $\hat{\rho}$,

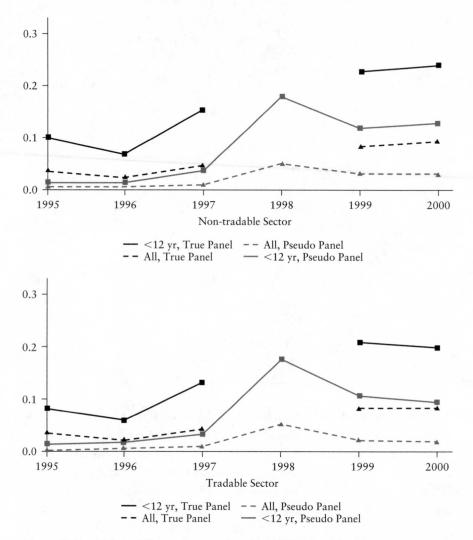

Figure 12.5. Vulnerability to Poverty Based on UWH: Pseudo- Versus True Panel Estimates, by Sectors of Employment

other parameters such as $\hat{\beta}^{j}_{t+1}$, average earnings, and the poverty threshold also differ across the data sets. In our second set of comparisons, both pseudo and true panel come from one data set but because the pseudo panel is not created from a balance panel, we are again looking at two different samples. In this case, we have more overlapping years, which allows us to compare the trend of vulnerability based on pseudo panel with that based on the panel.

CONCLUSION

This chapter explores a methodology that permits recovering some parameters of individual earnings dynamics from cross-sectional data under a set of simplifying assumptions that individual earning dynamics obeys some basic properties and follows a simple stochastic process. The knowledge of these parameters then permits one to simulate individual earning dynamics, and estimate vulnerability to poverty, making use of all the cross-sectional information available at a point of time.

The application of this methodology to Korean data yields rather satisfactory results. Two sets of comparisons were undertaken in order to check its relevance in comparison with standard panel data analysis. In the first comparison, estimates of a simple AR(1) earnings dynamics model are obtained from a pseudo panel derived from repeated cross-sectional surveys and a true panel of earnings data. The second comparison is between a panel data set and the pseudo panel constructed from it. In both cases, it is shown that the estimated parameters of individual earnings dynamic processes based on the pseudo panel approximate very closely the direct panel estimates. The point estimates of the measure for persistence of shocks, based on the pseudo panel of cohorts, are very close to those based on the true panel. Both estimates are not significantly different from each other. The other key parameter of individual earnings dynamics, the variance of the innovation in earnings, estimated from a pseudo panel of cohorts, tracks closely the direct panel estimates in the overlapping years.

Given that the pseudo- and true panel estimates of the earning dynamics are not exactly identical, the vulnerability measures derived from the earning dynamics are similar in trends but not identical in average point estimates.

The methodology developed in this chapter has some obvious weaknesses. First, by relying on aggregate data, the degrees of freedom of the estimation depends on the available number of cross-sections. As this number is necessarily limited, not very much precision may be expected. Second, and more importantly, this technique is valid only under the assumption that entries and exits from employment are random with respect to the distribution of individual earnings. Moreover, it focuses on the earnings dynamics of those individuals who are employed on a continuous basis. Practically, however, we know that the first assumption is unlikely to be satisfied and also that the main source of vulnerability to poverty may not be in variations in earnings but in the employment status of individuals. Losing one's job, and therefore leaving employment may be the most important event behind fluctuations in economic welfare and poverty dynamics. This is a dimension that was not considered in the present chapter. Yet, it is likely that the same kind of pseudo-panel techniques used for earnings may be used for employment status, and possibly simultaneous for both. This important dimension of vulnerability poverty and the way to approach it with cross-sections is left for further work.

Notes

1. For instance, Revenga (1997) finds that Mexico's trade reform of 1985–88 reduced employment modestly, but did not reduce wages. Cox Edwards and Edwards (1996) find that Chile's trade liberalization of the 1970s affected workers' duration of unemployment, but its effect was small relative to those of other variables, and declined over time. Arango and Maloney (2002) find some evidence of higher incidence of involuntary separation, mostly among skilled workers, in sectors that are opening to trade in Mexico and Argentina, but the impact is transitory.

2. We need estimates in equation (3) to behave in a certain way and must exercise caution when using the OLS. First, the OLS estimation of equation (3) must be done without an intercept. Second, we must take into account that residuals in equation (3) must be non-negative. Third, the estimated coefficient in equation (3) must be between zero and one. OLS estimation does not automatically satisfy these restrictions. For example, we can use more rigorous ways to impose the second restriction of nonzero residuals by having a half-normal distribution truncating to zero for the residual term in equation (3) (Battese-Coelli 1988). However, we didn't have to impose such restrictions in the chapter because OLS estimates always yield nonzero residuals and a coefficient between zero and one.

3. The survey collects information on firm's activity and workers' education, age, job tenure, occupation, and monthly wages. The sample size ranges from 450,000 to 500,000 each year. In particular, manufacturing is overly represented while retail trade and service sectors are underrepresented.

4. The households that left the sample were not replaced. As a result, the survey included 13,738 persons in 1998, but this number fell to 10,179 in 2001. The survey contains the information on working status, earnings, and job characteristics such as industry and occupation.

5. It samples 35,000 to 40,000 households each year and provides the information on total household earnings and heads' earnings and job characteristics.

6. See Fields (2000) for a discussion of the Korean labor market problems.

7. See for instance Atkinson, Bourguignon, and Morrisson (1992).

References

Atkinson, A. B., François Bourguignon, and C. Morrisson. 1992. *Empirical Studies of Earnings Mobility*. Philadelphia: Hardwood Academic.

Arango, Carlos, and William Maloney. 2002. "Unemployment Dynamics in Latin America: Estimates of Continuous Time Markov Models for Mexico and Argentina." World Bank, mimeo.

Battese, G., and T. Coelli, (1988). "Prediction of Firm-Level Technical Efficiencies with a Generalized Frontier Production Function and Panel data." *Journal of Econometrics* 38:387–99.

Bourguignon, François, and Chor-ching Goh. 2004. "Trade and Labor Vulnerability in Indonesia, Republic of Korea, and Thailand." In *East Asia Integrates: A Trade Policy Agenda for Shared Growth*, edited by H. Kharas and K. Krumm. Washington, DC: The World Bank and Oxford University Press.

Cox Edwards, A., and Sebastian Edwards. 1996. "Trade Liberalization and Unemployment: Policy Issues and Evidence from Chile." *Cuademos de Economia*, (33) No. 99:227–50.

De Ferranti, D., Guillermo E. Perry, Indermit S. Gill, and Luis Servén. 2000. *Securing our Future in a Global Economy*. Washington, DC: The World Bank.

Deaton, Angus, and Christina Paxson. 1994. "Intertemporal Choice and Inequality." *Journal of Political Economy* 102:437–67.

Fields, Gary. 2000. "The Employment Problems in Korea." *Journal of the Korean Economy* 1(2):207–27.

Revenga, Ana. 1997. "Employment and Wage Effects of Trade Liberalization: The Case of Mexican Manufacturing." *Journal of Labor Economics* 15 n3(2):S20–43.

CHAPTER THIRTEEN

Happiness Pays: An Analysis of Well-Being, Income, and Health Based on Russian Panel Data

Carol Graham, Andrew Eggers, and Sandip Sukhtankar *

The study of happiness, or subjective well-being, and its implications for economic behavior is a fairly new area for economists, although psychologists have been studying it for years. The findings of this research highlight the non-income determinants of economic behavior. For example, cross-country studies of happiness consistently demonstrate that after certain minimum levels of per capita income, average happiness levels do not increase as countries grow wealthier.[1] Within societies, most studies find that wealthier individuals are on average happier than poor ones, but after a minimum level of income, more money does not make people much happier.[2] Because income plays such an important role in standard definitions and measures of well-being, these findings have theoretical, empirical, and policy implications. The findings also inform a central theme of this volume: the relationship between outcomes in the labor market and mobility and inequality.

We would like to thank Bill Dickens, Gary Burtless, Robert Cummins, Clifford Gaddy, Michael Kremer, Andrew Oswald, George Perry, and Stefano Pettinato for helpful comments on an earlier version, as well as comments from the participants of the MacArthur Network on social interactions and inequality and at a Brookings work-in-progress seminar. We also thank two anonymous reviewers for extremely helpful comments. The authors acknowledge the generous support of the Tinker Foundation for this research. Please direct all comments to cgraham@brookings.edu. An earlier and slightly different version of this paper was published as "Does Happiness Pay: An Exploration Based on Panel Data from Russia," *Journal of Economic Behavior and Organization*, vol. 55 (2004):319–42. Graham is Senior Fellow in Economic Studies at the Brookings Institution and Professor in the School of Public Policy at the University of Maryland; Eggers and Sukhtankar are PhD candidates in political science and economics (respectively) at Harvard University.

Some of the earliest economists—such as Jeremy Bentham—were concerned with the pursuit of individual happiness. As the field became more rigorous and quantitative, however, much narrower definitions of individual welfare, or utility, became the norm, even though economics was still concerned with public welfare in the broader sense. In addition, economists have traditionally shied away from the use of survey data because of justifiable concerns that answers to surveys of individual preferences—and reported well-being—are subject to bias from factors such as respondents' mood at the time of the survey and minor changes in the phrasing of survey questions, which can produce large skews in results.[3] Thus traditional economic analysis focuses on actual behavior, such as revealed preferences in consumption, savings, and labor market participation, under the assumption that individuals rationally process all the information at their disposal to maximize their utility.[4] More recently, behavioral economics has begun to have influence at the margin, as an increasing number of economists supplement the methods and research questions more common to economists with those more common to psychologists.[5]

In this same vein, the research on subjective well-being relies heavily but not exclusively on surveys, and combines methods from both professions. Typically, the questions are very simple ones about how happy or satisfied respondents are with their lives, with responses ranging from not very or not at all to very or fully satisfied.[6] Although there are justified criticisms of how accurate such questions are in assessing life satisfaction at the individual level, there is remarkable consistency in the patterns generated by the answers to these questions aggregated across populations and over time. In addition, a number of psychologists have been able to "validate" the use of these questions through other measures, for example by showing that individuals who answer happiness questions positively also demonstrate other measures of positive affect, such as smiling more frequently.[7]

Some of the most recent work on subjective well-being has resulted in a new collaboration between economists and psychologists, and contributes to our understanding of seemingly nonrational economic behavior. Examples of such behavior are the remarkable contrast between predicted and experienced utility, such as individuals' valuing economic losses disproportionately more than gains; conspicuous consumption to demonstrate wealth at the margin; or the contrast between observed time preferences and the standard economic analyses of discounting.[8] Better understanding of such behavior helps explain unusual patterns in consumption and savings, in voting, in the structure of redistributive policies, in attitudes about insecurity and social insurance, and in support for market policies and democracy, among others.

Another of the many insights from the happiness research, which has been written about extensively in the sociological and economics literature, is the important role of adaptation and rising expectations. As individuals—and those in their reference group—earn more income, their expectations also rise or adapt.[9] Thus, higher levels of income are needed to achieve the same levels of well being.[10] Adaptations can also adjust downward. A good example is in the case of health and aging. Several studies show that individuals adapt to changes in health status—such as the onset of a serious disease—by changing their reference point for "good" health.[11]

An important unanswered question in much of this research is the direction of causality. In other words, it is difficult to establish cause and effect with many of the variables that are at play, and in many cases they may interact. For example, are married people happier, or are happier people more likely to get married? Are wealthier people happier, or are happier people more likely to be successful and earn more income over time? Similar questions can be posed in a number of areas, including the positive relationship between health and happiness, between happiness and support for market policies and democracy, and happiness and tolerance for inequality. A better understanding of the direction of causality question will help determine the extent to which the findings from this research should be incorporated into policy analysis.

One of the primary difficulties in establishing this direction of causality is the lack of adequate data. Most of the happiness research is based on cross-section data, while to answer these questions, we need panel data—that is, surveys that follow the same people over time. Such data are particularly rare for developing countries. A few isolated studies by psychologists in the United States and Australia shed some light, and establish that happier people earn more income in later periods than do their less happy cohorts.[12] Yet for the most part, research on subjective well-being has not addressed these questions.

In this chapter, we take advantage of a large panel for Russia, the Russia Longitudinal Monitoring Survey (RLMS), which covers an average of almost 13,000 Russians per year from 1992 to 2001, and from which we create a panel data set containing data in 1995 and 2000 (see Table 13.1 for

TABLE 13.1
Variable Means, Standard Deviations (in parentheses),
and Definitions

Variable	1995	2000	Definition
Happiness	2.209 (1.06)	2.355 (1.08)	To what extent are you satisfied with your life in general at the present time? (1 = not at all, 5 = fully)
Age	40.673 (19.17)	45.677 (19.17)	Age of respondent at time of survey in years
Age, squared	2104.208 (1674.04)	2453.682 (1822.74)	Age in years squared
Log equivalence income	7.873 (.86)	7.826 (.81)	Real household income in 1992 rubles/square root of the number of people in the household
Education level	8.684 (2.17)	8.741 (2.15)	School grade level completed, 0–12
Amount of drinking	2.329 (1.21)	2.353 (1.25)	How often have you used alcoholic beverages in the last 30 days? 1 = once, 6 = every day
Male	0.422 (.49)	0.422 (.49)	Gender dummy, 1 = male
Minority	0.164 (.37)	0.164 (.37)	Minority dummy, 1 = minority (non-Russian)
Married	0.599 (.49)	0.542 (.50)	Marital status dummy, 1 = married
Student	0.169 (.37)	0.116 (.32)	Employment status dummy, 1 = student*
Retired	0.236 (.42)	0.305 (.46)	Employment status dummy, 1 = retired
Housewife	0.043 (.20)	0.033 (.18)	Employment status dummy, 1 = housewife
Unemployed	0.064 (.24)	0.085 (.28)	Employment status dummy, 1 = unemployed
Self-employed	0.011 (.11)	0.012 (.11)	Employment status dummy, 1 = self-employed
Health index	0.838 (.22)	0.82 (.22)	Index of three equally weighted questions (0.33 = yes for each question):
			Have you in the last 30 days had any health problems?
			Have you been in the hospital in the last 3 months?
			In the last 30 days did you miss any work or study days due to illness?

(continued)

TABLE 13.1
(*continued*)

Variable	1995	2000	Definition
Smoker	0.247 (.43)	0.28 (.45)	Smoker dummy, 1 = yes answer to question "do you now smoke?"
Observations	5269	5269	

In a paired t-test, the difference between the 1995 and 2000 means was significant for all variables except male and minority (unchanging), self-employment, education level, and amount of drinking.

* The drop in the percentage of respondents who were students is a result of the aging of the respondent pool. Our data set consists of 5,269 people who responded to the survey in both 1995 and 2000. Since our youngest respondents are 10 years old in 1995 and 15 by 2000, there is a greater student population in the first round of the survey.

SOURCE: RLMS Round 6 and Round 9 data, authors' calculations.

summary statistics).[13] Among many other questions, there is a standard happiness question in the RLMS, which asks "to what extent are you satisfied with your life at the present time," with possible answers being "not at all satisfied," "less than satisfied," "both yes and no," "rather satisfied," and "fully satisfied."[14]

A very clear drawback of this data set is that it covers a time period of tremendous economic and structural change, with far-reaching changes for many people's livelihood and economic well-being, which limits the extent to which we can draw broader generalizations. On the other hand, data containing observations on both happiness and income for the same respondents at more than one point in time is extremely rare. In addition, the instability in economic conditions provides us with a better than average reference point for stability in subjective well-being despite extensive contextual change.

We depart in this study from earlier analysis by Graham and Pettinato, which compares happiness in Latin America and Russia. In contrast, we analyze happiness data on the same individuals for two points in time and examine a number of questions in which the direction of causality is not clear from cross-section data alone.[15] Our central goal is to test whether people who reported higher happiness in 1995 than would be expected based on their socioeconomic and demographic characteristics fared differently in 2000 than others. Presumably, these differences are due to psychological or other noneconomic or demographic factors. The purpose of this exercise is to determine whether these differences, appearing in people's reported happiness levels in the first period, have effects on outcomes such as income, marriage status, and employment in the second.

Psychologists find that there is a remarkable degree of consistency in people's level of well-being over time. They attribute this stability in happiness levels to homeostasis, in which happiness levels are not only under the influence of experience, but also controlled by positive cognitive bias, such as self-esteem, control, and optimism.[16] We use our panel data to create a "residual" or unexplained happiness variable, which is an attempt to capture or proxy this psychological element of happiness. We can then test whether it has causal properties in addition to the observed demographic and socioeconomic variables on future income. Of course, some of what is captured by our residual term could well be other unobservable socioeconomic, demographic, or stochastic characteristics that are unrelated to cognitive bias. It remains to be seen to what extent the causal properties of unexplained happiness depend on cognitive bias as opposed to other unobserved factors.

Our analysis is a first attempt to examine these questions in detail with this kind of data, and has an exploratory element. We first use the standard variables to explain as much as we can about happiness levels at a given point in time. We take advantage of having two observations on the same people to see if there are any changes in the relative weights of these variables over time. We then correct for the effects of individual traits or characteristics that could be driving the results (for example, happier people may be more likely to get married rather than marriage enhancing happiness) by using panel fixed effects to see whether changes in individual status make a difference to the results. We then turn to the effects of unexplained or residual happiness on our key variables, such as income, health, and marital status.

SOME NOTES ABOUT THE RUSSIA DATA

Any attempts to generalize from analysis based on Russia in the 1990s must take into account the far-reaching nature of the changes in that country's economy and polity over the course of the decade. During that period, Russia underwent a transition from a centrally planned economy and communist government to a free market, presidential-parliamentary democracy.[17] The transition had high social costs, with some of the worst losers being pensioners and others on fixed incomes. Poverty and inequality increased markedly. Depending on the data sources, the prevalence of poverty in Russia was between 22 and 33 percent in 2001, while the Gini coefficient increased from 0.29 to 0.40 between 1992 and 1998, with some estimates as high as 0.48, a level that is comparable to some of the most unequal countries in Latin America.[18]

There is considerable debate over the extent to which Russia's transition to the market has been a success or a failure, and whether the pace and sequencing of reform was appropriate. This is a debate that is well beyond the scope of this chapter.[19] Yet it is important to recognize that our panel data cover a period of extensive economic and political change, and the effects of those changes have not been even across individuals and across economic sectors. This, in turn, could affect the relationship between income and well-being.

There are some peculiarities in the data that seem to reflect the reality of the Russian situation—both in terms of a large black market and a large barter or virtual economy.[20] For example, we had fifty-four observations from respondents that reported zero household income. Yet the results of our econometric analysis including these respondents produced results that were quite counterintuitive, such as a consistently positive and significant sign on the zero income dummies in relation to both future happiness and future income. About half of the zero income respondents reported that they were employed. They may be earning substantial income on the black market, which they are reluctant to report, or have earnings in kind, which have effects on their well-being, but do not show up as reported income.[21]

Another caveat is that all panel data suffer from attrition bias. Those on the extreme tails of the distribution are the most likely to drop out of the panel, as the wealthiest may move to better neighborhoods and the poorest who "don't make it" may move in with other family members or opt for other kinds of coping strategies. Our analysis of the Russia data, however, finds no difference between the characteristics of those respondents in the panel and the entire group of respondents in the original 1995 survey, at least as measured by age, education, income, gender, marital status, and happiness.[22] A second problem, measurement error, involves possible error stemming from the difficulty of accurately measuring the incomes of those individuals who work in the informal economy or in the agricultural sector. This sector is very large in Russia.[23]

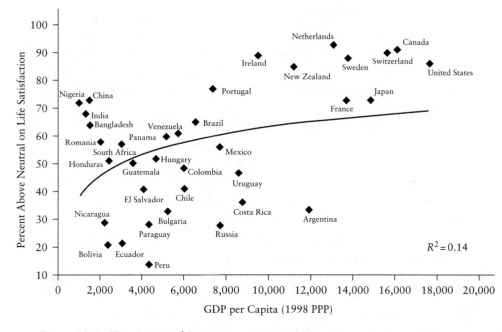

Figure 13.1. Happiness and Income per capita, 1990s
s o u r c e : Graham and Pettinato, 2002

Average happiness levels in Russia are relatively low compared to other countries of comparable per capita income levels (see Figure 13.1). There are concerns that because of Russia's political legacy, respondents might view survey questions with suspicion and answer them less honestly then they would in other contexts. Yet research by Veenhoven (2001) finds that the unusually low levels of happiness in Russia have more to do with the troublesome transitions than with Russian national character or other biases in responses. Despite these many caveats, the relatively large sample size and the intuitive nature of many of our results make us cautiously optimistic about their broader applicability.

MEASURABLE AND UNEXPLAINED DETERMINANTS OF HAPPINESS

A fairly wide body of literature has found consistent links between a number of demographic and socioeconomic variables and reported happiness.

These include income, health, marital status, gender, race, and life cycle effects. In this section, our objective is to explain happiness in Russia as accurately as possible based on these standard measures. Our first step was to examine the effects of the usual socioeconomic and demographic determinants of happiness, such as age, education, income, gender, and marriage, on happiness levels in Russia.

These variables have fairly consistent effects on happiness across societies and across time—in both the developed and developing economies for which there are data.[24] Yet there are a number of plausible reasons why these effects might not hold in Russia. These reasons include the dramatic nature of economic and political change in Russia during the period under study, as well as cultural differences in answering this kind of survey question.[25]

We ran standard happiness regressions for both 1995 and 2000, and conducted a T-test for equivalence to see if there was any significant difference in the results between the two years. As in many other countries, there is a quadratic relationship between age and happiness, a U-shaped curve with the lowest point on the curve being 47 years of age (this is slightly older than the turning point for most OECD countries, which is typically in the early forties). Men were happier than women in Russia, both in 1995 and in 2000 (Table 13.2). Higher levels of education are correlated with higher levels of happiness in Russia, as they are in most countries.[26] Retirees are less happy than others, which reflects the oft-described plight of pensioners there.

Minorities in Russia are, on average, happier than other respondents (16 percent are in the former group, 84 percent identify as Russian). This is distinct from trends in many other countries, where minorities tend to be less happy than other groups. In the United States, black people are, on average, less happy than other groups, and in Latin America, those who identify first as a minority rather than as the nationality of their country are less happy than other groups.[27] There are many plausible reasons for this, including the dramatic changes in Russia's status as a superpower and its effects on national morale. Similarly, in a related but separate question, those that identify themselves as Muslim—8 percent of the sample—were, on average, happier than others in 2000, although the coefficient was just short of significant at the 5 percent level. More generally, having faith or a religious affiliation is positively associated with happiness in most countries.[28]

Happiness research finds general patterns in the relationship between socioeconomic variables and happiness across countries and across time, but

TABLE 13.2
The Correlates of Happiness, 1995 and 2000

Independent Variables	1995		2000		t-stat for equivalence
	coef	z	coef	z	
Age	−0.0742	−6.27	−0.0668	−7.42	0.498
Age squared	0.0008	6.35	0.0007	7.15	−0.498
Male	0.1419	2.41	0.1521	2.80	0.128
Married	0.1490	2.15	0.0875	1.40	−0.659
Log equivalence income	**0.4777**	13.97	**0.3892**	11.48	**−1.839**
Education level	0.0305	1.87	0.0150	0.96	−0.688
Minority	**0.3835**	5.21	**0.1721**	2.46	**−2.082**
Student	0.4561	2.91	0.1991	1.59	−1.281
Retired	−0.3029	−3.05	−0.3783	−3.97	−0.548
Housewife	0.1814	1.34	0.0490	0.33	−0.661
Unemployed	**−0.2434**	−2.19	**−0.6568**	−6.51	**−2.756**
Self-employed	0.7676	3.00	0.5375	2.23	−0.654
Health index	0.2744	2.22	0.4462	3.82	1.010
Observations	4524		5134		
Pseudo R^2	0.0330		0.0331		

Dependent variable: Happiness (ordered logit regression).

NOTE: the coefficients in bold are those which had statistically significant changes between 1995 and 2000.

with subtle variations. Given the extent of economic change and mobility in Russia during the period under study, we expected there to be more than the usual variation across time. The 1990s crisis hit retirees, the unemployed, and lenders in particular very hard. Rather remarkably, there was very little change in the relationship among the standard variables and happiness during this time period. When we tested the difference between the two years' results, however, the only two coefficients in our basic happiness model that experienced a significant change in value were being a minority and being unemployed; even then there was not a change in direction in the sign of either coefficient (see column 3 of Table 13.2).

In 2000, while minorities were still, on average, happier than other respondents, they were far less happy than they were in 1995. The war in Chechnya has changed the image of Muslims and minorities in general in

Russia, and a number of surveys find that the majority of Russians support the efforts of their military against a mainly Islamic population.[29] Thus, respondents who are Muslim or minorities have, on average, higher happiness levels than Russians, but may have experienced a transitory decline in happiness due to the change in the status of Muslims related to the war.

The second coefficient that experienced a change in value was being unemployed. While unemployed people were less happy on average than others in both years, the negative effects of being unemployed were significantly greater in 2000 than they were in 1995 (see Table 13.2, column 3). This probably reflects the effects of the 1998 financial crisis and devaluation on the fixed and very meager incomes of the unemployed.

If our simple cross-sectional model completely captured the determinants of happiness, then conducting a panel fixed effects regression—essentially, measuring the effect of *changes* in the determinants on *changes* in happiness—would produce identical coefficient results. Yet panel fixed effects analysis corrects some of the bias associated with unobserved characteristics of the survey respondents in cross-sectional analysis. Although we observe a great many characteristics of each respondent, these factors leave much of the variation in happiness unexplained (the R-square in our happiness models is in the neighborhood of 0.03, suggesting that about 97 percent of the variation in happiness responses is due to factors we do not observe). For example, a person's disposition or personality is assuredly one of the determinants of his or her level of reported happiness, so we would expect a person with a generally sunnier disposition to report a higher level of happiness than a person who is identical in every other respect but has a gloomier outlook. Disposition, of course, is not captured in survey data.

These unobserved determinants of happiness will bias our coefficient estimates in cross-sectional analysis if they are correlated with the observed determinants. For example, if a person's disposition affects both his income and his happiness results in the same way, then our estimate of the effect of income on happiness will be biased upward, because disposition is unobserved. Using panel data allows us to filter out the set of unobserved determinants of happiness that are unchanging over time.

One potential problem with conducting panel fixed effects analysis with this data set comes from the volatility of Russian society in the period for which we have data. The relationship between observed characteristics and happiness changed between 1995 and 2000, which we believe reflects an

TABLE 13.3A
Income Mobility in Russia, 1995–2000

Quintile 1995	QUINTILE 2000					
	1	2	3	4	5	Total
1	**33%**	27%	16%	13%	12%	100%
2	25%	**28%**	20%	16%	10%	100%
3	19%	19%	**25%**	21%	15%	100%
4	14%	15%	23%	**25%**	23%	100%
5	9%	11%	16%	25%	**40%**	100%
Total	100%	100%	100%	100%	100%	

SOURCE: RLMS Round 6 and Round 9, authors' calculations using household equivalence income.

adjustment of Russians' priorities and concerns in the course of dramatic social change. Accordingly, some of the respondents' change in happiness that we analyze in this exercise will be attributable to this change in priorities rather than to a change in their observable circumstances.

On the other hand, the volatility in late-1990s Russia can be seen as a unique opportunity for analysis. Panel studies rely on changes in the observed variables to detect causal effects, so panel studies on populations that change very little tend to be unrevealing. Yet in this instance, the data reveal a high degree of mobility. There was significantly more movement among income quintiles in the second half of the 1990s (1995–2000) in Russia than there was during the entire 1980s in the United States, for example. Happiness levels also fluctuated a great deal during the period, with downward shifts more common than upward ones (see Table 13.3a–c). Although this is certainly an exceptional period in Russia, which suggests that caution is necessary in drawing some conclusions, there are also some very clear analytical advantages to the extent of change in the key variables.

As Table 13.4 shows, the only variables that have significant effects on changes in happiness are changes in income, which has positive effects; getting divorced, which has negative effects; and leaving school, which also has negative effects. The effects of income and divorce are both unsurprising, and would probably hold in any context. The effects of leaving school, which may or may not hold in other contexts, are intuitive in the Russian context, where the labor market is very precarious, and highly educated people are often unable to find satisfactory jobs.

TABLE 13.3B
Income Mobility in the United States, 1979–1989

Quintile	QUINTILE 1989					
1979	1	2	3	4	5	Total
1	**61%**	24%	9%	5%	1%	100%
2	23%	**33%**	28%	14%	3%	100%
3	8%	25%	**30%**	26%	11%	100%
4	5%	13%	23%	**33%**	26%	100%
5	3%	5%	11%	23%	**59%**	100%
Total	100%	100%	100%	100%	100%	

Numbers in bold indicate percentage of respondents who were in the same income quintile in 1995 and 2000.

SOURCE: Mishel, Bernstein, and Schmitt (1999) (using family income).

TABLE 13.3C
Happiness Mobility in Russia, 1995–2000

Happiness Score	HAPPINESS SCORE 2000					
1995	1	2	3	4	5	Total
1	534 (37%)	429 (37%)	173 (16%)	59 (8%)	23 (2%)	1218 (100%)
2	528 (22%)	**850 (44%)**	373 (20%)	135 (12%)	58 (2%)	1944 (100%)
3	233 (13%)	383 (36%)	**314 (30%)**	115 (15%)	37 (3%)	1082 (100%)
4	115 (13%)	221 (29%)	158 (25%)	**118 (26%)**	30 (14%)	642 (100%)
5	25 (13%)	34 (38%)	31 (22%)	32 (17%)	**24 (14%)**	146 (100%)
Total	1435 (102%)	1917 (180%)	1049 (113%)	459 (78%)	172 (27%)	

Percentages in parentheses indicate likelihood of obtaining a given happiness score in 2000, given 1995 happiness score.

SOURCE: RLMS Round 6 and Round 9 data, authors' calculations.

Happiness scores: 1: not at all satisfied; 2: less than satisfied; 3: both yes and no; 4: rather satisfied; 5: fully satisfied.

TABLE 13.4
First Difference Regression

		coef	z
Static Variables	Age	−0.0400	−1.70
	Age^2	0.0004	1.54
	Male	0.0390	0.35
	Minority	−0.0632	−0.51
Changes in Continuous Variables	Change in log equivalence income	**0.1875**	**4.21**
	Change in education level	0.0312	0.62
	Change in health index	0.0757	0.47
	Change in level of drinking	−0.0102	−0.31
Changes in Status Variables:			
Marriage	Got married	−0.3802	−1.20
(Omitted group: remained single)	Got divorced	**−0.5681**	**−3.20**
	Stayed married	−0.1905	−1.57
Employment	Got employed	0.0608	0.19
(Omitted: remained unemployed)	Got unemployed	−0.2054	−0.65
	Stayed employed	0.3554	1.35
Smoking	Quit smoking	0.1451	0.58
(Omitted: remained a nonsmoker)	Started smoking	0.2488	1.19
	Kept smoking	−0.0356	−0.31
Schooling	Entered school	*	*
(Omitted: remained a nonstudent)	Left school	**−0.8415**	**−2.38**
	Stayed in school	−0.7139	−1.29
Retirement	Became retired	−0.0699	−0.38
(Omitted: remained a nonretiree)	Came out of retirement	0.2638	0.55
	Stayed retired	−0.0731	−0.35
	Observations	1673	
	Pseudo R squared	0.0089	

* Dropped because of multicolinearity.

Dependent variable: change in happiness, 1995 to 2000 (ordered logit regression).

NOTE: Those figures in bold are statistically significant at the 5 percent level.

Finally, it is quite interesting that while both unemployment and retirement are negatively correlated with happiness in our standard regression, neither retiring nor becoming unemployed had significant effects in the panel regression. This may reflect the rather mixed fate of pensioners and the unemployed in Russia. Recent retirees are probably much better prepared to cope with the current economic environment than are those who retired many years ago on fixed incomes.[30] And many jobs in Russia pay unstable if any wages, while many highly educated workers are often overqualified for what they are doing, which may mitigate the usual effects of becoming unemployed on happiness.

HOW INCOME AFFECTS HAPPINESS AND HOW HAPPINESS AFFECTS INCOME

One issue that we have still not resolved is the direction of causality. In other words, do happier people earn more money, or does earning money make them happier? Are happier people more likely to get married, or does marriage make them happier? We turn to these questions in the following sections. Although we attempted to correct for the unobserved or unexplained differences in happiness among our respondents in the above estimations, we will now use this unexplained happiness to see how happiness affects behavior pertaining to earnings activities, health, and social relations.

Only part of what we are able to observe and measure as "happiness" can be explained by the demographic and socioeconomic variables available to us. There are clearly psychological traits that seem to account for consistency in happiness levels, which persist regardless of variations in demographic and socioeconomic variables. We took advantage of having over-time observations on happiness in the Russia data to attempt to capture this unmeasured or psychological component of happiness. We began with the standard regressions estimating the effect of the standard socioeconomic variables on happiness in Russia. Based on the residual from this regression we created a variable for each respondent's unexplained happiness. We then tested whether this element of happiness has any additional causal properties.

What do we know about residual happiness? We know that it is very close in value to happiness itself, since the pseudo R-squared statistics on our standard happiness regressions are quite low (in the neighborhood of 0.03).

In other words, a great deal of happiness is "unexplained happiness." We also know that while unexplained happiness is not correlated (by definition) with the observable socioeconomic variables that we believe affect happiness, it is positively correlated across time for individuals: people with high unexplained happiness in 1995 were likely to have high unexplained happiness in 2000. (The simple correlation between the two is 0.2198.) This result is consistent with the view that unexplained happiness includes stable factors that affect happiness and that might include cognitive bias.

The research on subjective well-being has focused a great deal on the relationship between income and happiness. Here we focus on the direction of causality question. Although we know that, on average, wealthier people are happier, the reverse may also be true: happier people may earn more income. We attempt to shed some light on these questions in this section.

We began by exploring whether happier people earn more income than less happy people. In order to do this, we first calculated the residual or unexplained happiness levels for each respondent from our standard happiness regression. We then regressed log equivalence income in 2000 on unexplained happiness in 1995, log equivalence income in 1995, and the usual sociodemographic variables.[31] We find that unexplained or residual happiness has positive and significant effects on second period income (see Table 13.5). To date, most analysis has focused on the effects of income on happiness. This result establishes that there is an additional causal effect of happiness on income.

We also separated the unexplained happiness residual variable by quintiles, to see if the effects of happiness varied according to respondents' position in the income distribution. In comparison to those respondents in the lowest quintile, happiness matters less to those in wealthier quintiles, although the difference is just short of significant. In other words, happiness matters more to future income to those at lower levels of income (see Table 13.5).

Having established that happiness has effects on income, we wanted to make sure that the usual effects of income on income still hold. We regressed second period income (log equivalence income) on initial period income and unexplained happiness, using dummies for the poorest (40 percent) and wealthiest (20 percent) of the respondents in the sample.[32] We found that the effects of unexplained happiness were still positive and significant on second period income. In addition, initial income was more important (significant)

TABLE 13.5
The Effects of Happiness on Income

Independent Variables	a		b		c	
	coef	t	coef	t	coef	t
Age	−0.0133	−3.00	−0.0132	−2.97	−0.0146	−3.25
Age^2	0.0001	3.18	0.0001	3.15	0.0002	3.52
Male	0.0102	0.42	0.0102	0.42	−0.0004	−0.02
Married	0.2053	7.84	0.2054	7.84	0.2050	7.84
Education level	0.0301	4.51	0.0301	4.51	0.0296	4.44
Minority	0.1213	3.98	0.1227	4.03	0.1216	4.00
Student	−0.0336	−0.34	−0.0301	−0.31	−0.0367	−0.38
Retired	−0.1906	−4.85	−0.1899	−4.83	−0.1659	−4.18
Housewife	−0.2488	−3.90	−0.2492	−3.90	−0.2388	−3.73
Unemployed	−0.3450	−8.16	−0.3435	−8.12	−0.3426	−8.07
Self-employed	0.1415	1.46	0.1411	1.46	0.1284	1.33
Health index	0.0601	1.11	0.0588	1.09	0.0559	1.04
Log equivalence income 95	0.2420	18.11	0.2429	18.12	0.2244	15.69
Log equivalence income 95, poor**	*	*	*	*	0.0094	2.60
Log equivalence income 95, rich**	*	*	*	*	0.0180	4.36
Unexplained happiness, 95***	0.0298	2.64	0.0634	2.32	0.0269	2.38
Unexplained happiness, 95***, 2nd quint	*	*	−0.0436	−1.14	*	*
Unexplained happiness, 95***, 3rd quint	*	*	−0.0361	−0.95	*	*
Unexplained happiness, 95***, 4th quint	*	*	−0.0626	−1.71	*	*
Unexplained happiness, 95***, 5th quint	*	*	−0.0229	−0.65	*	*
Constant	5.8325	36.35	5.8234	36.19	5.9365	34.62
Number of observations	4457		4457		4457	
Adjusted R-squared	0.1335		0.1333		0.1518	

Dependent Variable: Log equivalence income, 2000 (OLS).

* Omitted.
** "Poor" is defined as bottom 40 percent of the income distribution in 1995; "rich" is the top 20 percent.
*** The residual of basic happiness 1995 regression (Table 2).

Regression a: no income quintile distinctions.
Regression b: testing for a difference in the effect of unexplained happiness on 2000 income, by 1995 income quintile.
Regression c: testing for a difference in the effect of 1995 income on 2000 income, by 1995 income quintile.

Independent variables are from 2000 unless otherwise noted.

to second period income for the poor and the rich compared to the omitted, middle income category, with the effect being strongest for the rich. Initial period income seems to matter most for those at higher levels of income. It also matters more for the poor compared to those in the middle (see Table 13.5).

This suggests that initial period income provides advantages in earning even more income in the future for the wealthy, who can use their income as an asset in addition to consumption. Initial period income also matters more for the poor than for those in the middle, suggesting that some minimal amount of income (basic needs?) is necessary for people to increase their income in the future. Meanwhile happiness seems to matter to future incomes across the board, but more for those at lower levels of income. In other words, in the absence of income, a good attitude can make a difference to one's future earnings. At higher levels of income, income matters more than happiness, at least in relative terms.

Given that happiness has positive effects on income in Russia, does income still lead to happiness? We examined the effects of initial period income—controlling for residual happiness in 1995, and the usual socioeconomic and demographic variables, on happiness in 2000. We included income in both periods in order to control for the effects of income in 2000 on happiness in 2000. We found that income was indeed positively and significantly correlated with happiness, in addition to the positive and significant effects of unexplained happiness. Thus, income clearly does matter to happiness, even for happy people (see Table 13.6).

We broke this down by income levels, using our dummies for poor and rich categories as the independent income variables and controlling for initial period happiness. We found again that income matters for happiness, and evidence to suggest that the effect increases as people's income levels increase (the result is significant at the 10 percent level) (see Table 13.6).[33] Thus, initial period income seems to matter more for happiness for those at the top of the distribution.

It seems that income needs to be sufficiently above a minimum level to have effects on happiness—a sort of "greed" effect, where additional income increases happiness more for the very wealthy than for others. Some of the findings in the literature on happiness suggest that the relative importance of income as both a motivating force for behavior and in determining well-being is greater at very low levels of income, where basic needs are not yet met, while at higher levels of income, other variables have more importance.[34] In

TABLE 13.6
The Effects of Income on Happiness

Independent Variables	a		b	
	coef	z	coef	z
Age	−0.0781	−7.06	−0.0830	−7.41
Age^2	0.0008	6.97	0.0008	7.20
Male	0.1572	2.65	0.1430	2.39
Married	0.0698	1.08	0.0717	1.11
Education level	0.0211	1.27	0.0175	1.05
Minority	0.2088	2.80	0.2195	2.94
Student	−0.3473	−1.48	−0.2912	−1.24
Retired	−0.3972	−4.08	−0.3694	−3.75
Housewife	−0.0803	−0.53	−0.0446	−0.29
Unemployed	−0.6742	−6.34	−0.6434	−6.02
Self-employed	0.4541	1.89	0.4439	1.84
Health index	0.4000	3.05	0.3966	3.02
Log equivalence income 00	0.2438	7.21	0.3176	8.38
Log equivalence income 95	0.3199	8.46	0.2128	5.94
Log equivalence income 95, rich**	*	*	0.0163	1.62
Log equivalence income 95, poor**	*	*	−0.0146	−1.65
Unexplained happiness, 95***	0.4158	14.50	0.4096	14.24
Number of observations	4414		4414	
Pseudo R-squared	0.0474		0.0481	

Dependent variable: Happiness in 2000 (ordered logit).

* Omitted.

** "Poor" is defined as bottom 40 percent of the income distribution in 1995; "rich" is the top 20 percent.

*** the residual of basic happiness 1995 regression (Table 2).

Regression a: no income quintile distinctions.

Regression b: testing for a difference in the effect of 1995 income on 2000 income by 1995 income quintile.

Independent variables are from 2000 unless otherwise noted.

contrast, our findings suggest that when people reach a certain high level of income, money begins to matter more to them.

These findings are complementary to our findings for the effects of happiness on income, where residual happiness matters more for second period income for those at the lower end of the income ladder, while income matters most for second period income for those at the higher end of the income ladder. These findings suggest that income matters more for happiness to wealthy people. They may also reflect the peculiarities of the Russian situation, in which large numbers of people operate in the nonmonetary economy, and therefore reported income plays much less of a role in evaluating their well-being than it might in other contexts.[35]

In sum, unexplained happiness levels had positive and significant effects on future earnings.[36] This analysis supports the evidence from the psychology literature that happier people earn more income or, more broadly speaking, perform better economically. It is certainly plausible that the same positive cognitive biases that affect normal happiness levels—such as self-esteem, control, and optimism—may also have positive effects on people's performance in the labor market.[37] An additional finding is that the effects of unexplained happiness on future income and on future happiness seem to be more consistent across all income groups than are the effects of income on future income and future happiness. The effects of initial period income seem most important for those at higher levels of income, at least in the Russian context.

MARRIAGE, EMPLOYMENT, HEALTH, AND SMOKING AND DRINKING

One of our most important findings is that unexplained or residual happiness has positive effects on future income. An additional question, which we explore in this section, is whether unexplained happiness also has effects on other socioeconomic variables, such as on the probability of getting married or divorced, of being healthy, of being unemployed, and on behaviors such as smoking and drinking.

As expected, married people are, on average, happier than non-married people in Russia in 2000.[38] We created dummy variables for changes in marital status during the 1995–2000 period. Forty-five percent of the sample— 2,935 respondents—stayed married, while others experienced a change in status: 226 respondents or 3 percent of the sample got married and 529 respondents, or 8 percent of the sample got divorced. Our first set of regressions explored whether residual or unexplained happiness was a predictor of change in marital status. Rather surprisingly, given the strong relationship between marriage and happiness, there was no significant relationship between residual happiness and getting married. In other words, happier people are not more likely than others to get married (see Table 13.7).

Divorce is a marital status variable that has notable effects on happiness in most studies: divorced individuals are, on average, less happy than others. This is also the case in our Russia data set. Becoming divorced had negative and significant effects on both happiness levels in 2000 and changes in happiness levels from 1995 to 2000 in Russia. Yet we found that residual happiness—or more accurately put unhappiness—had no significant effect on the probability of getting divorced (Table 13.7).[39] Thus, although unhappiness does not cause divorce, divorce clearly causes unhappiness. In contrast, when we looked at the effects of getting married on happiness and HAPPYCHANGE, the sign on the coefficient was positive, but it was (rather surprisingly) insignificant for both happiness levels and for changes in happiness (see Table 13.4). Happiness (or unhappiness) also does not appear to cause marriage, but the implications of this finding are less clear because we failed to find a consistent relationship between marriage and happiness (see Tables 13.2 and 13.4).

Not surprisingly given the consistent negative effects of unemployment on happiness across countries and time, those that became unemployed in our sample were significantly less happy than other respondents (see Table 13.2). Unexplained happiness, however, had no effects on the probability of being unemployed. Although the sign on the coefficient is negative, it is short of significant (see Table 13.7). Interestingly enough, education levels also had no effects on the probability of being unemployed. This most likely reflects the dramatic nature of the economic transition in Russia, and the fact that many highly educated people are either overqualified for what they are doing or are unable to find jobs.[40]

Health is one of the most important variables affecting subjective well-being. In our first exploration on the determinants of happiness (discussed above), we find that health—as measured by a neutral index based on a number of questions about days missed due to illness, hospitalization, and so on—is positively and significantly correlated with happiness (see Table 13.2). (Three questions made up the index: In the last thirty days did you miss

TABLE 13.7

The Effects of Happiness on Marriage Status, Employment, and Health

DEPENDENT VARIABLE: CONDITION:	DIVORCED BY 2000 (GIVEN MARRIED 1995)		MARRIED BY 2000 (GIVEN UNMARRIED 1995)		UNEMPLOYED IN 2000		2000 HEALTH INDEX	
REGRESSION TECHNIQUE:	LOGIT a		LOGIT b		LOGIT c		OLS d	
Independent Variables	coef	z	coef	z	coef	z	coef	t
Age	-0.1061	-4.00	0.1023	2.12	0.1609	3.86	-0.0023	-1.89
Age^2	0.0012	4.57	-0.0017	-2.71	-0.0023	-4.62	0.0000	0.97
Male	-0.8974	-7.50	0.1331	0.62	0.8566	6.85	0.0319	4.76
Married	*	*	*	*	-0.3410	-2.55	0.0109	1.51
Education level	-0.0134	-0.43	-0.0171	-0.21	0.0356	0.71	-0.0001	-0.04
Minority	-0.2832	-1.77	-0.1190	-0.44	0.4020	2.94	0.0129	1.54
Student	**	**	-1.1540	-2.08	0.8497***	3.08	-0.0638	-2.38
Retired	0.1634	0.84	-0.7226	-1.39	-0.9747***	-2.15	-0.0507	-4.69
Housewife	*	*	*	*	0.8314***	3.59	0.0345	1.96
Unemployed	0.5603	2.79	0.1352	0.50	1.7353 ***	11.69	0.0332	2.84
Self-employed	0.1159	0.24	**	**	0.4387 ***	1.10	0.0014	0.05

(continued)

TABLE 13.7
(continued)

DEPENDENT VARIABLE: CONDITION:	DIVORCED BY 2000 (GIVEN MARRIED 1995)		MARRIED BY 2000 (GIVEN UNMARRIED 1995)		UNEMPLOYED IN 2000		2000 HEALTH INDEX	
REGRESSION TECHNIQUE:	LOGIT a		LOGIT b		LOGIT c		OLS d	
Independent Variables	*coef*	*z*	*coef*	*z*	*coef*	*z*	*coef*	*t*
Log equivalence income	−0.3646	−5.45	0.4490	3.40	−0.2341	−3.96	0.0040	1.00
Health index	−0.7259	−2.88	−0.2853	−0.65	0.7837****	2.70	0.1524***	10.68
Unexplained happiness, 95	−0.0365	−0.65	−0.0044	−0.04	−0.0886	−1.56	0.0127	4.09
Constant	4.0965	4.75	−6.2979	−3.78	−4.4105	−4.06	0.7368	16.09
Observations	3050		1397		4491		4457	
Pseudo R-squared	0.0759		0.1541		0.2077		0.0930	

* Omitted.

** Dropped: perfect predictor.

*** 1995 values employed.

**** The unexpected sign here is a spurious artifact of one of the three questions underlying the health index: "In the last 30 days did you miss any work or study days due to illness?" We obtain the expected negative relationship between good health and unemployment when we use other measures of health.

any work or study days due to illness? Have you been in the hospital in the last three months? Have you in the last thirty days had any health problems?)

We then examined the effects of residual or unexplained happiness on our health index. We found that residual happiness had positive and significant effects on health (see Table 13.7). Thus, not only does good health make people happier, but our findings suggest that happiness may have additional positive effects on health, something that is often alluded to in the literature but is more difficult to prove empirically with most data. The same cognitive bias or other attitudinal traits that seem to have positive effects on individuals' labor market performance may also influence the manner in which they take care of their health.

CONCLUSIONS

Studies by psychologists find that most individuals have fairly stable levels of happiness or subjective well-being, but that those levels are also subject to short-term fluctuations. Our findings support the idea that there are different elements of well-being, some of which are behaviorally driven, and others that are determined by socioeconomic and demographic variables. The latter are much more vulnerable to day-to-day events, such as changes in employment and marital status, and fluctuations in income.

Our study used panel data from Russia to identify "residual" happiness levels that are not explained by the usual demographic and socioeconomic determinants of happiness. We then tested whether our residual happiness variable had causal properties on future income and other variables. In other words, while we know that more income (up to a certain level) and stable marital status and more education make people happier, does happiness matter to future outcomes? Does happiness pay? Are happier people healthier or more likely to get married? Related to this, do positive expectations and perceptions also have an effect on economic behavior?

We find that residual happiness is associated with higher levels of income in future periods, controlling for income, education, and other sociodemographic variables. Thus, people with higher levels of happiness are more likely to increase their own income in the future. When we divided the sample by income level, we found that happiness matters more to future income to those at lower levels of income. In contrast, the effects of initial period income on both future income and future happiness seem more important for those at higher levels of income. Thus, at least in the Russian context, happiness matters more to future income for those with less income, while income matters more to both happiness and income to those with more income.

We also found that residual happiness had positive effects on health, but none on the probability of getting married or divorced. Although divorce made people significantly less happy, meanwhile, unhappier people were not more likely to get divorced.

Psychologists attribute stability in happiness levels over time—analogous to the "residual" happiness levels that we identify—to positive cognitive bias, such as self-esteem, control, and optimism. Our results suggest that these same traits may affect peoples' performance in the labor market.

Our findings about the effects of well-being on future economic performance—in particular that both happiness and high expectations seem to have positive effects on income in future periods and not only the other way around—suggest that better understanding of subjective well-being can contribute to policy questions, such as about labor market performance and about health. The results are tempered, however, by the exceptional nature of the time period and country from which they come. An important next stage is to test the broader relevance of these results against those from similar data—to the extent it exists—from other countries.[41]

Notes

1. Easterlin (1974).

2. See, among others, Blanchflower and Oswald (1999), Diener (1984), Frey and Stutzer (2002), and Graham and Pettinato (2002a). A contrasting view, in a study by psychologist Bob Cummins, starts from the assumption that subjective well-being is held within a narrow range determined by personality, and that then is influenced by a number of environmental factors, including income. This study finds that there are significantly different levels of subjective well-being for people who are rich, those who are of average Western incomes, and those who are poor. The study notes also that the effects of income are indirect, that is, in terms of the other resources that income allows people to purchase, ranging from better health to nicer environments. See Cummins (2000).

3. For a critique of the use of survey data, see Bertrand and Mullainathan (2001).

4. Assumptions about how much information individuals have and how they process it have become much more sophisticated over time, including the concept of bounded rationality. With bounded rationality, individuals are assumed to have access to local or limited information, and to make decisions according to simple

heuristic rules rather than complex optimization calculations. See Conlisk (1996) and Simon (1978).

5. A particularly important sign of support for this line of work was the granting of the 2002 Nobel Prize in economic science to Daniel Kahneman, a psychologist.

6. Most surveys use a four point scale, although more recently psychologists have begun to advocate the use of either seven or ten point scales as more accurate.

7. See, for example, Diener and Biswas-Diener (1999). More recently, Daniel Kahneman has been conducting studies to determine differences in the determinants of positive affect from those of life satisfaction at the Center for the Study of Wellbeing at Princeton. He presented preliminary findings at a Center on Social and Economic Dynamics seminar at Brookings, February 2002 (Kahneman et al 2002). Psychologists tend to make a distinction between happiness and life satisfaction, while economists tend to use the terms *satisfaction* and *happiness* interchangeably (as we do in this chapter). The correlation between responses to life satisfaction and happiness questions, meanwhile, tends to be on the order of 0.95.

8. Kahneman and Tversky (2000); Thaler (2000).

9. This literature is summarized in Graham and Pettinato (2002a).

10. This has also been referred to as the "hedonic treadmill."

11. Groot (2000).

12. These effects seem to be more important for those at the higher end of the income ladder (Diener and Biswas-Diener 1999).

13. The Russia Longitudinal Monitoring Survey (RLMS) is a nationally representative panel study for Russia, carried out in collaboration with the University of North Carolina at Chapel Hill, and with funding from USAID among others. More information on the survey can be found at www.cpc.unc.edu/projects/rlms/. Critics of the survey question its degree of representation. Accepting that some of these criticisms may have validity, we believe it is an extremely valuable data set.

14. Two possible problems with the question, however, which need to be taken into account, is that the question allows respondents to have a neutral option, which skews responses to the middle of the distribution, and the ordering of the question in the survey. Rather than asking the happiness question first in the survey, before respondents are given a chance to evaluate other aspects of their life, the RLMS happiness question is in the middle of the survey, after a series of questions about occupational and income status, which might skew the responses negatively.

15. The 2000 results were not available at the time of that analysis. See Graham and Pettinato (2002a). In addition, the *Journal of Happiness Studies* had a special issue on happiness in Russia (Vol.2, No.2, 2001) which was based on the analysis of a separate panel of households, the Russet panel, which ran from 1993 to 1995. The articles in that volume tracked changes in happiness over time, but did not attempt to evaluate the affects of happiness on other variables such as income. See, for example, Veenhoven (2001).

16. See, for example, Cummins and Nistico (forthcoming).

17. This is Freedom House's classification of the government in Russia in 2002.

18. There is considerable debate over these figures, in part due to problems with accurate over-time data. These figures are from the World Bank (www.worldbank.org.ru). For a more detailed discussion, see, for example, Ferreri-Carbonell and Van Praag (2001) and Klugman and Braithwaite (1998). For a description of the similarities and differences between Russia and Latin America, see Gaddy and Graham (2002).

19. For a critical view, see, for example, Stiglitz (2002). For a more optimistic view, see Aslund (1995).

20. For a description of Russia's "virtual economy," see Gaddy and Ickes (2002).

21. We initially attempted to include these respondents by adding one to each of the fifty-four observations that reported zero household income in order to take a log and include them. We also created a dummy variable for these respondents, in order to control for any effects that were specific to them or that result from our arbitrary specification of their income level (adding 1). We also substituted this specification with a Box-Cox income variable transformation, but found that it did not have a (statistically significant) better fit than did the zero-plus-one logarithmic specification with zero income dummies. Including them produces skewed results (for example, log income in 1995 was negatively correlated with log income in 2000). Because they comprise only fifty-four observations in a sample of over 5,000, we chose to drop them and to use a simple log equivalence specification throughout the analysis. Results of this econometric analysis are available from the authors on request.

22. Results available from the authors on request.

23. We attempted to deal with this error in our sample by creating dummy variables for the fifty-four respondents that report zero income. Rather ironically, at least half of these respondents display other traits that suggest they have substantial assets if not monetary income (discussed below). Because of this, including them often skewed our econometric results and thus we did not include them in most of our analysis.

24. For studies in the United States and Europe see, among others, Blanchflower and Oswald (1999) and Frey and Stutzer (2002). For happiness in Latin America, see Graham and Pettinato (2002a).

25. Veenhoven (2001), for example, notes that results from Russia could be distorted by translation as well as a culture of "negativism." His own analysis, however, based on a different panel for Russia—the Russet panel for 1993–95, finds that the results are not biased by these factors.

26. This is true for the developed economies and for Latin America. For the latter, see Graham and Sukhtankar (2004).

27. On the United States, see Blanchflower and Oswald (1999), among others; for Latin America, see Graham (2002).

28. For empirical evidence on this for Latin America and the United States, see Graham (2002).

29. See Gerber and Mendelson (2002).

30. This contrasts with findings for the United States, for example, where workers are least happy in anticipation of retirement, but then happier, on average, after they retire. See the chapter by Lowenstein et al. in Aaron (1999).

31. Our basic measure—the log of equivalence household income—is real household income in 1992 rubles divided by the square root of the number of people in the household. Although there are a number of other household equivalence scales, this is the most commonly used at the international level. For detail, see Figini (1998).

32. In contrast to happiness, which probably varies almost as much within each income quintile as it does over the whole sample, partitioning income-by-income quintiles loses much of the variation that occurs within the quintiles, particularly the higher ones. Therefore, we opted to split the sample in a way that better captured at least some of this variation. The omitted category—middle—is the middle 40 percent of the distribution.

33. The coefficient on the top quintile is short of significance at the 10 percent level but the point estimate suggests our result. When we include the quintiles without the income variable, the coefficient becomes significant.

34. The studies by psychologists that find that happiness has positive effects on future income also find that these effects are stronger at the higher end of the income scale. See Diener and Biswas-Diener (1999).

35. We also tried to capture the effects of changes in income on happiness to determine whether income mobility itself has additional effects. When we use percentage change in equivalence income (1995 to 2000), controlling for initial (1995) levels of income, we find a positive and significant effect on happiness. In other words, when one compares people that start out at the same level of income, a higher percentage change in income has positive effects on happiness.

36. An alternative exploration would be to use a kernel estimation of income. Unfortunately, we do not have a statistical package in house that is able to do so.

37. In an earlier version of this chapter, we found that positive perceptions in general—about individuals' economic situations and about their children's future, had similar effects on future income as did residual happiness. In contrast, negative perceptions, such as fear of unemployment, had the opposite effects. Results from authors.

38. One interesting finding is that in 1995, married people were not significantly happier than others, a finding that supports our intuition that overall happiness levels increased from 1995 to 2000 (For happiness in 1995, see Graham and Pettinato 2002a.) This is supported by the fact that 35 percent of the sample had positive changes in happiness levels, while 28 percent had decreases, plus the general improvements on the economic and governance fronts in Russia during the period.

39. The reverse of this was also true: residual happiness had no significant effects on the probability of staying married.

40. Another rather interesting result on unemployment is that the health index was positively and significantly correlated with being unemployed in 2000. This may well be the result of spurious correlation, as one question on the index asks "how days of work did you miss due to illness?" and obviously unemployed people would answer zero.

41. One author, Graham, is currently in the process of compiling second period observations on happiness and other variables with a research team in Peru.

References

Aslund, Anders. 1995. *How Russia Became a Market Economy*. Washington, DC: The Brookings Institution Press.

Bertrand, Marianne, and Sendhil Mullainathan. 2001. "Do People Mean What They Say? Implications for Subjective Survey Data." *American Economic Review* 91:67–72.

Blanchflower, David G., and Andrew J. Oswald. 1999. "Well-Being Over Time in Britain and the USA." Warwick University, Mimeo.

Conlisk, John. 1996. "Why Bounded Rationality?" *Journal of Economic Literature* 34:669–700.

Cummins, Robert. 2000. "Personal Income and Subjective Well Being: A Review." *Journal of Happiness Studies* 1:133–58.

Cummins, Robert, and Helen Nistico. Forthcoming. "Maintaining Life Satisfaction: The Role of Positive Cognitive Bias." *Journal of Happiness Studies*.

Diener, Ed. 1984. "Subjective Well Being." *Psychological Bulletin* 95:542–75.

Diener, Ed, and Robert Biswas-Diener. 1999. "Income and Subjective Well-Being: Will Money Make Us Happy?" Department of Psychology, University of Illinois, Mimeo.

Easterlin, Richard A. 1974. "Does Economic Growth Improve the Human Lot?" In *Nations and Households in Economic Growth*, edited by Paul A. David and Melvin W. Reder. New York: Academic Press.

Ferrer-i-Carbonell, Ada, and Bernard M. S. Van Praag. 2001. "Poverty in Russia." *Journal of Happiness Studies* 2:147–72.

Figini, Paolo. 1998. "Inequality Measures, Equivalence Scales, and Adjustment for Household Size and Composition." *LIS* Working Paper No. 185. Luxembourg: Luxembourg Income Study.

Frey, Bruno S., and Alois Stutzer. 2002. *Happiness and Economics*. Princeton, NJ: Princeton University Press.

Gaddy, Clifford, and Carol Graham. 2002. "Why Argentina '02 Is not Russia '98." *The Globalist* February 11.

Gaddy, Clifford, and Barry W. Ickes. 2002. *Russia's Virtual Economy*. Washington, DC: The Brookings Institution Press.

Gerber, Theodore P., and Sarah E. Mendelson. 2002. "How Russians Think about Chechnya." *PONARS Policy Memo* No. 243 and "The Disconnect in How Russians Think about Human Rights and Chechnya: A Consequence of Media Manipulation." *PONARS Policy Memo* No. 244. Washington, DC: Center for Strategic International Studies.

Graham, Carol. 2002. "Crafting Sustainable Social Contracts in Latin America: Political Economy, Public Attitudes, and Social Policy." Paper prepared for the Inter-American Development Bank Meeting on Social Policy, Santiago, Chile.

Graham, Carol, and Stefano Pettinato. 2002a. *Happiness and Hardship: Opportunity and Insecurity in New Market Economies*. Washington, DC: The Brookings Institution Press.

——— 2002b. "Frustrated Achievers: Winners, Losers, and Subjective Well Being in New Market Economies." *Journal of Development Studies* 38: 100–40.

Graham, Carol, and Sandip Sukhtankar. 2004. "Is Economic Crisis Reducing Support for Markets and Democracy in Latin America? Some Evidence from the Surveys of Public Opinion and Well Being." *Journal of Latin American Studies* 36:349–377.

Groot, Wim. 2000. "Adaptation and Scale of Reference Bias in Self Assessments of Quality of Life." *Journal of Health Econometrics* 19:403–20.

Kahneman, Daniel, Alan Krueger, David Schkade, Norbert Schwarz, and Arthur Stone. 2002. *Measuring Objective Happiness*. Work in Progress, Princeton University Center for the Study of Wellbeing.

Kahneman, Daniel, and Amos Tversky. 2000. *Choices, Values, and Frames*. New York: Cambridge University Press.

Klugman, Jeni, and Jeanine Braithwaite. 1998. "Poverty in Russia During the Transition: An Overview." *World Bank Research Observer* 13(1), February.

Lowenstein, Gorge, Drazen Prelec, Roberto Weber. 1999. "What, Me Worry? A Psychological Perspective on the Economics of Retirement." In *Behavioral Dimensions of Retirement*, edited by Henry J. Aaron. Washington, DC: Brookings Institution and Russell Sage Foundation.

Merton, Robert K. 1957. *Social Theory and Social Structure*. Glencoe, IL: Free Press.

Simon, Herbert. 1978. "Rationality as a Process and Product of Thought." *American Economic Review* 68:1–16.

Stiglitz, Joseph. 2002. *Globalization and Its Discontents*. New York: W.W. Norton.

Thaler, Richard H. 2000. "From Homo Economicus to Homo Sapiens." *Journal of Economic Perspectives* 14:133–41.

Veenhoven, Ruut. 2001. "Are Russians as Unhappy as They Say They Are?" *Journal of Happiness Studies* 2:111–36.

CHAPTER FOURTEEN

The Panel-of-Countries Approach to Explaining Income Inequality: An Interdisciplinary Research Agenda

Anthony B. Atkinson and Andrea Brandolini

Our purpose in this chapter is to review a recent strand of the empirical literature on the determinants of income distribution: econometric studies based on panels of countries, that is, combining time-series and cross-national evidence, in economics, economic history, political science, and sociology. We emphasize providing a framework within which the different studies can be assessed, bringing together the literature from different social science disciplines, and identifying areas that are fruitful for further research. It has to be stressed that the chapter does not aim to be an exhaustive survey of the time-series cross-country literature. First, we consider only *macroeconometric* studies. We exclude a large body of investigations of multi-country time series conducted in a narrative fashion, a tradition initiated by Kuznets (1963), using exploratory data analysis as illustrated by Fields (1991), or using decomposition techniques (e.g., Bourguignon 2002; Osberg 2003). Second, we concentrate less on the substantive conclusions than on the *methodological* characteristics of the literature under examination—how theory, data, and estimation are integrated.

Reaching conclusions about the determinants of income inequality requires a theoretical framework, reliable data, and appropriate statistical techniques. These requirements tend to involve different branches of social

Nuffield College, Oxford, and Bank of Italy, Economic Research Department, respectively. We are grateful to Arthur Alderson, Richard Hauser, participants in the ChangeQual meeting at Mannheim in April 2003, and participants in the International Summer School at Siena in July 2003, for their constructive comments. We thank Arthur Alderson and François Nielsen for sharing their data with us. The views expressed here are, however, solely those of the authors; in particular, they do not necessarily reflect those of the Bank of Italy.

sciences. A typical applied work takes a theoretical model "off the shelf" (such as the Kuznets models of structural change), and data from another shelf (or website), and then statistical techniques from an accessible software package. These "off the shelf" ingredients cannot, however, be used uncritically. The theoretical model may need to be adapted before it can be applied to the issue at hand; data are always imperfect, and their weaknesses need to be assessed in relation to the potential use; the estimation method needs to be tailored to the model under consideration and to the shortcomings of the data. In what follows, we consider in turn theory, data, and estimation, but these should be seen as a vertically integrated activity, not as a set of specialties.

Together with greater vertical integration of theory, data, and estimation, we need greater horizontal integration—across the different disciplines. Although the explanation of income inequality is a thriving research area, there tends to be parallel literatures, each with their strengths and weaknesses. Different issues are regarded as important; different hypotheses are tested; different methodological problems are highlighted; different solutions are invented, or the same solutions are reinvented. As we shall argue, there is considerable scope for mutual learning.

In the next section we briefly review the macroeconometric literature on income inequality based on a panel of countries. We summarize the main characteristics of twenty-nine studies in two tables to facilitate the comparison of different approaches and findings. To make the discussion in following sections concrete, we pick two questions with which much of the recent literature has been concerned: the extent to which globalization has caused rising income inequality, and the capacity of nation-states to moderate its impact through redistributive tax and social policy. The former is emphasized in the study "Globalization and the Great U-Turn: Income Inequality Trends in 16 OECD Countries" by Alderson and Nielsen (2002), that we take as an exemplar of state of the art research in this field. We deal with theory in Section 2, data in Section 3, and estimation in Section 4. At the end of each section, we draw lessons for future research.

I. THE MACROECONOMETRIC PANEL-OF-COUNTRIES LITERATURE ON INCOME INEQUALITY

Table 14.1 lists twenty-seven macroeconometric investigations of the determinants of *income distribution* that use cross-national time series, whereas

TABLE 14.1

Selected Results from Time-series Cross-country Studies of Income Inequality

Study	Publication	Period	Geographic Coverage (1)	Number of Observations on Inequality (1)	Inequality Measure	Inequality Variable	Inequality Data Source	Estimation Methods	Explanatory Variables, Sign and Significance of Coefficients (2)
Papanek and Kyn (1986)	*Journal of Development Economics*	1952–78	83 (36) unspecified countries	145 (98)	Gini index, share of bottom 40%	Unspecified income	Not indicated	OLS, fixed effects	*Table 3, Gini (fixed effects)* Log(real GNP per capita) +* Log(real GNP per capita) squared −** Difference in definitions dummies n.a.
Bulíř and Gulde (1995)	*IMF Working Paper* (in Czech in *Finance a úvir*, 2000)	1960–92	18 developed and developing countries	126 (121)	Gini index	Net income per household	National sources and studies	Fixed effects	*Table 1, equation 1* Real GDP per capita +** Real GDP per capita squared −** Government spending/GDP −** Inflation rate +***
Nielsen and Alderson (1995)	*American Sociological Review*	1952–88	88 developed and developing countries	279	Gini index, share of top 20%	Unspecified income (but probably gross and net income and consumption)	International compendia of statistics and cross-country studies	Random effects	*Table 2c, model 9* Secondary school enrolment ratio −*** Natural rate of population increase +*** Sector dualism +*** Share of labour force in agriculture −** Log(energy consumption per capita) −

Author (year)	Journal	Period	Countries	N	Inequality measure	Data	Method	Independent variable	Sign
								Log(energy consumption per capita) squared	−***
								Marxist-Leninist regime	−***
								Industrialising horti-cultural society	+
								Industrialising agrarian society	+
								Household-based income dummy	−***
								Gini based on quintiles dummy	−***
Ravallion (1995)	*Economics Letters*	1980s	36 develop-ing countries	52 (32)	Gini index	Consump-tion or income per person	Primary national data sets	OLS on differences	
								Equation in the text at p. 415	
								Real mean consumption per capita	+
								Inverse real mean con-sumption per capita	−
Jha (1996)	*World Devel-opment*	1960–92	76 developed and develop-ing countries	185 (181)	Shares of bottom 20%, bottom 40% and top 20%, ratio of shares of top 20% to bottom 40%	Unspecified income (but probably gross and net income and con-sumption, per person or house-hold)	World Bank database (World Bank, 1994)	OLS	
								Table 1, full sample, ratio of share of top 20% to bottom 40%	
								Log(real GDP per capita)	+***
								Log(real GDP per capita) squared	−***
								Primary schooling	−
								Secondary schooling	−***
								Growth rate	−
								Socialist country dummy	−***

(continued)

TABLE 14.1
(*continued*)

Study	Publication	Period	Geographic Coverage (1)	Number of Observations on Inequality (1)	Inequality Measure	Inequality Variable	Inequality Data Source	Estimation Methods	Explanatory Variables, Sign and Significance of Coefficients (2)	
Edwards (1997)	*American Economic Review Papers and Proceedings*	1970s and 1980s	44 developed and developing countries	43 (10-years averages)	Gini index	Unspecified income (but probably gross and net income and consumption)	Deininger-Squire	OLS on differences	*Equation in the text at p. 209*	
									Change in secondary schooling	$-$**
									Growth rate	$+$
									Inflation rate	$+$***
									GNP per capita in 1980	$+$
									Initial trade distortion	$+$**
									Initial trade distortion $\times$ developed country	$-$*
									Trade reform	$-$
									Trade reform $\times$ developed country	$+$
Ram (1997)	*Southern Economic Journal*	1950–92	19 OECD countries	239	Gini index, shares of bottom 40% and top 20%	Unspecified income (but gross and net income and consumption)	Deininger-Squire	OLS, fixed effects	*Tables 1, fixed effects, Gini*	
									Log(real GDP per capita)	$-$***
									Log(real GDP per capita) squared	$+$***
Sarel (1997)	*IMF Working Paper*	1950–92	45 developed and developing countries, excluding socialist countries	425, reduced to 45 by taking mean annual rate of change in each country	Gini index	Gross and net income and consumption, per person or household	Deininger-Squire	OLS	*Table 3*	
									Log(real income per capita)	$-$***
									Growth of real income per capita	$-$***
									Terms of trade change	$-$***
									Real exchange rate change	$+$***

Study	Journal	Period	Sample	N	Inequality measure	Data	Method	Source	Explanatory variables (results)	Sig.
									Real exchange rate change × log(real income per capita)	−***
									Investment/domestic demand	−***
									Participation rate	+++
									Participation rate change	+++
Bourguignon and Morrisson (1998)	*Journal of Development Economics*	Around 1970 and 1985	47 developing countries	71	Shares of bottom 40%, bottom 60% and top 20%, ratio of shares of top 20% to bottom 60%	Unspecified income and consumption, per person	Fixed effects	National sources and studies	*Table 3, model 3d, ratio of share of top 20% to bottom 60%*	
									Real GDP per capita	++
									Real GDP per capita squared	−*
									Secondary school enrolment ratio	−*
									Mineral resources dummy	+++
									Cultivable land per capita	−**
									Share of land of small-medium farmers	−**
									Non-farm/farm labour productivity	+++
Deininger and Squire (1998)	*Journal of Development Economics*	1960s–90s	49 developed and developing countries	529 (511)	Gini index	Gross and net income and consumption, per person or household	OLS on levels and first differences, fixed effects	Deininger-Squire	*Tables 6, column 3 (fixed effects)*	
									Real GDP per capita	+
									Inverse real GDP per capita	+

(continued)

TABLE 14.1
(continued)

Study	Publication	Period	Geographic Coverage (1)	Number of Observations on Inequality (1)	Inequality Measure	Inequality Variable	Inequality Data Source	Estimation Methods	Explanatory Variables, Sign and Significance of Coefficients (2)
Li, Squire, and Zou (1998)	Economic Journal	1947–94	49 developed and developing countries	573, reduced to 166 by taking 5-year averages	Gini index	Gross and net income and consumption, per person or household	Deininger-Squire	OLS, AR(1), IV	Table 6 (all methods) Mean years of schooling in 1960s –*** Civil liberty (Gastil index) +*** Initial Gini for land distribution +*** Financial development (M2/GDP) –***
Schultz (1998)	Journal of Population Economics	1947–95	56 developed and developing countries	509 (226)	Variance of logarithms of income	Gross income, per household	Deininger-Squire	OLS, fixed effects	Table 3, column 6 (fixed effects) Log(real GDP per capita) – Log(real GDP per capita) squared + Year –
Alderson and Nielsen (1999)	American Sociological Review	1967–94	88 developed and developing countries	488	Gini index	Gross and net income and consumption, per person or household	Deininger-Squire	Random effects	Table 2, model 3 Secondary school enrolment ratio –*** Natural rate of population increase +* Sector dualism +*** Share of labour force in agriculture –

Marxist-Leninist regime —***
Foreign investment/GDP +***
Foreign investment/ GDP × core country —*
Core country dummy —
Income (vs. consumption) dummy +***
Year +***

Table 1, full model, random effects, Gini
Real GDP per capita —**
Share of employment in industry —***
Import from developing countries/GDP +***
Unemployment rate —
Inflation rate —*
Government spending/GDP —**
Social security benefits/GDP —
Union density —***
Population share of young (aged 0–14) +***
Population share of elderly (aged 65+) +
Female participation rate (aged 15–64) +

Gustafsson and Johansson (1999) | *American Sociological Review* | 1966–94 | 16 OECD countries | 89 | Gini index, Mean logarithmic deviation, Theil index | Equivalent net income (equivalence scales differ), per person | Luxembourg Income Study and national sources | Fixed effects, random effects

(continued)

TABLE 14.1
(continued)

Study	Publication	Period	Geographic Coverage (1)	Number of Observations on Inequality (1)	Inequality Measure	Inequality Variable	Inequality Data Source	Estimation Methods	Explanatory Variables, Sign and Significance of Coefficients (2)
List and Gallet (1999)	*Review of Development Economics*	1961–92	71 developed and developing countries	892	Gini index	Unspecified income (but probably gross and net income and consumption)	ILO compendium (Tabatabai, 1996)	OLS, fixed effects, random effects	*Table 2, random effects* Real GDP per capita + Real GDP per capita squared –* Real GDP per capita cubed +** Year –** Difference in definitions dummies n.a.
Spilimbergo, Londoño, and Székely (1999)	*Journal of Development Economics*	1947–94	108 developed and developing countries	660	Gini index, shares of each quintile	Gross and net income and consumption, per person or household	Deininger-Squire	OLS	*Table 2, Gini* Real GDP per capita –*** Real GDP per capita squared +*** Arable land per capita +*** Capital per worker +*** Population aged 25+ with higher schooling –*** Arable land per capita × trade openness – Capital per worker × trade openness –*** Population aged 25+ with higher schooling × trade openness +*** Trade openness +***

Author (year)	Source	Period	Sample	Observations	Inequality measure	Data source	Method	Variables
Higgins and Williamson (1999)	*NBER Working Paper* (shorter version in *Southeast Asian Studies*, 2002)	1960s–90s	85 (44) developed and developing countries	600 (449)	Gini index, ratio of shares of top 20% to bottom 20%	Deininger-Squire	OLS, fixed effects	*Table 8, column 2, fixed effects, Gini* Real GDP per worker +*** Real GDP per worker squared −*** Trade openness (Sachs-Warner index) +* Share of adult population aged 40–59 −** Secondary school enrolment ratio −*** Year dummies n.a.
Barro (2000)	*Journal of Economic Growth*	1960s–90s	84 developed and developing countries	254 (196)	Gini index	Deininger-Squire, integrated with 48 observations	Fixed effects	*Table 6, part II, column 2, fixed effects* Log(real GDP per capita) +*** Log(real GDP per capita) squared −*** Net income or consumption dummy −*** Individuals (vs. households) dummy − Primary schooling + Secondary schooling −*** Higher schooling +*** Trade openness (export + import/GDP) +***
Chu, Davoodi, and Gupta (2000)	*IMF Working Paper*	1970s, 1980s, 1990s	Unspecified, developing and transition countries	85 (10-years averages)	Gini index	Deininger-Squire	OLS	*Table 8, equation 1.1.A.* Direct tax/indirect tax −*** Direct tax/indirect tax × direct tax/GDP +** Secondary school enrolment ratio −*** Urbanisation rate +***

(*continued*)

TABLE 14.1
(continued)

Study	Publication	Period	Geographic Coverage (1)	Number of Observations on Inequality (1)	Inequality Measure	Inequality Variable	Inequality Data Source	Estimation Methods	Explanatory Variables, Sign and Significance of Coefficients (2)
Li, Xie, and Zou (2000)	Canadian Journal of Economics	1950–92	84 developed and developing countries	583 (507)	Gini index	Gross and net income and consumption, per person or household	Deininger-Squire	Fixed effects	Table 7, column 2, full sample Real GDP per capita –*** Real GDP per capita squared +*** Government spending/GDP – Population growth – Trade openness + (export + import/GDP) Financial development (M2/GDP) +***
Cornia and Kiiski (2001)	UNU/WIDER Discussion Paper	1980, 1995 (or closest available years)	32 developing countries	64	Gini index	Net income	UN/WIDER World Income Inequality Database	OLS on logarithmic differences	Equation in the text at p. 36 Log(Gini) in 1980 –*** Index of policy reform +*** Former Soviet Union country dummy +*** Latin America and Caribbean dummy +*
Fields (2001), from Fields and Jakubson (1994)	Book	Not indicated	20 developing countries	62	Gini index	Unspecified income	Not indicated	OLS, fixed effects	Table 3.1, fixed effects Real GNP per capita –*** Real GNP per capita squared +***

Study	Journal	Period	Countries	N	Inequality measure	Income definition	Database	Effects	Variables
Galli and van der Hoeven (2001)	*ILO Employment Paper*	1973–96	15 OECD countries	60	Gini index	Net income, per household	UN/WIDER World Income Inequality Database	Fixed effects	*Table 7, model 3* Long-run inflation rate −*** Long-run inflation rate squared +*** Long-run real GDP growth +*** Government spending/GDP −***
Alderson and Nielsen (2002)	*American Journal of Sociology*	1967–92	16 OECD countries	192, 187 after 5 outliers are excluded (184)	Gini index	Gross and net income, per person or household	Deininger-Squire	Random effects	*Table 5, model 13* Sector dualism − Share of labor force in agriculture +*** Natural rate of population increase + Secondary school enrolment ratio −* Outflow of direct investment/labour force +* Southern import penetration/GDP +* Net migration rate +*** Union density −** Wage coordination (Kenworthy index) −** Decommodification −* Female labour force participation +*

(continued)

TABLE 14.1
(continued)

Study	Publication	Period	Geographic Coverage (1)	Number of Observations on Inequality (1)	Inequality Measure	Inequality Variable	Inequality Data Source	Estimation Methods	Explanatory Variables, Sign and Significance of Coefficients (2)
									Share of labour force in manufacturing − 1973–81 dummy + 1982–92 dummy −
Dollar and Kraay (2002)	*Journal of Economic Growth*	1950–99	137 developed and developing countries	953 (189)	Share of bottom 20% adjusted for differences in measurement	Gross and net income and consumption, per person or household	UN/WIDER World Income Inequality Database, Deininger-Squire, other World Bank databases	OLS on levels and differences, IV, System GMM	*Table 5, model with all growth variables,* OLS Log(real GDP per capita) + Trade openness (export + import/GDP) + Government spending/ GDP −** Log(1 + inflation rate) − Commercial bank assets/ total bank assets − Rule of law index − Regional dummies n.a.
Lundberg and Squire (2003)	*Economic Journal*	1960s– 90s	38 developed and developing countries	119 (5-year averages)	Gini index adjusted for differences in measurement	Gross and net income and consumption, per person or household	Deininger-Squire, integrated with 75 observations	Simultaneous growth-inequality model, IV	*Table 3* Years of schooling of population aged 25+ −** Government spending/ GDP + Financial development (M2/GDP) +* Inflation rate +** Trade openness (Sachs-Warner index) +***

Study	Journal	Years	Sample	N	Dependent variable	Income concept	Data source	Method
Mahler (2004)	*Comparative Political Studies*	1981–2000	14 OECD countries	59	Gini index	Equivalent net income (square root equivalence scale) per person	Luxembourg Income Study	GLS

Terms-of-trade changes +
Civil liberty (Gastil index) +***
Mean land Gini +*
Mean land Gini × less developed country +***
Initial income +***
1980s dummy −*
1990s dummy −**

Table 1, panel C

Imports from developing countries/GDP +
Outbound investment/GDP −
Financial openness (Quinn-Inclán index) +*
Cabinet ideological balance +
Electoral turnout +
Union density −***
Wage coordination (Kenworthy index) −***

N O T E S : (1) The number in parentheses is the number of observations for the estimate reported in the last column, when it differs from the maximum number of available observations. (2) Constant or country fixed effects are not reported. Significance levels are for one-tailed tests as follows: * significant at 10% level; ** significant at 5% level; *** significant at 1% level. It is unknown for Spilimbergo et al. (1999) whether test is one- or two-tailed.

Table 14.2 focuses on three studies of *earnings* inequality (of which one in common with Table 14.1). They are drawn from a variety of disciplines, including economics, political science, and sociology. This literature is fairly young. The oldest paper we have found in our search, admittedly incomplete and unsystematic, dates back to 1985 and then we jump directly to mid-1990s for the next ones. The study by Alderson and Nielsen (2002) used to illustrate many of the points in our review is shaded in Table 14.1.

The temporal and geographical coverage of the data used in these studies is very different. All postwar decades are covered, but data relate to periods as long as 1950–99 (Dollar and Kraay 2002), or as short as two years in the 1980s (Ravallion 1995). Five income studies and all three earnings papers focus on OECD countries only; four studies look at developing countries; the others have used data for both developed and developing countries, with up to 137 different countries (Dollar and Kraay 2002). These differing choices of sample periods and countries mean that the total numbers of observations differ considerably: from less than fifty (Edwards 1997; Wallerstein 1999) to about 900 or more (List and Gallet 1999; Dollar and Kraay 2002).

As regards the inequality measure, all but four of the income studies use the Gini coefficient, supplemented in some cases by an analysis of the shares of quantile groups. Of the four papers not using the Gini coefficient, three (Jha 1996; Bourguignon and Morrisson 1998; Dollar and Kraay 2002, which is however concerned with poverty more than inequality) look at income shares and one (Schultz 1998) at the variance of logarithms. The only other summary measures of inequality that appear in Table 14.1 are the mean logarithmic deviation and the Theil index, both used by Gustafsson and Johansson (1999) together with the Gini coefficient. Among the works on earnings distribution, two utilize the decile ratio and one the Gini coefficient.

Data on income and earnings distribution are derived from a variety of sources. In only one case (Ravallion 1995) the inequality figures are computed directly on primary sources; in two cases (Gustafsson and Johansson 1999; Mahler 2004) they are calculated from the microdata stored at the Luxembourg Income Study (LIS); in all other cases, inequality measures are drawn from national sources and studies, or secondary databases assembled at international organizations.[1] The lion's share of secondary sources is taken by the data set constructed at the World Bank by Deininger and Squire (DS), which has been used in half of the studies listed in Tables 14.1 and 14.2. The use of international databases, however, does not ensure the comparability of inequality figures, a fact of which many—but not all—users are aware. Although we have so far referred generically to "income distribution," as documented by Deininger and Squire and in other recent databases such as the World Income Inequality Database (WIID) of the United Nations University/ World Institute for Development Economics Research (UNU/WIDER), the actual variable for which inequality is computed can be consumption, gross (pre-tax) income, net (after-tax) income, or net equivalent (i.e., adjusted for household composition) income, and the distribution can refer to persons or households. This leads to problems of consistency both across studies and within studies. The fact that the same database was used does not imply that the results can be compared, because the econometric relationships may have been estimated on the basis of different definitions. Moreover, a number of studies mix various income concepts, sometimes accounting for these differences with additive dummies in estimation. Of the twenty-seven papers listed in Table 14.1, only six (Bulíř and Gulde 1995; Schultz 1998; Gustafsson and Johansson 1999; Cornia and Kiiski 2001; Galli and van der Hoeven 2001; Mahler 2004) appear to use a definition of income distribution relatively coherent across countries and years. Worries about comparability seem to be less important, at least at first sight, in the three earnings studies listed in Table 14.2. We return to questions regarding data sources and definitions in Section 3.

All studies in Tables 14.1 and 14.2 use time series (indexed by t) of countries (indexed by i) to estimate the relation between inequality, I, and the explanatory variable(s) of interest (vector X), possibly conditioning on some other variables (vector Z):

$$I_{it} = \alpha + \beta X_{it} + \gamma Z_{it} + \varepsilon_{it}. \tag{1}$$

(There are issues of reverse causality that we do not discuss here.) The advantage of panel data is the possibility to control for country fixed effects, representing (constant over time) differences across countries that are not captured by the independent variables. In Tables 14.1 and 14.2, there is a wide range of explanatory variables, reflecting the diverse focus of each study. These variables can be roughly grouped as macroeconomics, redistribution, financial development, globalization, natural resources, sectoral composition and demographics, education, labor market institutions, and political indicators. Several studies include variables to capture the level of development

TABLE 14.2

Selected Results from Time-series Cross-country Studies of Earnings Inequality

Study	Publication	Period	Geographic Coverage (1)	Number of Observations on Inequality (1)	Inequality Measure	Inequality Variable	Inequality Data Source	Estimation Methods	Explanatory Variables, Sign, and Significance of Coefficients (2)	
Wallerstein (1999)	American Journal of Political Science	1980, 1986, 1992 (or closest available year)	16 OECD countries	44 (41)	Ratio of top to bottom decile	Gross wages and salaries of full-time employees	Organisation for Economic Co-operation and Development (1996)	GLS, Fixed effects	Table 3, column 2 (no fixed effects)	
									Wage-setting centralization	−***
									Concentration of union membership	−***
									Collective agreement coverage	−***
									Cabinet share of left parties	+
									Cabinet share of right parties	−**
									Trade openness (export + import/GDP)	−***
									Government employment/total employment	−**
									Government spending/GDP	+**
									Period dummies	n.a.
Rueda and Pontusson (2000)	World Politics	1973–95	16 OECD countries	217	Ratio of top to bottom decile	Gross wages and salaries of full-time employees	Organisation for Economic Co-operation and Development database	Fixed effects (IV)	Table 4	
									Lagged dependent variable	+***
									Unemployment rate	−
									Trade with less developed countries/GDP	+
									Female participation rate	+**

Study	Source	Period	Countries	N	Dependent variable	Income definition	Database	Method	Independent variables
Mahler (2004)	*Comparative Political Studies*	1981–2000	14 OECD countries	55	Gini index	Income (unspecified if net or gross) from wages, salaries and self-employment of households with head aged 25–55	Luxembourg Income Study	GLS	Union density –** Bargaining centralisation (Iversen index) –*** Government employment/total employment –*** Cabinet ideological balance (Cusack index) +***

Table 1, panel A

Independent variable	
Imports from developing countries/GDP	–
Outbound investment/GDP	+
Financial openness (Quinn-Inclán index)	+**
Cabinet ideological balance (Schmidt index)	+
Electoral turnout	–**
Union density	+
Wage coordination (Kenworthy index)	–***

N O T E S : (1) The number in parentheses is the number of observations for the estimates reported in the last column, when it differs from the maximum number of available observations. (2) Constant or country fixed effects are not reported. Significance levels are for one-tailed tests as follows: * significant at 10% level; ** significant at 5% level; *** significant at 1% level.

or sectoral dualism in the Kuznets tradition, to which we turn at the outset of the next theoretical section.

To make our discussion more concrete, in the remaining of the chapter we shall focus on two explanatory variables: "globalization," G, and "redistribution," R. Thus, we shall have particularly in mind equations such as

$$I_{it} = \alpha + \beta_G G_{it} + \beta_R R_{it} + \gamma Z_{it} + \varepsilon_{it}, \tag{2}$$

where Z captures, as before, the role of other causes. Globalization is considered in half of the studies listed in Tables 14.1 and 14.2, where it is measured by the ratios to GDP of export and import, of import from developing countries, or of foreign investment, by terms of trade, by various indices of trade openness, such as the Sachs-Warner index or the black-market premium, or by the net migration rate. (For a recent study of the measurement of globalization, see Andersen and Herbertsson 2005.) The redistributive role of the state is analyzed somewhat less frequently: several studies include the ratio of government spending to GDP, one focuses on tax ratios, others use the government share in total employment and the ratio of social security benefits to GDP.

2. A THEORETICAL FRAMEWORK

Much of the literature on trends in income inequality draws on the Presidential Address of Kuznets (1955). This applies to political science and sociology as well as to economics. On the second page of their article, Alderson and Nielsen (2002:1245) describe how Kuznets "conjectured a general developmental pattern in which inequality traces a curvilinear, inverted U-shaped relationship with economic development." The inverse-U arises from the existence of "sector dualism," average incomes in the traditional agricultural sector being lower than in the modern industrial sector. Inequality is relatively less when either most people are in the traditional sector or when most people are in the modern sector.

Kuznets' conjecture has stimulated a large empirical literature, especially in development economics (see Kanbur 2000, for a survey). Of the twenty-seven studies using panels of countries listed in Table 14.1, fourteen estimate the nonlinear relationship between inequality and real income per capita (half of which conditioning on some other variables). The three papers by Nielsen and Alderson (1995) and Alderson and Nielsen (1999, 2002) test

Kuznets' hypothesis by using instead a measure of sector dualism. One reason that has made Kuznets' prediction particularly appealing to other disciplines is that sector dualism can explain an inverted-U shape, whereas "most theoretical discussions of the evolution of inequality in sociology [tend] to produce monotonic predictive statements . . . of the form 'the greater x (e.g. the spread of education), the lower y (income inequality)'" (Nielsen 1994:657).

A Model of Structural Change

A simple theoretical model allows us to see more precisely how the inverted-U comes about. Suppose that there is no within-sector inequality. (Our analysis is much less rich than that of Kuznets 1955, which allowed for within-sector inequality, and for other factors such as the concentration of savings.) There are then two income groups, one (in the modern sector) with a higher income; the wage differential between agriculture and industry necessary to cause movement between the two sectors is assumed to be a constant proportion of the industrial sector wage. This dual economy can be represented in terms of a Lorenz curve, which plots the share of income of the first $100x$ percent of the population against x. It is drawn between 0 and 1, is convex upward, and never lies above the 45° line that represents complete equality. The Lorenz curve for the dual economy is shown in Figure 14.1, where ϕ is the proportion of the population in the traditional sector (with lower incomes). The first segment has a slope equal to the ratio of the traditional sector income to the average income; the second segment has a slope equal to the ratio of the modern sector income to the average income. As the economy develops, the modern sector grows, so that the point P in Figure 14.1 moves to the left. The slopes of both segments of the Lorenz curve fall, because both the industrial workers and farmers find that they are worse off relative to the rising average. The gainers are those making the transition between sectors. This means that the Lorenz curve shifts inward (toward equality) at the top and outward (away from equality) at the bottom. It should be stressed that we are talking about relative inequality, not about absolute living standards or social welfare. The economy in this model is enjoying real economic growth, and no one becomes worse off.

Where the Lorenz curves intersect, different summary measures of inequality can give different answers. As seen in Table 14.1, most commonly employed is the Gini coefficient. The Gini coefficient can be calculated using the fact that it is equal to the ratio of the area between the diagonal and the

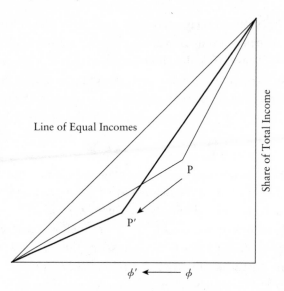

Figure 14.1.   Lorenz Curve for the Kuznets Model

Lorenz curve to the whole triangle. If ϕ is the proportion of labor force employed in the traditional sector and s is the wage premium paid in the modern sector (i.e., the industrial wage is $1 + s$ times the agricultural wage), the Gini coefficient I is equal to:

$$I = \phi - \frac{\phi}{\phi + (1 - \phi)(1 + s)}. \tag{3}$$

The value of I, in the simple case shown, is the difference between the population share ϕ and the income share (the second term in the right side of (3)) of the agricultural sector, which is the "sector dualism" variable used by Nielsen (1994), Nielsen and Alderson (1995), and Alderson and Nielsen (1999, 2002). Initially, both population and income share are close to 1, and the Gini coefficient is near zero; it rises over time, but as the economy matures the population and income share of agriculture both tend to zero. Hence the inverse-U shape. The opposite shape describes the evolution of the income share of the bottom 20 percent of the population ranked by increasing income, another distributive measure appearing in Table 14.1 (a measure of equality rather than inequality). In this simple model, the income share of the bottom 20 percent diminishes until the fraction of population in agriculture falls to 20 percent; as the latter declines further, the income share gradually increases, approaching its maximum value of 0.2 when the agricultural sector is about to disappear. Thus, both the Gini coefficient and the income share of the bottom 20 percent (or of any other population fraction) conforms to Kuznets' prediction that inequality varies non-monotonically as society develops. Where they differ, however, is in the turning point, that is the level of real income at which inequality starts to fall. This means that there is a range of values of ϕ (which has a one-to-one inverse correspondence with mean income) where the two measures give conflicting indications on the behavior of income inequality.[2]

Modeling the Effects of Globalization and Redistribution

The model of structural change takes us part of the way, but is not enough on its own. In fact it lacks both of the ingredients highlighted here. The economy is assumed closed to foreign trade, so that globalization has no direct role. There is no redistributive state.

Suppose now that we reinterpret the two sectors as using "skilled" and "unskilled" workers, and assume that the supply of skills is fixed. According to a widely held view, globalization has led to a shift in demand away from unskilled labor. As has been described by Krugman (1994) and Wood (1994), this view may have led to different outcomes in Europe from those in the United States. Where wages are freely flexible, a situation that may characterize the United States, then the shift in demand causes increased wage dispersion, and the Lorenz curve for wages unambiguously shifts outward—see the solid line in the left panel of Figure 14.2. On the other hand, if in the Continental European labor market wage differentials are held fixed, so that the wages of unskilled workers do not fall relative to those of skilled workers, then unskilled workers become unemployed. Among the *employed*, the average wage rises, causing the Lorenz curve to move inward at the top and outward at the bottom (by assumption, the ratio of the slopes of the two Lorenz curve segments is fixed). Similarly to the movement depicted in Figure 14.1, there is no unambiguous rise in inequality. In the extreme case where international competition completely eliminates the demand for unskilled workers, there is equality among the employed, who would all be skilled. But *among the whole population*, the distribution of *market* incomes becomes more unequal—see the heavy line in the right panel of Figure 14.2, where we now have three groups: skilled workers, unskilled workers, and the

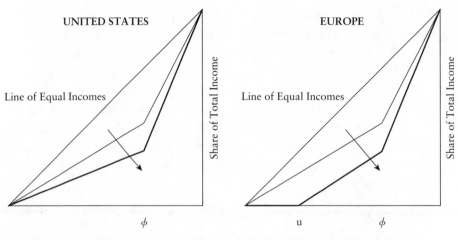

UNITED STATES   **EUROPE**

Line of Equal Incomes   Line of Equal Incomes

Share of Total Income   Share of Total Income

φ   u   φ

Population Ranked by Increasing Income   Population Ranked by Increasing Income

Figure 14.2.   Lorenz Curves for the Krugman-Wood Model

unemployed.[3] For the population as a whole, mean income falls, and the Lorenz curve moves outward at the top as well as at the bottom. So in the European case, as in the American case, there is an unambiguous rise in the inequality of market income among the population as a whole.

With three groups, the analysis becomes more complicated, and for the purposes of exposition we concentrate on the Gini coefficient, keeping in mind that it may conceal divergent movements at different points in the distribution. Some algebra may again be helpful. Skilled workers are assumed to account for a proportion $(1 - \phi)$ of the population and to receive a skill premium s. The Gini coefficient for market income in the "U.S. case" of flexible wages equals equation (3), or in a slightly rearranged form:

$$I_M^{US} = \frac{\phi(1 - \phi)s}{(1 - \phi)s + 1},$$ (4)

where subscript M indicates that I refers to market income. By assuming that the U.S. economy, in this simplified characterization, has no redistributive tools, equation (4) also provides the Gini coefficient for disposable income, or $I_D^{US} = I_M^{US}$ (where subscript D stands for disposable income). From (4), we can see that I is an increasing function of the skill premium s, so that if globalization raises the premium, then the Gini coefficient rises. The effect of a rise in the proportion of skilled workers is ambiguous, reflecting, as in the earlier model, the impact of structural change in leading first to increased, then reduced, inequality. In the "European case," introducing the unemployment rate, u, the Gini coefficient for the distribution of market income among the whole population becomes:

$$I_M^{EU} = \frac{\phi(1 - \phi)s + \boldsymbol{u(1 - u)}}{(1 - \phi)s + \boldsymbol{1 - u}}.$$ (5)

The new terms are shown in bold. If the effect of globalization is to raise unemployment, then (assuming that u is less than ϕ) the Gini coefficient is increased.

The rise in market income inequality is however moderated, in the distribution of disposable (or net) income, by the welfare state. Suppose that redistributive public policies are modeled as an unemployment protection scheme, whereby unemployment benefits are financed by contributions levied on wages at rate τ. More precisely, suppose that the program covers a proportion c (for *c*overed) of the unemployed, and that a subsidy is paid to each insured unemployed equal to a fraction b of the net-of-tax wage of the unskilled. (It is assumed that $0 \leq c \leq 1$, $0 \leq \tau \leq 1$, and $0 \leq b \leq 1$.) There are now four different classes of people (uninsured unemployed workers, insured unemployed workers, employed unskilled workers, and employed skilled workers), leading to the four-segment Lorenz curve shown in Figure 14.3 by solid lines. The Gini coefficient for the distribution of disposable income can now be calculated as:

$$I_D^{EU} = \frac{\phi(1 - \phi)s + u(1 - u) + \boldsymbol{bcuu} - \boldsymbol{bcu(1 - u + cu)}}{(1 - \phi)s + 1 - u + \boldsymbol{bcu}}.$$ (6)

As before, the new terms are shown in bold at the right of the numerator and denominator.

The introduction of tax and benefit parameters means that we have to consider the impact of changes in exogenous variables on the government budget. We cannot simply differentiate I with respect to s or u. Even where there is no change in the generosity of benefits, a rise in u adds to public spending, and this has to be financed. A policy response has to be specified. The requirement of budget balance is that

$$bc = \frac{\tau}{1 - \tau}\left[\frac{(1 - \phi)s + 1 - u}{u}\right].$$ (7)

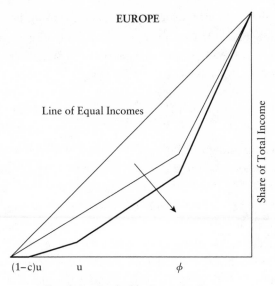

Figure 14.3.   Lorenz Curves for a Four-Class Model

If u rises, then raising the tax rate can finance the extra spending, leaving b and c unchanged. In this case, there is no feedback effect on the Gini coefficient: the benefit payment is scaled back in line with net wages. On the other hand, if the policy response is to cut b or c, then this will have repercussions for the level of inequality, in addition to those brought about by u and s. Even for the extremely simplified distribution sketched here, the Gini coefficient turns out to be a rather intricate function of the macroeconomic variables s and u, and the institutional parameters b, τ, and c. It is also evident that the impacts of globalization and of redistribution interact: for instance, the derivative of inequality with respect to the skill premium depends on the extent of social protection.

Interpreting the Models

The previous considerations have been derived from a rather mechanical application of the formula of the Gini coefficient. We have discussed the *impact*, or ceteris paribus, effect of changes in s or u. Whatever the form it takes, it is plausible that the policy response concerning b, τ, and c will affect the behavior of economic agents. There are feedback effects on s or u that should be taken into account. Here, two related questions arise: how should we interpret ϕ and s? Let us examine them in turn.

A key difference between the two models described above lies in the interpretation of ϕ. In the "stripped-down" Kuznets model, workers are inherently identical. They receive different incomes because, for historical reasons, they find themselves in different sectors of the economy. Inequality is a disequilibrium phenomenon: unless mobility is prevented, or relative wages are re-equilibrated, all workers will eventually move from the traditional to the modern sector. The fact that ϕ differs from 0 or 1 is a historical accident, which will be corrected provided that enough time elapses. In contrast, in the "stripped-down" Krugman-Wood story, people differ inherently in their skill. What are the origins of these skill differences? If skill is identified with education or training, inequality is again a disequilibrium phenomenon, because any excess economic advantage from skill will over time induce people to invest in human capital formation (wages may still be different, but only by enough to compensate for the period of education). But if skill is innate, parameters like ϕ are some "natural" constant, and then inequality is a permanent feature of society. This leaves us with the question as to the role of social science explanation. Should we be seeking "complete" explanation of observed differences? Or should we be satisfied with explaining the process by which differences in human characteristics are translated into differences in income? In contrast to the view of Pareto,[4] the latter position does not mean the distribution of income is unaffected by social and economic organization.

This premise is illustrated by the skill premium s, which governs the difference between the United States and Continental Europe in our simple version of the Krugman-Wood model. In the flexible U.S. labor market s is free to rise as a consequence of the increasing trade with developing economies, while in the rigid European labor market s is fixed, and it is an increase in unemployment to absorb the impact of globalization. But what is preventing s from rising? Here is where institutional variables play a role in the model. Unions, minimum wages, employment protection schemes, and wage bargaining mechanisms affect the structure of earnings. For instance, Blau and Kahn (1996:831) conclude that "wage-setting institutions are an important determinant of international differences in wage distribution," and DiNardo, Fortin, and Lemieux (1996:1039) remark that "labor market institutions [i.e., the unionization rate and the real value of the minimum wage] are as important as supply and demand considerations in explaining changes in the U.S. distribution of wages from 1979 to 1988." In the three studies included in Table 14.2, all from political science, the centralization of wage bargaining has a consistently negative effect on wage dispersion, while the evidence for union variables is more mixed.

The key role of institutional variables underlines how, while economic forces modeled above have influenced the approaches of other social science disciplines, the traffic goes in both directions. Shanahan and Tuma (1994: 748) in their review of the "Sociology of Distribution and Redistribution" note that empirical studies tend to corroborate Kuznets' hypothesis of an inverse-U shape, but move on to an explanation based on political power: "Most of the sociological literature on comparative income inequality following Lenski (1966) draws especially upon his central contention that political democracy, as an equitable system of power distribution, reduces income inequality." Modeling policy choices and responses is an important ingredient. There has been a large literature on the relation between cross-country differences in income inequality and social democratic governments. Maravall (1997: Appendix 3) provides a valuable summary. This literature in turn has been criticized for focusing on the nation-state in isolation. The world-system perspective (see Shanahan and Tuma 1994:748), for example, argues that the political determination of income inequality depends on the country's relations to the world economy. In this case, G and R interact.

Lessons for Future Research

The theoretical models described above are very simple, but allow a number of conclusions to be drawn:

- We need to look at different parts of the income distribution, and not rely solely on a summary measure such as the Gini coefficient. Analysis of the Lorenz curve in the Kuznets' process shows the upper part leveling, while the poor get left increasingly further behind.
- We must distinguish the distribution of wages among workers from the distribution of market incomes among the whole population (including the unemployed), and this in turn must be distinguished from the distribution of disposable incomes. These different distributions may move differently as a result of globalization. The distribution of wages among the employed may become less unequal, although the distribution of disposable income becomes more unequal.

- Even in a highly simplified model, the factors that determine income inequality interact in a rather complex manner. The effect of globalization depends on the degree of redistribution and on policy responses.
- We need to bring together economic and political explanations of inequality.

3. DATA FIT FOR PURPOSE

There has been a great improvement in the availability of data for the analysis of income distribution. When Kuznets gave his presidential address, he based his inverse-U hypothesis on five observations for the United States, six for the United Kingdom, two each for Prussia and Saxony, and three for united Germany. This is a rather slender basis for drawing firm conclusions. As he himself recognized, "I am acutely conscious of the meagerness of reliable information presented. The paper is perhaps 5 percent empirical information and 95 percent speculation" (Kuznets 1955:26). When Kuznets (1963) returned to the subject, his "long-term estimates" included, for the United States, averages of data for some forty-five years, and he added further countries: the Netherlands, Denmark, Norway, and Sweden. The range of the data has continued to expand. There has in particular been an explosion in the number of household surveys, several of them on a panel basis, which provide micro data on income distribution. Many secondary databases have also been assembled by international organizations and individual scholars (see Atkinson and Brandolini 2001:772–73). They have been widely used in social sciences, as shown in Tables 14.1 and 14.2. Here we consider two such sources that have played a key role: the database on earnings dispersion collected by the Organisation for Economic Co-operation and Development (1993, 1996) and the data set assembled by Deininger and Squire (1996) at the World Bank.

Distribution of What, Among Whom, and When

The theoretical framework has shown the importance of distinguishing between the distributions of earnings, market income, gross income, and disposable income. In the case of earnings, the OECD data set relates to the earnings of individuals, but this still leaves open many questions. Do we want to include all workers, or just males or just females? Do we want to consider only adult workers, or also young workers? Do we want to look at private sector workers only? Do we want to limit attention to full-time workers, or to cover part-time workers too? Do we want to focus exclusively on full-year workers, or to extend the analysis to contingent, temporary, and seasonal workers? How do we deal with the self-employed? Are we interested in annual earnings or in hourly pay? Do we take gross or net compensations?

These choices drive us back to the underlying theory. If the inequality is hypothesized to derive from individual educational characteristics, then this will show up whether we consider all workers or just male workers. On the other hand, in the Kuznets model of structural change, gender may be related to the sorting of workers between the high and low wage sectors, and we have to look at the whole distribution.

The "distribution of earnings" can therefore mean different things, and the problem of assuring comparability is acute. The problem for the 1993 version of the OECD data set is illustrated in Table 14.3, that is constructed from the information contained in Organisation for Economic Co-operation and Development (1993).[5] A wide range of definitions underlie the inequality measures (the ratios to the median of the upper and lower deciles of the distribution) reported for fifteen OECD countries. These differences lead to differences in the measured dispersion. For example, the top coding of earnings at the ceiling for social insurance contributions, as in Austria and Belgium, and the truncation of earnings below a certain threshold, as in Denmark, mean that the dispersion is understated (or the relevant percentiles cannot be reported).[6] The exclusion of agriculture, as in Italy and Portugal, is also likely to cause dispersion to be understated. Moreover, the difference caused by the difference in coverage is unlikely to remain constant over time; as the agricultural sector shrinks, so will the understatement. Some of the earnings data come from household surveys, some from income tax or social security administrative records, and some from surveys of employers. These sources may require care in their comparison. In fact, after discussing comparability problems, the Organisation for Economic Co-operation and Development (1993:166) concludes: "Differences between countries in both coverage and definition warn that these data should not be used for international comparisons of the level of dispersion."

Consistency over Time

The same comparability issues arise when we turn to the distribution of disposable income. The data set assembled by Deininger and Squire draws together more than 2,600 observations on Gini coefficients and, in many cases, quintile shares from a wide variety of studies covering 135 developed and developing countries for the years 1947–96. This data set has been made freely available at the World Bank's website, and has been very extensively used. The issues raised by this data set have been discussed at length in Atkinson and Brandolini (2001). Here we focus on the question of consistency over time, taking as an example the subset of DS data used by Alderson and Nielsen (2002).

Alderson and Nielsen helpfully graph at the end of their article the Gini coefficients for the sixteen countries that they consider. In some cases, such as the United Kingdom and the United States, the data are drawn from a consistent series over time, but in others there are apparent breaks that make us pause. Although the Gini coefficients can change substantially from one year to the next, a sharp rise or fall requires investigation. Visual inspection of the Alderson and Nielsen's graphs indicates several such examples. In Table 14.4 we report the six cases where the difference between two consecutive observations for the Gini coefficients equals 4 percentage points or more. (We ignore here the change between 1967 and 1975 in Sweden, which is discussed below.) In half of the cases, the sharp changes coincide with changes in the underlying sources. Where possible we have checked against alternative national sources that give a continuous run of years. For example, the estimates for France by Hourriez and Roux (2001:281, Table 2), based on the Tax Revenue Survey (*Enquête Revenus Fiscaux*), show a decline of the Gini coefficient for equivalized disposable income between 1975 and 1979 from 32 to 30 percent, compared with the 8 percentage point fall in the DS data used by Alderson and Nielsen. But breaks occur even where the source is apparently the same. Taking Canada between 1988 and 1989, the data used by Alderson and Nielsen exhibit a sharp fall of 4.5 percentage points from 31.9 to 27.4 percent, but the consistent series published by Statistics Canada (1996:34, Table 6) shows very little change, from 39.0 to 38.6 percent. (The levels of the coefficients are puzzlingly different, being all for gross incomes per household.) In the case of Italy, the underlying source is the same, but the methods changed: 1975 differed from 1976 in that high-income households were over-sampled, and in that interest and dividend income were included; if the latter are excluded the 1975 figure drops from 39 to 36 percent (Brandolini 1999:224, Table 13). There is therefore a break in continuity.

TABLE 14.3
OECD Database on Earnings Dispersion (1993 version)

Country	Source (1)	Period	Earnings Definition	Tax	Sex (2)	Age	Category	Sectors	Extreme Values
Australia	Earnings survey	1976–91	Weekly earnings	Gross	M, F	All	Full-time non-managerial workers, receiving pay in May	Exc. agriculture, armed forces, other unspecified categories	–
Austria	Social security archives	1980–91	Monthly earnings (daily pay multiplied by days worked)	Gross	M, F, All	All	Wage and salary workers, some civil servants, exc. apprentices	All	Top-coded
Belgium	Social security archives	1983–90	Daily earnings	Gross	M, F, All	All	Full-time workers	All	Top-coded
Canada	Household income survey	1973–90	Annual earnings	Gross	M, F, All	All	Full-time, full-year workers	All	–
Denmark	Tax registers	1980–90	Hourly earnings (annual pay divided by actual hours)	Gross	All	All	All	All	Exc. below 80% of minimum wage

Country	Source	Years	Earnings measure	Gross/Net	Sex	Age	Worker coverage	Industry coverage	Notes
France	Social security archives	1973–91	Hourly earnings (annual pay divided by hours)	Gross	M, F, All	All	Full-time workers	All	—
Germany	Household income survey	1979–90	Monthly earnings (incl. $\frac{1}{12}$ of all benefits)	Gross	M, F, All	All	Full-time, full-year workers	All	—
Italy	Household income survey	1979–87	Annual earnings	Net	M, F	18–65	Full-time, full-year workers	Exc. agriculture	—
Japan	Earnings survey	1979–90	Monthly scheduled earnings	Gross	M, F	18–59	"Regular" workers in establishments with at least 5 workers	Exc. agriculture, government, private household services	—
Netherlands	Earnings survey	1974–85 1985–90	Weekly earnings (exc. overtime) Annual earnings (incl. overtime and occasional payments)	Gross	M, F, All	23–64	Full-time, full-week workers Full-time, full-month workers	Exc. government and other social and personal services	—
Norway	Household income survey	1980–91	Hourly earnings (weekly/monthly pay divided by working hours)	Gross	All	19–55	All	All	Bottom- and top-coded
Portugal	Earnings survey	1985–89	Weekly earnings	Gross	All	All	Full-time workers	Exc. agriculture	—

(continued)

TABLE 14.3
(*continued*)

Country	Source (1)	Period	Earnings Definition	Tax	Sex (2)	Age	Category	Sectors	Extreme Values
Sweden	Household income survey	1974–91	Hourly earnings (weekly/monthly pay divided by hours worked, rates)	Gross	M, F, All	All	All	All	–
United Kingdom	Earnings survey	1973–91	Hourly earnings	Gross	M, F	Adult rates	Persons with pay not affected by absence in reference week	All	–
United States	Household income survey	1975–89	Hourly earnings (annual divided by hours worked)	Gross	M, F, All	All	Wage and salary workers	All	–

NOTES: (1) The type of source is inferred from published information. By earnings survey we indicate information that we understand is derived from a survey of employers.
(2) M and F indicate males and females, respectively.

SOURCE: Organisation for Economic Co-operation and Development (1993: 161, note to Table 5.2; 165–166).

Given that income distribution data generally do not move sharply, apparent large changes could play a particularly influential role in the resulting statistical analysis.

Extent of the Panel

Which countries should be included in a panel? Economists do not typically pay much attention to the issues involved in selecting samples of countries. In focusing on the OECD countries, for example, they are—often implicitly—seeking to hold constant the broad economic and social background. The logic has been described in the political science context as follows: "the most-similar systems design logically requires the student to select a sample of countries that have as many similarities as possible (such as culture, government structure, legal system)" (Perry and Robertson 2002:35). A common practice is to employ all countries for which data are easily accessible. This is not, however, the only possible strategy. It is possible to match comparable countries: for example, to compare the evolution over time of income inequality in Canada and the United States, as in the study of poverty by Hanratty and Blank (1992). The choice of sample depends on the hypothesis to be tested. If for example our interest is in the Kuznets hypothesis, linking inequality to structural change, then we need to ensure that the sample has a coverage over time and space that includes societies at different stages of development. On the other hand, if we are concerned with the impact of globalization, then we may wish to standardize as far as possible the level of development. If we are concerned with the impact of the welfare state, then we may wish to distinguish, as in the work stemming from Esping-Andersen (1990), different "regimes" of welfare state.[7]

The hypothesis to be tested equally influences the time period selected. There are dangers in considering a small slice of history, as is illustrated for the United States and the United Kingdom by the two ovals drawn in Figure 14.4. The first shows the period covered by the evidence that Kuznets had available to him in 1955; the second shows the rise in inequality in the 1980s that has been the main source of the view that we now have an upturn in the U shape. But looking at the period as a whole, we can see that these two episodes were separated by a period in the United States where overall inequality was not trending up or down: the U.S. Gini coefficient in 1971 was the same as in 1951. This does not mean that it was uninteresting—we have to ask why there was this relatively long period of stability. Is stability consistent

TABLE 14.4

Apparent Breaks in the Inequality Series Used by Alderson and Nielsen

Country	Year	DEININGER-SQUIRE SERIES		ALTERNATIVE SERIES	
		Gini index	Source	Gini index	Source
Canada	1988	31.91	} Statistics Canada	39.0	} Statistics Canada
	1989	27.41	} (IDS)	38.6	} (1996)
Finland	1984	30.84	Statistical Yearbook	–	
	1985	–		20.0	} Uusitalo (2002)
	1987	26.19	LIS	19.9	}
France	1975	43.00	United Nations (1985)	32.0	} Hourriez and Roux
	1979	34.85	LIS	30.0	} (2001)
Italy	1975	39.00		36.4	
	1976	35.00	} United Nations	–	} Brandolini (1999)
	1977	36.30	} (1981)	35.9	}
Norway	1976	37.30	} Statistical Yearbook	–	
	1979	31.15	}	–	
Sweden	1975	27.31	LIS	21.3	
	1976	33.12	Statistical Yearbook	–	} Gustafsson and
	1978	–		20.0	} Palmer (1997)

NOTE: DS data-set, "accept" figures. A "break" is defined as a difference between two consecutive observations of 4 percentage points or more.

with the theoretical models discussed above? Why did the United Kingdom see falling inequality in the same period? These considerations underline the significance of data with a long historical span. Here we should note the contribution of studies pioneered by Piketty (2001, 2003) of the long-run development of top income shares. He has shown how data from tax records, although limited in their coverage of the population, can throw light on almost the whole of the twentieth century.

The time dimension is important not only for its extent but also in terms of frequency. Panels are typically of N countries for a maximum of T years, although they are often unbalanced, with the number of years varying, and there being missing observations for many years. In the case of Alderson and Nielsen (2002), there are sixteen countries, with a maximum of twenty-six observations (the United States). If the panel were balanced, then the total number of observations would be 416, but in fact there are only 187. For Belgium and Ireland there are only three each, and for Australia, Denmark,

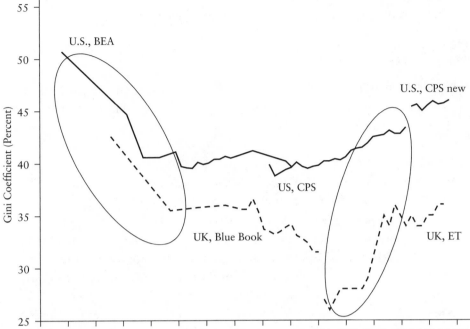

Figure 14.4.   Gini Coefficient for the United States and the United Kingdom: Different Foci

SOURCE: Brandolini 1998: pp 48–9, Table A1, columns 1a and 5; p, 52, Table A3, columns 1b and 3c.

France, (West) Germany, and Norway there are eight or fewer observations. Almost half the observations (89) are accounted for by the United States, the United Kingdom, Japan, and Canada. Where data only exist for infrequent years, the medium-term trends may be confounded with cyclical movements.

Lessons for Future Research

Data issues are important. In saying this, we are not concerned with the characteristics of data in abstract terms, but with their *fitness for purpose*. The question is—does the data specification capture the essence of the problem? This depends on the problem at hand. Data may be suitable for one purpose, but not for another. Data may be comparable in some respects, but not in others. In stressing data specification issues, we are not adopting a nihilistic · position. All data have their limitations and this is not a reason for rejecting them out of hand. Rather we need to be aware of the properties of the data when carrying out the statistical analysis, to which we now turn.

4. STATISTICAL ANALYSIS

Statistical analysis can take different forms. In this section, we consider in turn three elements: data description, specification of statistical relationships, and allowing for data deficiencies.

Describing the Evidence

Studies of income inequality pay considerable attention to "looking at the data," which we believe to be a crucial first step. It is not possible to make sense of reported regression coefficients without some idea of the behavior of the underlying variables. This applies to both explanatory variables and to the dependent variable, but the latter is particularly important. Is the variation across countries much greater than the variation across time? Is there a pattern of diffusion of rising inequality across countries? Alderson and Nielsen (2002) provide, as already noted, individual time series for all sixteen countries. They also give a scatter plot of the Gini coefficient against GDP per head, as other papers listed in Table 14.1 do, possibly using alternative indicators of economic development (e.g., List and Gallet 1999; Barro 2000; Fields 2001; Ravallion 1995, which uses consumption per capita). Gustafsson and Johansson (1999) begin with a chart of the annual observations by country, and then plot the Gini coefficient against selected explanatory variables. Edwards (1997) graphs the Gini coefficient in 1980 against each of the six alternative trade-policy indicators discussed in the paper.

An intermediate stage between graphic display and econometric analysis is the fitting of trends. De-trending is a subject much discussed in the macroeconomic literature and there are interesting parallels, not least in the controversy generated. Different approaches yield different "stylized facts" about the business cycle. But there are also differences: for example, the Gini coefficient, unlike U.S. GNP, has a limited range (see Jäntti and Jenkins 2001). Here the trend over time in income inequality is itself of considerable interest. Some studies have fitted linear trends to Gini coefficients for panels of countries. Li, Squire, and Zou (1998:26) using the DS data set over the period 1947–94 conclude that there is little intertemporal variation in income inequality: "income inequality is relatively stable within countries."

This finding is for all countries, developing as well as developed, but it will come as a surprise to those worried about widening inequality in industrialized countries. It is true that they find a "statistically large and quantitatively important time trend" (Li et al. 1998:33) for four OECD countries, but in two cases these are negative (France and Italy), and the two where the trend is large and positive (Australia and New Zealand) do not include the United States and the United Kingdom—in both of which there has been considerable concern about rising inequality. For the United States and the United Kingdom, they conclude that there is a small positive trend, where "small" is defined as an annual change less than 1 percent of the country's predicted 1980 value of the Gini coefficient (about 0.2–0.3 percentage points per year). From Figure 14.4, however, it is clear that fitting a linear trend to the period 1947–94 is a hopeless exercise, both in the United States and the United Kingdom.

A popular alternative is fitting a quadratic, to capture—on the Kuznets model—the inverse U, or, more recently, its reversal, which Harrison and Bluestone (1988) have christened as the "great U-turn." Cornia and Kiiski (2001:19–20), for instance, reexamine the Li, Xie, and Zou (2000) evidence and find that fitting a quadratic trend reduces the number of countries where the time trend is insignificant from thirty-two to nineteen (out of forty-nine), with a U-shaped pattern prevailing in thirteen countries. They also show that extending the time period until 1998 and the number of countries to seventy-three, using the first version of the WIID database, further reduces to sixteen the number of countries with stable inequality, while it increases the number of U-shaped profiles to twenty-nine. On the basis of these results, Cornia and Court (2001:7) describe how "[t]he Golden Age, a period of stable global economic growth between the 1950s and early-mid 1970s, witnessed declines in income inequality in a number of countries (with some exceptions). This trend was reversed over the last two decades as country after country has experienced an upsurge in income inequality."

Fitting a quadratic equation to explain the Gini coefficient as a function of time is, however, still too restrictive. It imposes a particular structure on the U. It does not allow for situations where the decline and rise in inequality are separated by a period of stability: a flat-bottomed U, as we have seen in the United States. Most importantly, the quadratic implies that the rise in inequality is continuing, and at an increasing pace. Given that we are especially concerned with the recent past, we need to be able to test whether or not inequality is continuing to trend upward. For this purpose, it may be preferable to fit a segmented trend.

Specification

In some statistical estimation there is a tight relation between the underlying theory and the specification of the empirical relation. Focusing on the Kuznets model, the use of the sector dualism variable by Alderson and Nielsen is a good example, where, in the simplest case, the Gini coefficient is equal to this variable. Another example is provided by the functional forms derived by Anand and Kanbur (1993) for the inverse-U relationship, which are shown to depend on the choice of the inequality index. As they stress: "the right index must be used with the right functional form for estimation purposes" (Anand and Kanbur 1993:39). For instance, the Gini coefficient should be written as $\alpha - \beta\mu_Y - \gamma/\mu_Y$, where μ_Y is mean income. This is different from the quadratic specification often adopted in empirical applications. Considering the studies in Table 14.1, eleven estimate a quadratic relation (either in levels, or in logarithms) and one a cubic relation; only two papers adopt Anand and Kanbur's specification.

There is however often only a loose connection between the variables studied in the theoretical models and those entering empirical investigations. This raises issues about their specification. We give two examples. The first concerns interactions. Suppose that we were to simply write down an equation like (2), where inequality is explained as a function of globalization G and redistribution R. This would ignore the interactions that we have seen to arise in several different ways. In the Krugman-Wood model, for example, the impact of globalization on the inequality I_D of disposable incomes depends on the extent to which social protection and labor market institutions provide a floor to wages, and the implications of unemployment depend on the replacement rate and coverage of benefits. In general, if $\partial I_D/\partial G$ is smaller where R is higher (the cross-derivative is negative), this could be allowed for by introducing a cross-term, $G \times R$, with an expected negative coefficient. However, this ad hoc response may not be a satisfactory solution. If the cross-derivative is negative, then its reverse implies that the derivative $\partial I_D/\partial R$ (which is negative by construction) is even more negative if G increases. Globalization increases the redistributive impact of the welfare state. This appears to be the reverse of what is argued by those who believe that the effectiveness of welfare states is under threat from globalization. Such a difference of view reflects differences in the mechanisms assumed to be in operation, but it underlines the need to go back to the theoretical framework in order to specify the relation to be estimated.

The second example concerns interdependencies between countries. The typical statistical analysis treats the panel as proceeding in columns; the countries simply happen to be on the same planet; there are no specific interdependencies. The same applied to the Krugman-Wood theoretical model. The United States and Continental Europe were analyzed in isolation. But what this formulation misses (as pointed out by Davis 1998) is the *interdependence* of Europe and the United States. The impact of internationalization on Europe is different on account of the existence of the United States pursuing different labor market and welfare state policies. In a unified analysis, if the United States and Continental Europe both produce the goods that face global competition, then the wage floor in Europe determines the relative goods prices. Assuming that the minimum wage is unchanged, this prevents the relative price from falling. The United States is therefore unaffected by increased trade. Europe bears the brunt in terms of unemployment (Davis 1998). By the same token, any move to greater labor market flexibility in Europe causes a decline in the relative wages of the unskilled in the United States. All this means that R^{EU} affects I^{US} and this must be taken into account in the estimation.

Allowing for Data Deficiencies

As shown in Section 2, the data available may not be fully comparable across countries; indeed it is only through projects such as the Luxembourg Income Study that we can hope to have data that are comparable in their definitions and sources. For example, some of the data used by Alderson and Nielsen (2002) relate to net, or disposable, income (Belgium and the United Kingdom) and some to gross income (Australia, Denmark, and the United States). The standard approach to dealing with such systematic differences in definition across countries is to use dummy variables. Use of a dummy variable assumes that the difference between net and gross remains constant over time. If this assumption holds, then the difference in definition can also be taken care of by a country fixed effect.

The theoretical models of Section 2 show, however, that the difference between the Gini coefficients for market income, gross income, and net income is influenced by economic and other variables. If we compare Equations (5) and (6), then the difference between I_M and I_D depends on the replacement rate and coverage of unemployment benefits. Empirically, the evidence suggests that in fact the redistributive impact of taxation and transfers vary over time. Estimates of the Gini coefficient in Canada for different concepts of income show that inequality in market income increased between 1971 and 1994, the Gini coefficient rising by some 5 percentage points (see Statistics Canada 1996:34, Table 6). This increase reflects among other things the increased size of the retired population. Because the retired receive state pensions, the degree of inequality in gross income (which includes state transfers) moves differently: indeed the Gini coefficient does not rise over the period as a whole. As a result, over the period the difference between the two series doubles. The Gini coefficient for net incomes declines from 1971 to 1993, so that its difference with respect to the Gini coefficient for gross incomes rises by about 1 percentage point by the end of the period; this change is almost fully reversed between 1993 and 1994. All this means that we would need separate equations for the different income concepts. The analysis would be enriched if we were to use all three series for Canada, and for other countries where available.

Extending the data set is one response to data deficiencies. An alternative is to explore the sensitivity of estimated relationships to weaknesses in the data. Here we refer briefly to two approaches. The first is to move beyond a binary classification of data quality, where data are treated as either acceptable (included in the analysis) or unacceptable (rejected). A good example is provided by the 1967 observation for Sweden, which predates the official series starting in 1975. Gustafsson and Uusitalo (1990:84) say of the 1967 figure "because of some differences between the two data sets the comparability is less satisfactory." Gustafsson and Johansson (1999) exclude the 1967 observation from their analysis of changes in inequality over time (see below). On the other hand, the 1967 observation for Sweden is included by Alderson and Nielsen (2002). An intermediate position is to include the observation but to "discount" it by assuming a larger error variance, as in generalized least squares estimation. The discount to be applied is a matter for judgment, informed by studying the sources. It is of course much easier to apply if the producers of the underlying data attach margins of error (see Feinstein and Thomas 2001).

The second approach is a development of the dummy variable method to allow for breaks in the consistency of data. Breaks are an almost universal feature of time series; in many cases they can be neglected but in other cases we have to take them seriously. The United States provides a good example. One notable break in the Current Population Survey (CPS) series was that in 1993 when the data collection changed from paper and pencil to computer-assisted interviewing, and when there was a large increase in the top codes (that for earnings rose from $300,000 to $1,000,000). This was important, because there was a large rise in recorded inequality in that year, and estimates (Weinberg 1996: 1, fn. 3) indicate that these changes could account for half of the recorded increase. This can be taken into account by introducing a dummy variable for years from 1993, which assumes that the impact is constant over time. An alternative approach is to rely solely on the intrinsic properties of the data. For any series we can examine the sensitivity of our conclusions to there being an unsignaled break in comparability (assumed to take the form of an additive shift). Such an approach resembles techniques for detecting influential observations (see, for example, Belsley, Kuh, and Welsch 1980). This technique was used by Gustafsson and Johansson (1999: 593, fn. 13) to exclude the 1967 observation for Sweden, confirming the a priori reasons for concern. Alderson and Nielsen (2002: 1271) used a newer algorithm (Hadi 1994) to identify five outlying observations, which did not include the 1967 observation for Sweden. Interestingly, none of these coincided with the cases identified here in Table 14.4.

Lessons for Future Research

The main points emphasized here are:

- The value of looking at the data
- The dangers in simply fitting trends or quadratics
- The need to relate the specification of estimated relationships to the underlying theory, in particular to take account of interactions and interdependencies
- Development of techniques to allow for data deficiencies that go beyond a binary classification (acceptable/unacceptable)

CONCLUSIONS

In this chapter, we have set out a research agenda to tackle the problems, theoretical and empirical, in the existing literature on explaining variations in income inequality across countries and time. Is progress possible? The flowering of the literature in recent years suggests that many researchers believe this to be the case. Others are more skeptical: Parker (2000) describes time-series analysis of income inequality as a "can of worms." Our view is intermediate. We believe that valuable lessons can be learned but that we require:

- An integrated approach to theory and estimation
- A proper specification of the data employed
- Techniques to address the deficiencies of the underlying data

This enterprise in turn will advance much more quickly if the different social science disciplines learn from each other.

Notes

1. The LIS microdata and a set of summary measures of inequality and poverty are accessible at the LIS website: http://www.lisproject.org. Tabatabai (1996) produced a compendium of figures on poverty and inequality for the International Labour Office (ILO). Many data sets have been constructed at the World Bank: for some of those referred to in Table 14.1, see World Bank (1994), Deininger and Squire (1996) (available at http://www.worldbank.org/research/growth/dddeisqu.htm) and Chen and Ravallion (2000) (available at http://iresearch.world-bank.org/PovcalNet/jsp/index.jsp). The World Income Inequality Database (WIID) of the United Nations University/World Institute for Development Economics Research (UNU/WIDER) is downloadable at http://www.wider.unu.edu/wiid/wiid.htm; a new version of the database, labeled WIID2, was released in June 2005. Data on the earnings distribution have been assembled by the Organisation for Economic Co-operation and Development (OECD) and are published in Organisation for Economic Co-operation and Development (1993, 1996).

2. By taking the partial derivatives of (3) with respect to ϕ and equating to 0, the turning point for the Gini coefficient is found to occur at $\phi^* = [1 + s - (1 + s)^{0.5}]/s$, which is greater than 0.5 for any positive value of s. Thus, in the range $0.2 < \phi < \phi^*$, any decrease in ϕ is associated with a decline in both the Gini coefficient and the income share of the bottom 20 percent.

3. This characterization of personal income distribution resembles that of Bourguignon (1990), who examined a three-class dual economy with workers employed either in the "traditional" sector, or in the "modern" sector, but his third class was that of "pure capitalists."

4. "The inequality in the distribution of incomes seems therefore to depend much more on the human nature itself than on the economic organization of the society. It could well be the case that deep modifications of this organization had but little impact on the law that governs the distribution of incomes" (Pareto 1897:363, §1012; our translation).

5. Two studies listed in Table 14.2 use the OECD database, although in more recent versions (Organisation for Economic Co-operation and Development 1996; a database directly provided to the authors). The following observations concerning the 1993 version carry over to these new versions.

6. MacPhail (2000) assesses the sensitivity of measured earnings inequality to top coding and to excluding bottom or top outliers, using Canadian data for male workers in 1981 and 1989. She finds, for instance, that the Gini coefficient in 1989 falls from 37.8 percent in the base case to 37.3 percent by setting a ceiling on earnings at 4 times the mean, and to 36.6 percent by excluding the bottom 2 percent of observations.

7. A related issue is the potential use of subnational data. For instance, Nielsen and Alderson (1997) tested the U-turn hypothesis by studying income distribution in the counties of the United States in 1970, 1980, and 1990, while Partridge (1997) and Panizza (2002) investigated the relationship between growth and inequality on a panel of the American states in the postwar period. In these papers, American counties or states are used on their own as a source of variation, but should we not consider combining state, or regional, data with national data? Saez and Veall (2005) point out that the rise in inequality at the top of the wage distribution has been less in francophone Quebec than in the rest of Canada, mirroring the fact that France has not seen the same rise in inequality at the top as the United States. The experience of the Italian South or the German East may be different from that of the North or the West, respectively. Although the use of subnational data may be conceived as a way of overcoming data deficiencies—as they are likely to be much more homogenous than cross-national statistics—they may have a distinct informational content.

References

Alderson, Arthur S., and François Nielsen. 1999. "Income Inequality, Development, and Dependence: A Reconsideration." *American Sociological Review* 64:606–31.

Alderson, Arthur S., and François Nielsen. 2002. "Globalisation and the Great U-Turn: Income Inequality Trends in 16 OECD Countries." *American Journal of Sociology* 107:1244–99.

Anand, Sudhir, and S. M. Ravi Kanbur. 1993. "The Kuznets Process and the Inequality-Development Relationship." *Journal of Development Economics* 40:25–52.

Andersen, Torben M., and Tryggvi T. Herbertsson. 2005. "Quantifying Globalization." *Applied Economics* 37: 1089–98.

Atkinson, Anthony B., and Andrea Brandolini. 2001. "Promise and Pitfalls in the Use of 'Secondary' Data-Sets: Income Inequality in OECD Countries." *Journal of Economic Literature* 34:771–99.

Barro, Robert J. 2000. "Inequality and Growth in a Panel of Countries." *Journal of Economic Growth* 5:5–32.

Belsley, David A., Edwin Kuh, and Roy E. Welsch. 1980. *Regression Diagnostics: Identifying Influential Data and Sources of Collinearity.* New York: Wiley.

Blau, Francine D., and Lawrence M. Kahn. 1996. "International Differences in Male Wage Inequality: Institutions versus Market Forces." *Journal of Political Economy* 104:791–837.

Bourguignon, François. 1990. "Growth and Inequality in the Dual Model of Development: The Role of Demand Factors." *Review of Economic Studies* 57: 215–28.

Bourguignon, François. 2002. "The Distributional Effects of Growth: Case Studies vs. Cross-Country Regressions." École Normale Supérieure, Départment et Laboratoire D'Économie Théorique et Appliqué, Working Paper, No. 23, December.

Bourguignon, François, and Christian Morrisson. 1998. "Inequality and Development: The Role of Dualism." *Journal of Development Economics* 57: 233–57.

Brandolini, Andrea. 1998. "A Bird's-Eye View of Long-Run Changes in Income Inequality." Paper presented at the 13th IEA World Congress, Lisbon, Portugal, 9–13 September 2002.

Brandolini, Andrea. 1999. "The Distribution of Personal Income in Post-War Italy: Source Description, Data Quality, and the Time Pattern of Income Inequality." *Giornale degli Economisti e Annali di Economia* 58:183–239.

Bulíř, Aleš and Anne-Marie Gulde. 1995. "Inflation and Income Distribution: Further Evidence on Empirical Links." IMF Working Paper, No. 95/86, August. Published, in Czech, in *Finance a úvěr* 50:207–23 (2000).

Chen, Shaohua, and Martin Ravallion. 2000. "How Did the World's Poorest Fare in the 1990s?" World Bank, Mimeo.

Chu, Ke-young, Hamid Davoodi, and Sanjeev Gupta. 2000. "Income Distribution and Tax and Government Social Spending Policies in Developing Countries." IMF Working Paper, No. 00/62, March.

Cornia, Giovanni Andrea, and Julius Court. 2001. "Inequality, Growth and Poverty in the Era of Liberalization and Globalization." UNU/WIDER Policy Brief, No. 4.

Cornia, Giovanni Andrea, and Sampsa Kiiski. 2001. "Trends in Income Distribution in the Post World War II Period. Evidence and Interpretation." UNU/WIDER Discussion Paper, No. 2001/89.

Davis, Donald R. 1998. "Does European Unemployment Prop Up American Wages? National Labor Markets and Global Trade." *American Economic Review* 88:478–94.

Deininger, Klaus, and Lyn Squire. 1996. "A New Data Set Measuring Income Inequality." *World Bank Economic Review* 10:565–91.

Deininger, Klaus, and Lyn Squire. 1998. "New Ways of Looking at Old Issues: Inequality and Growth." *Journal of Development Economics* 57:259–87.

DiNardo, John E., Nicole Fortin, and Thomas Lemieux. 1996. "Labor Market Institutions and the Distribution of Wages, 1973–1992: A Semiparametric Approach." *Econometrica* 64:1001–44.

Dollar, David, and Aart Kraay. 2002. "Growth Is Good for the Poor." *Journal of Economic Growth* 7:195–225.

Edwards, Sebastian. 1997. "Trade Policy, Growth, and Income Distribution." *American Economic Review Papers and Proceedings* 87:205–10.

Esping-Andersen, Gøsta. 1990. *The Three Worlds of Welfare Capitalism*. Princeton, NJ: Princeton University Press.

Feinstein, Charles H., and Mark Thomas. 2001. "A Plea for Errors." University of Oxford, Discussion Paper in Economic and Social History, No. 41, July.

Fields, Gary S. 1991. "Growth and Income Distribution." Pp. 1–52 in *Essays on Poverty, Equity and Growth*, edited by G. Psacharopoulos. Oxford: Pergamon.

Fields, Gary S. 2001. *Distribution and Development. A New Look at the Developing World*. New York and Cambridge, MA: Russell Sage Foundation and MIT Press.

Fields, Gary S., and George H. Jakubson. 1994. "New Evidence on the Kuznets Curve." Cornell University, Mimeo.

Galli, Rossana, and Rolph van der Hoeven. 2001. "Is Inflation Bad for Income Inequality?" ILO Employment Paper, No. 19.

Gustafsson, Björn, and Mats Johansson. 1999. "In Search of Smoking Guns: What Makes Income Inequality Vary Over Time in Different Countries?" *American Sociological Review* 64:585–605.

Gustafsson, Björn, and Edward Palmer. 1997. "Changes in Swedish Inequality. A Study of Equivalent Income 1975-1991." Pp. 293–325 in *Changing Patterns in the Distribution of Economic Welfare*, edited by P. Gottschalk, B. Gustafsson, and E. Palmer. Cambridge: Cambridge University Press.

Gustafsson, Björn, and Hannu Uusitalo. 1990. "Income Distribution and Redistribution during Two Decades: Experiences from Finland and Sweden." Pp. 73–95 in *Generating Equality in the Welfare State. The Swedish Experience*, edited by I. Persson. Oslo: Norwegian University Press.

Hadi, Ali S. 1994. "A Modification of a Method for the Detection of Outliers in Multivariate Samples." *Journal of the Royal Statistical Society* Series B, 56: 393–96.

Hanratty, Maria J., and Rebecca M. Blank. 1992. "Down and Out in North America: Recent Trends in Poverty Rates in the U.S. and Canada." *Quarterly Journal of Economics* 107:233–54.

Harrison, Bennett, and Barry Bluestone. 1988. *The Great U-Turn: Corporate Restructuring and the Polarizing of America*. New York: Basic Books.

Higgins, Matthew, and Jeffrey G. Williamson. 1999. "Explaining Inequality the World Round: Cohort Size, Kuznets Curves, and Openness." NBER Working

Paper, No. 7224, Shorter version published in *Southeast Asian Studies* 40: 268–302 (2002).

Hourriez, Jean-Michel, and Valérie Roux. 2001. "Vue d'ensemble des inégalités de revenu et de patrimoine." Pp. 269–284 in *In égalités Économiques*, edited by Conseil D'Analyse Économique. Paris: La Documentation Française.

Jäntti, Markus, and Stephen P. Jenkins. 2001. "Examining the Impact of Macro-Economic Conditions on Income Inequality." ISER Working Paper, No. 17.

Jha, Sailesh K. 1996. "The Kuznets Curve: A Reassessment." *World Development* 24:773–80.

Kanbur, S. M. Ravi. 2000. "Income Distribution and Development." Pp. 791–841 in *Handbook of Income Distribution*, vol. 1, edited by A. B. Atkinson and F. Bourguignon. Amsterdam: North-Holland.

Krugman, Paul. 1994. "Past and Prospective Causes of High Unemployment." Pp. 49–80 in *Reducing Unemployment: Current Issues and Policy Options*. Kansas City, MO: Federal Reserve Bank of Kansas City.

Kuznets, Simon. 1955. "Economic Growth and Income Inequality." *American Economic Review* 45:1–28.

Kuznets, Simon. 1963. "Quantitative Aspects of the Economic Growth of Nations: VIII. Distribution of Income by Size." *Economic Development and Cultural Change* 11, No. 2, part II:1–80.

Lenski, Gerhard. 1966. *Power and Privilege: A Theory of Social Stratification*. New York: McGraw-Hill.

Li, Hongyi, Lyn Squire, and Heng-Fu Zou. 1998. "Explaining International and Intertemporal Variations in Income Inequality." *Economic Journal* 108:26–43.

Li, Hongyi, Danyang Xie, and Heng-Fu Zou. 2000. "Dynamics of Income Distribution." *Canadian Journal of Economics* 33:937–61.

List, John A., and Craig A. Gallet. 1999. "The Kuznets Curve: What Happens After the Inverted-U?" *Review of Development Economics* 3:200–06.

Lundberg, Mattias, and Lyn Squire. 2003. "The Simultaneous Evolution of Growth and Inequality." *Economic Journal* 113:326–44.

MacPhail, Fiona. 2000. "Are Estimates of Earnings Inequality Sensitive to Measurement Choices? A Case Study of Canada in the 1980s." *Applied Economics* 32:845–60.

Mahler, Vincent A. 2004. "Economic Globalization, Domestic Politics, and Income Inequality in the Developed Countries: A Cross-National Study." *Comparative Political Studies* 37:1025–53.

Maravall, José María. 1997. *Regimes, Politics and Markets. Democratization and Economic Change in Southern and Eastern Europe*. Oxford: Oxford University Press.

Nielsen, François. 1994. "Income Inequality and Industrial Development: Dualism Revisited." *American Sociological Review* 59:654–77.

Nielsen, François, and Arthur S. Alderson. 1995. "Income Inequality, Development, and Dualism: Results from an Unbalanced Cross-National Panel." *American Sociological Review* 60:674–701.

Nielsen, François, and Arthur S. Alderson. 1997. "The Kuznets Curve and the Great U-Turn: Income Inequality in U.S. Counties, 1970 to 1990." *American Sociological Review* 62:12–33.

Organisation for Economic Co-operation and Development. 1993. "Earnings Inequality: Changes in the 1980s." Pp. 157–84 in *Employment Outlook*. Paris: Organisation for Economic Co-operation and Development.

Organisation for Economic Co-operation and Development. 1996. "Earnings Inequality, Low-Paid Employment and Earnings Mobility." Pp. 59–108 in *Employment Outlook*. Paris: Organisation for Economic Co-operation and Development.

Osberg, Lars. 2003. "Long Run Trends in Income Inequality in the United States, UK, Sweden, Germany and Canada: A Birth Cohort View." *Eastern Economic Journal* 29:121–41.

Panizza, Ugo. 2002. "Income Inequality and Economic Growth: Evidence from American Data." *Journal of Economic Growth* 7:25–41.

Papanek, Gustav F., and Oldrich Kyn. 1986. "The Effect on Income Distribution of Development, the Growth Rate and Economic Strategy." *Journal of Development Economics* 23:55–65.

Pareto, Vilfredo. 1897. *Cours d'économie politique*. Tome second. Lausanne and Paris: Rouge and Pichon. Reprinted in *Oeuvres complètes*, vol. I, edited by G.-H. Bousquet and G. Busino. Genève: Librairie Droz, 1964.

Parker, Simon C. 2000. "Opening a Can of Worms: The Pitfalls of Time-series Regression Analysis of Income Inequality." *Applied Economics* 32:221–30.

Partridge, Mark D. 1997. "Is Inequality Harmful for Growth? Comment." *American Economic Review* 87:1019–32.

Perry, Robert L., and John D. Robertson. 2002. *Comparative Analysis of Nations: Quantitative Approaches*. Oxford: Westview.

Piketty, Thomas. 2001. *Les hauts revenus en France au XXe siècle: Inégalités et redistributions,1901–1998*. Paris: Grasset.

Piketty, Thomas. 2003. "Income Inequality in France, 1901–1998." *Journal of Political Economy* 111:1004–42.

Ram, Rati. 1997. "Level of Economic Development and Income Inequality: Evidence from the Postwar Developed World." *Southern Economic Journal* 64:576–83.

Ravallion, Martin. 1995. "Growth and Poverty: Evidence for Developing Countries in the 1980s." *Economics Letters* 48:411–17.

Rueda, David, and Jonas Pontusson. 2000. "Wage Inequality and Varieties of Capitalism." *World Politics* 52:350–83.

Saez, Emmanuel, and Michael R. Veall. 2005. "The Evolution of High Incomes in Northern America: Lessons from Canadian Evidence." *American Economic Review* 95: 831–49.

Sarel, Michael. 1997. "How Macroeconomic Factors Affect Income Distribution: The Cross-Country Evidence." IMF Working Paper, No. 97/152, November.

Schultz, T. Paul. 1998. "Inequality in the Distribution of Personal Income in the World: How It Is Changing and Why." *Journal of Population Economics* 11:307–44.

Shanahan, Suzanne Elise, and Nancy Brandon Tuma. 1994. "The Sociology of Distribution and Redistribution." Pp. 733–65 in *The Handbook of Economic Sociology*, edited by N. J. Smelser and R. Swedberg. Princeton, NJ: Princeton University Press.

Spilimbergo, Antonio, Juan Luis Londoño, and Miguel Székely. 1999. "Income Distribution, Factor Endowments, and Trade Openness." *Journal of Development Economics* 59:77–101.

Statistics Canada. 1996. *Income after Tax, Distributions by Size in Canada. 1994.* Ottawa: Statistics Canada.

Tabatabai, Hamid. 1996. *Statistics on Poverty and Income Distribution: An ILO Compendium of Data.* Geneva: International Labour Office.

Uusitalo, Hannu. 2002. "Finland: Changes in Income Distribution." Central Pension Institute, Mimeo.

Wallerstein, Michael. 1999. "Wage-Setting Institutions and Pay Inequality in Advanced Industrial Societies." *American Journal of Political Science* 43:649–80.

Weinberg, Daniel H. 1996. "A Brief Look at Postwar U.S. Income Inequality." Current Population Reports, Series P60, No. 191. Washington, DC: U.S. Government Printing Office.

Wood, Adrian. 1994. *North-South Trade Employment and Inequality. Changing Fortunes in a Skill-Driven World.* Oxford: Clarendon.

World Bank. 1994. *Social Indicators of Development.* Baltimore, MD: Johns Hopkins University Press.